DAVID PUTTNAM is the Oscar-winning producer of *Chariots of Fire, Midnight Express, Local Hero, The Killing Fields* and *The Mission*. He was chairman of Columbia Pictures from 1986 to 1988 and now heads his own company, Enigma Productions. In 1995 he received a knighthood for his services to the British film industry and in August 1997 was appointed a Life Peer. He divides his time between England and a home in Ireland.

NEIL WATSON is a writer and researcher specializing in the film and entertainment industries. He lives in London.

DAVID PUTTNAM

WITH NEIL WATSON

The Undeclared War

*The Struggle for Control of
the World's Film Industry*

HarperCollins*Publishers*

HarperCollins*Publishers*
77–85 Fulham Palace Road,
Hammersmith, London w6 8jb

This paperback edition 1997

1   3   5   7   9   8   6   4   2

First published in Great Britain by
HarperCollins*Publishers* 1997

ISBN 0 00 638744 6

Printed and bound in Great Britain by
Caledonian International Book Manufacturing Ltd, Glasgow

For Terence Donovan,
a wonderful friend who loved books
and knew a good picture
when he saw one

ACKNOWLEDGEMENTS

This book was made possible through the help and enthusiasm of many people in many countries. It began life as a series of lectures delivered at the Hochschule für Film und Fernsehen in Berlin in the autumn of 1994. My particular thanks to Professor Wolf-Dieter Panse and Dr Renée Gundelach for their original invitation to deliver those lectures, and to the British Council for the support which made them possible.

The lectures were subsequently delivered in a slightly revised form at Oxford University in October 1995 under the auspices of the university's Film Studies Programme. Special thanks are due to Ian Christie, Anthony Smith and Wilf Stevenson for inviting me to Oxford and ensuring that the series was such a success.

For inspiration, help and advice I am indebted to more people than I can possibly hope to mention, but I am especially appreciative of the following: Sam Arkoff, Kate Beetham, Tina Brown, Kevin Brownlow, René Cleitman, Martin Dale, Peter Dekom, Stan Durwood, Lord Eatwell, Paolo Ferrari, Sir Denis Forman, Richard Fox, Christopher Frayling, Daniel Gélin, H. Mark Glancy, Lord Grade, Bill Grantham, Dominique Green, Peter Guber, Larushka Ivan-Zadeh, Tom Lewyn, Sandy Lieberson, Percy Livingstone, Marvin Meyer, Bernard Miyet, Janet Moat, Phyllis Mollet, the late Andrew Mitchell, Mark Phillips, Penni Pike, Terry Semel, Geoffrey Nowell-Smith, Richard O'Toole, Frank Pierce, James Royall, Gunnar Rugheimer, Raymond Seitz, Ric Senat, Bob Warby, John Wilkinson, Michael Williams-Jones and Sir John Woolf.

I am also grateful to a number of people who provided information on a confidential basis and for that reason have preferred to remain anonymous.

Thanks are due to staff at the following libraries: the British Film Institute Library, the British Library, the Margaret Herrick Library of the Academy of Motion Picture Arts and Sciences in Beverly Hills, and also to the staff at the Danish Film Museum in Copenhagen. Thanks also to the management and staff of the West Cork Hotel, Skibbereen, for their hospitality which enabled drafting and editing to be carried out in the most tranquil and well-provisioned surroundings.

I must also acknowledge the generosity of Leith Adams in providing invaluable information regarding Hollywood's response to the rise of television. My conversations with Jack Valenti over the years, as well as his responses to specific questions have been tremendously helpful in allowing me to understand and appreciate the context of many of the events mapped out in the pages that follow.

At HarperCollins, publishing director Michael Fishwick and editor Rebecca Lloyd steered the book through to publication with great dedication and skill. I am indebted to them and to all their staff for their commitment to the success of this book.

Also I am very grateful to Colin Young for his trouble in going through the final draft and offering any number of constructive suggestions.

I owe an enormous debt of thanks to Ed Victor not only for his sterling negotiating skills but also for his belief in this lunatic project, and for encouraging me to tackle new and somewhat forbidding territory.

I also owe a deep debt of gratitude to all the staff at my own company, Enigma Productions, for their support in bringing this project to fruition. In particular, I'd like to thank Valerie Kemp for her invaluable assistance with all manner of complex administrative and practical matters, Steve Norris for his help and input, and Sarah Wright and Paul May for their unstinting energy and cheerfulness over a whole range of irritating minutiae.

It's also true to say that this book would not have been possible without the tireless work of my colleague John Newbigin who involved himself far beyond the call of duty. He provided invaluable suggestions and ideas, most especially on those occasions when, unable to see my way forward, it seemed easier to abandon the entire venture. I am enormously grateful to him for his energy, support and friendship.

Finally, my wife Patsy who watched two precious summer holidays vanish under a deluge of paper with barely a word of complaint. As ever, she provided inspiration and encouragement, just as she has throughout the ups and downs of my entire career.

CONTENTS

List of Illustrations   xi

1   A Prologue   3

2   'An invention without any commercial future'   9

3   'All you needed was fifty dollars, a broad and a camera'   29

4   'No more licences! No more heartbreaks!'   52

5   'The very highest medium for the dissemination of
    public intelligence'   74

6   Film Europe   96

7   Movies and Money   115

8   'Who the hell wants to hear actors talk?'   135

9   'Last year alone we made fourteen films. How many
    were exhibited? None!'   148

10 'I am the King here. Whoever eats my bread, sings
    my song'   166

11 'Cinema is the strongest weapon'   186

12 'If I am compelled to choose between Bogart and bacon,
    I am bound to choose bacon'   202

13 The Star-spangled Octopus   216

14 Sleeping with the Enemy: Television   229

15 The Film-maker as Author: The Arrival of the
    Nouvelle Vague   248

16 Earth to Hollywood – You Win!   263

CONTENTS

17   'Films are made for one or maybe two people . . .'   291

18   A Bridge Too Far?   304

19   Films without Frontiers   329

20   'A permanent war, vital . . . An economic war'   349

     Notes   361

     Index   391

ILLUSTRATIONS

Section One

Thomas Edison (Kobal Collection)
Louis and Auguste Lumière (Kobal Collection)
Robert Paul (BFI Stills Archive)
Georges Méliès (Kobal Collection)
1907 Pathé poster
Early advertising poster showing Pathé cockerel (from the collection of
    M. Gianati)
Charles Pathé (Odile Boullouche)
Florence Lawrence (Kobal Collection)
Ole Olsen (Danish Film Museum)
Adolph Zukor (BFI Stills Archive)
A.P. Giannini (Camera Press)
Sam Goldwyn with his protégé, Anna Sten (Kobal Collection)
Carl Laemmle (Kobal Collection)
Irving Thalberg and Norma Shearer (Kobal Collection)
The Warner Brothers (Kobal Collection)
Illustration from 1920s German magazine
French poster revealing the dangers of free trade (Bibliothèque
    Nationale de France)
Renée Saint-Cyr in *Toto* (Archives Pathé)

Section Two

Darryl Zanuck (courtesy of Virginia Fox Zanuck)
Louis B. Mayer (Kobal Collection)
Harry Cohn with Stanley Kramer (Kobal Collection)
Will Hays (Kobal Collection)
J. Arthur Rank and Carol Marsh (Kobal Collection)
Alexander Korda and Vivien Leigh (BFI Stills Archive)

Alfred Hitchcock and James Stewart (Kobal Collection)

Sophia Loren (Kobal Collection)

Jean-Luc Godard (Kobal Collection)

1959 meeting of young French film directors (BFI Stills Archive)

Earth to Hollywood (artist J.C. Suares, reproduced by permission of Variety Inc.)

Lew Wasserman and his wife, Edie (Camera Press)

Bill Clinton and Jack Valenti (from Jack Valenti's collection)

'If we continue down the path we appear to have chosen, the danger exists that we will end up exactly where we seem to be heading'

Ancient Chinese proverb

The Undeclared War

1

A Prologue

ONE EVENING IN 1992, a high-ranking French civil servant, left his Paris office for a cocktail party at the headquarters of UNESCO. It promised to be one of those routine affairs of canapés, swizzle sticks and small talk designed to oil the wheels of international diplomacy. As he worked the room, he was introduced to a distinguished American woman who informed him that she was employed as head of public relations for a private foundation based in Dallas. They exchanged pleasantries and once the evening was over the civil servant promptly forgot about her. The following spring, however, after a brief spell working in the office of the Prime Minister Edouard Balladur, he was surprised to receive a telephone call from the woman, who seemed to have suddenly acquired an extraordinary interest in French politics, and in particular in his work for the Prime Minister's office. She quizzed him closely about the French approach to the ongoing negotiations on the General Agreement on Tariffs and Trade

3

(GATT) – hardly a subject to set the romantic pulse racing.

What the woman didn't know, as she assiduously courted the civil servant, was that her conversations were being monitored by French counter-espionage agents. For in reality the woman was employed not by a little-known organization in Dallas, Texas, but by a rather well-known one in Langley, Virginia – the Central Intelligence Agency. She was one of a team of five CIA agents who were cajoling and allegedly trying to bribe French officials in an effort to secure information about the ongoing GATT negotiations. The decision to spy on an ally in this way had already caused a furious row within the highest circles of American diplomacy. When the CIA's Paris station chief briefed Pamela Harriman, America's formidable ambassador to France, about the operation, she was outraged and immediately protested to national security advisor Anthony Lake in Washington. In no uncertain terms, Lake told her that given the precarious state of the GATT negotiations and the pivotal role of the French, the Commerce Department needed all the intelligence it could possibly get by whatever means.

Matters were certainly delicate. Originally hammered out in 1947, the GATT had been part of the post-war settlement designed to remove tariffs, taxes and other measures which impeded international trade. It was an American idea intended to foster closer economic ties between individual nations, preventing a recurrence of the worldwide depression experienced during the 1930s, while at the same time promoting the cause of peace. Twenty-three countries had signed up to the first agreement which over the following decades was extended in a series of complex negotiations. In this latest round of discussions, which had begun in Uruguay in 1986, negotiators had spent years haggling over everything from payments to European farmers to let their fields lie fallow to defence subsidies for aircraft manufacturers. So prolix were the discussions that in some quarters GATT had been dubbed the General Agreement to Talk and Talk. Slowly and painfully, during the autumn of 1993, the issues of agriculture and aerospace had at last been resolved. But there was one final sticking point which posed a threat to years of work: the USA wanted the film and television industries brought within the scope of GATT. Some European nations were totally opposed, arguing that the unique cultural nature of films made them quite unlike the normal run of internationally traded goods and services. They insisted on their right to protect their film and television industries through the continuance of a complex series of subsidies and quotas.

As a film producer who had spent twenty-five years working on both sides of the Atlantic, including a spell running a Hollywood studio, it was perhaps inevitable that I should find myself deeply embroiled in this debate. I had friends and allies on both sides of the battle and was desperately keen to help find a way out of the impasse. In September, the American directors Steven Spielberg and Martin Scorsese, both of whom had warmly acknowledged the influence of European cinema, had taken out a full-page advertisement in an American trade paper blasting the position of their overseas colleagues. 'If artists demand freedom to create without constraint, we must also demand freedom to travel without restrictions ... We cannot lock our borders, any more than we ought to close our minds.' I was a member of a group of European film-makers which also included Spain's Pedro Almodóvar, Italy's Bernardo Bertolucci and Germany's Wim Wenders who felt compelled to fire back, publishing a rather hastily prepared open letter in the trade press. 'We are desperately defending the tiny margin of freedom left to us,' it proclaimed. 'We are trying to protect European Cinema against its complete annihilation.'

Indeed, since my return from running Columbia in 1988, I had been channelling an ever-greater degree of energy into seeking a political solution to the problems faced by Europe's film and television industries in the face of the ever-increasing dominance of American movies across the continent. By 1993, with the European film industry firmly locked into a spiral of decline, these issues were consuming a growing proportion of my time. In October of that year I was invited to speak at a conference organized by the European Commission on future employment policies, where I highlighted the potential of the audio-visual industry to create hundreds of thousands of new jobs. With help from producers all over Europe, we made an eight-minute video entitled *It's Our Choice*, in which we argued that Europe had the creative genius and the financial resources to make our continent a power-house of world entertainment. Just a few weeks later I was appointed to a small think-tank assembled by the European Commission to reflect on policy initiatives to help Europe's ailing film and television industries meet the challenge from Hollywood. Our task was to help Europe find a future which would be creatively and commercially vigorous without resorting to the damaging and negative policies it had sometimes implemented in the past. We argued that it was time to move from an attitude of cultural defence to one of commercial success.

Barely had our discussions begun when the row over the film industry flared into life at the GATT talks. As the autumn dragged on, the rhetoric grew ever more heated. I found myself working with a small group of film-makers and politicians in a frantic attempt to find a compromise which would enable the two sides to resolve their differences in a constructive manner.

On one side, Hollywood's chief lobbyist, Jack Valenti, who as head of the Motion Picture Association of America had spent half a lifetime battling on behalf of his country's film industry, argued that 'the American audio-visual industry is everywhere under siege ... [its] very success in attracting world-wide viewers of all races, religions, nationalities and cultures has incited a counter-attack by foreign governments.' He pointed out that some 40 per cent of revenues of the American film and television industry were now earned overseas, with more than half of that total coming from Europe. Entertainment had become America's second largest export, after aircraft manufacturing. The American film and television industry brought back more than $3.5 billion a year in surplus balance of payments to the United States. Valenti and his colleagues were backed to the hilt by President Clinton who regarded the issue as so important that he personally telephoned Helmut Kohl, the German Chancellor, and Edouard Balladur, the French Prime Minister, to inform them that he had no intention of backing down over the audio-visual industry. Indeed, it was a big issue for Clinton himself; in early December, just a few days before the final talks in Geneva, the President had attended a star-studded dinner in Hollywood that raised $2 million for the Democratic Party.

The European counter-attack was led by the French. 'Creations of the spirit are not just commodities; the elements of culture are not pure business,' proclaimed President François Mitterrand. 'What is at stake is the cultural identity of all our nations ... it is the freedom to create and choose our own images. A society which abandons the means of depicting itself would soon be an enslaved society.' In response to the tirade of rhetoric from across the Atlantic, the Europeans pointed out that while Hollywood movies accounted for 80 per cent of box-office revenues across much of Europe, films produced in Europe accounted for less than one per cent of the American box office.

In France, the imbalance was dramatically symbolized by the box-office battle between Steven Spielberg's blockbuster *Jurassic Park* and Claude Berri's *Germinal*, the most expensive French film ever made. *Jurassic Park*, developed from Michael Crichton's novel, was packed with dazzling special effects and breathtaking action sequences. Supported by a huge advertising and promotional budget, it was turning out to be the highest grossing film the world had ever seen. *Germinal*, on the other hand, based on one of the great classics of French literature, was a three-hour epic about the struggles of a group of miners. It had been partly financed through a complex system of national subsidies. In October 1993, as the films were about to go head-to-head at the box office, the weekly news magazine *L'Express* ran a cover story featuring a colossal dinosaur striding across Paris under the headline, 'Culture: the American offensive.'

Amid all of this the GATT negotiating teams were dispatched to Geneva and told that if they failed to reach a resolution by 15 December then the whole agreement was void, with the risk that world trade would be plunged into chaos and acrimony. By the early hours of 14 December no such resolution had been reached;

everything now hinged on finding a settlement to the issue of film and television. Shortly before dawn in a spartan conference room on the eighth floor of an office block in the city centre, at the climax of the most critical and far-reaching international trade negotiations since the Second World War, two highly influential politicians found themselves sitting down and arguing about the movies. Mickey Kantor, a Californian lawyer and chief negotiator for the American administration, and Sir Leon Brittan, former British Home Secretary, representing the European Union, both found themselves unable to yield.

Amid the ferocious manoeuvrings and negotiations which led up to that cold dawn in Geneva, it increasingly struck me that the battle being fought was, in many respects, just one more in a war as old as cinema itself. In an uncanny way, the positions of the two sides had changed very little in the course of a hundred years. And it was a war that appeared destined to be fought ever more fiercely in the future as an array of new multi-media services and technologies came into being. Indeed, for all the nationalistic rhetoric, it was clear that, at some deeper level, the struggles over GATT were part of a long-running war of attrition over the very concept of culture. It was a battle about the status of mass culture and the potential of that culture to shape and transform our daily lives.

That was when I first had the idea of writing this book in an attempt to trace the roots of the whole affair. What follows is the story of a war which has raged for over a century and shows little sign of abating. To understand the genesis of this struggle we have to go back to the time when motion pictures were about to be born.

2

'An invention without any commercial future'

LOUIS LUMIÈRE, 1896

BY THE LATE 1880s, Thomas Alva Edison was universally hailed as the world's most celebrated inventor. In an age of increasing technical specialization he was an engineer in the tradition of the early Industrial Revolution, a creative and aggressive entrepreneur whose abilities seemed to encompass almost every branch of science and technology. In other respects, too, he resembled some of those early Iron Masters, possessing an ego that more than matched his talent. He claimed sole credit for inventions as diverse as the electric light-bulb and the phonograph. He insisted that he had played a part in the conception of scores of other devices which were beginning to transform the daily lives of millions of people throughout the industrialized world, including the telephone, the typewriter and the lead-acid battery. Throughout his homeland and across the world, he was honoured as a self-made prophet of progress, the seer of a new industrial age.

Edison was the supreme representative of a group of gifted

9

Americans who, from the early nineteenth century onwards, had been responsible for a series of inventions that had come to define the new industrial era. In 1807 Robert Fulton had launched the first steamboat, in 1844 Samuel Morse had created the first electric telegraph. For many Americans such technological innovation had become a measure of national stature. As the steel tycoon Andrew Carnegie put it: 'The old nations of the earth creep on a snail's pace; the Republic thunders past with the rush of the express.' For a nation founded on something as fragile as ideals rather than a shared language or a deep-rooted culture, the notion of progress as epitomized by men like Edison became a means of providing the country with a tangible identity.

Now, as the end of the century loomed, Edison turned to a problem which seemed to have defeated an army of inventors and scientists the world over: he set out to create a machine capable of projecting moving images. Throughout the nineteenth century, an endless array of bizarre contraptions for projecting moving pictures – the Actograph, the Phantascope, the Thaumatograph – had been registered with patent offices everywhere. But such devices were little more than toys, and had been quickly tossed aside. The true solution seemed as far away as ever.

None of these inventors, however, could lay claim to anything remotely resembling the reputation and influence of Thomas Edison. His life story has been encrusted with myth – much of it carefully nurtured by the man himself – but his remarkable journey from relatively humble beginnings in the backwoods of Ohio to his acknowledged position as the most successful inventor of the age was real enough. Born in 1847, the son of a timber dealer of Dutch descent, Edison was educated almost entirely by his mother and, perhaps, inherited from her that sense of iron resolve and puritanical self-denial so characteristic of the Protestant settlers of the eastern United States. At the age of twelve he took his first job as a newsboy and candy salesman on local trains. A growing interest in the new science of telegraphy spurred him to set up a laboratory in the corner of one of the baggage cars. In later life he claimed that his partial deafness was the result of having been boxed on the ears by a conductor for having set the carriage alight with one particularly outlandish experiment.

By the age of twenty-one Edison had patented his first invention – the ticker-tape machine, itself destined to become a symbol of the dynamism of American capitalism. Within ten years he had built a vast laboratory at Menlo Park in New Jersey, complete with its own electric railway in the grounds, funded with money he had made from the exploitation of his copyrights and patents. As ever more miraculous inventions poured forth from this laboratory, Edison became known as the Wizard of Menlo Park. Soon he built himself an even bigger laboratory at nearby West Orange, equipped with sleeping facilities so that he and his dedicated team could grab a quick nap in the course of their late-night sessions perfecting yet another startling new device.

In public, Edison loved to play the self-deprecating inventor, oblivious to everything but the disinterested pursuit of science, his bad hearing only serving to emphasize his apparent unworldliness. One contemporary recalled Edison materializing from 'a maze of wires and gadgets . . . the great shock of hair prematurely grey, the boyish look, eyes a baby blue, voice deep and friendly'. Behind this public façade, the Wizard was an incorrigible egoist and a somewhat shameless plagiarist, happy to take credit for what were in many cases other people's ideas. His commitment to scientific endeavour, considerable though it was, paled into insignificance beside his dedication to self-promotion and the elimination of competition, be it from friends, colleagues or rivals. It was speculated that he had mysteriously arranged the murder of a French inventor, Augustin Le Prince, as a means of ridding himself of a dangerous competitor. In fact, the Wizard retained his pre-eminence not so much by sorcery, murder or publicity stunts as by a ceaseless stream of law-suits alleging patent infringement by his rivals. This became the principal instrument with which he set out to seize control of the world of moving pictures.

Until the late 1880s, Thomas Edison had shown little interest in photography or in any of the early attempts to develop motion pictures. Then in 1888 he attended a lecture by the British photographer Eadweard Muybridge. With his shaggy, tobacco-stained beard, and hat pockmarked with holes, Muybridge looked like a tramp, but he was a skilled and inventive artist. Fifteen years earlier, he had been hired by Leland Stanford, the Governor of California, to undertake what had become a classic series of high-speed photographs demonstrating beyond doubt that a galloping horse lifted all its feet off the ground at once.

After the lecture Edison invited the great photographer back to his laboratory where they discussed the possibility of combining Edison's phonograph with the Zoopraxiscope, a motion picture device that Muybridge had just developed. It was an astonishingly audacious idea, a synthesis of sound and moving pictures which, had it been successful, would have pre-dated the arrival of the first full-length 'talkies' by almost forty years. The collaboration between the two men came to nothing. The Wizard's fertile mind, however, had become fully engaged by the potential of moving pictures. He assigned one of his young assistants, William Dickson, a Scot, to work on developing a machine which could both record and project moving images.

At first Dickson made little headway. Then, in the summer of 1889, Edison visited the World's Fair in Paris where he was treated to a demonstration of a new machine designed by a Frenchman, Étienne Jules Marey. Marey's 'Chronophotographe' fired Edison with new enthusiasm and, as he sailed back across the Atlantic, he sketched a draft of a machine of his own, based almost entirely on Marey's work.

Two years later, in May 1891, Edison unveiled the fruits of his labour, a crude arcade novelty which he named the 'Kinetoscope'. By dropping a coin through a slot in a large, heavy wooden cabinet, the spectator activated a tiny motor which moved spools of celluloid. An electric light flashed on to the film allowing the spectator to watch moving pictures of humans and animals through a peephole in the side of the box. The 'films' themselves were crude; snatches of vaudeville acts, boxing matches, circus performers and the like, few of which lasted more than twenty seconds.

Material for the Kinetoscope was shot in a studio hastily rigged up in the garden of Edison's laboratory. With its 'great flapping sail-like roof and ebony complexion', it was nicknamed the 'Black Maria' because of its resemblance to a police patrol wagon. The 'stars' of Edison's films, an exotic procession of vaudeville artistes, trapeze artists, performing bears and even a dancing cat, now trooped through the grounds at West Orange. 'No earthly stage has ever gathered within its precincts a more incongruous crew of actors since the days when gods and men and animals were on terms of social intimacy', observed William Dickson, with perhaps just a hint of exasperation.

Edison, his attention distracted by a plethora of other projects, demonstrated surprisingly little interest in the commercial exploitation of his Kinetoscope. Confident of its superior technical qualities, he patented the basic concept and turned to other things. Like so many prolific inventors, his interest waned once he felt he had successfully cracked the problem he had set himself. And like engineers a hundred years later, wrestling with the complexities of cyberspace, laser discs and virtual reality, his vision of the moving picture business focused almost exclusively on the technology. He failed to anticipate that its real significance lay in the images themselves. This may have reflected Edison's cultural roots, since the tradition of Dutch Puritanism carried within it a deep mistrust of both entertainment and the idea of representation. He probably found the notion that his ingenious device, the Kinetoscope, was obliged to survive on a diet of clowns and dancing cats extremely dispiriting.

As if to emphasize this, Edison later suggested that what really intrigued him about film was its potential as a teaching tool. 'It may seem curious, but the money end of the movies never hit me the hardest. The feature that did appeal to me about the whole thing was the educational possibilities ... I had some glowing dreams about what the camera could be made to do and ought to do in teaching the world things it needed to know – teaching it in a more vivid, direct way.' In this respect at least, Edison was firmly ahead of his time; almost one hundred years would pass before the potential of using moving images as a teaching tool would come to be fully realized.

In 1893 Edison licensed the commercial rights for the Kineto-scope to a pair of aggressive young entrepreneurs, Norman Raff and Frank Gammon. Within a year they had opened hundreds of Kinetoscope parlours throughout the United States. Two years later the parlours would stand shuttered and abandoned as new, far more sophisticated machines captured the public's imagination. Far from being the dawn of a new era, it seemed that Edison's Kinetoscope peep-show had done no more than mark the close of the first chaotic chapter in the evolution of cinema. Actually it had achieved far more than that. By virtue of his illustrious reputation, Edison's efforts galvanized other entrepreneurs in America and Europe into action. With Edison's attention distracted elsewhere, his rivals on both sides of the Atlantic prepared for battle.

By late 1893, in the French city of Lyon, one adversary was already hard at work. Antoine Lumière had just the mix of pride, flamboyance and gall required to join battle with Edison. The son of a wine-grower, he had begun his career as a sign-painter in Besançon, before establishing himself as a photographer. A ferociously im-patient character – who occasionally smashed furniture in a fit of temper – he quickly grew bored of taking snapshots for provincial family albums. After reading about a new technique for manufactur-ing photographic dry plates pioneered by the Belgian chemist Van Monkhoven, he determined to make his own plates in his cramped basement studio in the centre of Lyon.

Antoine's early attempts to manufacture the plates were a fiasco. He was simply too impetuous. In desperation he turned to Louis, his teenage son, who excelled at science in school. Louis quickly managed not only to emulate Van Monkhoven, but to surpass him. At the age of seventeen, he had created an entirely new form of dry plate, 'Étiquette Bleue' or 'Blue Label', far more sensitive than anything yet invented. With photographic portraits a fast-growing fashion for all but the very poorest families the Lumières quickly grew rich beyond their wildest imaginings. To meet the overwhelming demand for their product, they opened a huge new factory in the Lyon suburb of Monplaisir.

As the money flowed in, so Antoine's tastes grew ever more extravagant. He relished the good life and enjoyed nothing more than throwing banquets for family and friends, which frequently concluded with rousing patriotic songs and the smashing of a great deal of glassware. By 1882 he had all but bankrupted the family firm and his two sons, Louis and Auguste were eventually obliged to take control.

Antoine's competitive instincts continued to drive the business. A fervent French nationalist, he had already developed a fierce antipathy towards the Americans. He loathed the way they had excluded exports of French photographic products by using a punitive series of duties established in the wake of the McKinley Tariff of 1890. The bill had been engineered by the future president and fervent opponent of free trade, William McKinley, nicknamed the 'Great Protector'. It raised duties in the United States to their highest-ever levels and was seen as an instrument to allow the country to nurture its infant industries and become an industrial giant in the face of established competitors in Europe. In a report on the photographic trade prepared for the French government following his visit to the Chicago World Fair of 1890, Antoine Lumière presaged the sentiments, and even the terminology, of the American GATT negotiators a century later. 'It is not an entrance duty which hits our products', he complained, 'it is a form of prohibition, while we have left our own door almost completely open [to the Americans].' He went on to argue that the key to the popularity of American goods in overseas markets was not their intrinsic quality so much as their talent for boastful publicity, observing in passing that the actual quality of American photographic equipment left a great deal to be desired.

In the summer of 1894 a friend showed him one of Edison's

new Kinetoscopes. Here, Antoine realized with delight, was an opportunity to steal a hugely lucrative business from under the very noses of the Americans. He rushed to his son Louis' office. 'He took out of his pocket a bit of Kinetoscope film that he had got from Edison's agents', recalled Charles Moisson, a Lumière employee, 'and [he] said to Louis, "This is what you should make, since Edison sells it at hugely inflated prices and he wants to start manufacturing it here in France".' The impresario versus the Wizard. Lumière versus Edison. France versus America. Battle had been joined.

It soon became clear to Antoine and his sons that if they were to win a significant share of this new market they would have to develop a camera and a projector of their own. But like so many of their competitors, they were unable to find any way of moving the strip of film smoothly through a camera. Once again, it was the meticulous Louis who hit upon the solution. It came to him when he was lying in bed, prevented from sleeping by one of his habitual headaches and providing Auguste with his subsequent boast that his brother had invented the idea of cinema in a single night. Louis simply adapted the sprocket mechanism of the newly popular sewing machines in such a way as to allow a strip of film to glide along at a constantly controlled speed. Housed in a wooden box, the machine he created had the remarkable capacity to serve both as camera and projector. Even more significantly, his new device, instead of being limited to a single viewer, allowed large groups of people to watch the images it projected. Thus was born the idea of communal viewing, one which would remain at the heart of the cinema-going experience.

In the meantime, a fierce family row erupted over the choice of name for the new machine. The ever ebullient Antoine proposed to call it the Domitor, apparently because he believed it would dominate the competition. It was one more symbolic manifestation of Antoine's will to win, his desperate desire always to be the biggest and the best. His more cautious sons remained stoutly opposed, and eventually their choice of name, the Cinématographe, derived from the Greek word for movement, won the day.

By the end of summer 1894, the camera was sufficiently developed for Louis to shoot a rudimentary film, *La Sortie des Usines Lumière*, (Workers leaving the Lumière Factory). In March the following year, the Lumière family organized a number of screenings for French scientific institutions. To their astonishment, these moving pictures created far more interest than the revolutionary colour photographs which the brothers exhibited as part of the same demonstration. Word of the invention quickly spread. A daily flood of enquiries from inventors and showmen poured into the Monplaisir factory. All were anxious to acquire one of the new machines, but Louis and Auguste, wary of plagiarism, refused to contemplate selling to anybody.

Meanwhile Antoine, ever hungry for public affirmation of victory over his competitors, began agitating for a public demonstration of the Cinématographe in Paris. His sons at first resisted the idea. By convincing them that a pack of rival inventors would soon offer competing machines to Parisian theatre-owners, Antoine finally got his way.

The venue Antoine picked for the launch of the Cinématographe was the Salon Indien, an empty basement beneath the Grand Café, at 14 boulevard des Capucines, near the Place de l'Opéra. The Grand Café was a meeting point for cultivated Parisians, a place where they gathered to exchange literary and political gossip. Only with hindsight would it become clear just how fitting it was that moving pictures – which would long be regarded as a squalid and altogether immoral amusement fit only for the ignorant masses – should make their public debut in a shabby basement hidden from the genteel society dining above.

The first exhibition of the films was set for the evening of 28 December 1895. Just hours before this first show Antoine was still desperately drumming up support for the event, begging anyone he knew to make their way to the Salon Indien. 'You who amaze everyone with your tricks, you must come and see something which might well amaze you,' he told his friend Georges Méliès, a renowned magician. Méliès duly appeared, one of only thirty-three spectators who paid the 1 franc admission fee. He recalled:

> The other guests and I found ourselves in front of a small screen, similar to those we use for . . . projections. After a few minutes, a stationary photograph showing the Place Bellecour in Lyons was projected. Somewhat surprised, I whispered to my neighbour, 'Have we been brought here just to see projections? I've been doing them for more than ten years.' I had hardly finished speaking when a horse pulling a cart started to walk towards us, followed by other vehicles, then passers-by – in short, all the bustle of a street. At this sight, we sat with our mouths open, thunderstruck, speechless with amazement. At the end of the screening, all was madness, and everyone wanted to know how they might obtain the same results.

The films projected that evening were simple enough – a few images of Auguste Lumière and his wife feeding their baby, some shots of a train approaching a station platform along with a number of similar vignettes taken from daily life. They each lasted barely a minute and the entire show was over in less than half an hour. What made these clips far more striking than the flickering images glimpsed through the peephole of a Kinetoscope was that they were being amplified and thrown forwards on to a screen clearly visible to everyone in the room. Projected in this way, even the simplest moving images acquired a power and majesty which few could have anticipated. Audiences at the early Lumière screenings jumped aside in terror to avoid being hit by the train as it appeared to steam towards them. Crude as the images might now seem, their visceral impact on the audience anticipated the attraction that special-effect movies would have decades later. The basic appeal of the cinema as a form of heightened sensation has never really disappeared. Just as early films came to form an essential part of the attractions at fairgrounds, so the experience of watching many latter-day Hollywood blockbusters increasingly came to resemble taking a ride at a theme-park. A century later, some European intellectuals, notably in France, would spend a great deal of time denouncing the shallow, worthless pleasures offered by such American movies, apparently forgetting from where this particular kind of cinematic enjoyment had first originated. It was symptomatic of the way in which, in the debate over cinema, notions of cultural integrity would become increasingly confused with arguments about national identity.

Amid the chaos at the end of this first show, the director of the Folies-Bergère, one of the most powerful figures in the French entertainment world, offered Lumière 50,000 francs for a single machine. Antoine, fearing piracy, was adamant, insisting that no amount of money would induce him to sell. 'We left, enchanted on the one hand, but on the other disappointed and unhappy because we immediately understood the immense financial success which could result from this discovery,' recalled Méliès ruefully, realizing that the rewards were likely to be reaped by the Lumière family alone.

News of the images which could be viewed at the Salon Indien swept across France. Traditional amusements, like freak shows and waxwork museums, suddenly looked pitifully tame. Before long, 2500 people a day were queueing along the boulevard des Capucines, waiting for hours for a chance to see the Lumière show. Fighting broke out and the police were called to keep order. The owner of the Grand Café, a Monsieur Volpini, like generations of cautious European cinema-owners yet to come, nervously rejected a deal offering 20 per cent of the receipts, opting instead for a flat fee of just 30 francs a day, and then – too late – deeply regretted his decision.

It was Louis Lumière who perfected the technology that made the public projection of moving pictures possible. But in first exhorting his sons to take on Edison and then orchestrating the Grand Café screening, it was Antoine who had really transformed moving pictures into a public spectacle. Like so many successful entrepreneurs of the early cinema, Antoine was a self-made man, someone who relied on instinct rather than intellect as a means of achieving his goals. Unlike his more cerebral sons, he was naturally attracted to moving pictures, fascinated by the dream-like illusions conjured up in the dark from a tiny roll of celluloid. Auguste and Louis remained in Lyon on the night of the first public screening, thinking it more important to attend to routine business at the factory. 'The cinema is an invention without any commercial future,' Louis continued to assert, even after the screening. Together with Auguste, he took refuge in their belief that moving images were little more than a scientific curiosity. For all that, they were happy to cash in on it for as long as it lasted, perhaps because they saw it as a convenient and relatively painless way to fund their own scientific research.

As if to emphasize his indifference to the medium which he had brought to life, Louis soon gave up making films, although he assigned a team of specially trained apprentices, who doubled as cameramen and projectionists, to fan out across the world shooting new material as they went. He still maintained that it was all just a craze which would inevitably die down as quickly as it had started. 'You know, Mesguich, we're not offering anything with prospects, it's more of a fairground job,' he told one of these itinerant cameramen. 'It may last six months, a year, perhaps more, probably less.'

Louis' conviction that the crowds would quickly melt away, distracted by some other fad, may have been rooted as much in his bourgeois distaste for commercial spectacle as in any genuine scepticism about the money-making potential of the Cinématographe. For the rest of his life he seems to have harboured resentment about the way in which his invention had been undervalued and corrupted by commercial exploitation. 'Had I been able to foresee what the cinema would become,' he later confessed, 'I would never have invented it.'

This snobbish unease about a medium whose primary appeal was to the poorest in society found many echoes in the years to come. On both sides of the Atlantic, but particularly in Europe, scientific, artistic and even commercial interest in the cinema was tempered by a deep suspicion and unease among the cultural elite. Many of them openly despised the cinema, seeing it as dependent on vulgar showmanship and the patronage of the very lowest orders of society. For this reason its development was largely left in the hands of individual mavericks blessed with a combination of colossal energy and a low level of embarrassment. With the exception of Edison's firm, no established corporation on either side of the Atlantic showed any interest in the movies whatsoever. So it was that this strange and ghostly new medium, founded on nothing more tangible than a few rolls of celluloid film, took shape outside the established social and economic order. Little wonder that as it grew in popularity it should be blamed for all manner of depravities, regardless of the existence of any tangible link between the medium and the behaviour it was supposed to promote.

Meantime, word of this new phenomenon had crossed the Atlantic and the ever-watchful Edison was desperate to lay his hands on a Cinématographe. As early as October 1895 one of his subordinates had written to the Lumière Brothers asking if he could purchase one of their new machines. Auguste stalled, replying that the Cinématographe was still in early development. Within days of the screening at the Grand Café, Edison fired off another letter beseeching them to sell him the equipment needed to manufacture the Cinématographe. The Lumière Brothers, wary of Edison's reputation, demurred.

In the months that followed, suspicion turned to enmity. In May 1896 the organizers of a trade show in Geneva suggested to Louis that he might like to put the Cinématographe on display in a pavilion set aside for Thomas Edison. He furiously rejected the offer of sharing a stand. 'If there had been a pavilion for Marey,' he fulminated, 'then we might properly have sheltered under the French flag.' What mattered most was maintaining a united front against the Americans.

Whatever the misgivings of its inventor, the Cinématographe established itself as an international marvel with quite remarkable speed. One of the first overseas shows was organized in London by the illusionist Félicien Trewey, a friend of Antoine, at the Marlborough Hall in Regent Street on 20 February 1896. The initial screenings received a rapturous welcome and, after a fortnight or so, the show transferred to a far bigger venue, the Empire Theatre in Leicester Square, where it would play for almost eighteen months. Wherever the Lumière showmen went, from Bombay to Osaka, from Jerusalem to Rio de Janeiro, the reaction was equally powerful; an image as simple as that of a woman feeding her baby in an unknown and far-off country was enough to whip the audience into a frenzy of excitement.

The Lumière Brothers faced fierce competition, especially in America. The Cinématographe made its debut in the United States before a packed house at Keith's Union Square Theater in New York City on 29 June 1896. It was trailed in the *New York Times* as 'The Sensation of Europe – Exhibited before all the Crowned Heads and hailed universally as the Greatest Marvel of the 19th Century'. Within weeks the machine, now billed as 'America's greatest sensation', was playing in vaudeville theatres across the country. 'Never in all our experience have we seen an attraction draw such crowds as the Cinématographe,' wrote one journalist. American-made devices intended to rival the French machine were swept aside, among them the Vitascope, a crude projection system whose basic design Edison had lifted from an inventor called Thomas Armat.

American firms were furious that an upstart French concern could move into the United States and cream off profits that they felt should be pouring into their own coffers. They fought back desperately to regain control of their own market. The challenge was led by the American Mutoscope Company, formed in 1896 by Edison's former assistant, William Dickson, who had teamed up with two enterprising New York businessmen, Herman Casler and Harry Marvin. In October 1896, Dickson's company launched its own projector, the Biograph, which produced larger and far sharper images than those projected by the Cinématographe. 'It has the additional advantage of showing entirely American views,' added one provincial newspaper. Another device, the Vitagraph, followed. The Cinématographe was yesterday's sensation. By April 1897, the Lumière's American subsidiary had been broken up and sold.

Although the Lumière Brothers had been the losers in a battle against superior technology, there were also darker whisperings that they had been victims of political harassment. According to the Lumière projectionist Félix Mesguich, the company was the target of a brutal campaign of intimidation. He alleged that the Lumières faced a barrage of law-suits for supposed breaches of customs regulations. He claimed to have been arrested for filming in Central Park without a permit. He even suggested that Lumière's head of operations in America, fearing for his personal safety, had been forced to flee the country, secretly paddling by canoe to board a French liner waiting in the Hudson.

Perhaps Mesguich had been watching too many of his own film shows. There is little doubt that his tales were exaggerated, but it is also true that the American Mutoscope Company did have close ties to some of the more fervent protectionists who dominated Washington during the administration of President McKinley. It was certainly not beyond the bounds of possibility that the firm had leaned heavily on the administration in an attempt to squeeze the Gallic invaders out of a market which they regarded as their own.

As the leaders of the race to develop moving pictures, inventors from both France and America claimed credit for the invention. Economic rivalry between the two countries was only natural. Such tensions could also be seen in terms of the deeper ideological rivalry between the two nations. Both had been founded through revolutions which aspired to create a set of values – of enlightenment, liberty and progress – which they aspired to make universal. In France a series of repressive governments had betrayed many of these ideals. Equally, many French intellectuals no longer saw the United States as a democratic utopia but as a nation of rapacious philistines, obsessed with money, a position articulated by the poet Charles Baudelaire when he denounced America as a 'Gaslit Barbary'. The Statue of Liberty, designed by the French sculptor Frédéric-Auguste Bartholdi and unveiled in New York a few years earlier in October 1886, had been intended to help both sides put aside their suspicions. It was a gift from France to America, which would help rejuvenate the friendship between the two countries and boost trade, while symbolizing the liberal ideals which both countries shared. But the bond with France was quickly forgotten, the increase in trade failed to materialize and the statue soon became an icon of American values alone. Now it must have seemed to the French that moving pictures, too, were about to be appropriated by the Americans.

Whatever its role in the demise of the Lumière business in the United States, American Mutoscope was already engaged in an acrimonious domestic battle with Edison. By 1896, alarmed by his competitors' success, Edison had resurrected an old patent application from 1891 and, with suitable amendments, filed it anew with the Patents Office. He claimed that he had created a device for viewing moving pictures long before anyone else, and that any subsequent machines therefore infringed his patent even though they might be infinitely more sophisticated than the crude contraptions he had originally assembled. By 1898 he was confident enough to initiate law-suits against a host of rival companies. His suit against American Mutoscope sparked off a ferocious battle which dragged on for ten years, played out in courtrooms and in vicious confrontations in streets and theatres across the country.

Such acrimony was probably inevitable. With millions of customers flocking to witness the miracle of living pictures, there was clearly big money to be made. No one knew just how long the moving pictures craze would last. Many remained convinced it would all be over in a matter of months, perhaps even weeks. With so much at stake, competitors brutally elbowed each other out of the way in their determination to pile up wealth as quickly as they could. The mood was not so much that of a steadily developing industry as of a frantic and chaotic gold-rush.

Lumière's cameramen and salesmen travelled the world, with Edison's men, and a pack of other rivals, never far behind. Competition was particularly fierce in Great Britain. One early pioneer was William Friese-Greene, who took out a patent for a camera taking ten photographs a second. Despite the inventor's flair for publicity, such machines were too clumsy to achieve commercial success. When Friese-Greene collapsed and died at a cinema exhibitors meeting in 1921, his only asset was the money found in his pocket – apparently, one shilling and ten pence, equivalent to the price of a cinema seat. By February 1896, a brilliantly inventive British instrument-maker called Robert Paul had developed his own system for projecting moving images. Paul had become intrigued a few years earlier after a friend introduced him to a couple of Greek showmen who had bought some Kinetoscopes from Edison's agents in New York. The Greeks had installed the machines in a shop near London's Liverpool Street station where the public paid twopence each to see thirty-second films like *Boxing Cats* and *A Shoeblack at Work*. The showmen now implored Paul to help them acquire additional machines. On discovering that Edison had not bothered to take out a British patent, Paul quickly built six duplicate Kinetoscopes and, with public enthusiasm running higher than ever, decided to go into the moving picture business for himself. He developed his own camera and teamed up with a photographer, Birt Acres.

In the spring of 1895, Paul and Acres shot their first films. These included scenes from nature such as *Rough Sea at Dover*, which caused the audience to duck to avoid being splashed by the waves, as well as sporting events like the Derby and the Oxford and Cambridge boat race. The partnership soon dissolved. Next Paul created his own projector, the Animatograph, unveiled at Finsbury Technical College in London on 20 February 1896, the same day as Félicien Trewey gave the first British performance of the Lumière films. Within weeks the Animatograph had been installed at Olympia, London's largest exhibition hall, where it drew vast crowds.

As news of the Animatograph spread, an army of music-hall proprietors, magicians and fairground showmen from all over the world converged on the inventor's workshop. Cecil Hepworth, who became a leading British film-maker, recalled a visit:

> His work-room was at the very top of a tall building. I stumbled
> up the narrow staircase, trying not to tread upon the dozen or
> more sleeping Polish and Armenian Jews who had been waiting

. . . days and nights for delivery of "Animatographs". And there at the top was Paul himself, perspiring freely and cranking away at his big clumsy machines in a hopeless endeavour to run them in and make them usable by the weaker folk outside.

Some of Paul's customers proved excessively hasty. 'A gentleman from Spain, anxious to return quickly, proved too impatient to learn how to centre the arc light', he recalled. 'Arriving in Barcelona his first attempt at projection failed, so the disappointed audience threw knives at the screen. He . . . retired to serve a term in a Spanish prison.' Others were too slow; a group of Turkish customers spent so long learning how to use the machine that by the time they came to pay for one they discovered they had exhausted their funds on rumbustious explorations of London's night-life.

Paul's more tenacious and well organized customers ensured that films projected by the Animatograph were soon astounding audiences all over the world. Carl Hertz, an American magician, purchased the equipment just before setting off on an international tour. With Paul's machine as the star attraction, he played to huge crowds wherever he went. In South Africa, 'the audience . . . thought the pictures great, and we did wonderful business', he recalled. In Australia, 'the theatre [was] packed to suffocation . . . while hundreds were turned away from the door.' He even showed films in India billing himself as 'absolutely the world's greatest conjuror'.

There was no doubt that moving pictures were now firmly established as an international attraction. But they had yet to attain a kind of coherent, stable structure that might enable them to develop as an industry. Paul apparently attempted to sell shares in a company which would have taken over all his film activities. Few investors, though, were ready to risk money on such an apparently marginal business, particularly one stigmatized by its links to the ephemeral world of fairgrounds and penny arcades.

In one sense, perhaps, this financial caution was understandable. Two years after the first Lumière screening in Paris, the public's enthusiasm appeared to be on the wane. Although the cameras and projectors had vastly improved, the films themselves were still confined to three basic subject areas: scenics – essentially travelogues featuring 'exotic' lands such as Egypt, India and Japan; topicals – forerunners of the newsreel, covering events such as royal visits and major sporting fixtures; and simple comic skits, comprising scenes of knockabout fun in barbershops and circuses. It seemed as if Louis Lumière might have been right after all, if not in quite the way he imagined; so long as moving images were treated like mere novelties they were destined to have no real future. 'Kindly friends flagged us with predictions', remembered the early American film-maker Albert Smith, 'the day of moving pictures was over, audiences were tired of them, and we would be wise to salvage what we could with a quick sale of our Vitagraph.'

Other events served to diminish further the first flush of public enthusiasm. In May 1897 an exploding projection lamp set fire to a temporary wooden cinema at the Bazar de la Charité in Paris, killing over one hundred people. Showmen everywhere took fright. 'From Russia to England, we received telegram upon telegram containing the withdrawal of orders', recalled one manufacturer. 'We reduced the output of [film] positives by a ratio of ten to one.'

While crowds flocked to see pictures of boxing cats, exotic views and storms in the English Channel, in the months following Antoine Lumière's screening at the Grand Café there was little incentive for inventors to improve the quality of their pictures. Even if the audiences had been less enthusiastic, it is doubtful the story would have been substantially different. The men who had brought moving images to life – Thomas Edison, Louis Lumière, Robert Paul and others – were not showmen. They were technicians. They were fascinated by the intellectual challenge of creating a mechanical eye and, in as much as they were anything more than research engineers, they saw themselves as manufacturers of equipment. The film sequences they shot were intended simply as short-lived novelties, designed to demonstrate the convincing qualities of their projectors and cameras. As a result, none of them sensed the real commercial potential of moving pictures. Not one of them could see that, with customers besieging theatres all over the world, they had created a truly international retail business. After all, the only paying customers who mattered to them were those who purchased equipment and films. So the Lumière Brothers went back to their photographic plate factory; Edison delegated the commercial development of his Kinetoscope to a junior assistant, and Robert Paul, dismissing film as a 'sideline', eventually destroyed his stock of inflammable negatives and returned to his more reliable business as an instrument-maker.

'Animated photography is quite in its infancy,' Cecil Hepworth had warned in 1897. 'Let us hope it will not suffer the unhappy fate of so many infant prodigies and when the unwanted "boom" subsides, as it inevitably will, find itself entangled in a "slump" from which it has not the strength to extricate itself.' This was a fear that would haunt the fragile business of moving images for decades to come, with commentators perpetually poised to read the last rites for Hollywood and national industries around the world. It was true there were signs that the audience was already turning away from moving pictures, but Hepworth's fears of an impending slump turned out to be exaggerated. For what no one had realized was that the real potential of moving pictures had barely been tapped. Before that could happen the inventors, scientists and instrument-makers who had made moving images possible would be pushed aside by a new breed of entrepreneurs and showmen, with very different ideas about what might be the future of this strange new medium of ghost-like images.

3

'All you needed was fifty dollars, a broad and a camera'

EARLY INDUSTRY COMMENTATOR

THROUGHOUT HIS LIFE Charles Pathé was haunted by two things: the memory of the poverty which had blighted his childhood, and a fear of the recurrent illnesses which periodically brought his life to a temporary halt. These two anxieties energized his ferocious drive to succeed, as he sought to create a new life for himself, one in which poverty and pain played no part. Like so many of the pioneers who followed, Pathé would initially be drawn to the world of moving images, not out of some deep-rooted aesthetic interest in the medium, but simply because the fast-growing industry seemed to offer a man with little capital the chance to make large amounts of money relatively quickly. That in itself was enough to make him somewhat atypical in a nation which at that time attached far more importance to ties of blood, inherited wealth and a genteel approach to high culture than it did to the vulgar accumulation of money for its own sake. As the motion picture industry expanded and grew in sophistication, so Pathé's ambition would likewise grow in scope

29

and refinement, with consequences that would fundamentally transform the nature and purpose of moving images.

Pathé had been born on Christmas Day, 1863 in the hamlet of Chevry-Cossigny in the Alsace. His father bought calves, sheep and pigs in the surrounding district while his mother trudged from door to door selling the raw meat. Pathé's father was a brutish man who struggled to keep his business afloat, and the family lived in constant fear of financial ruin. Years later, Charles would recall how he shared his only pair of shoes with his mother.

After leaving school at fourteen he worked in a butcher's shop run by his older brother, Jacques. Determined to make his fortune, and thus escape his straitened circumstances for ever, Charles remained restless. A spell in South America, working as a customs officer, ended in a severe attack of yellow fever and his early return to France. Aged thirty, he was unemployed, penniless and cursed by sickness.

Then, in August 1894, Pathé visited a local fairground to hear one of Edison's phonographs, which had become the talk of the neighbourhood. Customers paid 10 centimes to listen to recordings through earpieces attached to the machine. Pathé was utterly captivated by this contraption capable of cranking out passages from *Carmen* and the *William Tell* overture. He immediately determined to acquire a machine of his own and establish himself as a showman.

After a long struggle he managed to borrow the funds needed to purchase a phonograph, and on the morning of 9 September 1894 he travelled to the fairgrounds around Vincennes without even having enough money to buy his ticket home. By the end of that first day he had made 200 francs, enough to pay his rent for the entire year. Within a few weeks, he was a comparatively rich man.

Pathé found that he thrived amid the noise, dirt and gaudy amusements of the fairground. Sharing their social background, he had an instinctive understanding of his customers. Indeed, they were the only business associates he ever allowed to address him by the familiar '*tu*' rather than the more formal '*vous*'. After working the fairgrounds round Paris for a few months, Pathé bought a shop which he packed with phonographs and various musical accessories. Soon afterwards, as a natural extension of this new business, he began selling Kinetoscopes. Curiosity drew him to one of the early Lumière screenings and he immediately realized there was likely to be a huge demand from the fairgrounds for both projectors and films. 'I decided to leave the sale of phonographs to my wife and two employees', he recalled, 'and devote myself exclusively to the cinématographe.'

He acquired a number of Edison's films, made some copies, and began selling them to fairground showmen. He was also ambitious enough to develop his own camera and projector. For a time the business thrived. But by 1897, battered by the apparent decline in appetite for films, and the impact of the fire at the Bazar de la Charité, the young company's profits from its film activities plunged.

Just as he was on the point of pulling out of the moving picture business altogether, Pathé was fortunate enough to receive an unexpected offer from Claude Grivolas, a wealthy and powerful industrialist from Lyon. Grivolas, a manufacturer of electrical equipment, also happened to be an enthusiastic amateur magician who had bought his films from Pathé in the past to add colour to his magic shows. Convinced of their commercial potential, he now offered to put up enough capital to allow the company to expand its activities in the phonograph and film business. In December 1897, Grivolas, in partnership with another financier, Jean Neyret and the Crédit Lyonnais bank, signed an agreement with Charles and his younger brother Emile which transformed Pathé Frères into a joint stock company with capital of a million francs.

That a relatively established bank like Crédit Lyonnais was prepared to invest in such a speculative venture was unusual. That such a thing should happen in France where the slow pace of industrial development was often blamed on the difficulty of securing capital from banks, was even more surprising. Indeed, most traditional financiers on both sides of the Atlantic would continue to regard the film business and the mercurial outsiders who ran it with undisguised contempt for another twenty-five years. In retrospect, the bank's decision probably had more to do with the fact that it had already established a relationship with Neyret than with any far-sighted conception of the financial potential of the film business.

For men like Charles Pathé the initial attraction of moving pictures had been that little capital was needed and a quick return could be virtually guaranteed. But so long as they lacked significant external finance, the showmen who screened films in tents and fairgrounds remained vulnerable to any sudden downturn in audience demand. By securing outside investment from Grivolas and his associates, Pathé ensured that he had the resources to weather short-term fluctuations and could plan a systematic expansion of his company's activities. An entirely new kind of film company was born.

Pathé was a punctilious man who retained a tight rein on his emotions. With his broad shoulders and his upright gait, he appeared bigger than he really was, enabling him to radiate a natural authority without ever raising his voice or losing his temper. But Pathé had a shrewd sense of the flamboyant, which became increasingly useful in the self-aggrandizing movie business, and helped to spread word of his company's activities. He quickly developed new cameras, new projectors and new techniques for processing raw stock. Business began to flourish. What really revolutionized his fortunes, though, was the decision to move into film production. To run this new department, in 1900 he hired Ferdinand Zecca, a one-time café singer who had recorded some songs for the company's phonographs. Zecca had absolutely no experience of film-making, or even of film-going; in fact, as he later confessed: 'At that time, I'd hardly even thought about the cinema.'

Within a few months Zecca, who because of his diminutive stature was quickly dubbed 'le plus petit grand homme du cinéma',. was pumping out vast numbers of films, serving as writer, producer, director and sometimes even as an actor. Meanwhile, Pathé concentrated his enormous energy on sales, marketing and distribution. Between the two of them they began to develop a more sophisticated understanding of their audience – a concept singularly lacking in the minds of most of their competitors. They quickly sensed that the public was getting bored with an endless diet of scenics and topicals. They wanted longer, narrative films. Zecca set out to exploit this development and in 1901 made *L'Histoire d'un crime*, with a story divided into six parts.

British film-makers had been among the first to respond to the demand for thrilling stories, and the result was movies like James Williamson's *Fire!* in 1902 and Frank Mottershaw's chase picture *Daring Daylight Burglary* made a year later. Despite their undoubted talent they lacked the financial resources to capitalize on their early success and, in what became a familiar story, their influence soon waned. Zecca, by contrast, had the resources to create and market large numbers of longer films. He based his plots on best-selling short stories, with a special emphasis on melodramatic tales of underworld crime and scandal, rightly believing that this was the kind of material which would find favour with the mass audience. In the process he helped create the sense that the film business might, after all, have a long-term future as an entirely new form of visual entertainment. The switch to longer films also had important implications for the way in which they were exhibited. Until that time the majority of film-shows in France, and throughout Europe, were still held in music-halls, magic theatres or even wax museums while, outside the cities, audiences had to make do with tents at travelling fairs. By 1905, as Zecca's longer films created a new confidence in the longevity of the medium, the first permanent cinemas began to appear.

Léon Gaumont, an optical craftsman whose backers included Gustave Eiffel (architect of the tower which dominated Paris), soon followed Pathé's example. Gaumont, the son of a taxi driver, had started work as an office boy for a precision machine company in 1881, before creating his own highly profitable business selling photographic equipment. Beginning in 1905, Gaumont secured outside capital from a number of financial institutions (including a forerunner of the Crédit Commercial de France) and undertook a major expansion into film production. The company's early films were directed by Alice Guy, Gaumont's former secretary, and Louis

Feuillade, who had once written about bullfighting. After the acquisition of a cinema chain, the company quickly became the second most powerful in France and for the next few years, with Pathé and Gaumont at its head, the French industry would tower above its counterparts in the rest of the world.

In other ways, too, the foundations of a modern industry were at last being laid. At the turn of the century producers had sold films outright to the travelling showmen. Sales were made, quite literally, by the yard – the longer the picture, the higher the price. In the USA, the rights to sell the film were sold state by state in what became known as a 'states rights' system. The showmen would then tour the area with the film until either the public grew bored or the print disintegrated. Quite apart from its lack of appeal to audiences, such a system was as expensive as it was inefficient; exhibitors often accumulated vast stocks of unwanted and eventually unusable prints.

Then, towards the end of 1903, a number of American producers – apparently independently – hit upon an entirely revolutionary idea. They began to buy films from other producers and rent them on to individual exhibitors. Among these pioneers were the Miles Brothers of San Francisco. Hearing that the Biograph company was about to sell off a pile of old films at bargain prices, they bought the entire stock and then travelled around the country renting the films out to individual theatres on a weekly basis. New companies began to emerge, specializing in the renting of films, in the process creating outfits that came to be known as 'film exchanges'. Thus was born the modern idea of the film distributor, the specialist middleman controlling the territory between producer and exhibitor.

This apparently simple switch from selling to renting transformed the American film business. Exhibitors were no longer obliged to tour a succession of carnivals and fairs with their cumbersome tents in the hope that if they stayed on the road long enough they would eventually recover the purchase price of their films. They could now establish permanent venues, constantly changing their programme in response to audience demand; this in turn encouraged audiences to return on a far more frequent basis, leading to an enormous surge in attendances and revenues. These new regular cinema-goers demanded a constant diet of innovation and American producers were soon obliged to emulate Ferdinand Zecca and experiment with longer, more ambitious films, in which increasingly complex plots at last supplanted comic sketches and aimless sequences of street life.

Before long these new films began to command a premium on the rental market. Exhibitors would bid fiercely against each other for the newest releases. Since the distributors were able to rent out the same film to several exhibitors at once they could quickly recover their costs, and some even began to generate huge profits. Film production, by its nature, was fraught with uncertainties that ranged from tempestuous actors to stormy weather. The business of distribution, on the other hand, which was not dependent on the fortunes of any one production, was far more predictable. Success for the distributor was almost entirely a matter of having a consistent supply of films and, as far as most early distributors were concerned, the production of those films could happily be left to others.

The American film industry now grew at an astounding rate. The public clamoured unceasingly for new product. A few years earlier, Edison had dismissed the moving image as a mere toy. Now that toy was transforming itself into a burgeoning industry worth millions of dollars. However fast it grew, demand always seemed to outstrip supply. To hundreds of aspiring entrepreneurs the great attraction of the film industry was that the costs of setting up in business were so extraordinarily low. Almost anyone could create their own film company and start cranking out movies, and indeed almost anyone did. 'All you needed was fifty dollars, a broad and a camera,' as someone bluntly put it. The contrast with the modern American industry, in which the gigantic cost of production and distribution prevents any but the richest multinational companies from operating a film studio, could hardly have been greater. If cameras were available they were rented or bought. If not, they were stolen. Bootlegging – of equipment and stock as well as completed films – was rife. The idea of any kind of distinction between the role of the producer (or financier) and that of the director had yet to emerge. The producer-director simply shot the story, developed the negatives, printed some positives and sold the film to a middleman.

Largely as a result of the move from buying to renting prints, by 1905 permanent cinemas were springing up all over the United States. Many were traditional theatres that had been turned over to the moving picture craze. Others were dime museums (so-called because admission was 10 cents) or converted penny arcades, which had once housed hundreds of peep-show machines.

Despite its phenomenal growth, the film business still failed to attract the interest of major investors or finance houses. The institutions which backed Pathé and Gaumont remained the sole exceptions. It is difficult not to conclude that, once again, crude snobbery clouded the judgement of usually astute financiers. The movies were neither respectable commerce nor respectable culture. They were run by what one observer called 'a variegated collection of former carnival men, ex-saloon keepers, medicine men, concessionaires of circus side shows, photographers and peddlers'. They were a diversion for the poor and rootless. Hardly surprising, then, that it was from exactly this group in society that the next wave of successful film pioneers emerged.

In 1905 the American film industry was turned upside down by the advent of an entirely new venue for showing films, called the nickelodeon. Like so much else in the early history of the movies, the nickelodeon was as much a creation of chance than of anything else. In June of that year an amusement arcade in Pittsburgh, owned by local vaudeville tycoon Harry Davis, had been destroyed by fire. Davis was a property speculator who had acquired a number of abandoned shops throughout the city. He decided to rehouse his moving picture show in one of these empty stores, located on the city's Smithfield Street. A few chairs, a projecting machine, a screen and a phonograph were all that was needed to create a venue ready for business. Borrowing a name used by existing amusement arcades, he christened it the Nickelodeon – admission was a nickel (5 cents), while the addition of the term 'Odeon' optimistically suggested a connection with the values of classical Greek theatre. Such was the success of his first venture that Davis quickly installed similar shows in other empty shops all over the city. His simple idea spread like wildfire. Soon the garish lights of the nickelodeon became a familiar sight throughout the slum districts of America's great cities. As one publication described it:

> The nickelodeon is usually a tiny theatre containing 199 seats, giving from 12–18 performances a day, seven days a week. Its walls are painted red. The seats are ordinarily kitchen chairs not fastened. The only break in the red color scheme is made by half a dozen signs, in black and white, No Smoking, Hats Off and sometimes but not always Stay As Long As You Like . . . Last year or the year before it was probably a second-hand clothier's or pawn shop or cigar store. Now the counter has been ripped out, there is a ticket-seller's booth where the shop window was, an automatic musical barker somewhere up in the air thunders its noise down on the passers-by and the little store has been converted into a theatrelet.

What one journalist called 'nickel delirium' now swept America. According to one early estimate, by 1907 there were between four and five thousand nickelodeons located across the country. With each of them offering a dozen or more shows a day, a new audience was being created on a scale that would have been unimaginable for any established forms of entertainment.

The members of this audience were, almost without exception, the urban poor; the new immigrants who could not in their wildest dreams afford the admission prices of the more conventional forms of entertainment to be found in the theatre, at the opera or in vaudeville houses. And even if they could afford the prices, millions of these slum-dwellers were excluded by the even more impenetrable barrier of language. They had come to America from every country in Europe, and most of them spoke little or no English. What enjoyment could they possibly derive from any entertainment which relied primarily on words they didn't yet understand? For them the theatre remained an alien world, as distant and unattainable as the wealthy middle-class suburbs to which the patrons of the respectable arts returned after an evening out. As one early historian put it: 'Ninety percent or more of the American population was not reached by any conventional method of story-telling.'

The nickelodeons changed all that for ever. They gave the urban poor a cheap, affordable entertainment of their own, located – unlike the traditional downtown theatres – in converted stores just a few yards from their homes. Most importantly of all, no one was excluded on grounds of origin or education. They spoke the universal language of visual images, what one writer later called the 'Esperanto of the Eye', and, in the process, created a common experience which drew together all the disparate communities that were then crowding into the New World. 'The newly arrived immigrant from Transylvania can get as much enjoyment out of them as the native,' observed one journalist. 'The imagination is appealed to directly and without any circumlocution.' The plots of the films, simple as they were, spoke directly to the dreams and aspirations of these new and hopeful arrivals. They were tales of fortunes made, of ordinary folk triumphing over adversity, of love won, of loyalty and courage rewarded. The most popular were invariably comedies or thrillers. Many were based on the audacious exploits of hardened criminals: *The Great Train Robbery* made in 1903 by Edwin Porter was something of a landmark and certainly one of the most successful. Since the shows were cheap and short – few ran for more than twenty-five minutes – small groups of friends might spend an entire evening racing excitedly from one venue to another, gazing with awe and wonder at everything they saw. To keep pace with the unceasing demand for new titles, some nickelodeons even changed their programme daily.

The real struggle for control of the booming American market had barely begun. Until the turn of the century, the international trade in films, such as it was, had been conducted largely through local companies which served as agents licensed to sell films on behalf of their overseas clients. The Lumière Brothers had preferred to launch a direct assault on the American market, but their experience hardly inspired others to emulate them.

By 1902, Georges Méliès, Antoine Lumière's magician friend, had grown weary of seeing his films bootlegged and distributed by American companies. Méliès had pioneered some of the earliest special effects in cinema history and had enjoyed remarkable success on both sides of the Atlantic with his dazzlingly inventive film version of Jules Verne's lunar adventure. Despite this he was hopelessly ill-equipped to compete seriously with men like Edison. Working alone in his own small studio, he continued to produce, direct and star in each of his films. He showed no interest in attracting outside capital, treating the business of making moving pictures as if it were a traditional craft in an era when, as a result of the efforts of Charles Pathé, Léon Gaumont and others, they had already become a form of mass entertainment. He decided that the only way to prevent bootlegging, known in the trade as 'duping', was for his company, Star Films, to establish an office of its own in America. He was convinced that this would enable him to exercise far tighter control over the circulation of his films, thus preventing large-scale duplication. 'In opening a factory and office in New York we are prepared and determined energetically to pursue all counterfeiters and pirates. We will not speak twice, we will act,' warned Méliès. It marked the beginning of a renewed French assault on the American film market.

Méliès had good reason to be worried. On one occasion he turned up at Lubin, an American production company, and, without revealing his name, told them he wanted to buy some films. Lubin, like many other companies, simply blocked out the original company trademark on any film it wanted to pirate. Then Lubin made the mistake of screening a film called *A Trip to the Moon*, based on a Jules Verne story, to their anonymous customer. A Lubin executive recalled:

> Suddenly he jumped up from his chair, shot out his arm in front of the beam of light from the projector, and shouted 'Stop the machine'. Startled I stopped grinding and turned on the

light wondering what was wrong. We found out soon enough when the prospective buyer shouted, 'You want me to buy that film?' Lubin wanted to know why not. 'I made that picture,' bellowed the man, thumping his chest. 'I am George Méliès from Paris.' The man, quite naturally, was in a wild rage. Lubin glared at him and, pointing to me, brazenly began telling Méliès what a hard time I'd had blocking out the trademark.

In any case, by 1905, with audiences demanding longer narrative films, the appeal of Méliès' contrived spectacles was rapidly fading. Within a few years, facing financial ruin, he would be forced out of the industry, and was eventually reduced to selling toys from a kiosk at the Gare Montparnasse in Paris.

Pathé, having consolidated his pre-eminent position in the French market, began moving into overseas territories. In 1904 his company opened offices in Moscow and Brussels. America with its vast, booming economy was the real prize. Despite the failure of previous attempts to establish normal trading relations with the United States, Pathé decided to try again. In July 1904, as he was about to open an office in New York, he fired off a warning to Edison: 'For more than a year we have watched the methods employed by your company who copy all our films which they think interesting in defiance of our rights of ownership.' He went on to suggest that the only way to end such piracy was to conclude a deal under which the two companies would once and for all agree not to duplicate each other's films. Edison spurned the offer. No sooner had Pathé opened his American office than a writ arrived from Edison, suing the French firm for breach of patent.

This time the Wizard of Menlo Park had miscalculated. Charles Pathé was a far shrewder, far more resolute adversary than anyone he had previously confronted. Helped by an aggressive pricing policy which enabled him to undercut Edison and other rivals, Pathé began pumping hundreds of films into the United States. Edison, and most of the other American producers, fought back furiously, determined to keep foreign competition out of their marketplace. The showmen who ran the nickelodeons and travelling shows – like the audiences themselves – could not have cared less where their films came from; the only thing that mattered to them was getting their hands on a consistent supply of well-made new titles at the right prices. Edison's fight back was hampered by a lack of management skills and his inability. to staff his company with reliable people. In an episode that typified these weaknesses, in 1904 William Markgraf, head of the Kinetograph Department, had travelled to England on motion picture business. When he arrived, he embarked on a month-long drinking bout and, with his mind befuddled by alcohol, purchased 200,000 feet of Lumière film stock without authorization. Unsurprisingly, he was fired on his return.

That Pathé, more than any of his American rivals, was able to guarantee such a consistent supply was largely due to the fact that he had already adapted the regimented techniques of mass production to the business of film-making, just as a few years later Henry Ford would apply them to the automobile industry. Pathé's industrial approach allowed the company to exercise an almost seamless integrated control over the entire operation. Raw film stock was manufactured at his Joinville factory near Paris and the films themselves were shot and edited by Zecca and his team at the company's Paris studios. Pathé even introduced the idea of employing a regular company of actors, anticipating the system under which the Hollywood studios would contract leading actors and actresses on an exclusive basis during the 1920s and '30s. The structure he adopted eventually came to be known as 'vertical integration', because of the way it brought the development, production, promotion, distribution and screening of films together under the control of a single company.

Without knowing it, and ten years before the creation of the first major American studio, Charles Pathé had laid the foundations of the system which would enable the Hollywood moguls to reign over the movie industry for decades to come. The system he adopted allowed him to minimize risk, using profits generated by the distribution of his films to fund the production of new ones. More than that, it ensured that the company had the capacity to churn out hundreds of movies a year, so that the risks that did exist were spread across a vast number of films. He saw that, in a market where the public was constantly clamouring for new films, power would inevitably accrue to anyone who had the capacity to supply a consistently high output of quality product. That in itself was enough to mark him out from the vast majority of his contemporaries in Europe and America. Nine decades later, the Hollywood studios still organize themselves according to the same core principle, so that control over the highly profitable business of distribution serves to finance the hazardous enterprise of producing a slate of increasingly expensive films.

Not that distribution has ever been without risk. Films were sent to exhibitors by train, and the distributor relied on the diligence of the baggage-handlers to ensure that the movies reached their intended destination. Sometimes this had unexpected consequences. 'Not realizing the importance of prompt delivery, they would often permit their baggage cars to be filled with film cans that should have been dropped off several stations back,' recalled one distributor. 'Their idea of righting matters was to throw the stuff off at the next stop, regardless of the destination on the label.' For an industry that would come to spend hundreds of millions of dollars every year ensuring that its films reached their target audience, this was hardly an auspicious start.

By the end of 1906, Pathé's studios were pumping out films at the astonishing rate of one a day, dwarfing the output of his competitors. They ranged from fantasy pictures like *Ali-Baba et les 40 voleurs* and *Puss 'n' Boots*, to dramas such as *Au pays noir*, the story of a mining catastrophe, and biblical epics such as *Passion et mort de Notre Seigneur Jésus Christ*. These were then sold in France and around the world through an extensive network of subsidiary offices. Within a few years the company's overseas offices would include branches in Calcutta, Singapore and Melbourne. It owned cinemas across Europe and in North Africa. So extensive were the company's tentacles that a French trade paper was soon boasting that a Pathé film would be seen by 300 million people around the world within a few months of being released. The entertainment business had never witnessed anything remotely like it.

By 1908 Pathé's domination of world cinema was complete. He was selling twice as many films in the USA as all the American companies put together. Subsidiaries were producing films as far afield as Rome and Moscow, the latter accounting for half the total number of movies produced in Russia by 1910. Pathé himself was a figure of such national prominence that when the actor Harold Lloyd wrote to him he simply addressed his letters to 'Monsieur Charles Pathé, France'.

The key to the astonishing success of Pathé's invasion of the United States and other foreign markets lay in the way he melded together two separate insights. On the one hand, he recognized that the movie business had to be organized like other mass manufacturing industries which had sprung up during the late nineteenth century. On the other hand, Pathé, unlike Edison, understood that the biggest profits could be reaped not from making cameras, projectors or film stock, but from the manufacture and distribution of movies themselves. He may initially have entered production because he saw it as a means of boosting sales of equipment. He was quick to realize his mistake. At heart Pathé remained a salesman, led by the market. It was that which gave him the edge over Edison, the complacent monopolist, more accustomed to organizing his companies according to his own needs rather than those of his customers.

While Pathé played no part in the actual creation of moving images, it was he, more than anyone else, who dragged them out of the laboratory and set the whole affair on the road towards becoming a vast international industry. As he later observed: 'I didn't invent cinema, but I did industrialize it.' In doing so, Pathé ensured that the passion for moving pictures would never again be confined merely to physiologists obsessed with improving their knowledge of animal locomotion, or bug-eyed inventors lugging primitive cameras around in huge wooden boxes.

All of this enabled Pathé to maintain a sizeable and consistent output of movies at a time when, especially in the United States, competitors simply couldn't turn out enough films to satisfy the public appetite. The great advantage of the American market was its sheer size; that was why it became so important to succeed there. As an industrial power, the United States may have lagged far behind trading partners such as Great Britain, France and Germany, to whom it was indebted to the tune of hundreds of millions of dollars, but the size of its movie-going audience dwarfed that of any other individual nation. The American market was also highly valued because of its relatively uniform regulatory regime; it was not necessary to file scores of patent claims in order to reap the commercial benefits offered by the country's vast cinema-going population. To have any realistic chance of reaching the same numbers of people in Europe, a film distributor had to find a way of slicing through a complex web of regulations in a host of different countries.

The basic shape of American society was also changing in ways that aided the distribution of goods like films. The pace of urbanization between the end of the Civil War and 1914 meant that many of its people lived huddled together in cities, making it that much easier to reach them in large numbers. By contrast, people in other highly populated countries like Russia, China or India remained dispersed in large numbers of tiny agrarian communities. In a business like moving pictures, which did not depend on the availability of natural resources or even on highly specialized machinery, the ability to reach large numbers of people relatively easily became an important factor in determining profitability. As the American film companies took control of their own market in the decades that followed, so they turned their nation's demographics to their own advantage. They realized they could afford to spend far more on producing high quality, star-laden films than their European counterparts, since they knew that they had every chance of recouping their costs at home.

It may have been a Frenchman who first demonstrated that one of the keys to success in the film business was the ability to adapt easily and quickly to the rapidly changing tastes of the newly enfranchised mass audience, but in the years to come it would be the Americans, far more than any other nation, who would really come to understand the importance of that lesson.

The number of spectators flocking to the nickelodeons now far exceeded audiences for theatres, vaudeville houses, circuses, waxworks and freak shows combined. As hundreds of millions of nickels poured through the ticket windows, and as more and more entrepreneurs clambered on to the movie bandwagon, opening scores of production companies, film exchanges and theatres, many wondered how long it could all possibly last. Surely the bubble must burst, and the nickelodeons, like the Kinetoscope parlours before them, would soon lie deserted, darkened monuments to just one more craze that for a few, brief months blazed fiercely amid the gloomy city slums?

What the sceptics did not see was that the revolution wrought by the 'nickel madness' was beginning to have profound social influence as well as an economic impact. Others did recognize it, and the more the movies prospered the more the forces of established society were mobilized against them. Cinemas were denounced as places 'where pickpockets could go through you as easy as an eel through water'. Self-righteous newspaper editorials fulminated against the nickelodeons. 'The fact that these amusement places are patronised largely by school children, and that the subjects in 90 per cent of them are far from moral is now being investigated by the police', thundered a Chicago paper in 1907, going on to castigate the theatres themselves, 'with their tawdry galvanised iron facades, and discordant graphophone [sic] attachments, screaming mechanical ragtime into the streets [which] have been encroaching steadily into residential districts.' In addition, the nickelodeons were seen as a severe fire hazard, although one local chief commented caustically: 'the people who go to 5 cent theaters are of the kind who know how to take care of themselves in a fire. They'll get out, never fear.'

'Nickel-delirium' began to look like an epidemic utterly out of control. And the fact that what little control did exist was exercised by men who bore no allegiance to the values of high culture meant that it represented a far more insidious – and thereby far more powerful – threat. Even the use of the word 'movie' became contentious. The term had first become common around 1906 or 1907, having been used in New York City's Bowery district as a shortened version of 'moving pictures'. Even some in the industry itself felt such a slang term might help to reinforce prejudice against motion pictures, a feeling that lingered for years. As late as 1914, cinema-owners in Los Angeles would unveil a campaign to boycott the use of the word.

Meanwhile, Edison fretted on the margins. Although his sales of film stock and projectors soared, his output of films had utterly failed to keep pace with the explosion in demand. Profits edged up by only a few percentage points each year. The capital his film division needed to compete effectively with the likes of Pathé was continually being drained by his enthusiasm for new ventures ranging from dental equipment to mining machinery. Ironically enough, his frustration may have been compounded by the fact that he belonged unmistakably to that white Protestant middle class who felt most uneasy about the popular culture of cinema. The idea of perching on a hard-backed seat in the company of factory workers, office girls and rowdy slum-dwellers would have been anathema to him. This fundamental ambivalence probably had as much to do with his failure to capitalize on the potential of this new industry as did his glaring ineptitude as a businessman.

Pathé's continuing dominance was only one of Edison's problems. Despite a stream of law-suits alleging patent infringement of both equipment and film, Edison had failed to destroy Biograph and Vitagraph, his most formidable domestic competitors. He hired private detectives and even outright thugs in his desperate pursuit of those who were allegedly infringing his patents. Independent producers soon learned how to outwit them. 'It became rather amusing, something like a game of hide-and-seek,' remembered one of them. 'When a company planned to work outdoors, they sent out a decoy group for the detectives to follow and spend the day watching, while the real shooting company left the studio later and worked unmolested.'

The battles continued. Eventually both sides realized they were in serious danger of bankrupting one another. That would have been a disaster for them all, since it would have meant watching control of the film business slip into the hands of those small-time entrepreneurs – many of them immigrants – who ran the nickelodeons. So on 18 December 1908 Edison invited representatives of the American Mutoscope and Biograph Company (AM&B) to a meeting at his West Orange laboratory. There they agreed not only to call a truce but to join forces and create a cartel. Perhaps Edison hoped that his invitation and the delightfully innocuous name he chose for the cartel – the Motion Picture Patents Company (MPPC) – would deflect attention from his downright predatory aims. He was wrong. Outraged competitors immediately branded it 'The Trust' and the name stuck. It was easy to see why. The MPPC was led by four companies: Armat, Biograph, Edison and Vitagraph. It was headed by Biograph's president, Jeremiah Kennedy, nick-named 'Fighting Jeremiah'. 'Kennedy was a sort of General Patton,' recalled one producer, 'hard, blunt, a born czar, not easily turned from a course.' Under his leadership, the MPPC licensed a limited number of motion picture firms to use its film stock and cameras in return for payment of a royalty. Exhibitors were to be offered licensed projection machines, also for a fee.

Only two firms with overseas connections were licensed as members of the Trust. One was Pathé, the other was Georges Kleine, a Chicago-based agency which was allowed to continue importing films from Gaumont and a British firm, Urban-Eclipse. Other foreign companies, however, including the Danish giant Nordisk, the British firms R. W. Paul and Hepworth, and Italy's Cinés were barred. The American independents may have been the principal target of the Trust, but for Cecil Hepworth and other foreign film-makers the formation of the Trust meant something else altogether. 'So far as we were concerned,' recalled Hepworth, '[the object of the Trust]

was to put a stop to the import of English and other European films.'
The Europeans launched a series of assaults on the Trust in the
trade press, often contrasting the openness of their own markets
with the barriers which protected the American market. 'We are
troubled with neither trusts nor combines, nor with custom duties,'
observed one British writer. And, in yet another extraordinary mirror-
image of the words used by the US negotiators at the GATT talks
in Geneva eighty-five years later, a European producer commented
bitterly: 'American, French and Italian films find an open door and
an open market in Europe. All are accorded a fair field and no favour.'
As one French producer put it, with some degree of prescience, in
an article under the heading 'Europe Pitted Against America': 'the
Americans will soon conquer the European market and impose their
regulations on Europe as soon as they have assured the final success
of their rule in the United States.'

Indeed, some members of the Trust such as William 'Pop' Rock,
founder of Vitagraph, had already railed against the foreign firms
which had seized a significant portion of the American market. In
early 1908, Rock had suggested shutting out 'the importation of
foreign stuff that was not suitable or good enough for the American
market', and lambasted those 'unheard-of small foreign manufacturers whose productions the American public will not stand for'.
Edison too had given voice to similar sentiments. '[T]he French are
somewhat in advance of us. But they will not long maintain their
supremacy,' he assured *Variety* in 1908. 'Americans in any department
of effort are never content to stay in second place.' The principal
rationale behind the creation of the Patents Company was to allow
Edison and AM&B to reassert what they saw as their rightful dominance of their home market, regardless of whether the competition
was American or foreign. The formation of the Patents Company
also gave Edison and his allies an excuse to wreak revenge on those
foreign competitors who had dared to challenge them on their home
ground. Even Pathé was now beholden to Edison, since although
he had been invited to join the Trust, he was obliged to pay royalties,
implicitly legitimizing Edison's claims to a form of sovereignty over

the entire American movie business. In March 1908, a group of European film-makers met in Paris and created a war chest of $15,000 'to be spent in a campaign in the American field', as a means of trying to protect their interests in the United States.

These changes had severe repercussions for European film companies, many of whom had come to rely on the United States as their largest and most profitable export market. Indeed, it was alleged that one of the most innovative British film-makers, James Williamson, was actually forced out of business when all of his US contracts were abruptly cancelled. In November 1908, just before the MPPC commenced formal operations, foreign importers accounted for 70 per cent of the total number of short films released in America. By October of the following year, the European share had been halved. The Europeans would never really recover.

Nordisk was now the only foreign company prepared to challenge the Trust. Its New York office which handled US distribution under the name of Great Northern – motto: 'Your Money's Worth' – defiantly remained open for business. That it managed to do so was largely a tribute to its indomitable founder, Ole Olsen. Like Charles Pathé, Olsen was a man set on making his fortune in whatever way he could, and he was quite accustomed to overcoming seemingly insurmountable barriers. Raised in poverty in rural Denmark, he had started work as a shepherd at the age of seven. After a spell as a sailor, he became a 'barker', standing outside shops and bawling out a catalogue of wares to passers-by in an attempt to attract custom. Before long he became a travelling showman and set up an amusement park in the Swedish city of Malmo.

In 1905, now in his early forties, he moved back to Denmark and opened the Biograf Theatre, one of the first cinemas in Copenhagen. After branching out into production he created Nordisk in November 1906. Within a couple of years he was employing almost two thousand people in what was, after Pathé, the second-largest film company in the world. His success encouraged other Scandinavians to become film producers. Soon the industry in neighbouring Sweden also started to thrive, following the formation of a company called Svenska Bio in 1907. Within a few years Swedish cameramen would create a series of brilliant innovations in cinematography. Olsen, like his rivals Pathé and Edison, was an instinctive monopolist, constantly seeking to lure actors, directors and technicians away from his competitors with exclusive contracts. If they refused to join him, he would simply buy out their companies. Like Pathé, Olsen also engaged in the predatory practice now known as 'block-booking', under which he forced cinema-owners to buy a whole string of pictures they didn't really want together with those they *did* want. It was an early form of that practice which would become a hugely contentious issue in Hollywood during the 1920s and '30s.

Olsen chose to direct many of Nordisk's early films himself, including a safari adventure, *Lion Hunt*, which, in defiance of geographical authenticity, was to be filmed in Denmark. The Danish authorities banned the production on the grounds that it would inevitably involve the maltreatment of animals. Olsen, however, went ahead and shot the film (if not the lion) and was promptly stripped of his licence to run cinemas. As was often to be the case with controversial films, the resulting adverse publicity served only to guarantee him a massive hit at the box office and the company's reputation suffered no lasting damage. He went on to produce a series of lurid melodramas about young prostitutes with titles such as *The White Slave Trade*, westerns such as *Texas Tex*, and even an extraordinarily compressed version of *Hamlet*, which lasted just seventeen minutes.

The Danish cinema audience was far too small to accommodate the ambitions of a man such as Olsen. Nordisk's success, to an even greater extent than that of Pathé, was founded on the effective exploitation of the international market. As well as opening an office in New York, Nordisk quickly established outposts in a cluster of European cities including London, Budapest and St Petersburg. And, like Pathé, Nordisk had become a vertically integrated company long before the Hollywood studios even considered it, not only producing and distributing films but operating chains of cinemas in Denmark, Holland, Switzerland and Germany.

Had he teamed up with Charles Pathé, Olsen might have been

able to crush the MPPC, or at least render it ineffectual, but Olsen
was excluded from the Trust, while Pathé was admitted. Even the
habitually myopic Edison seems to have realized that by excluding
Pathé, the world's most powerful film company, he risked provoking
a cataclysmic trade war which might engulf him along with his
fiercest enemies. By shrewdly inviting Pathé to join the MPPC
while excluding virtually all other overseas competitors, he ensured
that the foreign opposition was hopelessly divided and utterly
incapable of usurping the Trust's power over all aspects of the motion
picture business. And although Pathé's worldwide operation meant
it was less dependent on the United States than some of its rivals,
there were still powerful incentives for it to join. The challenge to
the Trust, if there was to be one, would have to come from elsewhere.

4

'No more licences!
No more heartbreaks!'

ALTHOUGH THE PANIC over nickelodeons among the guardians of public morality had been initially provoked by hostility towards the audiences who patronized them, there were increasing anxieties about the people who owned and managed them. The rapid expansion of the storefront theatre had attracted a new breed of showmen into the business who shared much in common with their customers. Mostly they were immigrants, or first-generation Americans. Many were Jews who had fled poverty in Eastern Europe, seeking to forge a new, more prosperous future in America. It was these émigrés – hungry for success, desperate for recognition, terrified of failure – who would eventually lead the charge against the Trust and in doing so transform the shape of the moving picture industry in America.

Carl Laemmle was one who had made the long journey from Europe to the New World. At first glance, this tiny mild-mannered man, not much more than five feet tall, looked an unlikely candidate to challenge the Edison Trust and all the power that it represented.

Despite his diminutive stature, he was, as one of his rivals recalled, 'full of fight and moved like a whirlwind, never sending a letter when a telegram would do'. His generosity was legendary, towards employees and family alike; indeed, they were often one and the same, leading one humorist to quip that 'Uncle Carl Laemmle has a very large faemmle'. Beneath the bonhomie and the self-deprecating humour which he dispensed in equal measure, Laemmle harboured a fiercely ethical spirit which had 'never sacrificed a principle to a dollar'. It was hardly surprising that he despised the self-serving machinations of Edison and his cronies, the ceaseless hounding by lawyers and private detectives, the endless assaults on his film crews by gangs of hired thugs.

Laemmle had been born in Laupheim in southern Germany. He began his working life at thirteen with a wholesale company dealing in stationery goods and novelties. For his seventeenth birthday, in 1884, Laemmle's father borrowed the comparatively large sum of 90 German marks and bought Carl a ticket to New York. Having arrived in the United States, Laemmle seemed to drift from one job to another. first in New York and later in Chicago. He worked as a bottle-washer, a clerk, a book-keeper and a farmer. Then, in 1894, he was offered a job as a book-keeper in a newly established clothing firm run by a former colleague in Oshkosh, Wisconsin. He soon became manager and, by 1905, had saved $3000. He remained dissatisfied. 'I was approaching forty,' he later recalled, 'I wanted better, but how could I find the career which – so I felt – must start now or never?'

Looking around for the opportunity to fulfil his belief in an independent destiny, Laemmle hit upon the idea of opening a chain of cheap retail stores, modelled on those of F. W. Woolworth. Searching for a suitable venue in Chicago, Laemmle chanced across a nickelodeon, and out of curiosity decided to pay a visit. He found himself captivated. 'It was evident that the basic idea of motion pictures and Mr. Woolworth's innovation were identical,' he recalled. '[A] low price commodity in tremendous quantities.' Laemmle abandoned his original course of action and threw himself wholeheartedly into the movie business. In February 1906, Laemmle opened his first nickelodeon on Milwaukee Avenue in Chicago. Right from the start he made a conscious effort to elevate his theatres above the tawdry standards of most of the rival venues, realizing perhaps that the huge new audience for moving pictures would quickly become more discerning and demand something better than a hard-backed chair in a stinking, unventilated room.

The first picture Laemmle screened was a Pathé western. 'There was a flavor about the manner of its production which baffled me; something told me that this picture which bore the Pathé trade-mark originated in an alien mind . . . They forgot for example that American Indians did not wear moustaches.' It was not until the following week that Laemmle learned that Pathé was a French company, but the incident may have encouraged him to believe that opportunities might also exist in the production business.

Laemmle may have understood little about the movies, but, having run a clothing store, he certainly knew a great deal about how to attract customers. His two nickelodeons were hugely successful, but he quickly grew dissatisfied with the quality of the prints he was obliged to rent from the existing film exchanges. 'You paid your money, and you had no choice. For example, a subject of eight hundred feet cost eighty dollars and would be rented and re-rented until the characters became blurred to the naked eye.' In frustration Laemmle came to the conclusion that there was no alternative but to go into the distribution business himself. In mid-1906 he set up his own film exchange, the Laemmle Film Service, based in Chicago, and he soon endowed the company with his own idiosyncratic style. He was a mischievous man who 'seemed to see humour in everything including himself'. As his advertisements put it: 'I'm Not Running a Bargain Counter. I wouldn't pay a cent for the cheap and rotten claptrap that has been flooding the market.' His films, he crowed, were simply, 'The Best, Newest, Liveliest, Finest stuff that human brains can conceive and human facilities execute'.

Laemmle, like many early distributors, handled most aspects of the business personally.

Each morning found me opening the mail and dumping the contents on my desk [he recalled]. There were checks, soiled dollar bills, money orders, inquiries, all in answer to my circulars and advertisements. I hustled to get more film. Trade was increasing rapidly, but the sharp practice of my unknown customers puzzled me ... In good faith, I would dispatch a film to an out-of-town exhibitor via express C.O.D. and after allowing him three days for usage and two or three days more for transit, weeks would elapse before the film came back to our office.

Laemmle's playful hyperbole and his easy identification with fellow showmen soon paid off. With the nickelodeon boom at its height, he was besieged by exhibitors desperate to secure new films to satisfy an ever-more hungry audience. In fact, the business was growing so fast that Laemmle found it almost impossible to supply all of his customers from Chicago. So he embarked on a flurry of expansion, opening an exchange in the basement of a bank in Evansville, Indiana, followed by other branches across the country. Laemmle's success convinced other operators in Chicago and New York to open their own exchanges, and soon distribution offices were being set up all over the United States. By 1907, it was estimated that there were more than a hundred film exchanges scattered around thirty-five cities.

When the owners of these exchanges arrived at the Imperial Hotel in New York for a trade convention in early January 1909, an unpleasant shock awaited them. On their chairs in the assembly room they found a paper from the MPPC setting out the terms on which all exchanges would have to operate if they wished to continue trading. Anyone who refused to sign, or sought to secure films from an alternative, unlicensed source, would find themselves the subject of a law-suit. The Trust document was brutally plain. If the exchange operators didn't like the terms on offer, there was a simple solution: find a new trade. At first, Laemmle and most of his colleagues felt they had little choice but to sign. They could not risk being put out of business, but neither could they afford to pursue endless rounds of costly litigation.

Laemmle was outraged. Furiously mulling over Edison's abuse of monopoly power, he changed his mind and, on 12 April, turned in his licence. 'I Have Quit The Patents Company', he announced in a full-page advertisement in the trade press. 'No More Licenses! No More Heartbreaks!'

Scores of independent exhibitors, equally angry about the punitive conditions, now asked Laemmle if he would be willing to supply them with films. Laemmle quickly concluded that the only way to meet this demand was to launch his own production company. He called it the Independent Manufacturing Company. Abbreviated to IMP, the name seemed a peculiarly appropriate choice for the elfin businessman. He rented run-down premises on East 14th Street in New York and, after sweeping away a carpet of rubbish 3-feet thick, converted the building into a film studio. He purchased his raw stock direct from Lumière, which was still operating as a manufacturing firm but which had been excluded from the Trust. In October 1909 the company released its first film, *Hiawatha*, based on the poem by Henry Longfellow.

Over the next few months, IMP worked to step up its production activities. However, if Laemmle was to triumph over the MPPC he urgently needed his own stable of popular actors and actresses and most of them were tied into long-term contracts with members of the Trust. Most of these companies had played down the individual identities of their stars for fear they would exploit their grip on audiences and start to demand exorbitant salaries, although a handful had experimented with publicizing the names of stars already known from the theatre. As a result, most prominent stars were known simply by the name of the company for which they worked – the Biograph Girl, the Vitagraph Girl, and so on. The surge of public interest in the private lives of the stars meant that this highly controlled system, convenient as it was for the producers, was becoming simply unsustainable. Already by 1909, the film companies and the trade papers were inundated with letters from the public addressed to their favourite stars. Since the correspondents had no idea of the names of the people they were writing to, they were forced to improvise; Charles Inslee who played a Red Indian in popular westerns received letters addressed simply to 'The Indian'.

Laemmle now moved to capitalize on this growing frenzy of public curiosity. In late 1909, the Biograph Girl, whose real name was Florence Lawrence, disappeared from her company's studios under mysterious circumstances. Some months later, in March 1910, stories appeared in newspapers in St Louis, over 1000 miles away, reporting that she had been run over and killed by a local tram. The following week an advertisement appeared in the trade paper *Moving Picture World*. Entitled 'We Nail a Lie' it observed that 'The blackest and at the same time the silliest lie yet circulated by enemies of the "Imp" was the story foisted on the public of St. Louis last week to the effect that Miss Laurence [sic] (the "Imp" Girl, formerly known as the "Biograph" girl) had been killed by a street car.' Lawrence, it turned out, was alive and well and working for IMP. The advertisement (placed by IMP of course) immediately roused suspicion that the stories of Lawrence's death were part of a publicity stunt engineered by Laemmle and his ally Robert Cochrane, a Chicago advertising executive. Still, Laemmle insisted on denying it, claiming that the whole episode was a plot by the Trust, 'a poor, half-witted ruse, intended in some nebulous way to unsettle the Independent public'.

Whatever the truth, the result was the same. Once the Biograph Girl was unmasked, Laemmle was free to cash in on the public's insatiable desire for gossip about her and their other favourite stars. Soon afterwards, Lawrence claimed that she had received 3000 proposals of marriage. Her move to IMP was soon followed by the defection of another 'Biograph Girl': Mary Pickford. A watershed had been reached and, from that moment on, the movie business became inextricably entangled with the lives and loves of its star performers. Celebrity had become the currency of success in the American movie industry.

Actors' names began to appear on posters and handbills, although it was some while before they would be credited on the screen. Around this time, celebrity-struck audiences became known for the first time as 'fans'. The earliest fan magazines, *Motion Picture Story* and *Photoplay*, started appearing in 1911. Their pages were packed with plot synopses, portraits of the stars and popularity contests. While the leading stage players of the period continued to be referred to as Mr Sothern, Miss Adams and so forth, movie stars quickly became known as simply Little Mary (Mary Pickford), Bunny (John Bunny) and Theda (Theda Bara). It became one more early sign of the manner in which the movies seemed to embody an egalitarian spirit which was increasingly identified with the very idea of plural democracy in the United States. For all their apparent aura of familiarity though, American movie stars increasingly came to represent a new aristocracy of wealth, a race apart from their fellow citizens. As with so much else that would be associated with the illusory world of the movies, it was perception that counted, not reality.

In Europe, by contrast, the stubborn sense remained that stars and all the attendant trappings of celebrity were somehow at odds with the creative ambitions of cinema. In the early European films, there was 'no personal exploitation or publicizing of cast, director, author and [a] hundred and one items that count for public popularity today', Carl Laemmle remembered in the 1920s. A handful of stars did emerge, notably in Scandinavia and in Italy, but even a decade later one respected British trade magazine was still claiming that:

> If far-sighted opinion is accurate, motion picture stars are fast approaching the day when their lustre may be dimmed. For several years now each successive season has witnessed larger salary demands from these men and women of the screen. No matter how great the drawing power of a star, it is fatal for a producer to sacrifice the production as a whole just to include them in the cast. The star system is dwindling already, and to such an extent that 1918 is bound to see it disappear altogether.

In part, this reflected a feeling throughout Europe that the promotional flair needed to create and sustain the star system was somehow peripheral to the real heart of the film business – making movies. It also reflected deeper cultural anxieties. Given the right blend of talent and opportunity almost anyone, it seemed, could become a star. Charlie Chaplin, for example, born in the slums of South London, a man whose films deliberately mocked all forms of authority, would soon rise to become the highest paid performer in the world, challenging the idea long cherished by Europe's cultural elite that a person's destiny was primarily determined by blood and lineage.

The new culture of celebrity seemed depressingly predictable. Salary costs soared. Charlie Chaplin, offered $1000 a week, demanded $1075, explaining that he needed the extra seventy-five to live on. Mary Pickford's weekly salary climbed from $175 to $10,000, with a yearly bonus of $300,000. In certain cases she had the right to select her directors and her supporting players. That any entertainer could command such a salary and such freedom was remarkable enough; for a woman to achieve this, in an era when in most states women didn't even have the vote, was even more astonishing. For the leading performers, acting rapidly became the highest paid profession in the world. For a few brief years, until the studios once more gained the upper hand, a handful of stars were able to dictate their own terms to studio bosses like Zukor and Laemmle. Not until the 1980s would most stars again command such power and financial leverage.

There were other, even less welcome consequences. When Roscoe 'Fatty' Arbuckle and other Hollywood figures became embroiled in sex and drug scandals in the 1920s (see Chapter 7), Hollywood was lambasted by the US federal government, the national press and moralists throughout the world, forcing the industry to adopt an onerous system of self-regulation. By that time, such was the lure and glamour of Hollywood that, overwhelmed by thousands of aspiring actors and actresses, the Hollywood Chamber of Commerce was obliged to run advertisements entreating, 'Please Don't Try to Break into the Movies'.

Such was the far-reaching process which Laemmle had set in train with his simple advertisement. In unmasking the Biograph Girl, Laemmle had revealed a far more important truth; success in the movie business did not, as those who ran companies like Edison, Biograph and others had believed, reside solely in the ability to control the means of supply, whether it be of films, cameras or projectors. While the business remained relatively small, that may have just been possible; a handful of companies could effectively police the boundaries of the East Coast industry, charging selected newcomers an entrance fee while barring other companies altogether. Once demand began to outstrip supply, as it did in the wake of the nickelodeon boom, all that irrevocably changed. The Trust's tactics for killing off competition now served only to provoke it. New producers surged into the marketplace, eager to meet the public's apparently insatiable appetite. With his distinctive advertisements and his shrewd exploitation of star power. Laemmle had shown just how adept he was at capitalizing upon this burgeoning popular demand. As the Trust's iron grip began to weaken, 'Uncle Carl' showed his true mettle. A series of cartoons began to appear in the trade press lampooning the Trust. Laemmle's associate Robert Cochrane had created a caricature, 'General Flimco', who was shown constantly 'grabbing, squealing and dragooning'. Other cartoons mocked the Trust's inflated sense of its own authority. 'Good morning, have you paid two dollars so you can kiss your wife?' asked one.

The Trust hit back. When filming on location, IMP's filmmakers were sometimes forced to hide their cameras in an ice-box to avoid detection. Laemmle even moved his entire company to Cuba, where they were plagued by mysterious 'tourists' who would appear on set saying they wanted to watch Mary Pickford, then start taking detailed photographs of the company's equipment. Attacks were also launched from other sources. The trade paper *Moving Picture World* launched a virulent personal assault on the independents. 'How can an ex-huckster, ex-bellboy, ex-tailor, ex-advertising man, ex-bookmaker know anything about picture quality?' it demanded. 'Hands that would be more properly employed with a push cart on the lower East Side are responsible for directing stage plays and making pictures of them.' The rhetoric smacked of the similarly strident language used to denounce the nickelodeons just a year or two earlier. The Trust wars had started out simply as a struggle for economic control. As the battle raged on, a second front had opened up, with other elements of the American establishment – newspaper editors, politicians and police chiefs – queueing up to condemn the movies. The hysterical denunciations that the political and cultural establishment directed at the entire institution of the movies may have been exacerbated by the anti-authoritarian themes associated with many of the movies. Authority figures often featured as objects of ridicule – in the form of exploding policemen and the like – while convicts and vagabonds and the dispossessed were treated as victims of an iniquitous social system; a theme taken up by Charlie Chaplin in films such as *The Tramp* released in 1915. The alarm among the middle classes, the church and the press over the moral impact of this one film revealed their concern that the movies had the capacity to unleash serious political turmoil.

Certainly, the movies became the glue binding together America's dispossessed. They offered downtrodden audiences a chance to dream of a better life, and a few immigrant entrepreneurs a chance to realize those dreams. And so it was that the movies developed into America's first truly indigenous form of mass culture.

In 1910, the Trust stepped up its assault. It quietly started buying up all the licensed film exchanges in the United States. The plan was to create its own directly controlled distribution operation. Once again, the firm's bland name, the General Film Company, masked its predatory intentions. The scheme very nearly succeeded. 'Hundreds of little rental bureaux faded overnight,' recalled Albert Smith, a member of the Trust committee responsible for acquiring exchanges. Within a year, General Film had acquired every exchange in the country, with just one exception, a company in New York under the control of William Fox.

Fox was another immigrant, his parents having left their native village in Hungary when he was nine months old. When his father lost his job, the young boy helped support his family, trudging 'up and down of the stairs of tenements, tapping on doors and selling stove blacking at 5 cents per can'. Leaving school aged eleven, he began working for a clothing firm until, following ten years of rather mixed fortunes – including a thoroughly ill-fated attempt at acting – he started his own clothing business in New York City. Within a couple of years he had managed to save $50,000. Looking round for an appropriate investment opportunity, he purchased a traditional penny arcade in Brooklyn and soon began to think that the new phenomenon of moving pictures might make a suitable addition to his small entertainment venture.

Fox rented the room above his arcade and equipped it with a screen and seating for about 150 people. He realized that if, after the show, he sent the customers out by the rear stairway they would have to walk past his arcade machines to get to the street, and might well be tempted to put a few coins in a few slots as they went. This early attempt at creating synergy was not a success. To his surprise he found it extraordinarily difficult to attract customers and sought assistance from a man who had worked at Barnum and Bailey's circus. The latter advised Fox to create a diversion, 'a ballyhoo' outside the theatre to attract patrons: 'I can get you a sword swallower for $2 a night or a fire eater for $3 a night.' 'Get me one of each!' Fox replied. 'The sword swallower did swallow a sword . . . Soon a crowd gathered, and then he said he would conclude his performance upstairs. It was two flights up, and the crowd followed him.' After a week or so, the theatre was besieged by crowds. 'We needed no more ballyhoos . . . This little bit of a theater into which I had put $1,600 brought in, in five years, approximately $250,000.' Fox was transformed into a master showman.

He started buying up theatres throughout New York and was soon attracting thousands of patrons every night. In some of them, film was mixed with vaudeville shows, but it was the former, however, that really seemed to pull in the crowds. In 1907, Fox expanded his involvement with the movie industry, creating the Greater New York Film Exchange, which began distributing movies throughout the city. Then in September 1911, he was approached by J. J. Kennedy, the Trust chief, who told him they wanted to buy him out. Fox refused to accept the price offered. An extraordinary battle now began. The Trust bribed an exhibitor to show some of Fox's films in a brothel, and then cancelled his licence on the grounds that he had allowed them to be screened in a house of prostitution. Without the licence granted by the Trust, Fox would face legal action if he continued to distribute films. Faced with such outrageous tactics, Fox agreed to sell his company and the Trust reinstated his licence. With his licence safely returned, Fox revoked his agreement to sell, and the Trust immediately revoked his licence a second time. Provoked beyond endurance, Fox instigated legal proceedings and encouraged the government to bring a federal suit against the Trust. When they did so, in 1912, the Trust was effectively finished.

Preoccupied as it was with endless legal wrangles, it was hardly surprising that the Trust had lost touch with the changing tastes of the audience. Few of the members of the Patents Company had been in the exhibition business and they had very little idea of how to gauge the changing tastes of the film-going public. The pictures made by the Trust were criticized for being confused and unintelligible, and were beginning to pay the price at the box office. Edison himself was a hardware manufacturer who understood little about the creative business of making movies. Like the Japanese electronics companies Sony and Matsushita which acquired Hollywood companies seventy-five years later, he quickly came to recognize that the creative community was best left to its own devices.

Some Edison executives felt that European film-makers might help rejuvenate the company's fortunes. This was perhaps unsurprising given that Edison's concentration on narrowly American subjects such as *The Rivals*, based on a cartoon strip in the *New York American*, seemed to have hampered sales in Europe. 'In our moving picture business we are very badly handicapped for the lack of skilled camera operators and stage directors,' wrote Frank Dyer, one of Edison's most senior executives, in a letter to the managing director of Edison's manufacturing subsidiary in Europe.

> [T]o get a good competent stage director, a man with sufficient originality to get up and direct the acting of a picture, seems to be almost hopeless ... It occurs to me that such a man

might be found in Paris, either out of employment or who might be willing to take a better position in this country. The leading manufacturers are there and they must have educated a good many men . . . For a really good man, we could pay $75.00 a week and travelling expenses from Paris, with a guarantee to pay expenses back if unsatisfactory.

This early attempt to import talent ended in failure. The real significance of the gesture, though, was that it anticipated the way in which, in the 1920s and '30s, Hollywood would regularly seek creative nourishment by recruiting stars and directors from Europe. It was already clear that, for the most part, film-makers and executives in Europe were preoccupied with the creative art of production, rather than with the business of distribution and marketing. Indeed, a very different kind of debate about the role of the industry was already beginning to unfold in Europe. Like so many other aspects of European cinema, the debate was at its most advanced in France. In America's burgeoning cities, the movies offered the prospect of being a unifying force in what was otherwise a fairly cosmopolitan melting pot, but in France all of this posed a serious dilemma. Since the seventeenth century, art had been regarded as an essential expression of the national spirit. 'The arts symbolize the power of a state just as much as feats of arms,' proclaimed the founding statement of the prestigious Le Journal des Savants which was widely read throughout Europe in the eighteenth century after having been originally authorized by Louis XIV in 1663. The rise of cinema's popularity posed the question of whether it could, or should, be assimilated into such a tradition. Some intellectuals believed that cinema provided a new and powerfully exciting means of disseminating the existing products of high culture. For example, by transposing stage productions on to celluloid it would be possible to make the very best of French art available throughout the world. Among those intrigued by this idea was Edmond Benoît-Lévy, a French lawyer with a passionate interest in the theatre, and founder of the Société Populaire des Beaux-Arts. In the early years of this century, he transferred a hugely popular mime show, L'Enfant prodigue, from the Parisian stage to the screen. Then in 1907 he joined forces with Charles Pathé to create a cinema chain called Omnia. To some it might have seemed that Benoît-Lévy must have forsaken his intellectual interests to pursue more overtly commercial aspirations. But that same year, writing under the pseudonym of Francis Moir, he published an astonishing article in a film trade-paper, *Phono-Ciné-Gazette*: 'What is a film? Is it a piece of ordinary merchandise that can be bought and used as one wishes? No, it's because of this belief that the industry has arrived at its present crisis. A film is a unique "literary and artistic property".'

The implications of Benoît-Lévy's statement were revolutionary. He was proposing that film be elevated from a low-life fairground attraction, a cheap mechanical novelty, to become an art-form in its own right. If that happened, films were therefore entitled to the same copyright protection as any other work of art. Furthermore, if cinema could legitimately be regarded as an art-form, then the film-maker must surely be accorded the status of an artist. In the midst of all this, there was considerable uncertainty as to who should be regarded as the real film-maker. Was it the director? The writer? Or even, perhaps, the leading actor? In an overwhelmingly literate culture like that of France, prevailing opinion rapidly came out in favour of the screenwriter. The vexed concept of 'author's rights' in relation to film would surface just four years later at the first International Congress of the Cinématographe in Brussels in 1911 when lawyer Charles Havermans claimed that film-making was a work of the mind and imagination, comparable to literature or art, rather than 'a mechanical profession' valued only for its ability to generate money.

It was a feeling shared by many across the Channel. In 1912, a writer in *The Times Educational Supplement* claimed: 'The great competition between picture palace companies is in itself harmful. It leads to a tendency to pander to the vitiated or uneducated tastes alike of the lower classes and the masses.'

The impact of this debate was not simply confined to a group of intellectuals huddled in the cafés along the Parisian boulevards or to lawyers gathered amid cigar smoke at erudite conferences. Charles Pathé, who had shown scant interest in artistic matters, claimed that Benoît-Lévy's argument asserting the cultural value of film triggered his decision to stop selling the rights to films and to rent them instead. He justified the change by saying that he now had a stake in the artistic rights of his productions, although it seemed more like a way of maximizing profits by retaining the underlying rights to his films.

In France, at least, this new culturally-oriented conception of film began to exercise a significant influence over the development of the industry itself. Before long, both French critics and entrepreneurs began to sense that there was potential for an entirely new kind of film, targeted at an educated middle-class audience, rather than the crowds which milled around amid the noise and dirt of the fairgrounds. The idea of basing films on stage plays or the work of prestigious literary authors became increasingly popular. In 1908, a new company, Film d'Art, began to put these ideas into practice, producing films which used established directors, writers and actors from the Comédie Française. One of its first productions, *L'Assassinat du Duc de Guise*, based on the famous episode from French history, was a hit both at home and in the USA. Pathé quickly negotiated distribution rights for anything the new company could produce. The creation of Film d'Art was followed the same year by the formation of Société Cinématographique des Auteurs et Gens des Lettres (SCAGL) which specialized in films based on recent literary classics and historical adaptations, such as *Cleopatra*. It also had close links to the Parisian theatre world. The idea of film as art had been born.

At the same time, producers in some countries were beginning to realize that if they were to do justice to their subject-matter, they needed to be more adventurous and make longer films. The resulting pictures, often several reels in length and a radical departure from the regular diet of short films, became the forerunners of what we know now as 'feature' films.

The term 'feature' was used in vaudeville to describe a programme's main attraction. Rather surprisingly, the first feature film – over an hour in length – had been produced in Australia in 1906 by the Tait Brothers, a family of theatrical entrepreneurs who had screened films at Melbourne town hall. Until then, Australian production had been dominated by the Salvation Army, which had been packing houses with films like *Our Social Triumphs* featuring their woman cadets in the streets selling the house magazine *War Cry*.

The Story of the Kelly Gang was somewhat different. It was based on the exploits of horse thief and bank robber Ned Kelly. At the Melbourne premiere live sound effects included the use of blank cartridges for gunshots, and the banging of coconut shells for horses' hoofs. The film was censored by the authorities on the grounds that it might deprave and corrupt. Perhaps because of this, it proved highly popular with local audiences, and spurred the production of further feature-length pictures in Australia in the years between 1906 and 1911. For a brief period the local production industry flourished, but was soon squeezed by American competition and would not recover until the mid-1970s.

In Europe, it was in Italy that the idea of the feature film was most enthusiastically embraced. From 1905 onwards, the Italian industry had begun to flourish, notably in the cities of Turin and Rome. Partly because it had been so slow to develop, cinema in Italy never really took root as a fairground spectacle as it had done in other European countries. As a result, by the time the Italians started to take an interest, the natural model to emulate was no longer that of an artisan like Georges Méliès, but rather that of an industrialist such as Pathé. As a consequence the industry in Italy was established by financiers and wealthy aristocrats who were really the first to show a sustained interest in the medium. Despite their tiny size, the leading film production companies created boards of directors and issued shares, and permanent cinemas sprang up much faster than in other European countries. The leading firm, Cinés, which included Baron Alberto Alberini as one of its backers, was even floated on the stock market by Ernesto Pacelli, a Vatican financier and uncle of Pope Pius XII. Indeed, although some clergymen denounced the cinema, the Catholic banks and others in the church saw involvement in the industry as a means of expanding their influence. In 1909, a cinema chain was created in Milan, backed by a local federation of parish oratories. Only films which conformed to certain moral standards were allowed to be screened in these venues. In this way, the church aimed to regulate or at least influence the Italian film industry which had established itself as the world's second largest exporter of films after France.

In Italy, the established cultural order, rather than attempting to marginalize cinema, sought to tame it by taking control of it for its own ends. Among other things, this helped ensure that cinema quickly won respect as an art-form along the lines suggested by Benoît-Lévy. As early as 1908, the Ambrosio company produced *The Last Days of Pompeii*, based on Bulwer-Lytton's historical novel. In 1911, longer Italian productions like the five-reel *Dante's Inferno* fanned the appetite of American audiences for still longer product. Subsequent epics such as *Quo Vadis?* and *Cabiria* achieved world-wide popularity as well as providing a crucial creative stimulus to the ambitions of American directors like D. W. Griffith. The Italians even created their own version of the star system, called the *divismo*, based around hugely popular actresses such as Lyda Borelli who typically starred in aristocratic love stories. If France and Britain had provided the early source of creative inspiration for American film-makers, now they looked predominantly to the Italians.

Meanwhile, across the Atlantic in New York City, one exhibitor had watched the spread of the multi-reel film in Europe with particular interest. By 1910 Adolph Zukor had become obsessed with the idea that these longer feature films could transform the future of moving pictures. Another member of that growing regiment of immigrants who were seizing control of the American industry, Zukor, born in the remote Hungarian village of Ricse, had built up a highly successful fur business after arriving in the United States as a teenager. 'Our house always smelled of fur,' his son recalled. 'And I used to wish that Dad would get into some other business.' Before long he did. In 1903, after visiting a penny arcade that had recently been started by his cousin, he opened his own. He leased a building on East 14th Street in New York, formerly a restaurant. '[Everything] was ripped out and the long room redecorated with bright colours and flashing lights. A hundred or more machines were installed, about sixty per cent of them phonographs and the rest moving pictures,' remembered Zukor. The venture was an astonishing success, and Zukor, having installed a cinema on the floor above the arcade, repeated the formula in cities all along the East Coast.

However, unlike the men of the Patent Company, Zukor kept a close eye on his audience. 'It was my custom to take a seat about six rows from the front . . . Probably they [the audience] had already concluded that my mind wandered for I spent a good deal of time watching the faces of the audience, even turning around to do so.' As he sat in the dark of the Crystal Hall, Zukor had the sense to realize that fundamental changes were in the air. The audience was bored with the increasingly predictable pictures put out by the Trust and seemed to prefer the more innovative and adventurous material put out by the independents. 'I felt the impact of [Edwin] Porter's *The Great Train Robbery*,' he remembered. 'But we couldn't run [the same film] every day, and the Edison company was simply having Porter grind out imitations of his masterpiece. The other companies flattered him with emulation. But there were no major changes.' He became convinced that the tired formula of chase scenes and short comedies was beginning to drive the audience away. 'The novelty wore off, and we had nothing to show that would attract a large public. That's when I realised that the only chance motion pictures had of being successful was if stories or plays could be produced which were like those on the stage or in magazines or in novels.' He tried to enlist supporters for his cause. First he sought to persuade a handful of producers to leave the Trust and join him in the creation of much longer films. He turned to an old friend, William Brady, a vaudeville promoter. Despite Zukor's best efforts, Brady remained unconvinced that the future lay in feature-length films. Wherever he turned, Zukor met a similar response. Few of his peers believed that the public would sit through longer movies.

Like Carl Laemmle, Zukor was small in stature but a giant in terms of energy. Just like 'Uncle Carl' he appeared outwardly calm, 'a quiet, almost timid-looking man', as the screenwriter William De Mille remembered him. There the similarities ended. Where Laemmle was full of expansive bonhomie, Zukor was cold and stiff. Where Laemmle preferred to disarm with humour, Zukor preferred savage attack. His visionary zeal was allied to a streak of megalomania which gave him the sense that he must conquer all he surveyed. Someone once called him a 'cross between Christopher Columbus and Napoleon'. He was prone to tearful outbursts, but such sensitivity was misleading. Cecil B. De Mille's memory of him was very different from his brother's: 'There would come a time when he would put his two clenched fists together and, slowly separating them, say to me: "Cecil, I can break you like that."'

Zukor, like Frank Dyer, the Edison executive, now looked to Europe as a means of reinvigorating his business. 'They were making the best pictures ... in France and Italy,' he later recalled. Having embarked on his own tour of Europe, Zukor saw a Pathé adaptation called *The Passion Play* a hand-coloured production which ran to three reels. The story was based on the famous play performed every ten years in the German town of Oberammergau. 'When I saw that picture', he said, 'I made up my mind to bring it to America.' In fact Pathé, still a member of the Trust, had already tried to introduce longer films in America, only to run into fierce opposition. 'The exchanges at that time had no use for multiple reels,' remembered Jacques Berst, one of Pathé's American chiefs. 'They would not stand for it, and in order to be able to get them to accept it, we had to release one reel one week and the second reel the following week.' To make matters worse, once the Trust decided to create its own distribution operation it had imposed strict limits on the number of films Pathé was permitted to import into America as a condition of allowing the French company to continue operations.

Zukor enjoyed great success with *The Passion Play*, disarming those who claimed the film was a blasphemous representation of sacred events by ensuring that sacred music accompanied the film wherever it played. Deciding to invest all his energies in feature-length films based on equally prestigious models, he now needed only a name for his new venture. Riding home on the New York subway one evening he hit upon a slogan he liked and jotted it down on the back of an envelope: 'Famous Players in Famous Plays.'

For its first release, Famous Players turned once again to Europe, acquiring the American distribution rights to *La Reine Elizabeth*, a feature-length French art picture starring Sarah Bernhardt and based on her performance in the hit stage play of the same name. Zukor paid $35,000 for the film, a vast sum at that time, and a further sign of his total confidence in the future of the feature film. That confidence was rewarded when the film turned out to be a huge success at the box office. In the meantime he had joined forces with Daniel Frohman, a prominent Broadway producer, in order to have access to a wider range of both plays and players. Zukor believed, however, that if he was to embark on any substantial productions of his own he would probably need a licence from the Trust. He went to see Jeremiah Kennedy. Having kept Zukor waiting for hours, Fighting Jeremiah lived up to his reputation by refusing him a licence: '[t]he time is not ripe for feature pictures, and I'm not sure if it will ever be.' Undeterred, Zukor pressed ahead with his plans and was rewarded with a string of successes, including *The Count of Monte Cristo* and *Tess of the D'Urbervilles*.

Zukor's triumph ensured that the feature-length film gradually became a mainstay of the business in the United States. He had taken a European idea and reinvented it for America. Other producers started to copy him and before long the old single-reel films began to seem crude, tedious and insubstantial. In later life, Zukor loved to describe himself as 'a visionary of the fillums' and it was true that he had changed many of the conventions of film-making. Zukor did something even more fundamental, transforming the very nature of the film-going experience itself. As well as creating prestige films, he ensured that they were shown in equally prestigious venues. The premiere of *La Reine Elizabeth* had been held at Daniel Frohman's Lyceum Theater, an illustrious venue in the heart of New

York City. It was a whole world away from the fairground tents of the Parisian showgrounds and the sleazy nickelodeons of Brooklyn. The advent of the feature film would soon spur the construction of an entirely new type of cinema, vast palaces capable of seating thousands of people with chandeliers, ornate lighting and smartly-clad ushers.

'In those early days', Zukor recalled, '"better" people had a great reluctance to go to the movies because of the unsavoury physical appearance of those early movie houses. And I could see very clearly that we would never be able to overcome this feeling until our industry was able to make them agreeable for that better element to be attracted by the comfort, good taste and fine service which pleasant and attractive theaters alone could offer.' More than any of his contemporaries it was Zukor who made cinema respectable in America. As one of his biographers later observed, he had set out to 'kill the slum tradition in the movies'. He had done so for the very practical and commercial reason that by creating clean comfortable theatres he believed he would increase his audience, and therefore his profitability. It was a lesson that, once learned, the American industry would never forget. Seven decades later, movie attendance plummeted in Europe partly because many of the cinema chains allowed their theatres to fall into an appalling state of disrepair. It was the Americans who came to the rescue, their investment of hundreds of millions of dollars in new multiplex cinemas leading to a dramatic increase in cinema-going in countries such as Germany and the United Kingdom. A brief examination of Adolph Zukor's extraordinary career might have saved the European industry, and most particularly its exhibitors, a great deal of unnecessary pain.

In their attempt to endow the humble business of the movies with a little prestige, European companies such as Films d'Art had concentrated almost exclusively on production. Zukor, with an eye to enhancing his profits, had focused instead on the audience. That too would increasingly become an article of faith for the entire American industry.

Not everyone, however, was yet ready to learn. The Trust

members, unconvinced by the success of features, preferred to concentrate on the more familiar single-reel films. In 1912 IMP won a crucial victory over the Trust when the US Circuit Court declared that independents were free to use any cameras they might choose. 'Victory! Victory!' trumpeted IMP. At the end of 1912, the US government finally issued an anti-competitive suit against the Trust. By then it was superfluous. Laemmle, Fox, Zukor and the other independents had already ensured the Trust's demise. Soon, these men too would be accused of trying to shut out competition. Monopoly, it seemed, was a terrible thing – until you had one of your own.

5

'The very highest medium for the dissemination of public intelligence'

WOODROW WILSON, 1917

AT THE END OF JUNE 1914 an assassin's bullet fired in Sarajevo unleashed war in Europe. Within days Germany, Russia, France, Great Britain and a host of other nations were caught up in the conflict. Although most Americans naturally reacted with horror to news of the resulting carnage, many also felt relieved that their country remained aloof from the hostilities taking place thousands of miles away, and hoped very much it would remain so. After all, from a purely selfish viewpoint, the sudden outbreak of war presented the American economy with a huge opportunity. Markets which had been previously controlled by European industry were suddenly ripe for conquest and the balance of economic power between the United States and the Old World was about to undergo a tumultuous change.

As well as expanding overseas, the American film companies were finally able to secure control of their home market, although in truth this process was well advanced even before hostilities broke out. After Carl Laemmle's IMP had moved into film production, a host of newly established independent companies began cranking out their own pictures. They included Reliance Pictures, which would eventually sign up director D. W. Griffith, and the Thanhouser Company, founded by Edwin Thanhouser, a former theatre manager and director of his own stock company. These firms rapidly stepped up their output and were soon producing scores of films every year; by the end of 1912 they were producing over half the movies made in the United States, while the ailing companies of the Trust saw their output fall. The European importers too, already battered by years of conflict with the Trust, and faced with an onslaught from a new and entirely unexpected quarter, now began to see their share of the American market steadily decline. 'Without doubt from 1910 an inverse movement became apparent,' recalled Charles Pathé. 'Any observer could see the fierce competition between France and America in cinema . . . We were being surpassed and we were angry.' By 1912 American movies accounted for some 80 per cent of new releases in the United States, with half those titles coming from the independent producers.

In their efforts to secure control of their home market, the American independents were helped by the fact that, in 1914, Charles Pathé, their strongest competitor, pulled out of feature production in the United States, deciding instead to concentrate on distributing short films made by independent producers. 'My intention is to become a picture publisher or editor – to publish films as others publish books. I accept negatives where they accept manuscripts,' he told an American journalist. 'I believe every effort of the editors or publishers of films must be to look out for good authors, for great authors. I would like to see writing for the screen such men as your late Mark Twain – men of genius.' With these remarks, Pathé echoed the sentiment of so many other pioneers of the early movie business who, while accumulating riches beyond their wildest imaginings, became obsessed with conveying an aura of gentility and refinement. It was perhaps no accident that it should be in the movies – that medium of illusion, imagined identities and public spectacle – that they finally found their true vocation. Ironically, Pathé was dismantling the vertically integrated structure which had been the cornerstone of his company's phenomenal worldwide success at precisely the moment that Zukor and Laemmle were beginning to create their own versions of the same model, companies that would eventually become the Hollywood studios, Paramount and Universal. In abandoning the distribution of features in favour of shorts he had made a serious miscalculation, and, by 1921, beset by financial difficulties, he would be forced to sell Pathé's American subsidiary to local interests.

Prior to the outbreak of the war, American companies had not launched any serious assault on foreign markets. In 1911, under the title 'Lack of American Enterprise in Foreign Countries', the American publication *Moving Picture World* had lambasted the indigenous industry for its timidity overseas;

> Those of us who are inclined to swell out our chests and point to the supremacy of American prestige would be decidedly shocked if we really knew how far behind the times some American manufacturers are in pushing their products beyond the borders of their own country. What is known to the picture trade as the 'foreign market' is, generally speaking, Great Britain and France. The American manufacturers seem to be unaware that there are thriving, teeming, countless millions of people in other centers besides the countries mentioned who must have amusement as well as their white-skinned brethren.

It went on to castigate American producers for leaving booming markets in countries as diverse as Russia and Uruguay entirely to the Europeans. Now the war gave the Americans precisely the opportunity they needed to redress the situation.

The outbreak of the Great War had an immediate and dramatic impact on most of America's competitors in the film business, especially France. 'The first shrill blast of the trumpet sounded the doom of the continental film business,' observed *Moving Picture World* in September 1914. 'European trade outside the British Isles has been throttled and completely strangled in the grip of war . . . In Germany,

Russia, France, Austria, Belgium, and the Balkans, the workers were called to the service of their country; the people were in too serious a mood for entertainment.' It predicted that, 'Within the next year or so the demand for American films in Europe will be large enough to justify a greater "invasion" than Europe has ever known before.' In France the industry came to a halt the moment the conflict started. The film stock factories were turned over to the war effort. Thousands employed in the industry were called up for military service. Cinemas were closed. When they reopened a few months later Charles Pathé had already moved the centre of his operations to the United States and the way was clear for American movies to fill the empty screens. The French surrealist writer and poet Phillipe Soupault remembered how the influx of American pictures changed the very look of the Parisian streets: 'One day we saw hanging on the walls great posters as long as serpents. At every street-corner a man, his face covered with a red handkerchief, levelled a revolver at the peaceful passers-by.' Italy, which as a production centre had been second in strength only to France, initially remained out of the war, its production relatively unaffected. When it joined the conflict, its film business, too, was quickly decimated.

Despite the turmoil engulfing Europe, the American industry was initially more preoccupied with expansion at home, pouring millions of dollars – the fruits of box-office success – into ever-bigger companies. The epicentre of production had also moved. One of the attractions of the West was the temperate climate. The sunshine in California enabled outdoor filming to continue all year round. Costs were lower, too, partly because Los Angeles remained for some time the country's principal non-unionized city. Wages were about half the level of those on the East Coast. For some, it also offered a haven from Edison's goons who found it far harder to hunt down alleged pirates in the Californian wilderness. Like so much else in the development of the early movie industry, the trail of events which led the industry to Hollywood was as much the result of chance as of logic. In 1913 Cecil B. De Mille had been preparing to shoot the Lasky Company's first feature *The Squaw*

Man. Earlier that year, Jesse Lasky, a former vaudeville promoter, had created his eponymous company with his brother-in-law Samuel Goldfish (later Goldwyn – he changed his name partly to avoid ridicule), a Polish émigré and former glove salesman. 'We were ready to go. Where? Well, we thought, Arizona might be good. It was western.' They considered California, knowing that other movie companies had already chosen to move there, 'but California was still further down the line than Arizona, and railroad companies had the unpleasant habit of charging by the mile.' When De Mille and his team got to Arizona they quickly realized they had made a mistake. De Mille wired Lasky and Sam Goldfish in New York: 'Flagstaff No Good For Our Purpose. Have Proceeded to California. Want Authority To Rent Barn In Place Called Hollywood For $75 A Month. Cecil.' Back came the reply: 'Authorize You To Rent Barn But On Month-To-Month Basis Only. Don't Make Any Long Commitment. Regards. Jesse.'

Hollywood itself was a recent creation. In 1883, a fervent prohibitionist from Kansas, Horace Wilcox, had bought some land in a suburb of Los Angeles and began developing it. According to one story, the suburb got its name when Wilcox's wife Daeida, travelling back to her home in the East, met a woman on a train who described the delights of her summer home which she had christened Hollywood. So taken was Daeida with the name that on her return to Los Angeles she decided to use the name for her own ranch, and soon it had been adopted for the whole surrounding area. There were, however, several other stories as to how Hollywood got its name, each of which passed into movie lore, and none has ever established itself as the definitive version.

Plots of land had been acquired by retired Methodist clergy and various other religious and community organizations. When the first movie-makers arrived around 1903, the suburb had a population of just 166. William De Mille, Cecil's elder brother, remembered that it 'was largely peopled by folks from Missouri and Iowa' many of whom 'had gone West to die'. Pepper trees lined the muddy streets, orange groves stretched across the fields for miles, and the hills were wrapped in 'heat waves you could actually see'. Rabbits and skunks vastly outnumbered people among the bungalows and the rickety wooden barns which were later pressed into service as studios. The church-going locals were deeply suspicious of the movie people, having already heard rumours of the debauchery and drunkenness which seemed to be an integral part of show business, an image hardly helped by the sleazy reputation of the nickelodeons. 'No dogs or actors allowed,' read the signs placed in the windows of rooming houses across Los Angeles. Locals called the studios 'camps' and referred to film people as 'the movie colony'. It was as if the film community were exiled in the desert, a feeling exacerbated by the fact that the train journey from New York lasted five uncomfortable days; first Chicago, then across the drab mid-West plains to the desert, where perspiring passengers would fling open the windows to escape the insufferable heat only to be assailed by waves of coarse sand. Finally to arrive in California was, recalled one early traveller, like 'coming out of an inferno into paradise'.

The physical and intellectual remoteness of Los Angeles from the rest of America, combined with the feelings of hope and optimism engendered by the Californian sunshine, all played a part in shaping the distinctive ethos of Hollywood cinema. The movies in America had initially developed outside the purview of those who shaped traditional culture, and as the industry matured it seemed peculiarly appropriate that a business which was so alien to the representatives of high culture and high finance on the eastern seaboard should take root in California, about as far away as it was possible to be without actually leaving the country. After all, it had always been part of the American tradition that outsiders and non-conformists should move westward to establish their settlements. The inhabitants of the 'movie colony' were just the latest in an endless stream of hopefuls who had made the same journey to seek their fortune. It was all very different in Europe, where film-making activities were overwhelmingly located in those cities – Berlin, London, Paris and Rome – which were also centres of traditional culture. Consequently, in Europe there was far more interaction between the film community and those involved with theatre and literature. The resulting exchange of talent, ideas and money did much to explain why European cinema, unlike its American counterpart, was so influenced by the values of traditional culture. Members of the Comédie-Française were hired for the productions of Film d'Art and other similar companies in France. As early as 1905, Carlo Rosaspina, a noted Italian theatrical star, was hired for costume dramas like *The Capture of Rome*. In Germany, from 1913 onwards, playwrights and theatre directors began to create pictures known as *Autorenfilm* or author's film.

Hollywood, on the other hand, was far removed from the established poles of culture. In fact, the entire movie community was permeated by an air of transience. The early pioneers didn't really live in Los Angeles, one Californian historian later surmised, 'they merely camped, prepared, like Arabs, to fold their tents and steal away in the night'. Even when much larger studios started to appear, there still seemed to be a temporary air about them. It was an impression reinforced by the flimsy movie sets, replicas of far-off cities and ancient places, which stood on the back lots for a few weeks, only to disappear and make way for whatever served the needs of the next production. This sense of transience and unreality continued to hang in the limpid Californian air long after the 'movie colony' had taken firm root. As late as 1930, only 20 per cent of the inhabitants of Los Angeles had been born in California. Perhaps it was because the physical products of the film industry were, in themselves, so peculiarly insubstantial, certainly unlike that of any traditional manufacturing industry. Millions of dollars, thousands of people, acres of buildings produced nothing more than a few rolls of celluloid, which might or might not prove popular.

Despite the lingering air of unreality, once they were established in the West the industry pioneers felt free to give expression to their overarching ambitions on a scale that simply dwarfed all that had gone before. As in so much else, it was Carl Laemmle who led the way. In 1912 Laemmle had created a new company, Universal Pictures, which quickly became the most powerful force in the film

world. The choice of name for the company seemed suggestive of
Laemmle's determination to plant his flag throughout the known
world, but, like so much else, it had been chosen by chance. He
had originally hit on it in the midst of a meeting with his colleagues.
'I've got the name ... Universal. That's what we're supplying –
universal entertainment for the universe.' Only afterwards did he
reveal how he got the name: 'I was looking down on the street as a
covered truck went by. On the top was painted "Universal Pipe
Fittings".' Laemmle now moved to create a suitably palatial home
for his new company. In 1914 he acquired a 230-acre ranch in the
San Fernando Valley and began building a giant studio. On a cold
Saturday morning in March 1915, 200 Universal employees queued
at Grand Central Station, New York, to board a special train bound
for Los Angeles, where the studio was about to open. The company
may have been called Universal but their progress across the continent was almost presidential. Along the way they were joined by
exchange men, now transformed into 'cheering Universalites'; in
Denver they were guests at a dinner presided over by the legendary
Buffalo Bill; and on arrival in Los Angeles, they were met by a party
of cowboys and Indians, who whooped and hollered and fired guns
into the air as they escorted the group to their hotel.

On Monday 15 March, in front of about ten thousand people,
a policewoman, Laura Oakley, handed Carl Laemmle a golden key.
He unlocked a gate, declared Universal City open for business and
his former adversary Thomas Edison, with whom Laemmle had
graciously made peace, flicked a switch to bring alive the studio's
electrical system which he had helped to create. The giant film
plants of Pathé in Paris seemed minuscule by comparison. Here
visitors found 'a city that had come into being within a few months,
solely and completely equipped for the large-scale production of
motion pictures', recalled Laemmle's official biographer.

> There was a main stage, four hundred feet by a hundred and
> fifty in extent, with every kind of natural scenery at hand for
> alternative use, and a smaller stage for minor productions.
> Eighty dressing rooms and the company offices were furnished

with electric light and running water. There were three pumping stations, a great concrete reservoir, a hospital, two restaurants capable of serving twelve hundred people, and an exhaustive range of shops, forges, garages and mills ... Macadamised roads, a police department, fire brigade, public utility services; libraries, greenhouses, an omnibus system and a school – here was a community, enjoying full municipal rights, supplied by a specially constructed spur of the Southern Pacific Railroad, self-contained and self-sufficient, ready to show the world what movies meant to do.

Lucky Laemmle, the vagabond émigré from Laupheim, had arrived in Hollywood. It was a powerful symbolic statement. Film had become a major industry, and not just an American industry but, as the name Laemmle had chosen for his company suggested, an industry that was truly universal, both in its appeal to audiences and in its ambitions. The creation of a giant studio like Universal City represented far more than simply a monument to Carl Laemmle's outsized ego; it signalled the dawn of a new era in production techniques. The increasingly sophisticated studio facilities available to Hollywood film-makers meant they were able to spend ever more time on lavish sets and costumes, expensive lighting and artful cinematography, creating a far more polished look for their finished pictures. This greatly enhanced their popular appeal at a time when European film-makers, starved of capital as never before because of the deprivations of war, lacked the resources to compete on anything like equal terms. By 1919, the overwhelming majority of the films made in the United States were being shot in Hollywood.

Once the production business had begun to move west, a frenzied series of mergers and takeovers rapidly transformed the shape of the industry. The most important of these changes was the creation of Paramount. Before the war films had usually been distributed on a state-by-state basis by the old and by now established film exchanges. Film, like most existing retail businesses, had operated on an essentially local basis. In 1914, a former telegraph operator and salesman of correspondence courses from Utah named W. W.

Hodkinson summoned a group of twenty distributors to New York and urged them to form a national organization for distributing films. His rationale was simple. Since many producers sold their films to the states rights' men for a flat fee they had no opportunity to share in the gigantic rewards that were beginning to accrue from a hit picture. They all went to the distributor. Because of this, and because many of the Wall Street banks and other financial institutions still regarded the film industry with something close to abhorrence, many producers were unable to raise the $20,000 or so needed to crank out five-reel features on a regular basis. Meanwhile the distributors, as always, were interested only in getting their hands on as many movies as possible, as cheaply as possible. By providing producers with a percentage of the gross box-office revenues instead of a flat fee for each picture, Hodkinson believed he could facilitate a vast expansion of output which would benefit both sides. To generate capital on a really significant scale, such a scheme would need to be carried out on a national basis. Accordingly, he proposed a grand merger of their interests. On his way to one of the negotiating meetings he noticed a building named the 'Paramount Apartments'. This gave him an idea. During the course of the meeting he sketched a picture of a snow-capped peak he knew in the Wasatch mountains of Utah. This, he announced, was the logo of their new company, Paramount Pictures.

When he first heard the name of the company that would now distribute his pictures, Jesse Lasky disliked it intensely: 'I didn't think it suggested film artistry. It sounded more like a brand of cheese or woollen mittens.' Lasky's overt misgivings merely disguised a deeper anxiety among producers regarding the likely power of this new distributor. Paramount demanded 35 per cent of the gross box office for every picture it released, based on the assumption that distribution costs accounted for 25 per cent of the budget of a picture, and allowing for a further 10 per cent profit margin. His fellow producer and friend, Zukor, shared his concern. 'The distributors seemed to be in the driving seat, observed the Famous Players boss, furious at the peremptory manner in which they were attempting to seize power. It was the arbitrariness of the arrangement that really annoyed Zukor. 'He was learning golf, and at about the twelfth hole would remark, "Well, I guess we're 65 per cent around the course",' remembered Lasky. Zukor began to manoeuvre for a takeover of the embryonic Paramount. 'Lasky, we [producers] are being throttled, strangled to death!' he told his associate. 'I have fought with Hodkinson to increase the cash advances and percentages of the gross for our pictures. The man has ice in his veins . . . we've got to get control of Paramount or we'll be forced out of business.' Zukor's seething anger was probably rooted as much in his megalomania as in genuine fear that he was about to be forced out of business. Zukor quietly began to buy up Paramount stock. At the next shareholders meeting, on 24 June, he successfully forced the immediate removal of W. W. Hodkinson, who instantly left the premises having been thrown out of the company he had founded less than two years earlier. Zukor installed his own candidate, Hiram Abrams, as Paramount president and, two weeks later, Famous Players-Lasky acquired control of Paramount in a $25 million cash and stock deal. Zukor had created what for most of the 1920s would become the world's most powerful movie company, an organization which one trade journal was already describing as 'the United States Steel Corp. of the motion picture industry'.

Before seizing control of Paramount, Zukor had already contacted Lasky and his associate Samuel Goldfish and proposed that they pool their resources to create a new production company, Famous Players-Lasky. Shortly after the Paramount deal went through, the two operations finally merged. The next clash, perhaps inevitable given the personalities involved, was between Zukor and Goldfish. The latter was renowned for subjecting terrified colleagues to what one writer described as 'a barrage of blue shoutings'. As one source later put it: 'You don't work for Sam, you enlist for the duration of the war.' Wherever he went he was busy pursuing lawsuits 'claiming anything from fraud to murder'. He became renowned for his alleged malapropisms, as when a director had allegedly mentioned that a story was too caustic and Goldwyn fired back, 'The hell with the cost, if it's a good picture we'll make it.' Another time, told that a sundial measures the time by the sun, he is supposed to have replied, 'My God, whatever will they think of next?' Many suspected though that such sayings were created by publicists as colourful fodder for copy-hungry journalists.

Zukor's megalomania and Goldfish's ferocious energy were bound to collide. Zukor had appointed Lasky as his head of production while Goldfish was appointed to the largely symbolic position of chairman, a move which could only lead to increasing friction. The struggle intensified. In August 1916 Zukor brusquely informed Lasky that he had a choice: either Goldfish must leave the company or Zukor would. 'I've never had a harder decision to make,' recalled Lasky. 'I hardly closed my eyes for the next forty-eight hours.' In the end, Lasky sided with Zukor partly because, as he explained to Cecil B. De Mille, he had 'a broader and bigger grasp of the picture business, [and] is considered the biggest man in the motion picture industry'.

Zukor's purchase of Paramount provided America with a giant motion picture conglomerate capable of producing more than a hundred full-length features a year. It helped establish an elaborate system of differential pricing for exhibitors, so that high-class theatres in prestigious downtown locations which were exclusively devoted to new features ('first-run' houses) would be charged anything up to $700 a week for a single film; while at the other end of the scale, the most dilapidated theatres, which could only afford older titles, might be charged as little as $35 a week. Zukor had achieved his ambition: he had become head of the biggest, most powerful movie company in the world.

Zukor remained in New York from where he ran the company's finances. Lasky ran the production side of the business from California. This eventually established itself as the classic structure for all the major studios: buttoned-down financiers in New York, free-wheeling producers in Hollywood. The relationship between the two centres was strained, what Lasky once described as 'an unremitting state of hostility'.

Perhaps because they were preoccupied with securing their sovereignty over domestic competitors, the moguls had been somewhat slower to take advantage of the opportunity presented by the catastrophic impact the war was having on many of their European competitors. Now as the industry began to assume a more stable structure, men like Laemmle, Zukor and Fox began looking overseas. By 1916 America was a creditor power for the first time in its history; New York had supplanted London as the centre of world finance. It was natural that in all sorts of fields the Americans should look to expand their exports and their influence.

For the first couple of years of the war, American strength had primarily been a reflection of European weakness as American movies flowed into countries like France, Italy and Great Britain to fill the gap left by the dearth of home-produced films. Beginning around mid-1916, though, buoyed by their new-found power, American companies began creating overseas subsidiaries on a regular basis, stepping up their export drive and actively scouting for business opportunities all over the world. Laemmle, Fox and Zukor led the charge. Having appointed Emil Shauer, a former department-store buyer as his foreign manager, Zukor began opening offices all over Europe. Entire regions of the world were annexed by the newly powerful American independents. Having seized control of the business in Australia and New Zealand during the early part of the war, they now moved on to Latin America. 'Not a foot of motion picture film is produced in South America,' the editor of *Moving Picture World* had observed in 1915. 'The market must be supplied exclusively by importation. The population of Latin America is greater than that of Germany and as great as that of France and Italy combined. The market is open to all producers on even terms.' By late 1916, the American takeover of Latin American movie markets was virtually complete. From that time on, Hollywood's dominance of the region would never come under serious threat.

The studios also began expanding their production activities overseas and Universal made pictures in places as far afield as Great Britain and Japan. Increasing production costs also spurred American movie companies to look to overseas markets to recoup some of their expenditure. As Carl Laemmle later remembered it: 'There was a time when the American manufacturer made so much profit in the American market alone that he was careless about the prices he got in foreign markets. Any money that his export business bought in . . . was like picking up unexpected money in the street.'

For a while, a few European companies managed to maintain a reasonably healthy level of overseas trade. Ole Olsen's Nordisk profited from the fact that Denmark remained neutral, and Germany remained one of the biggest customers for Danish goods. By 1917 the danger to shipping was so great that Nordisk could no longer risk sending its films abroad. In any case, the Russian market, vital to Nordisk, had collapsed in the chaos of revolution and civil war. As French film chief Léon Gaumont observed bitterly: 'This war was made for America.'

Many Americans agreed with him. Jesse Lasky later recalled:

I believe America's domination of the international film market can be traced to the interventions of the First World War. Europe really had the jump on us with such quality entertainment as *Camille* and *Queen Elizabeth* from France and the magnificent Italian productions of *Cabiria* and the eight-reel spectacle *Quo Vadis* . . . Our industry was slowly starting but expanded leaps and bounds during the European setback, and by the end of the war we were so far ahead technically and had such a grip on foreign audiences that our gross revenues put us in an impregnable position.

Until that point, the Americans had relied largely on agents based in London to sell their films into Europe. Now they began selling directly from New York and the city supplanted London as the centre for the distribution of American movies. For a while, some in the British trade refused to acknowledge that London was losing its pre-eminent position. '[We] express our unshakeable conviction that London is still, and will remain, the "film clearing-house of the world",' thundered the British trade-paper *Bioscope* in April 1917. It was already too late. The American companies realized that a vast expansion of their distribution network was necessary. 'The real problem in Europe will be the problem of distribution,' observed one trade journal. 'The prospect of increased demand for American-made films will greatly smooth the way of distribution but much remains to be done.' The fact that Europe's cinemas remained open while production had been almost completely shut down meant that this 'increased demand' rapidly became overwhelming, and was made even greater by the understandable craving of war-weary audiences for some distraction from the privations and terrors which permeated every aspect of their daily lives. For many people, an hour or more in the movie house, alone with their private hopes and fantasies, was a valuable antidote to the hardships brought about by war.

Meantime, a relationship of sorts had started to evolve between the tycoons in Hollywood and the political elite in Washington. Unlike the leaders of more traditional industries, the men who ran Hollywood had not initially been welcomed into the bosom of the political establishment. They were still regarded as vulgar, predatory hucksters. Contact between the two communities had been, at best, sporadic. It was Carl Laemmle who first tried to build bridges with Washington, largely for reasons of self-aggrandisement. He had been trying to arrange a meeting at the White House simply in order to shake the President's hand. Laemmle's secretary noted that his boss might create 'miles of motion pictures for the president simply by touching a button'. In early 1915, Laemmle had suggested in a letter to President Woodrow Wilson that he deliver a message to the American people via the nation's cinema screens. It was a brilliantly imaginative proposal – a populist coup that would surely have been almost irresistible to any politician, and at the same time the most public way for the industry to win presidential endorsement. Laemmle was a fraction ahead of his time. Wilson declined the offer for the same reason that Laemmle had made it – the movies still lacked real respectability. The President retained an open mind and, if not yet ready to appear in front of the camera, he was certainly prepared to sit in front of the screen. In 1915, after watching D. W. Griffith's *Birth of a Nation*, he is alleged to have remarked: 'It is like writing history in lightning. My only regret is that it is all so terribly true.' Indeed, Griffith's controversial civil war epic with its apparent support for racist sentiments would generate public uproar, and many politicians were furious that the film appeared to have received official approbation by being screened at the White House. Wilson tried to stay out of the controversy. Nevertheless, in a country for which cinema would help create a national identity, it was fitting that Griffith's film, the first really ambitious American movie, should deal with the roots of that identity. At any rate, within months the President had acceded to relentless pressure from Laemmle. On his own initiative, 'Uncle Carl' wrote a New Year's message for Wilson and then asked the President if he could show it on title cards in a short film to be shown in the nation's cinemas. Wilson personally rewrote the message more to his taste, and history was made.

With America's entry into the war in 1917, and with Europe's decline into barbarism seemingly without end, Wilson began to think seriously about the political value of cinema: that it was popular was undeniable; that it was increasingly associated in the eyes of the world with the modernity of the United States was equally clear. Why not, argued Wilson, put the movies at the service of a great crusade to uphold the values of liberal democracy which were being put at risk by the Great War? The project had a pleasing integrity to it; progressive liberalism and a new world order had become synonymous with the very essence of America, and any campaign to promulgate the former must, inevitably, promote the latter. It was almost inevitable that the movies, an industry increasingly identified with modern technological forms of production, should play a crucial role in the propaganda war. Wilson felt that America had a duty to lead the world towards a stable 'society of the future'. The age of American insularity was over. The country threw itself into the conflict with furious energy, training an army for deployment in Europe and sending its fleet out into the Atlantic to hunt down submarines. Wilson's project, however, was about far more than political idealism; it was underpinned by strictly practical politics. The dissemination of liberal values would be most effectively accomplished by the export of American goods. 'Western ideas go in with the western goods,' as he put it. In a speech entitled 'Men are Governed by Their Emotions', made in 1916, he was even more direct: 'Go out and sell goods that will make this world more comfortable and more happy and convert them to the principles of America.'

Economic arguments also began to be deployed. As early as 1918 the American Chamber of Commerce in London produced a memorandum on the cultural and economic value of the movie industry in an attempt to defeat proposals by the British to place restrictions on shipping space for movies, noting that Britain was 'probably the most important market in the world for U.S. film companies'. For Wilson, economics and ideology went hand in hand. The moving picture, which represented both an economic good and an ideological tool, was the perfect vehicle. It was a lesson that subsequent American presidents would never forget. A decade later, in 1926, a motion picture division would be specifically set up as part of the Bureau of Foreign and Domestic Commerce, whose duties included the promotion of overseas trade by dispatching agents abroad to be the 'eyes for the whole business community'.

Wilson had already created the Creel Committee on Public Information (named after its chairman George Creel) to spread his gospel of liberal democracy. Creel was a former journalist from the Midwest, a one-time editor of the *Rocky Mountain News* who had subsequently entered politics. He had organized a division of Four-Minute Men, public speakers who delivered brief patriotic speeches between reel changes at cinemas. The industry pushed for movies to be used as one of the instruments of propaganda utilized by the Creel Committee, partly no doubt to confer a new respectability upon cinema. '[T]he motion picture can be made the most wonderful system for spreading the National Propaganda at little or no cost,' William Brady, now president representative of the National Association of the Motion Picture Industry, wrote to Joseph Tumulty, Wilson's secretary. The movies could, he explained, 'in two weeks to a month place a message in every part of the civilised world . . . The method of doing so is already in existence – is organised efficiently and can be used for this great purpose, and is far more effective than the newspapers.' The images conveyed by the movies, after all, could be understood by anyone, regardless of whether they spoke English. Shortly afterwards, Wilson agreed to create an industry committee that could work with Creel. In what was for the film industry a landmark speech, Wilson proclaimed: 'The film has come to rank as the very highest medium for the dissemination of public intelligence and since it speaks a universal language it lends itself importantly to the presentation of America's plans and purposes.' In September 1917, the Creel Committee decided to establish a Division of Films.

In a move that echoed the efforts of the German Supreme Command, they commissioned a series of documentaries on American industry. But it seemed there was a subtle difference to the German approach. 'We did not call it propaganda, for that word, in German hands, had come to be associated with deceit and corruption,' wrote George Creel in a memoir which, with disarming frankness, he called *How We Advertised America*. 'Our effort was educational and informative throughout.' It may have been difficult to believe that, as one foreign trade representative put it, the Europeans 'are eager – it is not too much to say they are wild – for films that illustrate the various operations of American industry such as the manufacture of fountain pens.'

The real importance of all this lay elsewhere. Film company chiefs, including Adolph Zukor and Marcus Loew, another former furrier who had created one of the country's largest cinema chains, found themselves assigned to specific government departments to co-ordinate links between the Creel Committee and commercial industry. They took their place in the war effort alongside more established business leaders such as Bernard Baruch, a Wall Street financier who headed the War Industries Board, and Herbert Hoover a wealthy mining engineer (and future president) who served as Food Administrator. This practical arrangement proved highly successful and marked the beginning of what would, for the most part, prove to be a successful and harmonious relationship with successive administrations in Washington. Stars including Charles Chaplin, Douglas Fairbanks and Mary Pickford were encouraged to sell liberty bonds to help finance the war effort. Each Thursday evening a contingent of these celebrities, known as the Lasky Home Guard, would march behind a band down Hollywood Boulevard carrying rifles and wearing uniforms from the costume department in an attempt to encourage people to part with their hard-earned dollars. Lasky's company even produced a film called *The Great Liberty Bond Hold-Up* starring William Hart, Mary Pickford and Douglas Fairbanks in which Fairbanks displays such avid enthusiasm for grabbing liberty bonds from a teller at a bank that he is halfway out of the door before he remembers to pay for them. So it was that film became the continuation of war by other means.

An agreement was negotiated under which every export shipment of commercial Hollywood product had to include at least 20 per cent 'educational matter'. No films of any kind were to be sold to any exhibitor who refused to show this additional material. A Foreign Film Service was created and staff were dispatched to countries in Europe, South America and the Far East. Indeed, on occasion, the Creel Committee effectively took charge of the commercial distribution process as a whole. In Switzerland and Holland, where cinema screens were overwhelmingly dominated by German films, 'it was agreed by the leading film-producers that . . . the committee should have the absolute and unquestioned disposition of every foot of commercial film that went into the two countries . . . it was very soon the case that the Germans were being driven out of both markets.' In preventing German movies from reaching some of its key European customers, the Creel Committee enabled the American film business to snatch a small but valuable slice of international trade from an increasingly feared competitor.

All of this also had wider cultural implications for the image of America. As Creel put it:

It was not only that the Committee put motion pictures into foreign countries. Just as important was the work of keeping certain motion pictures out of those countries. As a matter of bitter fact, much of the misconception about America before the war was due to American motion pictures portraying the lives and exploits of New York's gun-men, Western bandits, and the wild days of the old frontier, all of which were accepted in many parts of the world as wholly representative of contemporary American life.

What we wanted to get into foreign countries were pictures that presented the wholesome life of America, giving fair ideas of our people and institutions. What we wanted to keep out of world circulation were the 'thrillers' that gave entirely false impressions of American life and morals. Film dramas portraying the life of 'Gyp the Blood' or 'Jesse James' were bound to prejudice our fight for the good public opinion of the neutral nations.

This debate about the potentially damaging impact of certain American movies would surface again from time to time, especially during periods of conflict. Such concerns largely remained subjugated to the overriding desire to expand overseas trade. The significance of this co-operation between industry and government went far beyond export assistance to a couple of relatively minor European markets. In helping the government to achieve their political and economic aims, the industry was building up a huge bank of goodwill in Washington. Industry leaders were keenly aware that somewhere in the future there would have to be some kind of quid pro quo. Hollywood had genuinely thrown its weight behind the government's push to export goods and ideas. It was only right that the government in turn should feel obliged to support the industry and, more specifically, to assist in its efforts to hold down any tariffs or other barriers that some misguided foreign government might be foolish enough to throw in its path. As one member of the Wilson administration put it: 'the government, while it cannot create trade, can give to trade an environment in which it can develop.' The movie business was declared 'an essential industry' in August 1918, enabling it to continue operating despite a shortage of materials. It had achieved official recognition at the very highest level. As Adolph Zukor put it, the industry had jumped at the chance 'to show its patriotism [and] to prove beyond all question its worth to the Government as well as to the people of the United States'. After the war, Treasury Secretary William McAdoo was even offered the presidency of the newly-formed United Artists, created by Charles Chaplin, Mary Pickford, Douglas Fairbanks Snr and D. W. Griffith and three creative partners. He turned the offer down. The movie bosses adopted a new slogan: 'Trade Follows Film.' It soon became a kind of mantra, or perhaps a battle-cry, in the crusade to demolish all taxes and tariffs threatened by foreign governments. It only remained for Hollywood to choose the issue on which it would call in the favours now owed by Washington.

To see Hollywood as a thing apart from the rest of America, some self-sufficient Shangri-La was, in fact, to be seduced by a myth that Hollywood itself did much to perpetuate. Notwithstanding its flimsy film sets, it was unquestionably an industry of growing power and influence. For, ironically, if it was the French who industrialized the movie industry, it was the Americans who politicized and legitimized it. And as it grew, it became increasingly dependent on the goodwill of politicians and bankers, stalwart members of that self-same establishment back East which had previously regarded the world of the movies with such disfavour. Hollywood's relationship with Capitol Hill, and with Wall Street, would evolve in very different ways and sometimes, particularly on the political front, the strains of maintaining those relationships would become enormous. Without help and support from the worlds of both finance and politics, Hollywood would have had a great deal more difficulty in achieving its overwhelming dominance of the world's cinema screens.

It would be a mistake to attribute these momentous shifts in the world's film industry entirely to the fortunes of war. It was true, of course, that war in mainland Europe had been in every respect a catastrophe. As far as the European movie business was concerned, it had decimated production at the very moment that audiences were flocking to the cinema in ever-greater numbers, as much as anything to forget the horrors of the conflict going on around them. The war also coincided with a vast expansion of American business which had little or nothing whatever to do with events in Europe. The American government also began to take the industry seriously and to support it. Indeed, if the Europeans used their traditional culture as a means of reminding them of their cultural identity, America used the movies as a way of forging a cultural identity. Without the war, it might have taken the Americans longer to complete their conquest of the key foreign markets, but the process was already under way when those fatal first shots were fired in Sarajevo. By the time the war ended in 1918, the American industry was in a commanding position not only across much of Europe, but in the Far East, South America and Australasia.

No sooner had the military hostilities ceased, than the battle for control of the film industry was renewed in earnest. And, somewhat surprisingly, the European counter-attack would now be led by Germany, the country which had just suffered such a catastrophic and humiliating defeat.

6

Film Europe

WHILE WOODROW WILSON and George Creel were busy integrating film into the national consciousness of the United States, the impact of war prompted some of the most powerful personalities in Germany to consider how the film industry might help the German war effort. In November 1916, the industrialist Alfred Hugenberg had quietly engineered the creation of Deutsche Lichtbild Gesellschaft (DLG, later known as Deulig), a privately-controlled film company formed from the merger of several smaller independent companies. Hugenberg, a towering figure in the national industry, was later dubbed 'Lord of the Press and Film'. He owned a majority holding in Scherl-Verlag, Germany's largest publishing company, as well as stakes in several leading German newspapers, and an advertising agency. He was described as: 'A small man, slim with white hair that is cut very short and sticks up like a brush, glasses and a funny moustache . . . An odd little man who is dressed as if he had to feed a family of five on the salary of a junior book-keeper.' He had always harboured political ambitions and would eventually become minister of economics in Hitler's coalition Cabinet in January 1933. DLG's initially modest ambition was to promote German industrial interests in short films intended to accompany commercial features at national cinemas. It was headed by Ludwig Klitzsch, a former advertising executive.

As the war dragged on, Erich Ludendorff, one of the most powerful figures in the German Supreme Command (and the man who first authorized the use of 'Yellow Cross' mustard gas), realized that films designed to promote the values of patriotism and national unity might play a vital role in promoting the German cause at home and abroad. Simultaneously, Lt-Col. Hans von Haeften, head of overseas propaganda of the German Foreign Office, who controlled BUFA (the Office of Photography and Film), argued that rival DLG needed to be brought under government control. In this way, DLG could be made into a truly effective vehicle for state, rather than industry, propaganda. Ludendorff therefore proposed the creation of a giant German film trust, which would merge DLG with BUFA, indigenous commercial firms and the local subsidiary of Ole Olsen's Nordisk. Ludendorff suggested that the company should be secretly controlled by the state. In a memorandum to the Prussian war minister in July 1917, Ludendorff observed: 'Precisely because of the powerful political and military influence that films will continue to wield for the duration of the war, our victory absolutely depends on our using films to exert the greatest possible persuasion wherever people can still be won over to the German cause.' The company would also be a powerful symbol of the strength of German nationalism, capable of demonstrating the might and majesty of the Fatherland in cinemas throughout Germany and around the world. As Ludendorff put it, the new company would constitute 'a further unification of our film industry so that it could undertake planned and energetic measures for influencing the masses in the interests of the state'.

Ludendorff, who once proclaimed that it was better 'the German Empire go under than that we make a renunciatory peace', really represented the past rather than the future. Nevertheless, his political influence was vital in facilitating a revolution in Germany's fledgling film industry. Soon afterwards Ludendorff and Haeften initiated discussions with Emil Georg von Stauss, the head of the Deutsche Bank and one of Germany's most influential financiers, to help secure finance for the plan. On 18 December 1917, the German Supreme Command, headed by Ludendorff and his military partner Paul von Hindenburg, announced the creation of Universum-Film AG (Ufa). This was an altogether different kind of entity from the free-wheeling enterprises which had sprung up around the world in the course of the previous twenty years. Ufa was capitalized at 25 million marks, a third of which was secretly put up by the German government. Stauss was made chairman and Robert Bosch, of the electrical group, was one of his deputies. The company was supported by an extraordinary group of private backers including Hamburg-Amerika, which before the war had been the largest shipping line in the world and which was represented by Wilhelm Cuno, later Reich Chancellor; North German Lloyd, another shipping giant; the Dresdner Bank; and Allgemeine Electrizitäts AG, a vast electrical company controlled by Walther Rathenau, later German foreign minister, who would be murdered by political opponents in 1922. Nordisk, which was producing over a quarter of Germany's films and owned a national chain of luxurious cinemas, was also integrated into the new enterprise, effectively placing its local subsidiary under state control. 'There was no choice for us,' recalled Olsen. 'As foreigners in a country at war we could only try to salvage as much as possible out of the deal.' In fact, the Reich used its power to acquire Nordisk's interests at a price well below market value, precipitating a decline that would culminate in Olsen's resignation from the company in 1924.

Ufa had a sparkling array of stars at its disposal, including Asta Nielsen, Pola Negri, and Emil Jannings, as well as directors such as Ernst Lubitsch and Paul Wegener. Ufa's mission, as prescribed by the Supreme Command, was not only to produce propaganda 'shorts' but, far more significantly, to make full-length dramatic features which embodied the supposed values of German *Kultur*, the 'blood and iron' evoked by Bismarck. With foreign films having been banned in February 1916, ostensibly to conserve the country's foreign currency reserves, Ufa's dominance in the domestic market was assured. Stauss was emphatic that the company had to operate as a vertically integrated firm so that 'it maintains complete superiority with respect to production, leasing [distribution] and theatres'. This was the structure, created by Charles Pathé, which had begun to serve the Hollywood studios so well. The company's first press statement also underlined the way in which it proposed to challenge those American firms which had previously dominated international markets.

Stauss was an extreme nationalist who later forged a close relationship with Hitler. He helped to found Lufthansa and would later serve on the boards of BMW and Daimler Benz. Ufa, like those other companies, would become a symbol of a future dominated by technology. At this time both Germany and America were countries which, for different reasons, had a relatively fragile sense of their own identity; both actively sought to create a clear sense of nationhood. After all, the unification of Germany had been achieved by Bismarck only in 1871. There was widespread enthusiasm for the spread of mass culture, unlike in countries such as France and Britain where this would cause deep anxiety among the intellectual elite. Thus it was that in Germany and America, more than anywhere else, the film industry, a powerful symbol of modern mass culture, was appropriated by political forces as a national symbol.

With the formation of Ufa, the Supreme Command had created the most powerful film company in Europe, towering over its French rivals, Pathé and Gaumont. Ufa quickly expanded into Eastern Europe, the Balkans, Scandinavia and the Low Countries. The principal architect of this expansion was Karl Bratz, a representative of the German jute trade and a member of Ufa's board. Even during the war Bratz had apparently established secret contacts with Hollywood. After the war, he would incur the wrath of his bosses when, without their knowledge, he signed an agreement for the distribution of Famous Players movies in Germany.

All this represented a staggering transformation of the German film industry, which had been far slower to develop than its rivals in smaller countries such as Denmark and Sweden. In part, this weakness was a direct consequence of the strength of Germany's vibrant theatrical tradition. Organizations representing playwrights, directors and actors had launched a formal boycott of the cinema in May 1912. They argued that cinema not only represented the very worst kind of inane popular entertainment, but that it actually served to corrupt the established arts by selectively adapting literary classics, often omitting characters and incidents which had been central to the original written work. '[T]he cinemas are a dangerous, almost invincible force that is working against all artistic effort,' claimed one intellectual manifesto. '[They] push aside the mighty word and the actor's noble gesture, and offer only a pitiable [visual] substitute . . . The cinema and the legitimate dramatic arts are born enemies.'

Their protests were eventually silenced by film producers offering well-known playwrights lucrative contracts for screen versions of prestigious literary texts, the so-called *Autorenfilm* (author's film). Unlike the *politique des auteurs* championed by the French New Wave in the late 1950s, in which the director was the pivotal figure, in these early German films it was the writer of the screenplay who was conceived as the author. The films featured famous actors from the theatre, such as Albert Basserman who starred in *Der Andere* (1913) and Paul Wegener, star of *Der Student Von Prag* made in the same year. These films were essentially the German version of the *Films d'Art* which had appeared a few years earlier in France. Despite the prestige they conferred on the industry, few of them achieved box-office success, and, until Ufa's emergence, the German industry remained little more than a scattered agglomeration of small companies.

The formation of Ufa created a flagship for the entire German movie business. As well as the production and distribution of films,

Ufa controlled the largest chain of cinemas in Germany. It embarked on a vast expansion of its production base at Neubabelsberg and Tempelhof in the Berlin suburbs and soon owned the biggest and best-equipped studios in Europe which, with their sophisticated facilities, could truly claim to compete with Laemmle's Universal City complex. The film studio was the perfect symbol of technological modernity which came to represent an important element in the ideology of German nationalism, even as, under Hitler, nationalists would simultaneously reach back to primitive mythologies.

A few years earlier the German establishment had fought a vigorous campaign to emasculate the movies through punitive forms of censorship. Now that same establishment had effectively seized control of the whole industry, not to kill it off but to transform and expand it. For the German state, determined to influence the hearts and minds of its people, the movies were no longer a target; instead, they had become a vital weapon. The government had not only recognized the positive power of cinema, they had accepted Ludwig Klitzsch's argument that feature-length dramas might prove an even more potent political tool for the dissemination of indigenous *Kultur* than tendentious shorts. Feature-length stories could promote the values of German nationalism throughout the world, simultaneously bolstering the economic strength of the industry. The German Reich, perhaps aware that the most effective propaganda was that which could not be readily identified, continued to keep its shareholdings in Ufa secret. It was only with the advent of the Weimar Republic after the war that the full extent of government involvement in the company leaked out. Shortly afterwards, the state sold its shares to Deutsche Bank.

The entry of financial titans into the movie business may well have been driven more by a pragmatic desire to cement invaluable political ties than by any sense that the film industry was a repository of huge, untapped profits. For politically ambitious men like Wilhelm Cuno and Walther Rathenau, taking a stake in Ufa alongside the German Treasury was just one more way of using their immense financial muscle to secure political influence. As regards its impact on the movie industry, it really didn't matter what their motives were. The simple act of investing in Ufa was enough to show that established financiers and industrialists were no longer turning their backs on the industry, that they no longer saw it as just a playground for idle speculators and small-time chancers. The merger of its leading film companies into one giant entity put Germany's movie business on a par with the country's coal, iron and chemical industries. Such a comparison was significant because these traditional heavy industries were, almost without exception, organized into effective cartels which shut out domestic rivals and provided a powerful springboard for assaults on foreign markets.

Despite the best efforts of Ufa, by the early 1920s the Europeans were losing an increasing share of their home markets to a confident and rapidly expanding American industry. The major American companies of the era, Fox, Universal and Famous Players-Lasky, had a comprehensive network of offices around the world. If European countries were to compete with the Americans in a serious way, it was clear that films produced in Europe would have to match the kind of high quality production values that were now the norm for major American films. Making such films was an expensive business. As remains the case today, few European producers could expect to recoup the production costs of a major film in their own, relatively small national markets. And their ability to earn revenues in foreign markets was severely limited by the absence of the complex multinational distribution networks deployed at the service of the Hollywood studios. In common with many of his European colleagues, Erich Pommer of Ufa concluded that some form of collective action was necessary: 'European producers must at last think of establishing a certain level of co-operation among themselves. It is imperative to create a system of regular trade which will enable the producers to amortise their films rapidly. It is necessary to create "European films" which will no longer be French, English, Italian or German films; entirely "continental" films, expanding out into all Europe and amortising their enormous costs, can be produced easily.' His ideas led to the creation of a new organization: Film Europe.

Film Europe was established on the premise that, if an appropriate distribution mechanism could be created, any producer, working
anywhere in Europe, could treat the whole continent as his home
market. Such ideas of European economic co-operation had gained
increasing currency in the wake of the Treaty of Versailles in 1919,
as nations sought to create an international trading framework which
would help to ensure peace. Ufa attempted to put this notion into
practice by negotiating a joint distribution deal with Aubert, one of
the largest distribution companies in France. This, in turn, triggered
other ambitious attempts to create a European 'major'. In 1923, one
of Germany's most powerful industrialists, Hugo Stinnes, joined
forces with a rich Russian émigré, Vladimir Wengeroff, with the
idea of creating a pan-European film company. Stinnes, the self-
styled 'king of the Ruhr', had long been an enthusiastic proponent
of European economic co-operation. 'European unity in the form of
increasing economic collaboration and interweaving of interests, that
was his great dream,' recalled his son. He well appreciated the
advantages that flowed from maximizing economies of scale. In 1920,
he had joined forces with Carl Friedrich von Siemens, of the great
electrical company, to create Siemens-Rheinelbe-Schuckert Union,
Germany's largest industrial combine, and one of the most powerful
conglomerates in the world, with interests stretching from coal, iron,
steel and electrical goods to paper and printing works. With his
personal interest in film, Stinnes seemed to offer something which
even the mighty Ufa could not accomplish: a truly pan-European
combine which could equal, and perhaps even surpass, the power
of the biggest Hollywood studios. In 1924, together with Wengeroff,
he created Westi, a Berlin-based film company with subsidiaries
in every corner of Europe. Later that year Pathé-Consortium, a
descendant of the original French firm, controlled by Jean Sapène,
publicity editor of the Paris newspaper *Le Matin*, joined forces with
this group to create Pathé-Westi. The new company had vast
amounts of capital at its disposal, and, with the involvement of
Pathé, access to the expertise of the most experienced film company
in the world. In France, many leading directors such as Abel Gance

and Germaine Dulac, were put under contract to make films for the new company. Here at last, it seemed, was an operation that could mount a serious challenge to the Hollywood majors.

Within a year Hugo Stinnes had died, leaving huge and unexpected debts. His companies, Westi among them, were forced into liquidation. The supporters of Film Europe gained fresh heart with the creation in 1926 of the Alliance Cinématographique Européen (ACE) a joint venture between the Swedish film company Svenska, Ufa and French investors. It was supposed to produce films in all three countries, but its primary function became the distribution of Ufa's films in France. In 1928 there were further agreements, leading Ufa's Ludwig Klitzsch to observe: 'A European film cartel is actually established now.' The Americans showed some signs of nervousness, with one official report claiming that 'America's dominant position on the world market, through an annual average output of 700 films, would seriously be challenged' if all companies in Europe formed a grand alliance. Film Europe, however, never had the remotest chance of fulfilling such an ambitious goal. With the rise of fascism in Germany and Italy, and the introduction of sound, the collaborative spirit which underlay the Film Europe movement started to dissolve. The talkies meant that individual countries were much more focused on producing films in their own languages for domestic audiences. After the end of the 1920s, little more was heard of such ideas.

The Italians and the Russians made their own attempts to mount a serious challenge to the Americans during this period. The Italian industry, which before the war had been among Europe's most prosperous, saw a sharp downturn in its fortunes after the outbreak of hostilities. In 1919, a group of producers, distributors and exhibitors got together to form a large, integrated film company called Unione Cinematografica Italiana (UCI). Its significance lay in the fact that it was financed by two Italian banks, Banca Italiana di Sconto and the Banca Commerciale, a sign that high finance was becoming increasingly intrigued by the potential of the industry. Italy, like the rest of Europe, had plenty of creative talent, but again had suffered from its inability to create a film company of any significant size. 'We are short of only one thing to make a good industry, and that is industrialists,' observed one Italian trade-paper of the period. 'We do not have people capable of understanding big business; we have only small shopkeepers.' UCI was desperately short of capital, the more so after Banca Italiana di Sconto collapsed. Its films, such as the serial adventure *Saetta Contro Golia* (*Saetta versus Goliath*), were poorly told and featured shabby sets and ill-defined characters. UCI eventually lurched into bankruptcy. The American production *Ben Hur*, shot in Rome in 1923, sent the wages of local technicians soaring and brought further chaos to the Italian industry from which it took years to recover.

At the same time, the film industry in the Soviet Union was becoming an increasingly influential force. In 1922, Lenin, acknowledging like Wilson and Ludendorff the ideological value of film, had allegedly declared: 'Of all the arts, for us the cinema is the most important.' Towards the end of that year, the government decided to organize the country's shambolic film industry into a central distribution monopoly called Goskino. The attempt failed and foreign films continued to dominate the market; an investigation in 1923 found that 99 per cent of all films distributed in the Soviet Union were of foreign origin, many of them German.

In 1925 the Soviet authorities tried again. They created a new nationalized film company, Sovkino, to control production and distribution. Sovkino backed young directors specializing in montage, an editing technique involving a staccato juxtaposition of images, sometimes designed to clash, and inspired by the work of D. W. Griffith among others. Indeed, it was rumoured that Lenin had once asked D. W. Griffith to head up the Soviet film industry. The foremost exponent of the technique was the director Sergei Eisenstein, and his film *The Battleship Potemkin*, a didactic epic dealing with the origins of the Soviet Union, achieved widespread popularity overseas after its release in 1926. This success was not matched at home. In an episode that symbolized the tension between direct state control of the cinema and the public taste, *Potemkin* opened to the Moscow public on the same day that *Robin Hood*, an American swashbuckler starring Douglas Fairbanks and produced some three years earlier, also made its Russian debut. *Robin Hood*, a swaggering tale of adventure set in a glorified medieval England, was emblematic of everything the Soviet regime hated. Nevertheless, just a few weeks later, *Potemkin* was quietly pulled from the grubby, second-rate cinemas where it had been playing to almost deserted houses. Even the rigging of audience figures by the Soviet authorities could not conceal the fact that it had been a dismal commercial failure. Ordinary Russians, no less than their counterparts elsewhere in the world, found themselves totally magnetized by the youthful exuberance of Fairbanks. Soviet directors were criticized by their masters for making films which were more suitable for educated audiences abroad than for those mass audiences at home that the authorities felt should be the real target of state film-making. Eventually, in 1930, Eisenstein left the country to pursue his film-making career first in Hollywood and then in Mexico. Despite the creative influence overseas of montage, the country's film industry remained financially fragile.

Ufa rapidly built up a resident company of hundreds of actors, producers, directors and technicians at its magnificently equipped studios outside Berlin. Over the next few years it began producing big-budget spectaculars, deliberately intended to challenge the supremacy of the Americans. On a visit to the set of Lang's *Siegfried*, the British film-maker George Pearson recalled, with envy, that he had stood 'amazed before the gigantic forest of studio-built trees, some thirty feet high, through which Siegfried would ride. The overall cost of that one scene would have exhausted the whole budget of one of my own films'. In late 1921, an American-based observer reported that the German industry was 'indisputably second in the world in order of size and, dare I say it, merit', adding that it was still 'progressing at an alarming speed'. He noted that their studios were 'larger than anything we have on this side of the Atlantic, their offices resemble the Ritz Hotel, and their outside sets which are most elaborate and accurate in design and construction, sometimes cover dozens of acres'. As in Hollywood, what was perhaps most noticeable was the air of unreality that hung over everything. At Neubabelsberg, noted one observer, 'They construct whole cultures and destroy them again'. The inflation which engulfed Germany during the early 1920s, and which led to the hyper-inflation of 1923, provided a further boost for the German film industry. The dramatic slump in the value of the mark meant that foreign distributors could buy German films at incredibly cheap prices. Conversely, few German exhibitors could afford the millions of marks needed to acquire foreign films and so had to content themselves with locally-made material.

In early 1920, *Madame Dubarry*, a sumptuously mounted costume drama set just before the outbreak of the French Revolution, became a huge hit worldwide. Released in the United States under the title *Passion*, its success, together with that of a handful of other German movies, sparked fears that the Germans were about to seize control of the entire American film market. Some American workers began to demand a tariff on foreign films entering the country. In an extraordinary move, the American actors' union (Actors' Equity), together with other groups including the American Legion and Adolph Zukor's Famous Players, called for a blanket ban on all foreign films, on the grounds that they were causing unemployment in the American film industry. Such protectionism anticipated the response in Hollywood to a prolonged downturn in domestic movie production during the 1960s. The real target in the 1920s, however, was unmistakably Germany. The American Legion and its allies stirred up antagonism in Los Angeles towards the remarkable *The Cabinet of Dr Caligari*, preventing it from being screened there. It was some time before such hostility evaporated.

This hostility to foreign films coincided with a wave of antipathy towards immigrants generally – so-called 'hyphenated Americans' – culminating in the repressively anti-immigrant Johnson-Reed Act of 1924. It was hardly surprising that in such a feverish atmosphere some American industry publications resorted to the crudest kind of racial caricature. 'There are no two countries so widely separated in their aspirations, ambitions and manifestations as Germany and America,' observed one writer. Germany was depicted as a society riddled by class hatred, in which the sexual immorality of its citizens manifested itself in a voyeuristic enjoyment of 'horror and suffering on the screen'. By contrast, Americans believed in 'the eternal splendid youth, in the glory of motherhood, in the square deal, in the equality of sexes' and, most crucially, 'in equal opportunities for all'. The supposed contrast between the democratic impulses of American society and the class-ridden structure of Germany gave rise to a further twist in the story. It was argued that while the United States produced films for the masses, Europe tailored its films for an intellectual elite. In a review of Fritz Lang's film *Siegfried*, the American trade paper *Variety* haughtily observed:

> the picture is purely artistic and holds but few things to interest the average picturegoer of today. It's an artistic but not a commercial film . . . The rave about these German pictures is that the directors are artists to their fingertips. But . . . their artistry consists in playing the film story before settings of a very stagey nature and in playing the various scenes in a slow and stodgy pace, not only tiresome to an American audience, but ruinous to the picture . . . Just an 'artistic success' which doesn't mean 10 cents in Mexican money at the box-office.

The protectionist impulse was well wrapped in the cloak of commerce.

It was ironic that the American film industry had itself been built almost entirely by 'hyphenated Americans' – the moguls and their allies, many of whom had emigrated from Eastern Europe. In fact, there were over 7 million German-Americans in the United States as a whole. Naturally, they were wary of the extreme nationalism which fuelled so much of the American hostility to German pictures. 'This "German Invasion" fright is the oldest and silliest of alarms,' proclaimed Adolph Zukor. 'One might think that the Germans had some magical recipe for making great pictures. A European might just as sensibly, after seeing *Birth of a Nation*, *Miracle Man* or *Four Horsemen*, fall into a panic and believe that every American film was of equal calibre.'

Ufa had further consolidated its grip on the German industry. In 1921 it had absorbed Decla-Bioskop, a leading independent firm. The head of Decla-Bioskop, Erich Pommer, was made chief of production at Ufa in February 1923. At Decla-Bioskop he had nurtured such directors as Fritz Lang and Robert Wiene and introduced the world to German Expressionism with Wiene's *The Cabinet of Dr Caligari*. Pommer soon established himself as Ufa's most influential executive. Like so many of his American counterparts, he was blessed with almost inexhaustible energy. 'He simply didn't know what fatigue was,' recalled the Danish director Carl Theodor Dreyer. 'He often worked 24 and 48 hours at a stretch.' Pommer was an instigator, not a creator, happy to give his artists the autonomy they sought. Although best known for his Expressionist films, they constituted only a small part of his output at Ufa. 'The mass of non-stylised films were the economic backbone of the company,' Pommer recalled. Ufa resembled a giant movie factory in which specialized labourers, working under the command of one all-seeing figure – the producer – churned out films on a veritable production line: 'Each producer has his own suite of rooms, his reception office, his private cutting and joining room, his private projection room, ready for viewing each day's work as it comes through – complete with piano.' Everyone, from the director and screenwriter to the carpenters and electrical workers, had his or her clearly defined role to play in the process which took a film from drawing-board to cinema screen. The system closely resembled that of the centralized producer system originally developed in a rather crude form by Thomas Ince of the New York Motion Picture Company in the United States before the Great War, and subsequently adopted by all the major Hollywood studios. It was this mass manufacturing ethos that later prompted actress Lillian Gish to describe Hollywood as the 'Detroit of the emotions'. It was hardly surprising, perhaps, that Mac and Dick McDonald, who gave their name to the McDonald's burger chain (for many, another symbol of American mass manufacturing), originally went West in the 1930s to try their fortune in Hollywood, before opening their first drive-in restaurant near Pasadena in 1937.

By the mid-1920s, America was in vogue in Germany. The hostility towards Germany among some sections of the Hollywood community did nothing to dampen the enthusiasm for American goods. 'America is currently in style. We imitate it in order to steal a march on it and would like if possible to be more American than the Americans,' acknowledged one German industry observer. This reflected a broader fashion among many Europeans for worshipping America as, above all, the home of technological and commercial innovation; a land where machines and startling new production techniques had revolutionized people's lives. Such a utopian vision exercised a powerful grip on the imagination of political radicals from both the left and right. Socialists such as Bertolt Brecht believed that the energy and efficiency which they associated with America's technological revolution could be harnessed to transform the lives of the masses in Europe. Ufa director Fritz Lang sent a long memorandum to Emil Georg von Stauss explaining that, in historical terms, America's equivalent of Siegfried was the gun-slinging sheriff and that the cowboy film represented the American epic. He suggested that the Germans could usefully emulate American production and advertising techniques, enabling them to expand their home market. Lenin was an admirer of American engineering and production methods, particularly the scientific management techniques developed by Frederick W. Taylor, inventor of the time and motion study. It was even reported that, as he lay on his death-bed, Lenin told his followers to 'Americanize yourselves'.

The ferment of political radicalism which surrounded the creation of the Weimar Republic provided fertile ground for the development of *Amerikanismus* (Americanism) within Germany. More than any other European nation, Germany was receptive to the influence of American ideas about technology and efficiency. As a symbol of this, the German translation of Henry Ford's autobiography sold more than 200,000 copies by the end of the decade.

The establishment of the Dawes Plan in 1924 helped harden attitudes towards the United States. Under the plan the United States, in partnership with other nations, provided loans to stabilize a German economy still sunk in the chaos of hyper-inflation. In addition to the official loan, American investors poured almost $4 billion into Germany over the next few years. Perversely, the sudden stabilization of its currency swept away the massive price advantages which German industry – including the movie business – had enjoyed in the international marketplace. The cost of German exports soared, while import prices plunged. A wave of American goods flooded the German market, riding on the crest of America's own booming economy. Everything American – from jazz and dance troupes like the Tiller Girls to the Model T Ford and the movies of Charles Chaplin and Buster Keaton – seemed to be embraced with wild enthusiasm by the German public.

American movies were at the epicentre of the cultural invasion. In 1920, German films had overwhelmingly dominated their home market. By the end of 1924, according to one estimate, as many as 40 per cent of the films screened in Germany were of American origin and the German government began to implement quota restrictions which had been on the statute book since 1921. Rather than setting a limit to the amount of foreign footage that could be imported into the country, these regulations allowed a German distributor to release one foreign film for each German picture they had handled in the previous year. Even Ufa could not be shielded from the dramatic effects of these developments. As one writer later put it, as far as the Deutsche Bank was concerned, 'Ufa sucked money the way Murnau's *Nosferatu* sucked blood'. Its problems were similar to those of Daimler-Benz, which also became a strain on the resources of Deutsche Bank. Like the film industry, the car industry was a new and expensive mass manufacturing business whose primary competitor was the United States. While Ufa executives asked for government help in keeping out foreign films, the leaders of the automobile industry similarly complained about high taxes on cars.

By autumn 1925 Ufa was facing bankruptcy and was saved only

by a $4 million loan from Paramount and Metro-Goldwyn-Mayer (MGM). (The latter was an increasingly powerful studio formed by the merger of Marcus Loew's Metro with an independent company formerly headed by Samuel Goldwyn; see Chapter 7.) There had been fierce competition between moguls in the race to secure a stake in Ufa. Paramount and MGM executives had secretly boarded the liner *Majestic* in New York, on the same day in December 1925 that Carl Laemmle had set out for Europe on the *Leviathan*. When they arrived in Great Britain, the Paramount and MGM team hurriedly took a plane to Berlin, while Laemmle continued by surface transport. Having got their foot in the door first, Paramount and MGM pressed home their advantage and later that month finally saw off a rival bid from Laemmle. They created a new distribution venture, Parufamet, to distribute films throughout Germany. There was fury among members of the Ufa board when the American companies distributed *The Four Horsemen of the Apocalypse*, a film about the First World War, which portrayed the Germans as destructive 'Huns'. The movie, directed by Rex Ingram, had been a great success in the United States, but, unsurprisingly, it flopped in Germany. This together with continuing financial problems eventually forced the sale of Ufa to Alfred Hugenberg's Scherl group in March 1927. Hugenberg promptly installed Ludwig Klitzsch as the new head of Ufa. The loan to the Americans was paid off. The forces of rabid German nationalism were back in control of Ufa.

Throughout this period, executives from the Hollywood studios would make regular visits to Europe trawling for talent. The migration of European film-makers had begun in earnest in Germany in the mid-1920s. Ernst Lubitsch had been the first leading German director to be lured away by Hollywood in 1923. By 1926, stars such as Conrad Beidt and Emil Jannings had also moved from their native Germany to the US. Erich Pommer left Germany the same year. During his short spell in Hollywood, he worked for Paramount and MGM, where he produced *Hotel Imperial*, directed by the émigré Swede Mauritz Stiller. However, Pommer failed to adapt to Hollywood and returned to Ufa's Babelsberg studios late the following year.

In 1927, William Fox scored a significant coup when he persuaded the director F. W. Murnau to cross the Atlantic. Murnau was given a huge budget to direct his first American film, *Sunrise*, scripted by Carl Mayer. Although made for a Hollywood studio, the film was remarkably uncompromising. Murnau did nothing to dilute the influence of German Expressionism. Despite its artistic brilliance the film failed to achieve sufficient commercial success to justify its budget. In the years that followed, Fox assigned Murnau ever smaller projects, and by time of his death in a car crash in 1931 it had become apparent that the director was ill-suited to work within the confines of the studio system.

Other European film-makers, such as Mauritz Stiller and Victor Sjöström, found it even harder to adapt. Stiller had been brought to Hollywood by MGM after its executives saw a screening of *The Story of Gösta Berling* in Berlin in 1924. They also hired two actors from the film, Greta Garbo and Lars Hansen. But Stiller was unable to strike a rapport with Irving Thalberg, head of production at MGM, and could not come to terms with the rigorous financial discipline imposed by the studio. As a result, he was replaced as director on his very first American film *The Torrent*. The effect on him was severe – he returned home to Sweden a broken man and died shortly afterwards.

Sjöström, renamed Victor Seastrom, fared better for a while. But his austere directorial style, exemplified in *The Wind*, starring Lillian Gish, did not endear him to studio executives or to the American public. He, too, eventually returned to Sweden.

Despite Greta Garbo's phenomenal success, it wasn't all smooth sailing for the imported foreign stars. The Russian actress Anna Sten was brought to Hollywood in the 1932 by Samuel Goldwyn in the apparent belief that he had discovered another Garbo – despite the fact that Sten didn't speak a word of English. Unsurprisingly, she failed to win over American audiences and was soon christened 'Goldwyn's Folly'. Although Goldwyn lavished money on his protégé, nothing could be done, and by 1935 the two had parted company.

The experience of the second wave of émigrés from Germany,

many of whom were fleeing political persecution, was very different. This was especially true for directors. This group made many of their finest films in Hollywood – in fact these films are among the finest ever made anywhere. They recognized that they would have to negotiate and often struggle hard with the studios with whom they were working. They were under much greater pressure to adapt to Hollywood than their predecessors since, in the wake of the political upheavals in Europe, they simply did not have the option of returning home.

In Germany, the change in Ufa's ownership chimed with other events. The film industry was now intimately caught up in the furious national debate over *Amerikanismus*. In terms that echoed those of the French lawyer Edmond Benoît-Levy some twenty years earlier, the argument was made that film was a cultural, not simply a commercial product. 'Film is not merchandise! ... Indeed, precisely *because* film is not merchandise we can compete with America ... In the cinema, *Geist* [spirit] can balance the monetary supremacy of the competition,' observed one cinema critic in 1926. So it was that the question of economic values, of the cultural status of the movies, of the reaction to America as a symbol of technological modernity, all became caught up in the German response to Hollywood. Each of these issues would soon be played out on the larger European stage, as other countries sought to defend themselves against an increasingly ferocious assault by the growing and seemingly omnipotent Hollywood studios.

7

Movies and Money

THE MEN WHO DID MORE than anyone to revolutionize the relationship between movies and money were two brothers from the Santa Clara Valley, near San Jose in northern California. Amadeo Peter Giannini ('A.P.') and his younger brother Attilio (known as the 'Doc', because he held a degree in medicine) were the sons of an Italian immigrant farmer. Like the men who built the studios, the Gianninis were outsiders, determined to forge a cultural identity of their own in the New World.

It was A.P., a giant of a man in every respect, who took the first steps. He had started out as a fruit salesman and was possessed of a ferocious energy that was soon to become legendary. On the way to close an early deal with one of his clients, he had seen a competitor riding in his buggy towards the same ranch. Spying a short cut, A.P. tethered his horse to a tree, swam across a river holding his clothes above his head, and raced to the front door. By the time his competitor arrived, Giannini had closed the deal. 'I don't think he ever lost an account or a contest of any kind,' recalled one rival. 'No one could bluff, intimidate, or outgeneral him.'

In 1902 Giannini inherited his father-in-law's position as director and principal shareholder in the Columbus Savings and Loan Society, a small bank catering to the Italian–American community in North Beach, California. But he fell out with his fellow directors, and before long left to found his own bank. This, he believed, would enable him to meet the needs of ordinary people, rather than simply serving the demands of the local elite and the institutions of Wall Street.

Then came the cataclysm which transformed Giannini's life and set him on course to becoming the most powerful banker in America. At 5.13 on the morning of 18 April 1906, A.P. was thrown from his bed by a series of massive earth tremors. Running to the railway station, he made his way to the devastated centre of San Francisco where panic-stricken crowds milled around in the streets while looters pillaged the shops. The Little Italy district, where the bank was situated, had miraculously escaped serious damage. Even so, Giannini shrewdly reckoned the bank's money would be safer elsewhere. He took $300,000 in cash and more than $1-million-worth of other securities and bonds, threw them into a handcart, covered the booty with crates of fruit and vegetables to deter thieves, and set off for home. Once there, he stowed the money in an ash can next to the fireplace. By the next morning the Bank of Italy, along with every other bank in San Francisco, had burned to the ground. With his cartload of money, A.P. was almost the only banker ready to do business in a city that needed to be rebuilt from the ground up. 'The idea of the crates worked,' he later observed, 'but for weeks afterwards the bank's money smelled of orange juice.'

Soon afterwards the Gianninis made their first, modest, loan to the motion picture industry. A seventeen-year-old nickelodeon owner in San Francisco, Sol Lesser, approached A.P. for $100 to pay for delivery of a rented film. Lesser was firmly told that the bank did not lend money on motion pictures, but when pressed A.P. relented and not only advanced the money but did so from his personal account, because the boy was under age and the bank had no legal means of ensuring repayment. In later years the Doc claimed that it was he, rather than A.P., who had been responsible for this act of sympathetic generosity, but, whoever was responsible, Lesser repaid his $100 loan and went on to become one of the most successful exhibitors on the West Coast.

Over the next few years the Giannini brothers rapidly expanded their business with a variety of movie companies. In the eyes of their fellow bankers, it was now their customers, rather than their money, which had a strange smell. The Doc, though, was gruffly dismissive. 'Who cares if they smell of cheese and garlic? They meet their obligations.' The motion picture industry had found its bankers at last.

Attracted by the nickelodeon boom, a number of speculators had already begun to show interest in the film industry. 'The moving picture is sharing the fate of everything that comes under the heading of popular novelty,' observed an editorial in *Moving Picture World* in 1912. 'It is attracting the hawklike gaze of the professional financier . . . There are some "get-rich-quick" schemes in the moving picture field that have failed disastrously . . . The most recent of these is a talking picture proposition which was hawked about on the Wall Street curb and is being hawked about in some part of the country even now.'

By 1916, the climate was little changed. The journal *Photoplay* ran a series of articles under the heading 'Investing in the Movies', but the thrust of articles was cautionary. Observing that it had received 'hundreds' of requests from people interested in investing in the motion picture industry, the paper observed that 'in many cases investigation showed that these people were being solicited to invest money in concerns that, in the face of existing conditions, did not have one chance in a hundred to succeed'. It went on to note: 'There are no motion picture companies today paying bonanza dividends . . . There are not many motion picture companies paying dividends at all.'

For the public at large, investing in movies remained a dangerous business. It was best left to those who had developed some real expertise in the sector, such as A.P. and the Doc. At first, the Gianninis loaned money to the smaller companies like Biograph, Vitagraph and Lubin. But helped by his new friend Sol Lesser, the Doc began to develop relationships with some of the most powerful tycoons in the business, including Jesse Lasky, Marcus Loew, Samuel Goldfish, Carl Laemmle and two rising stars, Joseph and Nicholas Schenck. Gruff, square-jowled, with a savage temper to match, the Doc was just the man to deal with the moguls. He created a system whereby the bank loaned money to fund individual movies, using the film's negative as security. Only when the loan had been repaid would the bank allow the negative to be released from the laboratory. Sometimes the loans were made on the strength of the cast. 'If a film is offered me starring Doug [Fairbanks], Charlie [Chaplin], or Harold [Lloyd], it's as good as cash,' he once said. Indeed, it was the brothers who loaned $250,000 to First National in 1921 enabling them to make Charlie Chaplin's first full-length feature, *The Kid*.

The Doc occasionally employed other, more idiosyncratic, methods for assessing the risk attached to his loans. If a distributor needed funds to release a picture, the Doc would insist on previewing the film before an audience of young women aged eighteen to twenty-two, recruited from a local college. 'If the girls reacted favourably, I'd finance the picture,' he recalled, offering what to some might have sounded suspiciously like an excuse for spending time in the dark with attractive young females. A few years earlier, D. W. Griffith had introduced the idea of previewing films before an invited audience. Such methods of judging a film's commercial potential were the forerunners of market research designed to test every aspect of a movie's popular appeal. In 1924, the Doc provided $100,000 to three men – Harry Cohn, Joe Brandt and Harry's brother, Jack – to form the CBC Sales Company, the letters standing for the names of the founders. That same year, the name of the company was changed to Columbia Pictures Corporation, and the founders stepped up their ambition to become a significant force in the movie business. Columbia would grow during the 1930s to become one of the industry's leading companies. It was said that Doc Giannini was one of the handful of individuals Harry Cohn, the most tyrannical and brutal studio boss of them all, regarded with something like respect. Indeed, the banker (played by Walter Huston) who supports the 'little people' in Frank Capra's *American Madness*, made by Columbia in 1932, was rumoured to be based on one of the Gianninis.

Giannini stuffed the board of each of his branch banks with producers, directors, actors and actresses as a way of trying to seduce even more Hollywood figures to invest their money with him. He even went so far as to appoint Cecil B. De Mille as vice-president of the Commercial National Trust and Savings Bank, one of the institutions he controlled in Los Angeles. De Mille promptly made a $200,000 unsecured loan to Samuel Goldwyn. Giannini let out a 'roar' when he was told of the deal, worried that Goldwyn 'had no assets', but De Mille's decision was shrewder than it appeared. Goldwyn would become one of Hollywood's most successful independent producers, and MGM, by the mid-1930s, became the most powerful of the Hollywood studios.

In 1928 A.P. purchased the Bank of America, one of the leading banks on the East Coast. As a result of a policy of almost frantic growth – in 1927 alone he acquired almost a hundred banks – he was by the end of the decade one of the most powerful bankers in the country. 'The Gianninis have so much power', said one banking authority, 'they could start a depression throughout the West ... simply by calling in their loans.'

The Gianninis were the first bankers to recognize the motion picture business as a legitimate industry. In a given year, they would invest anywhere in the range of $3–12 million. By the end of the 1930s, it was reckoned that they had pumped around $130 million into the US industry, always as straight loans rather than in the form of profit-sharing deals.

The extent of the affinity between the Gianninis and pioneers of the movie colony was extraordinary. It was easy to see why they were able to form such a deep-rooted and enduring alliance. Just like the film people, the Gianninis were outsiders, immigrants based in the far West, initially loathed, distrusted and thoroughly misunderstood by the financial establishment. A.P.'s evangelical drive to 'open up' banking by creating hundreds of branches scattered throughout California, creating a financial system for the masses, was a precise corollary of the way in which the movie pioneers brought an increasingly sophisticated entertainment to an audience long excluded from any form of culture. Like all the moguls, A.P. revelled in all aspects of advertising and showmanship that were critical to the development of what he saw as, above all, a retail industry. A.P. sold banking to the American people just like the moguls, former merchants themselves, sold entertainment. Indeed, in the end A.P. and the Doc had really committed the ultimate act of apostasy in the eyes of Wall Street blue-bloods like J. Pierpont Morgan and his peers: in effect, they made banking into a branch of show business. Therein lay the real reason why the movie colony flocked to the Bank of America during the 1920s, '30s and for many decades to follow.

With incomparable flair, the Gianninis had shown that it was possible to make money from financing a maverick industry. Now, at last, some rather more conservative bankers began to follow in their footsteps. Among the first was Otto Kahn, of the Wall Street firm of Kuhn, Loeb & Co. The bank had been founded by two Jewish immigrants: Abraham Kuhn, who had started as a peddler in 1849, and Salomon Loeb. They later ran a clothing store in Indiana, and in 1867 they opened a private bank in New York City. With that kind of cosmopolitan background, it was perhaps unsurprising that the bank was sympathetic to the film industry.

Kahn was also a German émigré, a professional banker and a passionate supporter of the arts who had worked tirelessly for the Metropolitan Opera in New York. A small, lithe man who liked to wear black opera capes, he was a familiar figure at first nights. A habitual socialite, he received so much attention in the gossip columns that one columnist referred to New York as 'a town frequently mentioned in connection with the name of Otto Kahn'. The inmates at San Quentin jail even named one of the prison cats after him.

Kahn was a close associate of Edward Harriman, the railroad magnate, acting as his right-hand man during the reorganization of the Union Pacific. He was also a powerful and unashamed member of that East Coast financial establishment which had hitherto disparaged the movie business. He built a vast castle on Long Island which had 170 rooms, a private zoo and an eighteen-hole golf course complete with resident professional. It was later used as a set for *Citizen Kane*.

For all the ostentatious display of wealth, Kahn was a passionate advocate of egalitarianism, seeing universal access to the arts as a vital expression of the essence of a democracy. '[T]he visitor who pays twenty-five cents for a gallery seat at Century opera is richer than the man who sits yawning in a box at the Metropolitan,' he declared. It was beliefs like these which eventually persuaded him to embrace the idea of investing in a medium like the movies, which by its very nature so clearly symbolized the idea of democratic participation. In 1919 Zukor had approached him for a loan of $10 million to help launch his proposed Famous Players company. According to Zukor himself, Kahn 'held that the request for so large a sum was preposterous. I pointed out that if we got it, motion pictures would overnight be regarded as an important industry.'

Kahn was sufficiently interested to commission a study of the entire motion picture industry. He and his bank were impressed by the report and agreed to underwrite a stock issue which raised the $10 million Zukor needed. But Kuhn, Loeb wanted to ensure that its money was being wisely used, and tried to enforce a series of cost-efficiency measures on Famous Players. 'We were in the habit of writing our telegrams in the form of letters, with the salutation "Dear So-and-So" and closing with "Regards",' Jesse Lasky recalled. 'But such gushing sentiment was entirely superfluous in the bank's eyes. Their accountant argued that getting rid of three unnecessary words on each of thousands of telegrams would mean a saving of countless pennies. He thereupon issued an edict that no more regards were to be bandied carelessly between the two coasts.' Unsurprisingly, the order unleashed a storm of animosity between the two offices. 'Without the softening effect of the accustomed "Regards", routine criticisms and friendly suggestions took on the sting of a slap of a face,' said Lasky. It wasn't long before he and others were reinserting fulsome greetings into their communications.

Otto Kahn eventually became a fervent supporter of the movie industry. In one of his passionately argued defences of the industry he observed: 'It has produced untold millions of new national values and wealth. It has created employment for hundreds of thousands. It has brought a new means of enjoyment and education into the lives of the masses, and has broadened their horizons. It has conquered the world for the American movie.' Kahn's conversion to the movies was immensely important, as much for the prestige and air of financial respectability which he conferred upon the industry as for the capital Kuhn Loeb & Co. pumped into it. All of these developments served as catalysts for drawing even more East Coast capital into the industry, while at the same time contributing to its social and political profile.

In the wake of Kahn, other Wall Street financiers began scouring the industry for investment opportunities. Among them was Motley Flint, head of the Security First National Bank. He was close to four brothers, Sam, Jack, Albert and Harry Warner, who entered the industry when they opened a nickelodeon in New Castle, Pittsburgh, in 1903. The brothers had subsequently expanded into distribution and production. By the early 1920s they were looking for outside capital to expand their rapidly growing business. Flint offered them a credit line, telling Jack, 'I never worry about your debts, you and Sam are going in the right direction and I know you'll make it.' To help them raise more money he introduced them to Waddill Catchings, who along with J. P. Morgan had symbolized the American banking establishment before moving to Goldman, Sachs.

Goldman, Sachs had been founded by Marcus Goldman, an immigrant from Bavaria who, like Kuhn, had begun his career as a peddler. In the early 1900s he began specializing in the market for securities in small, privately-owned manufacturing and retailing firms whose needs had been overlooked by established financial institutions. This became a booming business for the bank as more and more manufacturers of consumer goods and retail store chains began to emerge. Indeed, for both Goldman, Sachs and Catchings, their involvement with a company like Warner Brothers was a natural extension of their existing interests. Catchings had already agreed to help finance the expansion of two small retail firms – Woolworths and Sears, Roebuck – which had ambitious plans to become national giants, and he was convinced that Warner Brothers had similar potential. Catchings persuaded a group of banks, including the National Bank of Commerce, to create a credit line worth several million dollars which enabled the Warners to buy the Vitagraph studio. It ensured that the Warner Brothers had access to an invaluable new source of working capital. This would also provide the springboard for an ambitious plan which, the Warner Brothers hoped, would enable them to start making sound films.

Motley Flint met an untimely and rather grisly end. In 1932, after testifying on behalf of the producer David Selznick, who had got himself into financial difficulties, Flint was attacked in the courtroom by an aggrieved real estate man who blamed him for his losses. He shot him in the face, in full view of the judge, killing him instantly.

Wall Street money was also attracted into the industry by the growth of theatre chains. From around 1915 opulent film theatres, later known as picture palaces, began to spring up in major cities across the United States. One of the first was the Regent, which opened in New York in 1913. It was the creation of S. L. 'Roxy' Rothapfel who, helped by lines like 'Don't give the people "what they want", give 'em something better', became the movie industry's leading showman. With their large and lavishly designed interiors featuring architectural motifs inspired by visions of oriental exotica, the picture palaces' contrast with the squalid nickelodeons could hardly have been greater. What men like Rothapfel realized was that it was not only the quality of an individual movie which attracted the public, but also the environment in which those pictures played.

During the 1920s, on the West Coast, a Los Angeles showman called Sid Grauman created his famous Egyptian and Chinese theatres, where the soon-to-be obligatory star-studded premières would find their first home. Grauman loved using pranks to promote his movies or simply as a means of pricking inflated Hollywood egos. Such pranks were intended to be affectionate but sometimes had unexpected consequences. When 'he learned that director Ernst Lubitsch, who hated to fly, was forced to take a plane from Los Angeles . . . to San Francisco, he hired two stuntmen to dress as pilots, run down the aisle, and then parachute out during the flight.' It gave Lubitsch 'a minor heart attack', although he quickly recovered. It was reputedly Grauman who persuaded the stars to imprint their hands and feet into wet concrete creating the now famous tourist attraction outside his Chinese Theater in Hollywood. According to one source, Grauman had been walking by the Chinese Theater when he fell from a builder's plank into wet cement. When he realized what he had done, he supposedly shouted to a friend, 'I am going to have all the stars recorded here'.

After the Great War, encouraged by the example of national department stores such as Woolworths and Sears, Roebuck, a number of cinema exhibitors had begun to think about organizing their operations on a national basis. Chain stores had demonstrated how costs could be kept to a minimum by taking advantage of the extraordinary economies of scale available to an operation with outlets across the country. Companies such as Loews, the New York firm controlled by Marcus Loew (dubbed the 'Henry Ford of Show Business'), and the Stanley Company based in Philadelphia, had built up powerful regional chains. Such companies did not as yet have significant interests in production or distribution. The more far-sighted among them soon realized, however, that expansion into making films and releasing to cinemas, thereby creating a vertically integrated structure, was greatly to their advantage. It gave them the means to ensure their theatres had access to a regular supply of product. Indeed, the Loews theatre circuit formed the kernel of a company which would eventually take Paramount's place as the most powerful studio in Hollywood. In 1919, Loew acquired the distributor Metro Pictures, created by a fiercely ambitious exhibitor called Louis Mayer, and in 1924 the company merged with Samuel Goldwyn's firm to create Metro-Goldwyn-Mayer (MGM).

Jules Mastbaum and his brother Stanley, founders of the Stanley Company, learned about chain-store techniques from an early pioneer, Gimbels, which had a branch in central Philadelphia. They quickly built a thriving local cinema chain simply by following the new trolley lines, which marked the expansion of the city.

The first company to build up a truly national cinema circuit along the lines of the great department stores was a Chicago-based company controlled by Barney Balaban and Samuel Katz. It was Balaban who sowed the seeds of the company when he opened a nickelodeon with his brother in a Chicago ghetto in 1908. While acquiring more theatres across the city they also opened a restaurant, the Movie Inn, as a meeting place for film people. It was here that they met Samuel Katz, who had started his career in movies playing piano in a nickelodeon on the city's south side. They joined forces and decided to open a giant theatre modelled on those recently created in New York City. The venture was a great success and Balaban and Katz soon began planning new ventures. But Katz realized that, if they were to have any chance of implementing their schemes, they needed access to significant amounts of capital. After a good deal of effort, he brought together a group of Chicago-based backers who had both the resources and the enthusiasm to finance just such an expansion. They included Julius Rosenwald, who would build Sears, Roebuck into one of America's biggest retailers; William Wrigley, Jr, whose company was expanding at breakneck speed as Americans flocked to buy chewing gum; and John Hertz, who had created Chicago's biggest taxi firm and who would go on to create the eponymous car-rental company.

Besides the straightforward merits of investing in movie theatres themselves, each of these backers would also reap some specific advantages from the growth of film exhibition; many Sears, Roebuck stores would eventually be located near movie theatres, chewing gum was widely sold on the concession stand while the taxi firms transported as many patrons as possible to and from cinemas. These backers may not have been able to see the precise benefit that would accrue from investing in movies, but their willingness to invest anticipated the drive in the 1980s by companies involved in consumer electronics and the drinks business to acquire control of Hollywood studios, because they believed it would boost sales of their existing products, a business philosophy of variable credibility that came to be known as 'synergy'.

Throughout the early 1920s, Balaban and Katz acquired cinemas across the Midwest. No expense was spared in an effort to attract patrons. They created the world's first air-conditioned theatre, a haven from the torturous humidity of summer in Chicago, decorating their advertisements with icicles to remind potential customers of the comforts that awaited them. The Public Health Commissioner even issued an edict stating that the company's theatres had such pure air that people with a lung disease or women in the final stages of pregnancy could benefit from regular visits to the movies. It was just another demonstration of the remarkable dedication that American showmen brought to the business of retailing movies to the public. In one sense, the comfort and attractiveness of the venue was seen as even more important than the appeal of the individual films. 'We sell tickets to theaters, not movies,' claimed Marcus Loew.

In Europe, on the other hand, the overriding emphasis on producing movies meant that the crucial business of making cinema-going an attractive and desirable activity was too often neglected. In 1925, Balaban and Katz merged with Zukor's Famous Players-Lasky to create Publix, the world's largest theatre chain, adopting the slogan: 'You don't need to know what's playing in a Publix House.' Sam Katz moved to New York to head the new operation, and the idea of a truly national circuit became reality. New 'scientific' forms of management, much in vogue elsewhere, were now applied to cinema retailing; Katz and his team controlled everything from the booking of the films to the patterns of the cinema carpets.

That men like Loew, Balaban and Katz seemed to be marketing cinemas rather than movies had as much to do with the underlying economic value of those theatres as it did with any belief in the fundamental primacy of retailing. For movie theatres were also a form of real estate, providing the collateral to underwrite Wall Street's expanding investment in the industry. The capital that companies like MGM, Paramount, Warners and Fox pumped into their theatre chains provided much of the security which in turn enabled such rapid expansion of their distribution and production capacity.

Indeed, the vast majority of the industry's capital was tied up in exhibition. Encouraged by the example of people like Otto Kahn and the Gianninis, American financial institutions from Wall Street and elsewhere had, by 1926, invested about $1.5 billion in the country's film industry. Of this, some $1.25 billion went into exhibition, with the remaining $250 million going into production and distribution. These were astonishing figures for an industry that was still barely twenty years old. The creative community also realized what benefits might be reaped. Many writers began to realize that they could make huge amounts of money in Hollywood. Such earnings dwarfed the amounts they might expect to make from more conventional sources.

When in 1919 Herbert Hoover became Secretary for Commerce in President Harding's administration, the economic arguments regarding the value of film were taken a step further. Hoover was a progressive who embraced the idea of corporatism as a means of negotiating a middle course between the free market and direct state intervention in the economy. The role of government on this model was to favour those mechanisms which would facilitate the expansion of all industry at home and abroad. In particular, the gathering of data and information was seen as crucial in the effort to expand foreign trade. Privately-run trade organizations, operating independently of the government, were seen as vital instruments for achieving the same goals. In 1921, one of Hoover's assistants wrote to William Brady, head of the industry's trade body, the National Association of the Motion Picture Industry:

The government is considering the establishment of a small section devoted to the study of the motion picture industry in relation to its export and import problems, foreign film production etc.

Mr. Hoover has asked me to inquire from you whether you know of any individual who has a real knowledge of the industry in this country, and who is at the same time familiar with the import and export problems which the industry has to face.

The government had other reasons for taking a close interest in the movie industry. In the early 1920s, Hollywood was hit by a series of highly-publicized scandals. Mary Pickford was involved in an apparently fraudulent divorce testimony. Then, during a wild drinking party at a hotel in San Francisco, a starlet called Virginia Rappe was seized by convulsions, apparently after having been sexually assaulted by the actor Roscoe 'Fatty' Arbuckle. She died a few days later and Arbuckle was tried for manslaughter. Two trials ended with a hung jury but he was eventually acquitted. Finally, in 1922, the director William Desmond Taylor was murdered in circumstances which, as his colleague Cecil B. De Mille put it, 'gave the press its opportunity to ring the changes on all manner of rumours about drink, dope, blackmail and indescribable orgies'. Opprobrium was heaped upon the industry from all sides, not just from the press but from Washington and state authorities across the entire country. The store of goodwill which the industry had built up as a result of its valiant efforts during the Great War looked as if it would be swept away. The government demanded action and threatened to impose a strict programme of censorship. But before it could act, the studio heads in a rare demonstration of collective wisdom invited Will Hays, the Postmaster General, to head a new trade body, the Motion Picture Producers and Distributors of America (MPPDA). This organization would implement what amounted to a healthy degree of self-censorship by the studios. Much more importantly, from the industry's point of view, it would provide a single corporate voice enabling it to engage in active lobbying at home and abroad.

The baby-faced Hays was a Protestant layman from Sullivan,

Indiana, an archetypal 'Hoosier' as natives of the state were known. Recalling the 'Christian' neighbourhood of his youth, Hays remembered, 'our home had the kind of spiritual "air conditioning" in which it was a joy to live', adding, 'If we Hoosiers are accused of provincialism, we don't apologise'. Hays' mother told him if he agreed not to drink or smoke until he was twenty-one, she would give him $100. He kept the deal. After becoming involved in local Republican politics, he had first made a real mark on the national stage when he organized President Harding's successful election campaign in 1920. He was rewarded with the job of running the US Post Office, a task he was considered to have performed extremely well. He was once characterized as 'a 100% American who belonged in the Bureau of Standards rather than in the Post Office Department'.

Such was the man who now took charge of the studios' public image, and their relationship with Washington. Hays had never previously visited Hollywood and didn't make his first trip there until four months after his appointment. When at last he did arrive, he was the first and probably the only person to describe the spirit of Hollywood as analogous to 'a great university'. At an initial banquet given by industry tycoons the atmosphere was tense. Hays was later introduced to almost the entire population of the film business at a vast all-industry rally at the Hollywood Bowl, attended by some 50,000 people. The Bowl was still being built, and so vast were the crowds that many were forced to sit and watch from neighbouring hillsides. An American Legion band played before Hays stood up and read a roll-call of the studios. He then spoke 'to the entire fellowship of the university', telling them of the need to develop systems of moral self-regulation. As he left for San Francisco, he reflected: 'The folks of Hollywood had bought the goods.' So closely was its boss identified with the organization that the MPPDA became widely known as the Hays Organization. He was nicknamed the 'czar' of motion pictures, one part of a trio whose other members were Judge Kenshaw Mountain Landis, 'czar' of baseball, and Augustus Thomas, 'czar' of the theatre. Like the movies, baseball, which had been established as a national institution since the late nineteenth century, had recently been swept by a national scandal. In the so-called 'Black Sox' affair, eight members of Chicago's White Sox team were convicted of accepting bribes to lose World Series games. Just like Hays, Judge Landis was brought in to purge the miscreants, and to ensure that appropriate ethical standards were maintained.

The alliance between Hays and the movie industry was, in many ways, a strange one. He once described the drive to cleanse American cinema as 'a case of inherited American standards – products of a Christian civilisation – against alien customs variously considered "modern", "liberal" or "pagan"'. Such sentiments might have made men like Laemmle, Zukor and Mayer feel a little uneasy. But without such an alliance, the American industry might once more have become a target for the moralists who had unleashed such a torrent of fury during the nickelodeon era. And in the end, Hays' crusade against what he considered morally undesirable 'alien customs' converged with the desire of the moguls to ensure that American movies dominated markets the world over. Indeed, in his battle against the protective measures put in place by foreign governments, Hays would invoke ideals with which the moguls themselves could naturally identify. 'There is a special reason why America should have given birth and prosperous nurture to the motion picture and its worldwide entertainment,' he proclaimed a few years later. 'America in the very literal sense is truly the world state. All races, creeds, all men are to be found here – working, sharing, and developing, side by side in more friendship among greater diversities of tribes and men than all previous history of the world discloses.' These were ideals which stretched way back to the American Revolution.

Clearly the relationship between Hays and Hollywood was one riddled with contradictions, although these almost never surfaced publicly. True, there were occasional rumblings in both Hollywood and Washington about Hays' performance. The industry sometimes felt that Hays had failed to represent it vigorously enough, while the administration were periodically agitated because he seemed insufficiently sensitive to the cultural concerns of foreign govern-

Thomas Edison – the wizard of Menlo Park

Below
Louis (left) and Auguste Lumière (right) – they wished that the technology of moving pictures had never left the laboratory

Robert Paul, creator
of the Animatographe,
who later dismissed
film as a 'sideline' and
burnt his stock of
negatives

Georges Méliès, who after his business was destroyed –
partly as a result of the illegal copying of his films by
American companies – ended up selling toys from a
kiosk at the Gare Montparnasse

By 1907 a Pathé
film would be seen by
300 million people
around the world

A LA CONQUÊTE DU MONDE

scène vécue
PAR
PATHÉ FRÈRES

1894-19...

Above Charles Pathé at Francis Doublier's
house in 1945. 'I didn't invent cinema but
I did industrialize it.'

Left The Pathé cockerel celebrates the
company's supremacy in the American
market – an early advertising poster

Florence Lawrence, the 'Biograph Girl', who became one of the world's first movie stars

Ole Olsen, the former shepherd who founded Nordisk, the Danish firm which became one of the most powerful film companies in the world by 1908

Left Adolph Zukor surveys what he sees as his empire

Below A. P. Giannini, the movie industry's first banker. 'No-one could bluff, intimidate or outgeneral him'

Sam Goldwyn cuts a deal for his European protégé Anna Sten. But she failed to win over audiences and Goldwyn eventually terminated her contract

Carl Laemmle, the elfin mogul –
one-time bottle washer and
failed farmer – who took on and
defeated Edison and the mighty
Trust

Irving Thalberg celebrates his
marriage to Norma Shearer

The Warner Brothers – (left to right) Jack, Harry, Albert – celebrate the fact that millions *did* want to hear actors talk

Left By the early 1920s, Hollywood films already dominated Europe's cinemas. This illustration appeared in a German magazine, one of the country's which led the fightback against American supremacy

Below left More than 70 years before the acrimonious GATT negotiations in Geneva the French were already fretting about the dangers of free trade

Below right There was no Production Code in France in the 1930s, as illustrated by this still of Renée Saint-Cyr from *Toto* (1933)

ments. But his position as head of the MPPDA would never be seriously threatened. What mattered were Hays' public triumphs, not the private scepticism.

During the 1920s, Hays fought against the protectionists responsible for introducing domestic tariff Acts in 1922 and 1930. This resistance was doubtless more the product of sound economic pragmatism than of any underlying ideology. The American film industry, supreme in its home market, felt no need for such defensive measures. Had the US industry been weaker, the situation might well have been very different, but it would also have made it far harder for Hays to argue convincingly against the quotas introduced by foreign governments later in the decade.

By 1924, foreign markets had become an increasingly important issue for the MPPDA. Articles had started to appear in overseas newspapers deploring the cultural effects of America's domination of cinema screens. In the same year, Hays appointed Frederick Herron, his brother-in-law and old college friend, as manager of the MPPDA. Herron had served in the United States diplomatic service, and after the Great War had remained in Europe for a period of special service to advise on matters arising from the aftermath of the conflict. Herron's diplomatic skills would become increasingly valuable to the MPPDA as the decade wore on.

By 1923 the United States government was in no doubt about the importance of the overseas market. 'We are becoming more and more interested in this matter of the trade promoting possibilities of American films,' observed Jules Klein, a former Harvard academic who had become head of the Bureau of Foreign and Domestic Commerce, adding: 'our films are having a profound effect upon Chinese trade, in the main a favourable one; so much so in fact, that we are considering the appointment of a special trade commissioner in our China organisation for the purpose of getting advice as to the character and distribution of films for that area.' As Hollywood's overseas exports expanded in the 1920s, so this interest markedly increased. In July 1926, the American administration established a separate Motion Picture Division, with a budget of $15,000, within the Bureau of Foreign and Domestic Commerce. Headed by Clarence J. North, its chief task was to gather information about the size and nature of individual overseas markets, and the competitive position of American movies within those markets.

The *Film Daily Yearbook* explained:

[T]he Motion Picture Section endeavors to serve the industry in every legitimate way in maintaining and developing the exhibition of American motion pictures in foreign markets. To this end, information in the shape of reports and trade notes is received from the 44 foreign offices of the Department in the chief capitals and commercial centers of the world, and also from the 400 consular offices of the Department of State stationed abroad. These reports are distributed to the trade through the appropriate associations and through the motion picture trade press. They aid in keeping the industry advised of all foreign market possibilities and also the activities of our competitors, in their endeavors to build up markets within their borders ... it can [also] supply information as to the tariff treatment and duties on American films into all foreign countries.

So, once again, it was the Americans who first recognized the role that government might play in promoting a prosperous industry. Their strategy was aggressive and outward-looking, directed towards expanding their overseas markets. When European governments moved to assist their film industries a couple of years later, their strategy – defensive and inward-looking, directed primarily towards protecting their home markets – would be very different. Another, crucial, step had been taken in the American government's drive, after its own unique fashion, to politicize the film industry. Such a mission converged neatly with the self-appointed task of the MPPDA: '[S]teps have been taken to make certain that every picture which is made here shall correctly portray American life, opportunities and aspirations to the world, and, too, that we correctly portray to America the life of other peoples. We are going to sell America to the world with American pictures.' What had started out as an internal matter of morality had now become inextricably linked to far broader issues of international trade. The formation of the MPPDA had its roots in a moral crusade to purge the movie industry of disreputable elements, but this effort to create a new image for the movie industry neatly converged with the administration's desire to promote American ideals and trade generally, through the export of moving pictures.

Paradoxically, it was the American government more than the movie industry itself which first sought to exploit fully the cultural and economic value of the industry abroad. Of course, once the MPPDA was up and running it became entirely natural for it to be involved in promoting trade. As Hays later put it: 'The organized industry plunged into the sphere of foreign relations ... [and] it assumed responsibilities that have made it almost an adjunct of our State Department.' In the early years at least, the film industry was very much a tool of government not the other way around. As time progressed, and as the movie industry sought more autonomy, relations would quite naturally sometimes become strained. By 1968 Jack Valenti, head of the MPAA, successor body to the Hays Organization, could credibly claim that 'the movie industry is perhaps the only American industry which has the authority to negotiate on its own with foreign governments'. This was almost certainly true, but it was the initiative of the American government which had made it all possible in the first place.

The creation of the MPPDA and the appointment of Hays also had the effect of reassuring nervous financiers on Wall Street. At a stroke, the middle-class, Anglo-Saxon establishment had won the power to determine the destiny of the American movie industry, certainly in political terms and perhaps in other ways too. The MPPDA made it easier to attract and hold new money as well as creating an immensely powerful lobbying organization which, to this day, enables Hollywood to speak with a single voice in its dealings with the federal government in Washington. The movie industry, for so long treated as a pariah by more traditional businessmen, had striven hard to assume the trappings of a traditional industry. Hays' most critical contribution to the American movie business, however, would not really become apparent until the late 1920s, when his tireless lobbying against foreign trade barriers would be enormously important in helping Hollywood to extend its dominion around the world.

The struggle for control of the movie trade was no longer purely a matter of economics or simple patriotism; it was caught up in the debate over national and spiritual values. In Hays and the MPPDA, the Americans had found a weapon to take the battle into a new era, an era dominated by a new technology (of their own invention), and one which for a time threatened to wipe out their hard-won domination of the world's cinema screens. The movies were about to start talking.

8

'Who the hell wants to hear actors talk?'

HARRY WARNER

BY THE MID-1920s, the principal players of the Hollywood drama were well established. Laemmle, Zukor and Louis Mayer fought each other for stars, theatres and overseas markets. Others were waiting in the wings, eager for an opportunity to grab centre stage, among them the Warner brothers. Even in Hollywood, where most people were outsiders of one kind or another, the Warner brothers were regarded with disdain. Their most important star was Rin Tin Tin, a stray dog rescued from the war-time trenches of Europe and christened the 'mortgage lifter' because of the financial benefits his films brought to the studio. So valuable was the dog that he even had his own stand-ins to perform stunts.

Jack Warner, who rapidly established himself as the driving force behind their new company, was untroubled by its cheap image. If anything, he revelled in his role as maverick. Where men like Zukor and Mayer aspired to raise themselves and their businesses by eagerly courting literary and society figures, Jack preferred to play the wise-cracking vulgarian. Accepting an award in New York he discarded his speech and launched into a comic tirade so laced with obscenities it couldn't be quoted in the papers. And when Albert Einstein visited the studio Warner told him, 'Well, professor, I have a theory of relatives too – don't hire 'em.' The comedian Jack Benny was not alone in believing that Warner was a man 'who would rather tell a bad joke than make a good movie'. Others saw it as a defence mechanism. 'Jack's not a bad guy,' said Humphrey Bogart, 'he's just so uncomfortable with everyone he has to make jokes to prove he's regular.' Inevitably, though, Jack's blunt manner made him enemies in Hollywood and elsewhere. He even carried a business card inscribed 'Jack L. Warner, President, Bon Ton Woolen Company, Youngstown, Ohio'. He claimed that it helped confuse agents and put starlets off the scent if they pestered him in the street. 'You can't pull the wool over my eyes,' he would quip, handing the card to bemused acquaintances. But in truth the card seemed like one more manifestation of Jack's disdain for the more devious trappings of power and status.

The journey of the four Warner brothers – Sam, Jack, Harry and Albert – from a small rural town to the glittering world of the movies was every bit as extraordinary as those of their contemporaries. Their father originally ran a shoe repair shop in Youngstown, Ohio. Sam was working as a railway fireman when he ran into an old friend who was repairing an Edison Kinetoscope. Fascinated by the crude device, Sam persuaded his father to pawn the family horse so that he could buy a machine of his own. Soon afterwards, in 1903, Sam, Harry and Albert opened a nickelodeon in New Castle, Pennsylvania. Being short of chairs, and with no spare cash, they struck a useful deal with the undertaker next door. If they had a popular film to show, the funeral service would be postponed while they borrowed the chairs. For their part they would delay the start of a movie whenever the undertaker had a big ceremony on *his* hands. Unlike men such as Adolph Zukor and Louis Mayer, the Warner brothers never really attempted to reinvent themselves as genteel figures with a sartorial elegance to match. After Harry's death, an actor was being kitted out in the Warners' wardrobe department when he came across Harry Warner's name attached to a piece of clothing. The actor looked surprised and was informed that on Harry's death his clothes had been removed to wardrobe. How terrible, said the actor. Why? asked the wardrobe man. After all, he got them from here in the first place.

The Warners followed the now familiar path of the other moguls. By the end of the decade they had expanded into distribution and then into production, but it was not until 1917 that they had their first hit, *My Four Years in Germany*, based on the memoirs of a former American ambassador. Jack produced the films in Hollywood, while Harry, 'a small, strong swarthy man ... with a cupid-bow mouth' who loathed his brother's flip manner, settled in New York where he cultivated Wall Street financiers. (The hatred between the two brothers was so fierce that Jack did not even bother to attend Harry's funeral.) Albert became company treasurer, while Sam worked with Jack in production.

Following the fashion of the time, Sam and Jack were keen to promote their films on radio and, unable to find a suitable station for sale, they created their own. They hired Major Nathan Levinson, a young sound engineer with Western Electric, to set up a station with the call sign KFWB at their studios on Sunset Boulevard. Soon afterwards, on a visit to New York, Levinson visited the Bell Laboratories where a system had been developed to synchronize sound and moving pictures.

For years, the industry's leading pioneers, from Léon Gaumont to Thomas Edison, had been struggling to create a workable system which would weave together the magic of the moving pictures with sound. Levinson persuaded a somewhat sceptical Sam that it would be well worth his while making the trek back East to view the latest efforts of the Bell technicians. When he arrived in New York after a journey lasting several days, Sam found that Harry 'was icy cool, and flatly declared that he had no interest in any invention that had already been found useless'. Sam was determined that his journey should not have been entirely in vain. On the pretence of a meeting with some Wall Street bankers, he tricked Harry into accompanying him to Bell Laboratories, with deeply gratifying results. Harry was astounded by what he saw and heard. 'Now *that* is something,' he said, after watching a film of an orchestra playing the classics, with the music pouring out from nearby speakers. 'Think of hundreds of small theater guys who can't afford an orchestra or any other kind of an act . . . What a gadget!' Sam pointed out that the same gadget could also enable the audience to hear the voices of the on-screen players. 'Who the hell wants to hear actors talk?' Harry snapped. 'The music – that's the big plus about this.'

Just as thirty years earlier Louis Lumière had mistakenly believed that the real value of the Cinématographe lay in its potential as a tool for scientific research, so Harry Warner now fiercely insisted that the future of the sound film lay in its role as a musical 'gadget' for impoverished theatre-owners. As the later development of television, video and laser discs would demonstrate, the advent of new technologies will always be laced with uncertainty, as a fresh army of entrepreneurs scramble to find the quickest and most profitable use for any new device.

Whatever the limitations of Harry's vision, it was sufficient to make him an enthusiastic convert to the development of sound. He concluded an agreement with Western Electric to develop jointly the new technology. On 6 August 1926, at the Warner Brothers' theatre in New York, *Don Juan*, a short based on the exploits of the famous philanderer, was unveiled before an audience stuffed with celebrities. None of the film's performers actually spoke, but the film was accompanied by a synchronized soundtrack, so that the audience heard the clashing of swords and the clattering hoofs of the horses as John Barrymore fought his rivals for the hand of Mary Astor. Reactions veered from wild enthusiasm to deep scepticism. 'It's a fad, it won't last,' sneered Adolph Zukor, a sentiment shared by many other members of the Hollywood community, including D. W. Griffith and Mary Pickford, who observed tartly that 'adding sound to movies would be like putting lipstick on the Venus de Milo'.

It was not until the following year, with the première of Warner Brothers' *The Jazz Singer*, the first feature-length picture incorporating spoken dialogue, that the momentous impact of sound really began to hit home. The film, starring Al Jolson, premièred in New York on 6 October 1927. 'C'mon Ma – listen to this,' wheedled Jolson, as he broke into a version of 'Blue Skies'.

The film was greeted with wild applause and a standing ovation, but none of the Warner brothers was there to enjoy the moment of triumph. A few days earlier, Sam, only in his late thirties, had suffered a massive cerebral haemorrhage in Los Angeles. The others raced out to see him, but they were too late. The man who had first understood the real potential of sound died just one day before the world première of the first feature-length talkie.

Two months later, *The Jazz Singer* was shown in Hollywood. This time the reaction was more complicated. At the end of the film, the audience – a sparkling array of moguls, stars and directors – sat in a momentary state of shock, until the applause finally began to ring out. Aware that the film had revolutionary implications for the whole of the American moving picture business, none of them could predict exactly what those implications would be. Did the coming of sound herald an exhilarating new chapter in Hollywood's conquest of the world, or did it spell the end of the American film industry's popular appeal around the globe?

In a community which, then as now, was ruled above all by fear and insecurity, the overwhelming reaction, in private at least, was one of outright panic. Samuel Goldwyn's wife, Frances, later recalled that as the crowd left the cinema there was 'terror on all their faces, as they realized that the game they had been playing for years was finally over'. The Goldwyns drove home that evening with the producer Irving Thalberg and his wife Norma Shearer. There was complete silence in the car, each occupant lost in thought, pondering what all this meant for their future and that of Hollywood. Frances Goldwyn felt sure that a similar scene was being played out in every car returning home from the screening that December night.

One of the chief anxieties of the Hollywood moguls concerned the economic implications of sound. It would cost hundreds of millions of dollars to wire every cinema in the United States for the new technology. Studios, too, would have to undergo expensive conversions. All that expenditure for something that might turn out to be a simple fad, a momentary blip in the glorious march of the silent movie.

There were other worries, too. Charlie Chaplin feared that the cumbersome technology needed to produce talking pictures would have a deadening impact on cinematic inspiration. His first visit to a sound stage left him in a state of despair: 'Men dressed like warriors from Mars, sat with earphones while the actors performed with microphones hovering over them like fishing rods. It was all very complicated and depressing. How could anyone be creative with all that junk around them?'

There were also deeper cultural anxieties, intimately bound up with America's idea of what the industry had come to represent. Sound could destroy the very essence of the movies as a cosmopolitan popular cultural form. It was, after all, the absence of language that had made the movies uniquely accessible to their immigrant audiences, creating a medium open to all regardless of status, culture or ethnic origin. Now Warner Brothers had built something of a Tower of Babel. The concerns even transcended the issue of mere language. 'A good picture', said Chaplin, 'has universal appeal both to the intellectual and to the rank and file. Now with sound, it is all to be lost.' Silent movies had helped define the democratic ideals which many felt were synonymous with the very idea of America itself. Sound threatened to reopen a cultural divide, polarized along traditional lines between an intellectual elite and the masses.

With foreign markets already representing as much as 30–40 per cent of their revenues, the studios had good cause to worry that overseas audiences would now flock to hear films in their own language, deserting the American movies which for over ten years had dominated the world. There was also the danger that the loss of those markets would severely weaken the cultural impact of the United States overseas at the very moment when a gigantic outpouring of American products designed for mass consumption – everything from automobiles to jazz – was sweeping into developing markets across the world. As a commercial commodity in their own right, the movies were an enormously valuable part of that economic and cultural assault on foreign markets, generating millions of dollars in export revenues. But they also served – just as they do today – as a vehicle for the promotion of other American goods: cars, clothes, music, drinks and packaged food which adoring fans would identify with the stars.

The nationwide success of *The Jazz Singer* soon made it obvious that, in the United States at least, talking pictures represented a huge commercial opportunity. The Warner Brothers were way ahead of the competition and soon reaped their reward as the company's value skyrocketed from $6 million to $230 million in just two years. The established giants of the industry – led by Paramount and MGM – suddenly found themselves obliged to throw all their resources into talkies. Theatre chains across the country began an equally frantic race to gear up for sound, completing the process with quite astonishing speed and, by the end of 1930, virtually all American cinemas were fully equipped. It was, said *Fortune* magazine, 'beyond comparison the fastest and most amazing revolution in the whole history of industrial revolutions.' Producers, directors and writers all scrambled to jump on the bandwagon.

Other changes also swept through the movie business. The headlong rush into sound was largely made possible by blue-blooded East Coast financiers. These were the men who, only a few years earlier, had recoiled at the very mention of the 'movies'. Now they swarmed to invest in film. As the 1920s progressed an increasing number of investment firms had shown an interest in Hollywood. Even more powerful backers began to join the party and, significantly, some of them were not banks but the major communications companies. Among these was Western Electric, a subsidiary of American Telephone and Telegraph (AT&T), one of the world's largest companies, which was controlled by banker J. P. Morgan. Another new investor was RCA Photophone, a subsidiary of the Radio Corporation of

America (RCA), owned by interests tied to the Rockefellers, America's richest family. Between them, these two groups were largely responsible for financing the construction of new 'sound' studios and the re-equipping of the nation's cinemas.

Within the United States, the transition to sound had been astonishingly smooth. By the beginning of the 1930s, those who had predicted that sound would spell the end of the industry had been proved entirely wrong. Even in the export markets, the impact of sound had been nowhere near as disastrous as some had feared. The major American studios began to export sound films late in 1928. There were few cinemas wired for sound overseas, though, as many of the companies which controlled foreign theatre chains lacked the capital to make the transition. In Europe, as elsewhere, the advent of the talkie was viewed both as an opportunity and as a threat. On the one hand, if audiences did take to sound in any significant numbers – something that in the late 1920s was still far from certain – it seemed obvious that they would prefer to watch films in their own language. On the other hand there was a fear, reinforced as Hollywood films began to arrive with their English-language dialogue, that if American pictures retained their huge popularity, the coming of sound would pose a real threat to the cultural identity of non-English-speaking countries. Indeed, in early 1928 Louis Mayer had confidently asserted that the popularity of American films would ensure that English would be adopted as a universal language.

In Europe there was mounting alarm, particularly among the cultural elite. The majority of European intellectuals had been nurtured within an aesthetic tradition dominated by the spoken and written word. 'Noise yes, words no,' as one French anti-sound slogan had it. In America, literary and theatrical traditions were not nearly so deep-rooted, and did not command the same kind of social or political influence. The first major battle faced by the Americans was in Germany, where, with the encouragement of the government, a cartel had emerged with its own technology for producing and screening talking pictures. Tobis-Klangfilm had been created as a joint venture in 1929, and was led by Siemens and AEG, the German electrical giants. In May that year, as Warner Brothers were about to premiere *The Singing Fool* in Berlin, Tobis-Klangfilm sued and successfully halted the première on the grounds that the Americans were infringing its exclusive rights to use sound equipment. Until the case was resolved, no American talkies could be shown in Germany. In retaliation the Hollywood studios, led by Will Hays, launched a boycott of the German market. Meanwhile, Tobis-Klangfilm succeeded in securing further injunctions against the use of Western Electric's technology in Hungary, the Netherlands and Switzerland.

In June 1930 representatives of Tobis-Klangfilm gathered in Paris to meet with executives from Western Electric, RCA and the Hollywood studios. Eventually they hammered out an agreement under which the various parties divided the world into four sectors, with each company guaranteed exclusive access in certain specified territories, in a market whose profitability was estimated to be worth at least a quarter of a billion dollars. The initial agreement quickly broke down, but a series of further agreements kept the informal cartel alive until the outbreak of the Second World War finally put paid to the idea of any kind of co-operation, allowing the American system to emerge triumphant. The one serious attempt to fuse European electrical giants with the interests of the film industry had ended in failure, even if that failure was more the result of external political events than the inherent weaknesses of the technology.

In Hollywood, on the other hand, films have featured as one element of a wider communications and electronics industry ever since the introduction of sound. This not only opened up major new sources of investment capital, but it also helped create a climate in which the film, television and video industries would learn to co-exist on a far more productive and harmonious basis than would ever be the case in Europe. It continues today as American telecommunications firms have once again become involved in financing the movie industry, largely because of their conviction that movies may soon be delivered to homes down telephone lines through so-called 'video-on-demand'. This, they believe, will dramatically enhance sales of all kinds of additional services such as home shopping and banking which can be made available using their technology. And just like Western Electric and RCA, Japanese electronics manufacturers such as Sony, JVC and Matsushita have also seen fit to invest heavily in the hope that controlling large libraries of films will provide them with a reliable stream of product for any new consumer goods that they might develop.

In the years immediately following the conversion to sound, Hollywood simply exported films in English without any kind of translation. Since mixing was unknown, all sound had to be recorded simultaneously, so that what we now know as 'dubbing' was out of the question. There were reports from some countries that the talkies had boosted the study of English; a report from South America revealed that after screenings of the first talkies in Rio de Janeiro, audiences would emerge reciting the dialogue to their friends. But the novelty soon wore off.

When it became clear that foreign audiences were clamouring to see films in their own language, some of the more adventurous US and European companies tried shooting several versions of the same film in different languages. Paramount opened a studio in the Paris suburb of Joinville to make local language versions of its major features. Rivalling the Hollywood studios in size and sophistication, by the early 1930s, actors and technicians at Joinville worked round the clock, producing a single film in as many as twelve different languages. But within a year it was clear that Paramount had made an expensive mistake. For one thing, stars were by now the driving force behind the popular appeal of movies all over the world, and foreign audiences did not take kindly to films which featured unknown actors instead of their favourite celebrities. Multilingual versions of a movie were hugely expensive, and in most cases there was little chance of recouping the cost in individual markets.

Meantime, dubbing and subtitling had vastly improved, enabling talkies to begin to overcome the language barrier. From 1931 onwards, these two methods became the standard means for translating films. Dubbing was the preferred method for markets where audiences spoke German, French or Italian. Elsewhere, subtitling was the norm. This reflected the relative strengths of the local industries. The Americans were apparently worried that in Germany, France and Italy, where the national film industries were relatively healthy, audiences, weary of reading subtitles, would start flocking to local films. In other parts of Europe and throughout the rest of the world, where the national industries were much weaker, the Americans were far less concerned about the likely impact of subtitling on their market share. Still, the quality of translations provided in the early days of dubbing and subtitling sometimes left a good deal to be desired. When a cowboy in an American western went into a bar, and yelled, 'Gimme a shot of red-eye', it was rendered in French as *'Donnez-moi un Dubonnet, s'il vous plaît'.*

Not surprisingly, it was in Great Britain that the impact of sound was most dramatic. Here was a chance for the British to start exporting movies to English-speaking countries all over the world on a much bigger scale than before. New capital flooded in. In November 1928, with the help of investors from the City of London, a Scottish solicitor named John Maxwell created Associated British Cinemas (ABC), with interests in production, distribution and exhibition. One month later, Gaumont-British, originally a subsidiary of the French parent company, which had been quietly expanding since the early 1920s, acquired one of the country's biggest cinema chains, which became Gaumont-British Picture Corporation. In the same way that the Wall Street banks had finally taken Hollywood seriously in the mid-1920s, so investors in the City of London, encouraged by the advent of the talkies, now played a crucial part in the expansion of British cinema. Within the space of a few months, the British film industry had been transformed. For the first time, it was spearheaded by two large, well-capitalized companies which, although they did not rival the giant Hollywood studios, at least had the financial resources to produce big-budget pictures for audiences at home and abroad.

As a result, Great Britain was one of the first countries outside the United States to equip its cinemas and studios for sound. With audiences all over the world flocking to 'talkies' in ever greater numbers, British producers seized their opportunity and began creating bigger, more expensive pictures for the world market.

In 1930, Sir Gordon Craig proposed the creation of a centre for the production of 'International Talking Pictures', arguing that such a studio, capitalizing upon the development of sound, might help to address the problem of unemployment. The Midland Bank apparently agreed to underwrite the scheme if the government signalled its approval of the project, but the government remained sceptical, suggesting that since only around 1500 people had been employed in film studios the previous year such a scheme would be unlikely to have much effect. The same objections would still be aired fifty-five years later, once again ignoring the wider impact of a labour-intensive industry like film production which promotes scores of jobs in other sectors.

Various organizations put forward their own schemes for boosting the fortunes of the industry. One of the more extravagant ideas was a plan to create a financial institution with the capital resources to acquire outright control of American cinema chains, and to produce films especially for audiences in the United States. The Federation of British Industries observed that 'the apathy and short-sightedness . . . of the financial powers of this country in neglecting the possibilities of an industry, which, if directed by responsible and influential persons capable of attracting the necessary public moneys, would be a source of immense revenue and of incalculable assistance in rehabilitating the industrial welfare of the Empire.' Such a venture, it was observed, by launching an assault on the American market, would have the resources to 'carry the war into the enemy's camp'. In a letter to the British ambassador in Paris, a Foreign Office civil servant enumerated the advantages which now accrued to Britain: '[T]he talkie for various reasons, the improvement in lenses (which now laugh at murky atmospheres), the increases of studio as opposed to outdoor work, etc., all have considerably diminished Hollywood's natural advantages'. He went on to suggest that this new body could finance a picture starring Charlie Chaplin who was, after all, British by birth, about the first governor of Virginia and the native American, Pocohontas: '[W]ith Chaplin's name and experience behind it, it would be bound to "go".' The idea failed to gain serious political backing.

One of the spurs for the creation of the British Council in the 1930s was the belated realization in Great Britain that cultural relations and trade promotion went hand in hand. The authors of a report to the Prince of Wales on a British economic mission to South America in 1929 had argued that 'we have not sufficiently understood the direct relation between culture and trade' and called for the export of more and better British films.

An article in the American *Saturday Evening Post* of July 1933 explained: 'John Bull is determined that Hollywood shall not continue to supply the product and reap the profits from what he considers his rightful inheritance.' As the British industry began to flex its muscles for the first time in thirty years, the American writer Dalton Trumbo predicted: 'It is safe to say that within two years foreign films – notably British – will be offering competition in Hollywood's back yard.' He anticipated a remark made by Colin Welland, an English writer, fifty years later. When collecting his Oscar for *Chariots of Fire*, he announced that 'the British are coming'. Both predictions proved sadly hollow.

9

'Last year alone we made fourteen films. How many were exhibited? None!'

BRAZILIAN JOURNALIST, 1927

AS EARLY AS 1901, the British writer William Stead had published a book called *The Americanisation of the World*. The idea that America was an alien, exotic land had deep roots. In the first three decades of the twentieth century, as its influence – politically, culturally, economically – expanded overseas, so a perception of the existential strangeness of the New World was bolstered by new emotions, including suspicion and fear. These anxieties became particularly powerful during the 1920s in the face of the huge outpouring of American cultural artefacts.

The overwhelming dominance exercised by Hollywood movies became, for many European social commentators, the most visible and most threatening symbol of cultural colonization. By 1927, such was the level of concern that an editorial in Britain's *Daily Express* protested: 'The bulk of picture goers are Americanized to an extent that makes them regard the British film as a foreign film. They talk America, think America, dream America; we have several million people, mostly women, who, to all intents and purposes, are temporary American citizens.'

It is easy to see why Hollywood movies attracted such opprobrium. They symbolized everything that the European bourgeoisie found most threatening. They were highly visible, using glamour and hard-sell advertising techniques to attract the public. They championed the values of cash over culture, embodying what Thorstein Veblen called a 'sense of costliness masquerading under the name of beauty'. They often championed the underdog and they had developed largely outside the control of the dominant social and cultural groups; in fact, they had originally developed in outright defiance of the wishes of powerful cultural elites. Indeed, in some respects the popularity of American films owed as much to changes in European society as to the intrinsic merits of the films themselves. The Great War had destroyed many of the class rigidities of European society, and the stultifying social distinctions that went with them. The working people and the unemployed who flooded into the cinemas of Europe were newly receptive to the subliminal message that America was a place where anyone, regardless of birth or social rank, had the opportunity to acquire wealth, fame and freedom beyond their wildest fantasies.

The most popular movie stars were a living proof of this. Mary Pickford, for example, was the daughter of a manual labourer who had been killed at work when she was five years old, forcing her to find a job as the family's sole breadwinner. Yet within a few years, 'Little Mary' had become one of the world's best-known celebrities, earning thousands of dollars a week. American silent films, particularly those featuring Chaplin's 'little tramp', often depicted the triumph of ordinary individuals over unjust or wilfully stupid authority. The world of the movies was the antithesis of hidebound societies in which blood and class determined most things, and where social mobility was extremely restricted.

As the decades passed and the influence of American movies became ever greater, this feeling would grow more intense. By the early 1960s, it would be quite possible for Europeans brought up on cinema and visiting America for the first time, to feel that they were arriving home. Such was the power of the moving image.

The values of American cinema posed a different but related challenge to the intellectual elite who had long served as the self-appointed guardians of 'high culture' in Europe. What they found threatening was not so much that Hollywood set out consciously to attack the tradition of high culture, as that it seemed at times oblivious to its very existence. It treated the great classics of European literature with much the same cheerful abandon as it treated slapstick comedy. It not only posed a threat to the cultural identity of European nations, it posed a threat to the concept of culture itself; hardly surprising, then, that Europe rang with strident denunciations of Hollywood and everything it stood for.

In keeping with the perceived need to preserve the integrity of their own cultures, throughout the 1920s and '30s, most European countries introduced legislation to provide at least some measure of protection against the flood of American films which threatened their national industries. Germany had been the first to introduce protective measures some ten years earlier, during the Great War, with an outright ban on imports. This was subsequently modified in 1921 to a system of quotas which restricted the number of imported foreign films to just 15 per cent of the total produced in Germany in any given year. In France after the Great War, Charles Pathé attempted to rescue the fortunes of the ailing film industry by proposing 'the institution of a percentage on cinema receipts as well as a quota system for the importation of a foreign film negative into France'. The idea was fiercely, and successfully, opposed by distributors and exhibitors who feared that they would be starved of the popular American films which provided their principal source of income. In Italy, production plummeted from around 500 films a year in 1915 to a mere ten by the end of the 1920s, while cinema audiences had soared, with receipts doubling between 1924 and 1927 alone. With the birth of the talkies, even more American films flooded into the market to meet the new demand.

In Britain, the indigenous industry was even weaker. As early as 1917 a leading British film trade paper proposed protective legislation but, as ever, different sections of the industry found themselves at odds. One producer argued that unless at least a third of screen time was reserved for British films, the industry might not survive in the face of what had become a 'hopeless struggle' against foreign imports. A cinema-owner retorted: 'If the British film is all that its advocates claim, why does it need "protection"? . . . The public and the public alone, is the best and sole arbiter,' suggesting that 'the British film has suffered from the poverty-stricken imagination of its producers'. Nothing came of the quota proposals.

In June 1925, a group of prominent British political, cultural and business leaders renewed the call for protection in a letter to the *Morning Post*. They pointed out that British films commanded just 5 per cent of the national box office, with American movies accounting for almost all the remainder. They touched on commercial arguments about the importance of the film industry as an employer, but they paid far more attention to cultural arguments claiming that 'high national and patriotic interests are involved . . . The bulk of the films shown in this country have, to say the least of it, a non-British atmosphere . . . Many of them are inferior productions, neither healthy nor patriotic in tone, while the psychological influences which they convey may have far-reaching consequences.'

The signatories to the letter included the composer Edward Elgar, the novelist Thomas Hardy, the newspaper tycoon Cecil Harmsworth and the department-store magnate, Gordon Selfridge. Their argument was taken up by Stanley Baldwin, the Conservative Prime Minister, in a parliamentary debate on unemployment. He suggested that the film industry deserved protection because of 'the enormous power which the film is developing for propaganda purposes, and the danger to which we in this country, and in our Empire subject ourselves if we allow that method of propaganda to be entirely in the hands of foreign countries'. Although Baldwin referred to 'foreign countries', it was clear that he had only one target in mind: America.

In the same month, there was uproar in Parliament after a senior executive of Universal's UK subsidiary tricked the army into supplying a guard of honour, complete with regimental band, to play 'The British Grenadiers' to mark the London première of *The Phantom of the Opera*. The army protested that it had agreed to participate only on the grounds that the event would be used to promote recruitment. To make the humiliation complete, the stunt was filmed to provide yet more publicity for the movie. In an effort to demonstrate their patriotism, exhibitors boycotted the film which did not go on general release until three years later. The incident served only to feed the growing animosity of many politicians towards America. 'No mention was made to them of an American film to be met and escorted, and nothing was said to make them suspect the real purpose for which they were required,' thundered Sir Laming Worthington-Evans, Secretary of State for War, speaking in Parliament. The Foreign Office complained haughtily that it was 'deplorable that the Army should have been trapped into making of itself a humorous advertisement for an American motion picture company'. Underlying many of the more extreme statements of anti-Americanism was the unmistakable sense, born of a cultural arrogance and distaste for marketing, that the popularity of American movies somehow rested on nothing more than a confidence trick. The public were presented as powerless victims of a conspiracy cooked up by the Hollywood studios. If only they realized they were being duped, ran the argument, then of course they would once again flock to see British films, rather than pictures made by 'foreigners'.

In spite of all this righteous indignation, there were those who recognized that the popularity of American movies rested on something more substantial than a sinister conspiracy to bamboozle the public. In an essay entitled *Notes for English Producers*, prepared for the Foreign Office in 1927, John Grierson, who went on to become a highly respected documentary-maker, set out to address precisely this issue. Among many passages which strike a chord today, he wrote:

It is clearer than most things that the outcome of a picture must be positive rather than negative, that it must concern itself with youth and achievement rather than age and disintegration, with matters that instil optimism rather than those that suggest a reason for pessimism.

To this drabness English pictures have been peculiarly liable. Their preoccupation with slums, their harping on poverty, their tendency to represent workmen and workgirls in a dismal atmosphere of obvious conscious and complacent inferiority, do not serve them well in the larger cinema market.

In many ways, Grierson's subsequent documentaries, didactic exercises in gritty social realism, seem to exemplify precisely the dourness against which he was fulminating. That in no way invalidated his argument. As compared to their American counterparts, British films did seem dreary, depressing and monotonous.

Eventually the British government did introduce a system of 'quotas' with the Films Act of 1927. Cinema-owners were obliged to ensure that at least 5 per cent of the total footage of film screened each year was made up of British pictures, and this proportion was to rise to 20 per cent by 1936. The Italians also passed legislation in 1927, requiring cinemas to reserve one day in ten for local productions. The French introduced quotas in 1928 but their chosen instrument, the so-called Herriot decree, named after the Minister for Public Education, was significantly weakened as a result of lobbying by Will Hays. In any case, the French industry, which no longer had large, vertically integrated companies like Pathé at its core, was too weak to take advantage of the opportunities afforded by these quotas. When, in 1929, as the argument over quotas rumbled on, American firms suspended the supply of films to France, the gap was largely filled not by French movies but by German ones.

However crude and ineffective they were, quotas had become accepted as a means of protecting 'national identity' throughout Europe. Perhaps it was hardly surprising that cinema, born at the end of a century in which the idea of nations and nationalism had gained almost universal currency, should for so many countries become closely identified with the idea of national identity. In France, where this concept was closely identified with the civilizing values of literature, philosophy and art, the debate about the dominance of American cinema took on a more strident tone. The relationship between France and America had long been an ambivalent one. During the nineteenth century some French thinkers, disillusioned with the disorder of their own society, increasingly looked to America as a democratic Utopia, while others characterized it as a country full of rapacious philistines obsessed only with making money. As early as 1835, one French intellectual had denounced America 'as a nation of ignorant shopkeepers and narrow-minded industrialists whose entire vast continent contains not one single work of art that was not inherited from various tribes which antedated Christianity'. Even a liberal French intellectual like Alexis de Tocqueville, in so many ways deeply sympathetic to America, felt compelled to condemn the 'tyranny of the majority'. For some, America represented ideals which had been betrayed in France. As Bartholdi, the inspiration behind the Statue of Liberty, had put it: 'I will try to glorify the republic and liberty over there ... in the hope that someday I will find it again here in France.' The strength of feeling about America – whether positive or negative – suggested that in some way the reaction of French thinkers towards America really had far more to do with an ambivalence towards their own country. For those who detested the creeping mechanization of French society, viewing it as a threat to the values of the cultural elite, America was the perfect scapegoat. On the other hand, those who wanted to see a modern, progressive French state, spreading the gospel of enlightened liberalism throughout the world, lauded America as a model to be emulated.

In the eyes of many French intellectuals, the very popularity of the movies was sufficient to damn them. 'No true art has ever been a popular craze,' asserted the writer Georges Duhamel, in a best-seller suggestively entitled *America – The Menace*.

A more sinister reason for alarm surfaced in an influential essay entitled *The American Cinematic Invasion*, published in February 1930 by the celebrated French commentator René Jeanne. He claimed to detect 'a deliberate plan carefully nurtured and patiently put into practice by the leaders of the American film industry' to use cinema as a weapon of political propaganda, distorting even the most famous historical events. He cited the example of an MGM film which showed American troops marching past the Arc de Triomphe at the end of the Great War, as if, he claimed, it had been General Pershing and his troops who had been solely responsible for defeating the Germans. He complained that European stars, such as Greta Garbo and Pola Negri, who had emigrated to Hollywood were subjected to the deadening influence of a system of mass production which robbed their work of all vitality. He objected to the way that Victor Sjöström, the Swedish director, had been forced to change his name to Seastrom in a desperate attempt to make his work more palatable to parochial American audiences. And at the root of it all was his complaint that the Americans had appropriated and debased a once noble French invention.

For all the heat and passion, there was surprisingly little popular interest in cinema in France. In 1929 one magazine observed, perhaps a little wistfully, that 'only 7 per cent of the population goes to the cinema, whereas in the United States, 75 per cent of the population goes'. Those who did go to the cinema went on average only five or six times a year, a fifth of the figure for Britain, and a seventh of that for America.

Since film was viewed as a form of cultural expression, an increasing number of French intellectuals put forward the idea that, like most forms of traditional culture, it should be developed under the aegis of the state. In 1932, a French government representative told film industry executives:

> a collection of enterprises such as the cinema, that is at every moment in contact with the economic, intellectual, moral and aesthetic interests of an entire Democratic nation, cannot live apart from the Government, just as the Government cannot live apart from you ... [The talking film] must be turned to

profit . . . to organize production in France, for . . . only a film *made* in France can be representative of French culture . . . It is your duty . . . to collaborate with the French Government in such a manner that the French cinema industry may be directed towards the highest and noblest aims, and that French productions may hold their premier place in all the world.

Such elevated aspirations ignored hard commercial realities. In France, as in most of the rest of Europe, the fragmented nature of the industry meant that there was neither the means nor the desire to create the kind of star system which lay at the heart of Hollywood's worldwide popularity. Since there was no contract system in France, and production companies were isolated from the business of distribution, producers had no interest in marketing their stars, as their success would not be reflected in future profits. In any case, an increase in the value of a star was not always welcome since it usually meant that the company would have to pay higher fees for the actor's services in the future. Without a studio system, it was difficult for fans to contact stars and there was no publicity machine to promote them on a consistent basis. As a result, European actors and actresses worked in both theatre and film, while in the United States the best performers could afford to devote themselves full-time to the cinema.

In July 1934, the French government set up a commission under Maurice Petsch to report on the difficulties facing French cinema. Petsch's report, delivered in 1935, concluded that the industry was hopelessly fragmented, consisting of hundreds of under-capitalized companies, many of which went bankrupt each year. He proposed two principal measures to redress the situation: a national credit organization funded by several forms of tax, including one on foreign films, which would fund film production through the use of a controlled interest rate; and a technical committee made up of twenty-five representatives from all sections of the industry and from government which would advise on the expenditure of these funds. Petsch turned out to be no more successful than the industry he was analysing. His proposals were rejected, both by the film-makers who feared regulation of their activities, and by the Americans who instinctively opposed taxes on their films.

'Details of the system [may] differ in different lands,' an American journalist had concluded in 1930 in an article for the *North American Review* which was brashly entitled 'War in the Film World', '[but] in intent, it is uniform: it amounts to asking the Americans to subsidize the foreign, and competitive industries.' What no one questioned, at least in any serious fashion, was whether defensive measures such as quotas were actually an effective means for rejuvenating film industries in the face of overwhelming American success. In the United States, the government, originally at the behest of President Wilson, had long since recognized that the American movie industry represented both a potentially huge export earner for the country, and a means of advertising the merits of the American way of life to people all over the world. As the London *Morning Post* had put it a few years earlier: 'If the United States abolished its diplomatic and consular services, kept its ships in harbour and its tourists at home, and retired from the world's markets, its citizens, its problems, its towns and countryside, its roads, motor cars, counting houses and saloons would still be familiar in the uttermost corner of the world . . . The film is to America what the flag was once to Britain.'

The American approach was in many ways the direct antithesis of that adopted by the Europeans. The former saw that the most effective way to maximize the cultural impact of their cinema was to market it aggressively, as if it was any other commercial product for trade. European governments, on the other hand, believed that the only way to give their film industry commercial support was by surrounding it with a bulwark of culturally motivated legislation.

In the intervening sixty years, very little has changed. In every country that has ever considered legislation to 'protect' its local film industry from the overwhelming dominance exercised by Hollywood, the arguments at the heart of the debate, and the way in which the industry has polarized around those arguments, have been much the same. The creators of European cinema – writers, producers, directors and others – have tended to argue that a system of quotas and tariffs is the only viable way to fend off the American challenge and thereby create breathing space for the local industry. The Americans, they argue, have a huge competitive advantage simply because of the size and coherence of their domestic market. This imbalance is so great that it can be tackled only by protective legislation. On the other side, those who sell movies to the public, the film distributors and particularly the exhibitors, have consistently argued that any attempt by the state to determine what films are shown on a nation's cinema screens is a violation of individual freedom and is ultimately self-defeating. The public choose Hollywood movies not out of cussedness, but because they offer the kind of drama, action and excitement which is all too often absent from their own, domestically-produced films.

The quotas introduced in various European countries at the end of the 1920s and the beginning of the '30s, did produce the desired effect, at least in the short-term. The Americans' share of local markets fell and the film industries of Germany, France and Great Britain underwent a brief renaissance. Before 1930, the typical Hollywood film generated between 30 and 50 per cent of its revenues from overseas. Of this figure, almost half came from the English-speaking countries, principally Great Britain. During the early 1930s, overseas revenues fell to around 20 per cent, but then quickly returned to their earlier levels. Hollywood was now producing 75–80 per cent of all movies shown across the world, generating $200 million in annual revenues for the American distributors out of a total world gross of $275 million.

If any one man symbolized the brief rejuvenation of the British industry, it was Alexander Korda. Born in Hungary in 1893, Korda emigrated to Paris in 1911 where he persuaded Charles Pathé to give him a menial job in his studio. With the benefit of his French experience, Korda returned to Hungary and began producing and directing his own films. After spells in Vienna and Berlin, he moved to Hollywood in 1927. But, resenting the heavy hand of the studio bosses and the way they imposed their views on individual producers, he soon packed his bags for Europe. Arriving in England in 1932, Korda formed his own company, London Films, and just a year later had an enormous worldwide hit with *The Private Life of Henry VIII*, an historical pastiche starring Charles Laughton.

Such were his powers of persuasion that Alexander Korda was able to secure a distribution deal with one of the Hollywood studios, United Artists, which was virtually unprecedented for a British producer. The resources which the studio was able to put behind *Henry VIII* undoubtedly played a major role in helping it to achieve such box-office popularity in the United States.

The film cost £60,000, a huge amount at the time, but its backers were rewarded with a ten-fold return on their investment and twenty years later it was still making them £10,000 a year. In the United States, where commercial success had so long eluded foreign film-makers, the immense popularity of the film seduced other British producers into believing that they, too, could produce big-budget pictures and recoup their costs in the American market. What they overlooked was that the film's success in America was in large part due to United Artists' marketing and distribution campaign. Without effective American distribution, it was impossible for such big-budget films to recoup their costs; the same holds true today.

In practice, it was almost impossible for foreign producers to secure effective American distribution for their movies, so much so that many of them regarded it as, in effect, a particularly American form of quota. As early as 1926, a contemporary observer of the industry, William Marston Seabury, noted: 'British producers are denied access to the American market . . . This market can now be profitably reached only through one or more of a group of not more than ten national American distributors . . . each of which is busily engaged in marketing its own brand of pictures through its own sales or rental organisation, and through the theatres owned, controlled or operated by one or more of this group.'

The success of *Henry VIII* encouraged the City of London to pour new money into the British industry. In 1934, the Prudential

Assurance Company made a major investment in London Films, while Korda also received further backing from United Artists, which agreed to distribute a package of his future movies in America. Armed with this capital, Korda built the largest studio complex in Britain which opened at Denham in 1936.

Korda was the nearest equivalent to a movie mogul that the British industry possessed and he shared the taste of men like Louis Mayer and Sam Goldwyn for bombast and the grand gesture, although he looked 'more like a professor than a film magnate'. He occasionally worked with his brothers Zoltan, a director, and Vincent, a set designer. All three men had an uncertain grasp of English, and it was rumoured that their speech, like that of the American mogul Samuel Goldwyn, was littered with malapropisms. Responding angrily to a critic who had questioned his knowledge of film, Zoltan is said to have retorted angrily, 'You think I know fuck nothing about pictures! I tell you, I know fuck all!'

While Korda established himself as the leader of a renascent British industry, his increasingly profligate ways merely served to encourage the industry to grow beyond its means. Between the late 1920s and the mid-'30s, the number of production companies more than doubled to over 200. Studios sprang up all around London. Some even talked excitedly of a 'Hollywood on Thames'. Much of the funding came in the form of loans and was being made to companies with virtually no working capital. It was all too reminiscent of the over-heating in the German industry, in the early 1920s, which had been built on the shaky foundations of easy credit and protectionist legislation.

The crash came in 1937. Hundreds of British production companies collapsed as City investors, realizing that the anticipated profits were failing to materialize, began calling in their loans. Many of the companies had never even made a film. One such, with paid-up capital of £4, had outstanding charges on its books of £415,000. In late 1938 Korda, beset by financial difficulties, was forced to sell Denham Studios. The Bank of England launched an enquiry into the affairs of the industry. The British challenge to

Hollywood, like that of Germany ten years earlier, had ended in ignominious failure.

The swift and inevitable collapse of the British industry was as much the result of creative inadequacy as economic mismanagement. Korda himself, in a 1933 interview, had said that 'to be really international a film must first of all be truly and intensely national ... The greatest folly is to set out to try and suit everybody. It is the sure road to insincerity and artificiality. The result will be a mongrel film which belongs to nobody.' Yet when it came to his own films, Korda consistently flouted this admirable precept. Films like *Sanders of the River*, a trifling adventure story set in Africa, or *The Ghost Goes West*, a mystery tale of a spirit haunting a Scottish castle, starring Robert Donat, conveyed only the most superficial impression of the culture in which they were set. It was a fault common to many British films of the period.

The most successful examples of European cinema have almost always been rooted in the specific. The films of Ingmar Bergman, Federico Fellini and Pedro Almodóvar impart a feeling of cultural particularity which is underpinned by universal emotions in such a way that audiences everywhere can identify with the dreams and anxieties of the central characters. By contrast, attempts to make third-rate imitations of successful American movies, or efforts to produce movies which are self-consciously 'international' in theme or style, have invariably ended in failure. The history of the European industry is littered with films sunk by futile attempts to reproduce formulae imperfectly copied from Hollywood.

Despite the hectic expansion of the 1930s, Hollywood still dominated British screens, accounting for 70–80 per cent of the box office, and Britain remained America's most lucrative foreign market, accounting for over a third of its overseas earnings. According to one estimate, between 1921 and 1936 an astonishing £100 million was repatriated from Great Britain to Hollywood, a trade deficit which in the years since has continued to climb remorselessly. The 1927 Films Act which had encouraged a sense of security among investors was, in practice, deeply flawed. The British subsidiaries of the Hollywood studios which had been established during the 1930s had rendered the legislation almost completely ineffective, simply by cranking out hundreds of inexpensive, short films, 'quota quickies', to enable cinemas to fulfil their obligations to devote a percentage of screen time to British pictures. As an act of kindness these 'British' films were usually shown *after* the main Hollywood feature, when the vast majority of the audience had already left the cinema.

In 1936, the government formed a committee, headed by Lord Moyne, a former government minister, to study ways of revising the legislation governing the film industry. This led to a new Films Act in 1938, but this time in the face of fierce lobbying on behalf of the Hollywood studios by Will Hays, the head of the MPPDA, and Joseph Kennedy, who had been appointed American ambassador to Britain in the same year. Once again, quotas reserving screen space for British films were at the heart of the Act. This time the quotas were set at a slightly higher level. Apart from that, nothing had changed.

In every other major European country, and further afield in English-speaking territories like Australia, Canada, New Zealand and South Africa, the story was the same. In all these countries, American films regularly accounted for as much as 85–95 per cent of the national box office during the 1920s and early '30s. Everywhere ministers, bureaucrats and newspaper editors alike pontificated on the grievous harm to cultural identity that was being inflicted by Hollywood's dominance of the box office. When in 1928 an Australian senator argued that 'American pictures are destroying our national outlook,' he might have been speaking for any number of politicians around the world. 'The portrayal of extravagance and luxury creates a feeling of discontent and gives to pictures abnormal views of life,' argued one of his colleagues. Frank Thring, a former projectionist who had risen to become Australia's leading independent producer, led a campaign which resulted in the introduction of quota legislation in September 1935. There were widespread calls for protectionist measures to boost the fortunes of national film industries, and they enjoyed varying degrees of success. In Canada, after an attempt to prosecute the local subsidiary of Adolph Zukor's Famous Players for anti-competitive behaviour had been thrown out by the judge, the proponents of quotas seemed to lack the stomach for further legislative battles.

In South America, Hollywood movies dominated the entire continent, with local films often finding it difficult even to secure a release. 'Last year alone we made 14 films. How many were exhibited? None!' complained one Brazilian writer in 1927. 'The photographs of motion picture "stars" of the United States are repro-duced in Brazilian magazines and many are almost as well known in Rio de Janeiro as they are in the United States,' observed a Department of Commerce report on *Motion Pictures in Argentina and Brazil* in 1929, going on to note: 'There is a feeling that although North American films represent the life of a great people and a nation which has a great future, they do not entirely typify the art of the Latin races. Naturally, a film which in any way belittles Latin customs or shows Latin life disadvantageously tends to create an unfriendly feeling between the two countries.'

Mexico was the only country that really tried to turn back the tide of American influence. What exercised the Mexicans, however, was not so much the threat to their cultural identity as a thoroughly justified anger at the way in which Hollywood persistently charac-terized all Mexicans as villainous but ultimately spineless thugs. This resulted in a series of bans on selected American films throughout the 1920s.

Significantly, several of the countries that had the most success in building robust national film industries during the 1930s, India and Japan among them, succeeded in doing so without resorting to protectionism. In the case of India, as in Hong Kong, the multiplicity of local dialects meant that there were already strong local sub-cultures. After the introduction of sound gave people the opportunity to hear films in their own language, the immense popularity of a new genre of movies featuring flamboyant and repetitive song and dance sequences transformed the fortunes of the local industry. The head of the cinema chain which showed the first talkie in India recalled that at the screening, 'the booking office was literally stormed by jostling, riotous mobs hankering to secure anyhow a ticket to see a talking picture in the language they understood'. By the end of the 1930s, India was the world's third largest producer of movies.

The Japanese film industry was effectively wiped out by the huge earthquake which ripped through Tokyo in September 1923, reducing the city to smouldering rubble. The energy which animated the country's effort to recover from the catastrophe fed through to the film industry, and within a few years the business had its own thriving version of the Hollywood studio system. Leading firms such as Shochiku and Toho used the profits from distributing films to fund the production of local movies, while the cinemas they owned closed their doors to American product.

Nevertheless, Japan was slow to adapt to sound. Audiences did not take kindly to dubbed movies from overseas, uncomfortable with the image of foreigners apparently speaking fluent Japanese. There was fierce resistance too from the *benshi*, the garrulous and highly-paid commentators originally provided to explain the action of silent films to the audience, who were now threatened with redundancy. At first the *benshi* simply tried to ignore sound by shouting their commentaries over the dialogue of the film. When that failed, they forced cinema managers to switch the sound off, providing narration as they had done for silent films. Finally, they tried intimidation, dispatching gangsters to attack the head of one leading firm at his home and engaging in a series of violent strikes before eventually conceding defeat.

The *benshi*'s threats and bullying were the most dramatic symbol of the resistance to sound encountered in so many other countries. These struggles, the blunt refusal to adapt to the fundamental changes which had swept through the movie business, all ultimately proved futile. With the arrival of television and video, the same battles against innovation would be taken up by those who feared that these new technologies would spell the end of the film industry as they knew it. But the revolution unleashed by the Warner Brothers was unstoppable. By taking a huge gamble on talkies, rather than waging war on them, they transformed themselves from underdogs to industry leaders. For those who cared to notice, this offered a valuable lesson about the way in which the movies could deal with, and even benefit from, the challenges thrown up by technology. Few did, and as a result, in the 1950s with television and again in the 1970s with video, many film-makers around the world would pay a heavy price.

10

'I am the King here.
Whoever eats my bread,
sings my song'

HARRY COHN

NO SOONER HAD HOLLYWOOD'S long-cherished dream of better
access to bank and corporate finance come true, than problems
began to emerge. One of AT&T's executives who had helped the
Warner Brothers develop talkies, John Otterson, secretly hatched a
plot which would have allowed AT&T and Chase National Bank,
two of the largest investors in the industry, to seize effective control
of the whole of Hollywood, merging all the studios into one giant
entity. The attempt never really got off the ground, since it would
have required massive capital, but during the depression of the early
1930s the relationship between Hollywood and Wall Street became
increasingly fraught with mutual mistrust and suspicion. As Cecil B.
De Mille later lamented: 'When we operated on movie money, there
was joy . . . When we operated on Wall Street money, there was grief.'

The emergence of sound, the 1929 Wall Street Crash and the
subsequent depression all contributed to making the early 1930s a
turbulent time in Hollywood. For a while, it looked as if the movies

would escape the impact of the crash, as admissions continued to rise. The conventional wisdom was that cheap amusements were immune to recession. Within a year that myth was shattered as admissions plunged. Theatres were forced to slash the costs of tickets. Production costs soared. This heightened the sense of crisis engendered by various corporate upheavals. In April 1930, William Fox, the one-time nickelodeon operator, had been thrown out of the company he had created but not before fighting a momentous battle with AT&T's Otterson and his allies at Halsey Stuart, the Wall Street investment firm. Fox was replaced by Harley Clarke, a utilities tycoon from the Midwest. Clarke's attempt to impose 'scientific' management techniques on a Hollywood studio proved disastrous, and he, in turn, was swiftly replaced by Edward Tinker, a former chairman of Chase National Bank, who fared no better. Only with the appointment of industry veteran Sidney Kent in 1932 did Fox Film start to prosper once again.

The story was much the same at Paramount. When the depression hit the company's fortunes in 1931, its Wall Street backers installed John Hertz (founder of the rent-a-car empire and an investor in the theatre chain, Balaban and Katz) as chairman of the finance committee, and most of Zukor's management team were fired. Within eighteen months Hertz was gone, and after further years of unrest, during which the company went into receivership, the banks finally reinstated Zukor, who swiftly returned it to profitability.

The outside interests that took control of some of the studios during the depression, in the belief that they could rescue them from financial catastrophe, only succeeded in making things worse. In the 1920s, the Wall Street investors had left the job of running the studios to the moguls themselves. Interference was minimal. For all its desire to be accepted as just another industry in need of investment, the fact remained that the dynamics of film finance required a very special combination of nerve and intuition. (The harsh experience of Sony, Matsushita and Crédit Lyonnais in the 1980s suggests that this remains as true in our day as it did in the

1930s.) As Irving Thalberg put it in a 1933 article entitled 'Why Moving Pictures Cost So Much': 'It is hard . . . to explain the whole motion picture situation to a banker . . . It is a creative business dependent, as almost no other business is, on the emotional reaction of its customers. It should be conducted with budgets and cost sheets, but it cannot be conducted with blueprints and graphs.'

Throughout the 1930s, the studio system grew ever more complex. At its heart were the 'Big Five' companies: Adolph Zukor's Paramount, Fox Film, Warner Brothers, RKO and Loews. RKO, the smallest of the Big Five, had been created in 1928 after RCA president David Sarnoff joined forces with Joseph Kennedy (father of President John F. Kennedy) who ran a small production company, and the Keith Albee vaudeville theatre circuit. It was intended that the resulting company, Radio-Keith-Orpheum, would use its film production capacity and ownership of theatres to promote the use of the Photophone sound equipment created by RCA. The heavily mortgaged company went into receivership in 1933, and spent much of the 1930s tied up in legal wrangles. It would eventually be acquired by maverick billionaire Howard Hughes in 1948.

Loews, on the other hand, had become the most powerful company in the American motion picture business by the early 1930s. It controlled a highly prestigious chain of theatres as well as MGM, the producer and distributor. It was headed by Nicholas Schenck, another émigré from Eastern Europe. He had roamed the streets of the Bowery with his brother Joseph until the latter eventually got a job 'doling out pills and powders behind the scarred counter of [a] little local drug store'. Working their way up through the ranks, the Schencks eventually acquired a couple of drugstores, then purchased an amusement park in New Jersey. Joseph, who married Norma Talmadge in 1917, branched out into independent production, and eventually became president of United Artists. Nick, 'friendly and generous, but more conservative than Joe', joined Loews then acquired the company in 1927 after the death of founder Marcus Loew. The real moving power at MGM, however, was Louis B. Mayer.

Mayer's parents had arrived in St John, New Brunswick, from Russia when Louis was just a few years old. His father worked as a peddler, before becoming a scrap merchant salvaging materials from wrecked ships lying along the coast, assisted by the young Louis. Mayer eventually moved to Boston in search of bigger things, although when he arrived in the city he was without any means of paying his way. After a brief and unhappy spell in the scrap metal business, he started looking for other commercial avenues to explore. As he trudged the streets of Boston pondering his future, he made friends with a nickelodeon owner. Intrigued by his first visit to the man's theatre, Mayer began to visit frequently, occasionally helping to sell tickets and, eventually, decided to go into the business on his own. He took out a lease on a small theatre in Haverhill, Massachusetts, and gradually built up a successful chain of theatres in New England. In 1914 he branched out into distribution, making huge profits from one of the first films he handled, D. W. Griffith's *The Birth of a Nation*. Next he moved into production and in 1924 he was hired by Marcus Loew to become vice-president and general manager of the newly-born Metro-Goldwyn-Mayer.

The mixture of ruthlessness and sentimentality that characterized men like Zukor was demonstrated to even greater extremes in Mayer. As he made his way around the studio, 'he strode – ready for battle,' an impression reinforced by his booming voice. Always impeccably groomed, he was a gifted speaker who worked hard on his orations and was capable of launching ferocious verbal assaults – a useful quality in the turbulent world of the big studios. It was said that after watching Mayer savage an employee, one of his senior colleagues had stumbled from the room and been physically sick. Despite his stocky build, Mayer would sometimes resort to using his fists, and board meetings at MGM were known to degenerate into outright brawls. In a hotel restaurant, Mayer hit Charlie Chaplin so hard that 'he was lifted a foot off the floor' before keeling over and landing in a potted palm. He once threatened to pummel a man who imitated a noted opera singer at a party – until told the man was part of the act. He was equally impetuous in his approach to sex. 'Why don't you sit on my lap when we're discussing your contract the way the other girls do?' he asked one actress. It was somewhat ironic that Mayer, speaking of his altogether softer boss Nick Schenck, should refer to his 'two faces – the smiler and the killer'.

Despite his ruthlessness, Mayer was also a sentimentalist, quickly moved to tears, immensely protective of his daughters and a fierce patriot. One Hollywood executive recalled that if an actor refused to appear in one of Mayer's pictures, Mayer would 'stage his own command performance. [He] would get down on his knees. He'd shed real tears ... He'd sob, "You're destroying me. If you don't do this, I'll be penniless".' So strong was his desire to identify with his adopted country that he claimed the fourth of July – American independence day – as his birthday, and on that day each year the MGM studio would shut down for a giant party in honour of the boss.

Each of the Big Five produced a stream of films, distributed them throughout the world, and owned substantial chains of cinemas. They were shadowed by the so-called 'Little Three' – Universal, Columbia and United Artists – which confined themselves to production and distribution, and by a handful of significant independent producers such as Monogram and Republic.

Of all the studios, Warner Brothers, under its boss Darryl Zanuck, who had started as a scriptwriter for *Rin Tin Tin*, was the most ruthless in its insistence that the demands of individuals should be subordinated to the efficient running of the company. Edward G. Robinson, one of Warner's leading stars, who had earned millions of dollars for the studio, once asked Zanuck if there might be a way for him to make some contribution to the process of script development. Zanuck's response was swift and brusque: 'We will accept anybody's ideas or suggestions, but the treatment of the subject in script form should be left largely to the judgement and intelligence of the "system".'

The studio system, 'the private grammar' of the pictures, as Scott Fitzgerald called it, with its rigorous division of labour and its assembly-line approach to manufacturing, owed much to the techniques of mass production which were simultaneously being developed in other industries. In 1924, Henry Ford had observed: 'the ideas we have put into practice are capable of the largest application . . . they are nothing particularly to do with motor cars or tractors, but form something in the nature of a universal code.' Directors and writers weren't, for the most part, hired for their own ideas. Instead, they were put under contract, and assigned to whatever project the studio thought most suitable for them at the time. This was the studio system mythologized in films such as Vincente Minelli's *The Bad and the Beautiful* and the Coen brothers' *Barton Fink*.

Just as they treated the creation of films as a manufacturing process, albeit a highly sophisticated one, so the moguls treated the finished film as a product to be sold using the most sophisticated retailing techniques. For the studios, it was the stars who provided the clearest and most effective means of attracting an audience. They were the 'brand names' who could create a distinct identity for each film, distinguishing it from the hundreds of others which jostled for audiences in the marketplace.

It was the stars who were the most visible sign of the power the movies now exercised. The worship of celebrity had become akin to a new religion in America and around the world. From a trickle of fan-mail to Florence Lawrence, Mary Pickford and Charles Chaplin, it rapidly turned into something much bigger and much crazier. By the mid-1920s, the star phenomenon was threatening to get completely out of hand. Fans became obsessed with imitating not only the way their favourite stars looked, but the way they talked and even what they ate. As one press agent put it: 'a goddamn star could fuck an ape and it might create a vogue.' It was Rudolph Valentino, with his legions of adoring female fans, who best symbolized this new form of mass hysteria. 'A man should control his life,' Valentino once said. 'Mine is controlling me. I don't like it.' After his sudden death in 1926 there was a riot at the funeral home where his body rested and thousands of hysterical women flocked to his funeral.

There were even reports that some committed suicide, such was their despair at the loss of their idol.

During the early 1930s, as the depression hit Hollywood, star salaries began to tumble and the studios moved to take advantage of the situation. Stars were placed under onerous contracts, usually lasting seven years, which gave them almost no choice over the roles they were offered. The exploitation of star power became a highly managed affair in which little was left to chance. Stars were created, not born. The studios would test potential talent in a variety of roles, measuring the resulting audience response through sneak previews, reviews, the opinions of cinema managers and comments in fan-mail. In the latter half of the 1930s, as the worst of the depression finally began to lift, the increasing sophistication of the methods used by the studios demonstrated that motion pictures had become a modern American retail industry. The chaotic days of the nickelodeon had been left far behind, but one thing remained constant: the belief that members of the public were the ultimate arbiters of everything that the studios did.

The mechanisms for marketing stars and movies to the public had also become highly sophisticated. In the 1920s, press agents had routinely pulled outrageous stunts as a means of publicizing movies. The most notorious of them all was Harry Reichenbach. Hired to promote *The Return of Tarzan*, Reichenbach secretly let a lion loose inside New York's Belleclaire Hotel, and left the management to deal with the problem of recapturing the beast. Just before the release of Universal's *The Virgin of Stamboul*, he persuaded a group of New York journalists that a party of 'Turks' who were staying at a hotel in the city were there to hunt for a lost virgin, and as a result, the police dragged the lake in Central Park. It was only a matter of time before legislation was introduced to put an end to such pranks.

Gradually the studio publicity departments evolved into highly sophisticated and well-oiled machines, primed not only to raise the public profile of particular stars but also to ensure that the impact of the suicides, turbulent divorces and other scandals which occasionally engulfed their performers was minimized. The major stars had their own publicists whose duties often extended to the management of their personal affairs. Perhaps inevitably, as the manipulation of the stars' public images became ever more rigorous, so too did the efforts of gossip columnists such as Louella Parsons, Hedda Hopper and Walter Winchell to uncover dirt and scandal. Trade papers, including the *Hollywood Reporter* and *Variety*, were set up to cover the affairs of the industry. An ever-increasing profusion of fan magazines spread across America and the English-speaking world. Top stars would receive thousands of letters a week, most of them asking for photographs and other souvenirs. The visibility and influence of the stars meant that they were persuaded to promote a galaxy of other products from cosmetics to toothpastes. Merchandising tie-ins became popular. When *Gone with the Wind* was released in 1939, wristwatches, corsets and hats were just a few of the goods marketed to an eager public alongside replicas of Scarlett O'Hara's barbecue dress. A chain of stores called Cinema Fashions Shops was set up, its owner Bernard Waldman working closely with the studios to secure advance sketches of clothes which would be worn by the stars in forthcoming movies. Such was the popularity of these lines that the company quickly grew to 400 stores spread across the United States.

Throughout the 1930s, Hollywood made increasing use of radio, still a relatively new medium, to promote its movies. With the coming of sound, and the sudden need to find performers with proven speaking and singing ability, the studios also turned to radio as an important and reliable source of new talent. Like cinema, radio had been greeted with snobbish distaste by some intellectuals. As H. G. Wells had scathingly described it in 1927, it was a medium designed for 'very sedentary persons living in badly lighted houses or otherwise unable to read, who have never realized the possibilities of the gramophone and the pianola and who have no capacity nor opportunity for thought or conversation'. It was perhaps natural that the movies and radio should form an alliance.

Even a very short roll-call of the stars of that period gives some idea of the rich and diverse talent pool that was available to Holly-wood by the 1930s: Bette Davis, Henry Fonda, Greta Garbo, Clark Gable, Jean Harlow, William Powell, Norma Shearer. It was hardly surprising that thousands of young girls flocked to Los Angeles desperate to get into the movies. They became known as 'starlets' which, as screenwriter Ben Hecht put it, was soon no more than a euphemism for 'any woman in Hollywood under thirty not actively employed in a brothel'. The easy availability of an army of young women was one of the significant and enduring attractions of the movie industry for many male executives, and for more than a few investors.

Another method of marketing films was to offer an increasingly clear-cut variety of film styles. The studios began to group their productions into standard narrative forms, the most prominent of which were the musical, western and the gangster film, though the system also included horror movies, screwball comedies and war films. Despite the common features of the system as a whole, individual movies began to acquire a clearly identifiable 'brand identity' which greatly facilitated their marketing and advertising, both at home and overseas.

In addition, each studio had its own particular character. During the 1930s, for example, Warner Brothers became renowned for its tight-fisted approach to production costs and star salaries, turning out a stream of gangster movies like *Public Enemy*, *Little Caesar* and *Angels With Dirty Faces*.

Jack Warner, unlike some of his rivals, made little secret of his contempt for the creative talent that fuelled the studio machine. It was rumoured that he had banned actors from the executive dining room with the contemptuous remark, 'I don't need to look at actors when I eat.' Those lower down the studio hierarchy fared even worse. Warner was ruthless in his quest to drive down costs. He would prowl around the studio late at night snapping off unnecessary lights to save money. On one such night, he heard a gatekeeper singing Verdi arias in a beautiful voice. Warner started talking to the man, who told him that he was a student and practised every day. 'Which would you rather be', asked Jack, 'a singer or a gatekeeper?' The gatekeeper, warming to the conversation, replied, 'Oh, a singer.' 'In that case, you're fired,' Jack told him simply. Unsurprisingly, such attitudes engendered a good deal of ill-will. As one scriptwriter put it: 'Working for Warner Brothers is like fucking a porcupine – it's one hundred pricks against one.'

MGM, on the other hand, with Louis Mayer at the helm, specialized in classy, upmarket films such as *Grand Hotel*, *Mata Hari* and *Queen Christina*, and was known as the Tiffany's of the movie business after the opulent New York store. While Darryl Zanuck's predilection for costume epics led to his studio being dubbed 'Sixteenth Century Fox'.

This conscious and highly targeted use of brand identities, built equally on stars, genres and the individual studios themselves, gave Hollywood the essential characteristics of many other emerging retail industries. Far from creating a series of unique bespoke products the studios were, in a sense, manufacturing product-lines, each with certain tried and tested ingredients which the public recognized and trusted. But that was not the whole story.

For much of the 1930s, the real creative control of Hollywood's output rested not so much with the actual bosses of the studios as with a select group of producers whom they employed, men such as David Selznick, Hal Wallis and Darryl Zanuck. These men gave Hollywood its creative energy and, to a very considerable extent, its aura as a place of youth and opportunity. Selznick was just twenty-nine when he was appointed vice-president in charge of production at RKO; Hal Wallis was chief executive producer at Warner Brothers by the time he was thirty-two.

It was these men, the heads of production, rather than the directors, stars or the nominal studio chiefs, who more than anyone else determined the kinds of films which were made in Hollywood throughout the 1930s. They were first-generation Americans, rather than immigrants. It was they who had the power to turn some 'wall-eyed', 'bow-legged' girl in her early twenties, like Norma Shearer, into an international celebrity, the 'First Lady of the American Screen' whose name would flare as brightly in the public consciousness as it did on the neon hoardings of thousands of cinemas around the world. It was they who developed the characters and shaped the stories which had the power to make audiences shake with laughter, recoil in fear or dissolve in tears.

The films made during the heyday of the Hollywood studios – the 1930s and the early '40s – were the product of a system in which the work of a vast army of individuals was synthesized under the control of a single individual, the producer. The director, the writer, the set designer, the composer, as well as a hundred others, all played crucial roles in crafting different aspects of a picture, but there was no doubt that ultimate power and authority rested with the producer. Screenwriter Philip Dunne, who worked with Darryl Zanuck when he moved to Fox, summed up the way this system worked: 'writers did not write scripts for directors; they wrote them for Darryl. Directors were assigned, as writers and actors were assigned: by his decision.'

Dunne described a typical story conference with Zanuck in the latter's long green office. As Zanuck strode up and down with a sawn-off polo mallet:

> He declaimed, as was his custom, the most outrageous clichés which he trusted the writers to transmute into playable scenes. 'And now,' Zanuck asserts, 'and *now* her love turns to hate.' A pause. He stops, stares at the writers, and repeats, 'Her love turns to hate'.
>
> Another pause. Then Kitty Scola [his collaborator] says, 'Why, Mr. Zanuck? Why does her love turn to hate?'
>
> Zanuck glares at Kitty for a moment, then strides into the dressing room behind his office ... The writers ... sit in bemused silence. They hear the sound of the toilet flushing and Zanuck reappears, paces the length of the office, and turns dramatically, pointing the polo mallet at Kitty Scola. 'All right,' he says, 'her love *doesn't* turn to hate.'

David Selznick, on the other hand, preferred to do much of his work via an endless stream of memoranda dispatched to almost anyone who happened to come into his orbit. These communications invariably marked 'rush' or 'urgent' often began with the phrase, 'I was horrified to learn that . . .' and became known to his colleagues as 'horrifiers'. They were packed with suggestions, criticisms, observations about films, art and the business of life in general. He would dictate for ten or twelve hours at a stretch, pumping out as many as 80,000 words a day. As Selznick's career flourished and grew in complexity, so the memos got longer. One afternoon, executives in his New York office were greeted by a Western Union messenger with what appeared to resemble a roll of paper towels. It was an interminable memo, subsequently celebrated as the 'Ten Yarder'. Just as they were about to start poring over this gigantic missive, two of his executives held it up to measure it. As they did so, one of them happened to glance at the final paragraph: 'I have just received a phone call that pretty much clears up the matter. Therefore you can largely disregard this wire. Anyway, I'm coming in tonight on the red-eye. Both of you plan to have breakfast with me. Regards. DOS.' That was the Selznick way of doing things.

At Columbia, it was Harry Cohn who indisputably ran the show. After writer Herman Mankiewicz had been fired by just about every studio in town for drunkenness and insulting behaviour, his friends eventually persuaded Cohn to hire him. Mankiewiecz was warned to stay out of the Columbia dining room, where each lunchtime Cohn sat at the head of a long table ritually insulting everyone who worked for him. 'If you go in there, Mank, you're through,' the writer was told. After hearing laughter coming from the dining room every day, Mankiewicz could stand it no longer. One day he entered the room and when Cohn arrived, found himself at the receiving end of a stream of barbed insults. The writer stuck it out, and didn't utter a word in reply. Then Cohn changed tack and began explaining his method for assessing the merits of a picture. He had, it seemed, an infallible test of a film's success or failure, and it was his own behind. 'If it itches,' Cohn proclaimed, 'the picture stinks. If it doesn't itch, then the picture's going to be a hit.' There was a brief silence, then Mankiewicz could resist no longer, crying out: 'I never knew before that the entire American motion picture audience is wired to Harry Cohn's ass.' The room shook with laughter. With that the writer got up and, without needing to be told what to do, went down to his office, cleared his desk and left.

Unlike Zukor and Mayer, Cohn, a former trolley conductor, had never had any aspirations to appear more refined or learned than he really was. On one occasion, his brother Jack, who also worked at Columbia, suggested that the company should make a biblical epic. 'What the hell do you know about the Bible?' asked Harry. 'I'll bet you fifty bucks you can't recite the Lord's Prayer.' 'Okay, it's a bet,' said Jack and they laid down $50. 'Okay, say it,' Harry said. 'Now I lay me down to sleep –' Jack began. 'That's enough,' interrupted Harry, handing him the $50. 'I really didn't realize you knew it.'

Though he had a shrewd eye for talent, Cohn accumulated many enemies over the years. So great was the antipathy he generated that, seeing the large crowds flocking to his funeral in 1958, the actor Red Skelton speaking on national television was moved to remark, 'Well, it only proves what they say – give the public something they want to see, and they'll come out for it.'

It was Irving Thalberg, more than anybody else, who was both the architect and symbol of the producer system. 'Twenty-five years old. Fifty thousand a year. Hundred per cent chance to be the biggest man in the picture industry. That's Thalberg,' was the way one profile writer described him in 1924. The glittering appearance was marred by an underlying darkness. Thalberg was born with a rheumatic heart condition, and doctors told his mother that he would be lucky to live beyond thirty. His illness only served to energize him. 'I was struck by his look of frailty,' recalled screenwriter George Oppenheimer, 'his thin form, the pallor of his cheeks, his hunched posture . . . However, when he started to talk, all frailty vanished; he had dynamic energy and the decisiveness and security so lacking in most producers.' He worked sixteen hour days at his bungalow on the MGM lot. 'I never had a conversation with him about anything except movies,' recalled one publicist. Thalberg was not the monomaniac he seemed. He read widely, his favourite authors including Epictetus, Bacon and Kant. Such literary and philosophical interests were the first sign that a shift was taking place in the management of Hollywood's creative affairs, not simply a generational change, but a cultural one, too. Zukor and Mayer may have loved mingling with writers, but they rarely, if ever, read books.

Thalberg's upbringing was staid and conventional, in sharp contrast to the men he later worked for, Carl Laemmle and Louis Mayer. A second-generation American, the son of a lace importer from Brooklyn, he started work as Laemmle's private secretary at the age of twenty. Laemmle was so taken with Thalberg's beguiling mixture of charm, judgement and quiet authority that he soon promoted him to supervisor of production. Thalberg's age and personality put him on an immediate collision course with Erich von Stroheim, notorious as a profligate, strutting autocrat, who had become one of Universal's most cherished directors. In 1921, they were both working on a picture called *Foolish Wives*, which, thanks to von Stroheim's self-indulgence had cost over $1 million – twenty-five times the cost of each of the five westerns which director John Ford shot in the same year – and which, at 320 reels, had consumed over fifty hours of film stock. After von Stroheim had cut the film down to three and a half hours, Thalberg demanded still more cuts. The director refused so Thalberg, aged twenty-one, simply locked him out of the editing suite and supervised the job himself. Although the picture did well enough at the box office, the enmity between the two men continued to fester. Soon after shooting began on von Stroheim's next Universal picture, *Merry Go Round*, Thalberg fired him. 'The age of the director was over,' one of their number later remarked wistfully. In brusquely pricking von Stroheim's ballooning ego, Thalberg had achieved something else too. He had established himself, rather than Laemmle, as the focus of authority in the studio, at least as far as production was concerned.

Thalberg felt he deserved more money than the parsimonious Laemmle was prepared to pay him, and was soon lured away to Louis Mayer's fledgling production company, Metro-Goldwyn-Mayer. Here he clashed with, and duly fired, a further clutch of obdurate directors, men like Marshall (Mickey) Neilan, Maurice Tourneur and Mauritz Stiller who bitterly resented the way in which he had apparently usurped their power over the film-making process. What Thalberg had created was a system in which the ultimate authority over all aspects of creative work had become vested in the studio production chief, with individual movies overseen by a subordinate team of production supervisors.

Thalberg was a great enthusiast for the practice of previewing movies, holding advance screenings in the Los Angeles suburbs. If the audience failed to respond to the picture, or seemed confused by it, Thalberg had no hesitation in reshaping, recutting and, if necessary, reshooting or adding entire scenes. Culver City, home of MGM, became known as Retake Valley. This went far beyond the kind of system used at European firms like Ufa, where the producers confined themselves to organizing the logistics of production and would rarely attempt to influence the creative shape of their movies. The idea that a producer, rather than the director, might order the recutting of a film would have been unthinkable in Europe, and largely remains so today. In Europe where an industrialized conception of cinema never really took root, the director would almost always be credited as the sovereign power behind a film.

Across most of Europe in the 1920s, film-making was largely conducted by small independent production companies. In France, for example, after Pathé ran into difficulties in the wake of the Great War, production was in the hands of hundreds of tiny firms. Such companies were in no position to exercise the same authority over their film-makers, because they could offer neither the lavish rewards nor the continuity of employment which were the carrots dangled in front of talent by the Hollywood studios. In Europe, film-makers who perceived their authority under threat might simply defect to another company, where they could easily negotiate greater freedom.

'The writer was very important in Europe, but here [in Hollywood] he is transformed into a mechanic,' complained German émigré director Fritz Lang. 'In any major studio, there are ten writers working on a single script. You never know which was the first.' With the development of the *auteur* theory in France in the 1950s, the myth began to take hold that it was really the long-suffering director who, in the teeth of the greed, blatant profiteering and double-dealing supposedly endemic to Hollywood, would somehow manage to impose his personal vision on work that otherwise would have been utterly devoid of soul. It was a myth whose legacy would come to have devastating consequences for the later development of much of the European industry.

In Hollywood, personal expression seemed to be stimulated rather than stifled by the discipline of the studio system. It was, after all, within the constraints of this system that directors as diverse as John Ford, Howard Hawks and Alfred Hitchcock made such richly rewarding films as *Stagecoach*, *Bringing Up Baby* and *Rebecca*.

Nothing better symbolized the gulf between Hollywood and European high culture than an encounter between Irving Thalberg and the composer Arnold Schoenberg. The meeting had been arranged by the German *émigrée* Salka Viertel, who, knowing that the exiled Schoenberg needed work, suggested that he might like to score a film called *Good Earth* for Thalberg. Thalberg explained to Schoenberg why he was interested in hiring him after hearing some of the composer's early, more melodic work. 'Last Sunday when I heard the lovely music you have written –' he began but was immediately interrupted by the composer who, having long since moved on to embrace dissonance, replied, 'I don't write "lovely" music.' Schoenberg went on to explain that he thought most music in films was dreadful, and that he would work on the movie only if he had complete control over the sound. 'What do you mean by complete control?' asked an incredulous Thalberg. 'I mean that I would have to work with the actors. They would have to speak in the same pitch and key as I compose it in. It would be similar to *Pierrot Lunaire*, but of course, less difficult.' When Thalberg explained that the director would want to handle the actors himself, the meeting was quickly terminated. A few days after the débâcle, Viertel recalled, the film's technical advisor 'bought some folk songs which . . . inspired the head of the sound department to write some very lovely music.'

Thalberg's assault on the established power structure in the 1920s and '30s proved commercially effective, and broadly similar regimes began to be implemented at other studios, most particularly by Jesse Lasky and B. P. Schulberg at Paramount, Darryl Zanuck at Warners and, briefly, by David Selznick at RKO.

Despite the manifold temptations that came with achieving success so young, Thalberg never succumbed to the rampant egotism which tended to be an inherent feature of the Hollywood industry. 'While everyone else was bent on plugging his own personality, Irving remained aristocratically aloof,' recalled screenwriter Anita Loos. He refused to allow his name to adorn any of the pictures he produced. 'Credit you give yourself is not worth having,' he explained. Thalberg's reluctance to grab the limelight was remarkable in a community dedicated to self-glorification.

In the end, Thalberg's aloofness may have been less a matter of personal modesty than a reflection of his view of film-making. In salary negotiations with Laemmle or Mayer, he fought ferociously for the bonuses and stock options which he felt belonged to him and his staff. He believed that the producer was the pivotal figure in the business of cinema, responsible not just for the creation of a single movie, but ultimately for the entire style of film-making which conferred a distinctive character upon each studio. The studio's signature was really synonymous with that of the head of production. That was why he came to define an era.

The power of the producers induced its own form of cynicism especially among screenwriters who felt themselves to be at the mercy of a bunch of brazen philistines. They were happy enough to take the money. 'For a thousand a week I'd dramatize the Sears, Roebuck catalogue for a producer who couldn't spell "cat",' was how one screenwriter put it. Still, a deep-rooted resentment festered among most of them. In a novel published after his death, Raymond Chandler had one of his characters musing somewhat acidly, 'There are grave difficulties about the afterlife. I don't think I should really enjoy a heaven in which I shared lodgings with a Congo pygmy or a Chinese coolie or a Levantine rug peddler or even a Hollywood producer.' Most writers in Hollywood had little expectation of remaining there for long. Those brought out from New York on the luxury train, the Super Chief, would be warned by veterans, 'Don't buy anything you can't take home on the Chief'. In any case, as Ben Hecht observed: 'Movies were seldom written. They were yelled into existence in conferences that kept going in saloons, brothels and all-night poker games.'

For all his qualities, Thalberg also made his fair share of mistaken judgements. Most famously, when Louis Mayer sought his advice on the rights to a novel entitled *Gone with the Wind*, he responded without a moment's hesitation, 'Forget it, Louis. No Civil War picture ever made a nickel.' Mayer turned it down but *Gone with the Wind* went on to become the biggest grossing picture the industry had ever known.

Thalberg died of pneumonia in 1937 at the age of thirty-eight. His death marked the beginning of the end of the producer system he had pioneered. In 1939, Frank Capra wrote a letter to the *New York Times* in which he remarked:

> About six producers today pass upon [reject] 90 per cent of the scripts, and cut and edit 90 per cent of the picture . . . [and] there are only half a dozen directors in Hollywood who are allowed to shoot as they please . . . I would say that 80 per cent of the directors today shoot scenes exactly as they are told to shoot them without any changes whatsoever, and that 90 per cent of them have no voice in the story or the editing.

But the system had already passed its zenith. From the late 1930s onwards, the power of the production chiefs began to decline. There were no longer pivotal producers at each studio; instead, supervising producers were temporarily assigned to oversee individual pictures, while the emerging power of directors like John Ford and Howard Hawks ensured that power within the studios became more diffuse.

If there was one thing that bound the bosses together, moguls and production chiefs alike, it was their passion for gambling. Cards, horses, roulette – despite their cultural differences it became an all-embracing passion from Laemmle, Zukor and Warner to Selznick and Thalberg. It was hardly surprising that such men should find their natural home in a high-risk business like the movies. Prodigious amounts of money were lost in a single evening. Some like David Selznick risked everything. 'He was a very poor man with a very big salary,' recalled his wife, Irene. 'He could blow in a few hours more than I could save in two years.' According to one source, when David Selznick went off to Columbia University in the early 1920s his father Lewis, an alcoholic, gave him $750 dollars, a huge allowance for the time. 'Spend it all,' his father told him. 'Give it away. Throw it away.' His son did not disappoint. Such was the Hollywood passion for the horses that Groucho Marx once showed up at the offices of MGM dressed in a jockey's uniform because, he explained, 'This is the only way you can get to see a producer these days.'

By virtue of their commitment to mass production, the Hollywood studios, perhaps unwittingly, were creating assets, analogous to real estate, which today account for all of their security and much of the profit: their large and ever-growing film libraries. For what those libraries would come to represent was a treasure trove which could be freshly exploited with each new development of technology: television, video, on-line services and anything else that is to come. These libraries came into being not as the result of any deep strategic thinking or visionary inspiration, but just as a by-product of the studio system itself, and of decisions made to store films on the off-chance that they could be re-released in the cinema at some future date. During the 1940s most film titles were valued on the books at $1 each. But in the decades that followed television turned them into enormous assets against which the studios could seek loans to fund expansion and new production.

Europe managed to build up very few film libraries of any comparable size, principally because the industry did not develop the kind of large, well-capitalized companies capable of producing, marketing and retaining ownership of a consistent stream of films over a number of years. What was left was a hopelessly fragmented industry, in which the ownership of the rights to those films which had been made constantly passed from one set of hands to another as companies were bought and sold in the wake of what often seemed to be perpetual financial difficulties. As a result, there was hardly any opportunity for anyone to build up a valuable library of product. With the market for audio-visual entertainment set to increase exponentially over the next few years, the value of such libraries can only increase, but few European companies are positioned to take advantage of this.

What no one could foresee was that, within twenty years, those libraries would provide Hollywood's salvation in the face of a new threat which looked likely to wipe out the movies altogether: television.

11

'Cinema is the strongest weapon'

On a poster behind Mussolini as he laid the
foundation of Cinecittà Studios, Rome

THE DESPERATE NEED to pull the American economy out of the depression of the early 1930s gave rise to an unprecedented series of initiatives on the part of the federal government in Washington. An essential component of President Roosevelt's comprehensive rescue programme, the New Deal, unveiled in 1933, was the National Recovery Administration (NRA). Among many other proposals, the NRA suspended anti-trust legislation in return for promises by industry (including the film business) to adhere to a series of voluntary codes. Though it deeply offended his sense of justice, Roosevelt believed that to allow the continued operation of some of the country's major cartels was a necessary trade-off in helping to underwrite his plans for a systematic and sustainable recovery. The symbol of the NRA, a blue eagle, appeared on flags, buildings and newspapers throughout America. But on 27 May 1935, 'Black Monday', the NRA was declared unconstitutional by the Supreme Court and the government's attitude towards cartels suddenly swung through 180 degrees, from benign acceptance to active hostility. Despite the political setback which this represented for Roosevelt, temperamentally he found this new situation much more to his liking. He had grown increasingly fretful about the way in which control of vast manufacturing sectors, such as the steel and automobile industries, was vested in a handful of giant corporations. Moreover, he felt that such sectors had shown little, if any, gratitude for the way in which he had rescued them from the depression. He launched what he called 'the first real offensive in our history' against the concentration of economic power. It was an offensive that fundamentally changed the face of Hollywood, and made the struggle for control of foreign markets more critical than ever.

The man chosen to spearhead this onslaught against the cartels was Thurman Arnold. Arnold headed the anti-trust division at the Justice Department and had been a leading figure in Roosevelt's 'brains trust', a group of youthful, hard-driving politicians whom he had gathered round him to oversee the New Deal policies. He was a flamboyant, combative figure who looked, said one observer, 'like a small town storekeeper and talks like a native Rabelais'. Arnold now ordered a dramatic increase in the number of anti-trust lawyers employed by his department, from just eighteen to over 300. This army of 'trust busters' proceeded to lay siege to some of the most illustrious giants of American industry, including General Electric, the Aluminium Company of America and the Hollywood studios.

On 20 July 1938, Arnold filed suit in the Federal District Court of Southern New York against the major studios, alleging that for almost twenty years they had 'combined and conspired with each other to unreasonably restrain . . . trade and commerce in the production, distribution and exhibition of motion pictures in the United States'. History had come full circle. The system of movie-making which had come into being as a result of the battle against Edison's Trust, was now itself being run as a cartel. What really filled the studios with fear, though, far more than the catalogue of alleged abuses, was the suggested remedy. Arnold proposed that the studios sell off their cinema chains. The moguls knew this would deal a devastating, possibly a mortal blow to the entire system.

The government wanted to tear apart the whole edifice of vertical integration of production, distribution and exhibition with which the studios had exercised power over the world's movie industry for two decades. Quite apart from anything else, the cinema chains were the most valuable financial assets the studios possessed, the collateral which effectively underwrote all their other activities. Indeed, *Variety* estimated that the 2000 cinemas owned by the five major companies were together worth over $300 million. Will Hays was immediately dispatched to warn Roosevelt that the studios would be 'wrecked at a blow' if the government won, but the President was unmoved. With the suit entitled *United States vs. Paramount Pictures Inc. et al*, the administration had effectively declared war on Hollywood.

The suit, striking as it did at the very heart of the extraordinary power exercised by the studios, detonated an explosion of panic throughout Hollywood. Pious pronouncements that the studios' sole function was to give the public the movies they wanted to see suddenly looked embarrassingly hollow. According to the government, the public were effectively being force-fed whatever the studios decided they should see, by a system whose very profitability was founded on this restriction of choice. It made a mockery of the industry's protests against the protective measures imposed by foreign governments. In the United States, it seemed, there was no need for the government to intervene to shut out independent or foreign-made pictures; the studios were doing it themselves.

The Justice Department maintained that it had launched the suit 'in response to numerous complaints by independent producers, distributors and exhibitors, and by the theater-going public'. The Roosevelt administration claimed to be acting in the name of free enterprise. As Arnold put it when the case came to trial two years later, 'If we are to maintain an industrial democracy we must stop the private seizure of power,' and he hinted that the studio bosses might face criminal charges. The suit named eight studios, twenty-four subsidiaries and 133 individual executives. *Variety* aptly summed up the outbreak of panic. 'Never before has the film industry faced a situation so potent with dangerous reactions to the millions which are invested in tangible properties, and to the several hundred thousand men and women who earn their living in the far-flung film enterprises, which American ingenuity, skill and talent have created.'

The success of preceding years now began to appear in a very different light as evidence against the studios was marshalled. Since the early 1920s, hundreds of independent exhibitors had been forced out of business by belligerent purchasing agents known as the 'dynamite gang' or the 'wrecking crew'. These agents had gradually become an integral part of the studios' smooth exercise of power, using methods which, while no longer relying on the threat of outright physical violence, were undoubtedly coercive and intimidatory. Under a system known as 'block-booking', cinema-owners were denied access to the most popular movies unless they also bought packages of less prestigious pictures they really didn't want. The government had already launched a number of probes into allegations of sharp practice, bullying and sometimes worse, but had been unable to gather hard evidence. No one, it seemed, was prepared to challenge the traditionally cosy relationship between the politicians and the moguls.

Thurman Arnold was determined to bring all that to an end. As well as singling out block-booking, he accused the studios of price fixing, shutting out independent producers and creating secret deals to ensure that cinemas which would otherwise have been in competition with one another were run to the mutual advantage of their owners rather than their customers. And the owners of these cinema chains were, of course, the studios themselves. Some 80 per cent of the 'first-run' cinemas – the city-centre showcases for new releases – were owned by or affiliated to the five largest studios. While such theatres represented less than a sixth of the total number of cinemas in the United States, in some areas they provided as much as four-fifths of all revenues. The government's argument was that the public were being obliged to pay artificially inflated prices for the right to see new movies in first-run cinemas. On top of all this, the studios produced 70 per cent of all feature films, and their distribution arms accounted for an astonishing 95 per cent of total film rentals.

Confronted with such damning evidence, it might appear that the studios would have little to offer by way of defence, but when faced with such a direct assault on their power, they fought back with everything they had. In their attempt to head off the threat of anti-trust legislation, the studios placed great emphasis on reminding the government of the critical importance of Hollywood movies as vehicles for American goods and ideas. In March 1939 Harry Warner wrote to Harry Hopkins, the Secretary of Commerce, pointing out that American films earned $150 million overseas every year, calling them 'America's world ambassador' and pointing out that 'our films fairly shriek "buy American".' The studios' opposition to the anti-trust suit became even more fierce as the possibility of another European war loomed. Later that year, just before the threatened war became a reality, Harry Warner made a trip to Europe. He wanted the President to dismiss the anti-trust suit so that the studios could concentrate on the threat to their foreign business posed by the war. He quickly realized that war could virtually wipe out European markets for the company's films. He wrote to the President pleading with him to cancel the anti-trust suit or at least to postpone it until after the conflict was resolved, indicating that the entire future of the studios might now be in jeopardy.

There is no firm evidence that Hopkins and Roosevelt were won over by Warner's arguments. But this pressure, together with the memory of the strategic importance of the film industry during the war of 1914–18, may have convinced the administration that a more conciliatory attitude towards the studios would probably be to the benefit of all. Certainly, by August 1940 *Variety* was claiming that 'administrative officers high in Government places are urging the Dept. of Justice to settle the suit against the majors at any cost', partly because 'the film industry is co-operating as an important factor in defense preparedness plans'. It seemed that, as during the Great War, the American administration was prepared to provide economic favours in return for ideological support. This softening of attitude was now reflected in a compromise suggested by the government, a series of so-called 'consent decrees', by which the studios would be able to hang on to at least some of their theatres in return for a voluntary agreement not to compel any cinema to book particular films against their wishes. To widespread amazement, Thurman Arnold accepted. The studios, flushed with victory, reneged on the deal and carried on much as before.

Soon afterwards, Arnold was promoted to appeals judge and the studios assumed they had been let off the hook. Their relief proved temporary. In 1944, Robert L. Wright, the new assistant attorney general (and son of the architect Frank Lloyd Wright), relaunched the government's anti-trust suit against the studios. With the government having been duped by the studios first time around, he was in no mood for compromise. Both sides began digging in for a battle that looked likely to last for years.

The outbreak of the Second World War added new but equally unwelcome pressure on Hollywood, threatening to draw personnel into the war effort and disrupt overseas trade. At first, the matter was treated lightly. 'In case of an air raid, go directly to RKO – they haven't had a hit in years,' as one gag had it. Jack Warner had a sign painted on the roof of his studio proclaiming 'Lockheed Thataway', alongside a large arrow pointing to the nearby aerospace factory. He removed it only when Lockheed's boss threatened to retaliate with a sign of his own pointing towards Warners' studio lot.

The Japanese attack on Pearl Harbor brought this light-hearted war of words to an abrupt end, and America's entry into the conflict, in December 1941, found Hollywood embroiled in a far more serious propaganda battle. As had been true in 1917, the outbreak of war made governments on both sides of the Atlantic suddenly aware of the power and usefulness of their film industries. In the summer of 1942, the Office of War Information in the United States formed a Bureau of Motion Pictures to goad the studios into pumping out films that would give a rousing lift to the war effort. 'Will this picture help win the war?' the studios were instructed to ask themselves as they contemplated each new production. They were to send proposed scripts to the Bureau for review, to enable government officials to monitor output and possibly even insert patriotic material of their own. Many studio executives – notably Darryl Zanuck and Jack Warner – responded eagerly to the administration's call for industry support by turning out government-backed training films. Indeed, to some in the administration, it seemed that with the anti-trust law-suits still pending, the studios were, if anything, a little over-eager to come to the aid of the government. Certainly they were quick to see the economic and political benefits that might flow from co-operation. After all, even the contracts to produce propaganda films could be relatively lucrative. That may explain why, as one government official observed, Warner was 'ahead of us in wanting to see defense incorporated into pictures'. Barney Balaban, president of Paramount, told Commerce Secretary Harry Hopkins that he wanted to arrange for Hollywood to broadcast entertainment to Latin America by shortwave. This played to the government's desire to counter German and Italian influence in the region. It also provided a means by which Hollywood could promote its films in Latin America at a time when many other foreign markets had been all but destroyed.

By 1943 the studios were under investigation again, this time by a Senate committee headed by Harry Truman, examining allegations that they had been profiteering at the expense of government-sponsored films, and had mercilessly squeezed out smaller producers seeking similar work. The committee suspected that the studios' apparent enthusiasm for the war effort was driven as much by their thirst for government film contracts as by any patriotic fervour. As a consequence, from 1943 onwards, contracts for government films were awarded through a system of competitive bidding. The studios continued to curry favour with the government by ostentatiously supporting the war effort, but this time the Washington establishment was less than convinced. They were growing tired of the industry's overt monopolistic practices, and the cynical way in which it appeared to advance its own economic interest even in the midst of war.

Despite the fact that many of its difficulties were self-inflicted, some of Hollywood's headaches were real enough. The foreign markets, which had been steadily shrinking since the mid-1930s, were now evaporating at an alarming rate. With legal investigation of their domestic business still under way, it was more important than ever that the studios ensured an uninterrupted flow of overseas revenues; revenues which, now, were not so much a bonus on the balance sheet as an essential element in their basic financial viability. With so much beyond their control, there were lean times ahead.

Spain was the first market to disappear, following the outbreak of civil war in 1936. Before long, political pressure meant that Hollywood was obliged to stop selling films to Germany and Italy. In the Far East, Japan's increasing dominance shut American films out of most of that once profitable region. Finally, the outbreak of full-scale war in continental Europe meant the end of business in France, the Benelux countries and much of Scandinavia and Eastern Europe. Only the two neutral states, Sweden and Switzerland, remained open for business as usual. In desperation, the studios made strenuous efforts to keep films flowing into markets like Australia, New Zealand and Canada. Most of all, the studios were terrified at the prospect of losing the United Kingdom – and for good reason. 'In many cases, loss of the English market would transform satisfactory profits into sizeable deficits,' observed a report by a Wall Street investment house in December 1940, claiming that one American company relied on the UK for as much as 35 per cent of its total earnings.

For Hollywood, what really mattered was that movies should keep flowing into any foreign market that remained open lest local industries equipped themselves to plug the gap, with disastrous long-term consequences for the American industry. They channelled all their energies into getting their pictures shipped overseas, whatever the price. Despite 'almost insurmountable transportation problems . . . the foreign departments have managed to get their films to their destinations, by plane, boat, railroad, street car and horseback,' observed one journalist in 1942. 'There has been no instance in any open country that a theater has been left dark due to the failure of an American picture to arrive.'

This obsession with the economic impact of the war might have seemed somewhat callous and self-serving, but for anyone familiar with Hollywood there was really nothing surprising in that. In the end, moguls like Jack Warner, Harry Cohn and Louis Mayer had always instinctively treated movies as a commodity. True, almost all of them harboured individual aspirations to cultural gentility or some sort of political influence. In times of crisis, however, that façade tended to fall away, their primal instincts came to the fore and they focused on the overriding necessity of maintaining domination of the world's film industry. Nothing was allowed to get in the way of that all-embracing imperative. When Mussolini precipitated an international crisis with his 1935 invasion of Ethiopia, a producer, asked if he had heard any late news, snapped: 'Yes. Italy just banned *Marie Antoinette*!'

In Europe the situation was very different. The abiding preoccupation of those who ran the European industry had generally been with the cultural rather than the commercial significance of cinema. This had now taken a rather more sinister turn in the two European Axis powers, Germany and Italy. The fascists revelled in their capacity to entertain and mobilize the masses. They viewed the advent of mass culture not as a threat to be deplored but as a huge political opportunity which would help generate support for their cause. Thus the qualities that made cinema anathema to the cultural conservatives of Europe were precisely those that made it attractive to the fascists.

As early as June 1933, Joseph Goebbels, Hitler's Minister of Propaganda, and Ludwig Klitzsch of Ufa had created a financial institution called the Filmkreditbank, specifically to provide capital for the expansion of the film industry. It was backed by the Deutsche Bank among others and had reserves of 10 million marks. As with the creation of Ufa in 1917, the government saw the Filmkreditbank as a means of acquiring influence over the film industry, so that it could more easily be used as a weapon of propaganda. The Nazi administration did not take a direct stake in the bank, but they packed its supervisory board with their own supporters as a means of ensuring effective control. The film business was accorded special priority since, along with the aircraft and automobile industries, it was seen as symbolizing a new era of technological progress. In 1935 at the Venice Film Festival, in a move which paralleled the creation of Film Europe a decade earlier, an organization called the International Film Chamber was launched at the instigation of the Nazis. It was intended as a body which would counter the work of the MPPDA, the trade association representing the studios, and was designed to sweep away American dominance of European film markets. The Chamber had an obvious and powerful appeal, quickly gaining members from every major European country except Britain, as well as from major film production countries such as India and Japan.

Keen though the Nazis were to build on the anti-Americanism of their neighbours, they were at least as keen to learn what they could from the Hollywood studios. While the International Film Chamber publicly campaigned to stop the import of American films, Goebbels privately invited chosen German producers to screenings of new American releases, in the hope that they could re-create Hollywood's successful chemistry in their own films. Although the liberal-democratic values that underpinned much of Hollywood's output had absolutely nothing in common with the racist totalitarianism of Nazi philosophy, Hitler's regime had few qualms about seeking to emulate the popular success of the American industry. It appealed directly to their unqualified enthusiasm for the revolutionary powers of technology. For Hitler's regime, shameless imitation of the American film industry, far from undermining indigenous culture, was seen instead as a celebration of the new society they themselves were claiming to build.

As in the Great War, German movies were treated as a potentially powerful instrument for spreading a rigidly controlled message of national strength and pride. 'Films constitute one of the most modern and scientific means of influencing the masses. Therefore, a Government must not neglect them,' declared Goebbels in 1933. Hitler, like Stalin and Churchill, regularly watched movies, screening films as after-dinner entertainment, and enjoyed socializing with actors and directors. He was particularly passionate about American movies; in 1943 when the Germans confiscated a consignment of recent releases from a Swedish liner, including Walt Disney's *Bambi*, they were immediately rushed to the Führer for a private viewing.

In 1937 the Nazis had begun secretly buying shares in the country's leading film concerns, including Ufa, the firm which had dominated the country's industry during the 1920s. By 1942, the entire industry had been consolidated into one giant, state-owned combine, Ufa-Film, known as Ufi. It was said that Goebbels now personally scrutinized every film, newsreel and 'short' prior to its release in Germany.

In Italy, Mussolini's government was a similarly enthusiastic supporter of cinema as the quintessentially modern medium. As in so much else, where the Nazis imposed rigorous state control, the Italian fascists were content to see private firms flourishing alongside the wholly state-owned sector. In recognition of the immense social and economic importance accorded to cinema, Mussolini laid the foundation stone of the huge Cinecittà studio complex in Rome in 1937, posing before a giant slogan which read '*La cinematografia è l'arma più forte*', ('Cinema is the strongest weapon'). The studio, built with state finance, provided Italian film-makers with the most sophisticated technical equipment in Europe. The man who oversaw its construction, Luigi Freddi, a former head of the fascist party's propaganda office, was the moving force behind the government's involvement in the industry. With Freddi's enthusiastic backing, the domestic industry flourished. Attendances surged despite an American boycott of the Italian market, and production soared to unprecedented levels to meet the increased demand. Ironically, though, in 1937, just as the American majors were pulling back from Italy, Mussolini's son Vittorio was in Hollywood negotiating a deal with independent producer Hal Roach to shoot Italian operas.

Mussolini could even claim that his influence had spread to Hollywood. In 1933 Harry Cohn, head of Columbia Pictures, was invited to Rome to meet Il Duce to celebrate the release of a Columbia documentary entitled *Mussolini Speaks*. Cohn was much taken with Mussolini's imperial style, and especially by the way he sat on a raised platform at one end of a vast office. 'By the time I arrived at his desk, I was whipped,' admitted Cohn. On his return to Hollywood, he rebuilt his entire office suite in emulation of the baronial style favoured by Mussolini and a photograph of the dictator was given pride of place on his desk.

No movies produced in the Axis countries of Europe were allowed into the American market. Only the British industry remained entirely free to export its products across the Atlantic, even though securing distribution with major studios remained difficult. To the surprise of many, some of these films proved extremely popular with American audiences so, once again, apparently undaunted by their disastrous experiences during the late 1930s, British producers became dazzled by the idea of snatching a large chunk of the American market from right under Hollywood's nose.

The British invasion began in earnest in 1942. Sidney Bernstein, founder of the British cinema chain Granada, had persuaded the major Hollywood studios to agree to distribute one British feature a year to help bolster support for the British war effort among the American people. Bernstein's scheme soon scored its first big hit: Noël Coward and David Lean's war picture *In Which We Serve* became the most successful British film in the United States for years. This, together with a string of other movies like *This Happy Breed* and *The Way to the Stars*, seduced many British producers into believing that the American market was there for the taking.

If any one man could be said to symbolize this unexpected renaissance of the British industry, it was the thoroughly unlikely figure of J. Arthur Rank, a Methodist flour-miller from the north of England. He was described by one American journalist as 'a burly grandfather-clock of a man who at fifty-nine is tick-tock solemn and sure. He stands 6ft 1in, with his limp brown hair stuck down flat, and bulks a solid 15 stone'. A more cynical observer reckoned that 'his large face reveals so little of brilliance or even shrewdness that many people feel his bland expression is a mask'. In person, he combined the bluntness characteristic of his native Yorkshire with a self-consciousness betrayed by his regular habit of jingling coins in his pockets while he talked. If his manner was suggestive of a prudent, small-town businessman, that impression only seemed to be confirmed by his conservative social habits. A teetotaller and devout Methodist he would interrupt meetings with American studio executives to fire off postcards to his Sunday School pupils. He requested that none of the stars of his films should ever be shown with a drink in their hands. He even confided to fellow British producer Michael Balcon that he prayed for him every night. As one journalist put it, 'there's Methodism in his madness'.

In contrast to the flamboyant Alexander Korda, Rank's suburban pragmatism made him seem rather pinched and austere. The actor James Mason claimed that 'Arthur Rank is the worst thing that has happened to the British film industry . . . He has no apparent talent for cinemas or showmanship'. That was not entirely true for, despite his puritanical façade, Rank proved an enthusiastic backer of director Michael Powell, whose films revelled in an emotional extravagance utterly alien to the prevailing British convention of dour realism.

Rank had become involved with the film industry almost by accident. Looking for a way to enliven his Sunday School lectures, he had hit upon the idea of buying a film projector to show religious films. Oblivious to the antipathy which many of his fellow Methodists felt towards cinema on principle, Rank became treasurer of the newly formed Religious Film Society which soon afterwards expanded its activities into film production.

Backed by his already substantial wealth, his ambitions grew. He teamed up with Lady Yule, the eccentric widow of a Calcutta jute tycoon, and together they launched into commercial film production. She helped him build Pinewood Studios on the site of a rambling country house outside London. Shortly afterwards, when

Alexander Korda was overwhelmed by financial difficulties, Rank acquired control of Denham too.

Having built his production base, Rank soon expanded into distribution and then went on to buy a 25 per cent stake in Universal when Carl Laemmle was forced to sell in the wake of a financial crisis. In autumn 1941 he snapped up two British cinema circuits, one of them the prestigious Odeon chain which was up for sale following the death of its founder, Oscar Deutsch. The son of a Hungarian scrap-metal merchant, Deutsch was an enthusiastic proponent of brand names and, so he claimed, had named his chain Odeon not only because of the classical reference to Greek theatre but also because it was an acronym for Oscar Deutsch Entertains Our Nation.

Rank now controlled a fully integrated movie operation. With two of the country's three leading cinema chains, two of its major studios and a web of associated production and distribution interests, it matched the size and scope of the major Hollywood studios. He also controlled a stable of independent producers, of whom the most controversial was a high-spending Italian émigré Filippo Del Giudice who, in order to impress, was partial to quoting from Juvenal: *Duas tantum res anxius optat, panem et circenses* ('The anxious longings of the people were for two things only – bread and circuses'). Rank even founded a short-lived animation subsidiary, G-B Animation, an ill-starred effort to challenge Walt Disney with such long-forgotten characters as Ginger Nutt and Ferdy the Fox.

By 1944, Rank's organization had assets of over $200 million, making it more valuable than MGM. Clearly it was time for him to take on the majors. He created his own worldwide distribution company Eagle-Lion and, over the next two years, bought up stakes in cinema chains in Canada and Australia, even building a luxury cinema in central Cairo. With soaring confidence he predicted that 'before long . . . Britain would be turning out pictures that would make more money in the American market than Hollywood'.

The extraordinary success of Rank's empire was made even more remarkable by the nature of the man himself. His involvement in cinema was motivated by something much more personal than a crude desire for profit or market share. He was fighting a crusade in the quiet conviction that cinema audiences could be won over to decency and morality rather than what he saw as the cynical and aggressive values espoused by so many Hollywood films. 'Quality tells in the end,' he would inform the sceptics who told him that he would never conquer the American market.

Whether it was a belief in film as high art, as an ideological vehicle, or as an instrument of moral education, it was this willingness to sacrifice economic imperatives for what they felt to be more exalted ideals which principally distinguished those who ran the European film business from their American counterparts. Of course, in their unrelenting quest to build the world's most powerful movie industry, the American moguls had been driven by a wide variety of motives, worthy and unworthy, as well as the more obvious desire to acquire wealth and power. In the end they knew it always came back to money. It was money which enabled them to acquire cultural gentility – or at least the trappings of such gentility – not, as the Europeans seemed to believe, the other way around.

Perhaps it was precisely because a man like Rank already *had* money and power that he could afford the luxury of other motivations. The American moguls had made the long journey to their Bel Air mansions from the slums of the Lower East Side. They were genuinely driven men. Whatever else happened to them they were determined to have the priceless sense of security that came from wealth and power. That was why, when it came to fighting for overseas markets, they found it so easy to put aside all the personal hatreds, the internecine rivalries and the quarrels over talent. Cinema might aspire to become an art-form or be a wonderful vehicle for the dissemination of political and ethical values but, in the end, it was a business like any other. They knew that without the twin pillars of investment and profit, the entire edifice would crumble. For the men who built and ran Hollywood, this was the truth which underpinned all their extravagant ambition. It was a lesson well remembered by the conglomerates which, from the 1960s onwards, would start acquiring control of the Hollywood studios. The Europeans, on the other hand, never really seemed prepared to address these obvious and simple truths. In the 1970s and '80s they would pay an increasingly heavy price for their intransigence.

Meantime, the end of the Second World War was to present the Hollywood moguls with new opportunities to demonstrate their unyielding dedication to the pursuit of profit as they sought to re-establish their control over those markets which just a few years earlier seemed as if they might be lost for ever.

12

'If I am compelled to
choose between Bogart and
bacon, I am bound to
choose bacon'

ROBERT BOOTHBY MP, 1947

AT THE END OF the Second World War, the American economy
was in buoyant shape, in stark contrast to the shattered and indebted
nations of Europe. The American film industry was once again in
an aggressively expansionist mood, unlikely to take kindly to any
challenges to its power. It had survived the loss of most of its overseas markets by tenaciously fighting to keep movies pouring into
those few overseas territories – the United Kingdom, Australia
and New Zealand – which had remained open to it. Now it had
to set about the task of regaining its dominance in the rest of the
world.

Despite the threat of continuing investigation by the Justice
Department, the immediate prospects for the industry looked bright.
There was especially good news on the home front. Millions of
people had been called up for military service or had been requisi-
tioned to work in munitions factories. The return of the military
personnel to their families unleashed a massive pent-up demand for

leisure activities of every kind. Weekly cinema attendances in the US hit an all-time high of 98 million in 1946, a record which would still stand fifty years later. Movie shares were 'sail[ing] the financial stratosphere,' reported *Business Week* in May of that year. 'Many stock-traders . . . believe that movie-going has become an ingrained habit that won't easily be dislodged, especially when stimulated by shorter hours of work and today's higher incomes and savings.' Not for the first time, Wall Street was mistaken.

Abroad, the Allied victory reopened the markets which had been denied to the American distributors since the late 1930s. In its determination to recover its lost territories, Hollywood formed the Motion Picture Export Association (MPEA), an overseas arm designed to complement the activities of the newly renamed Motion Picture Association of America (MPAA). The MPEA was estab-lished as a legal cartel under the provisions of the Webb-Pomerene Export Trade Act of 1918, which enabled it to claim exemption from anti-trust laws as an organization exclusively engaged in overseas trade. The success of the industry in restoring its pre-war position was startling. Already by 1946, one paper was reporting that foreign sales were earning $175 million a year for the studios up from a pre-war average of $135 million.

Eric Johnston had by now succeeded Will Hays as head of the MPAA, which was fighting a vigorous campaign against the government's anti-trust suit on behalf of its member companies. Johnston, a one-time door-to-door salesman of vacuum cleaners, had most recently served as president of the US Chamber of Commerce. Like Hays, he was drawn from traditional American stock. One producer recalled him as a 'lean, voluble [man] . . . given to quick, chopping chirps of laughter that seldom seemed genuine'. An ardent anti-communist, he promised among other things to 'wash the Red stain out of the industry's fabric'. However extreme his views might come to seem, the administration approved of Johnston and in the early 1950s he would briefly serve as a special envoy to the President in the Near East. Indeed, the ties between the MPAA and govern-ment were as close as ever; Frank McCarthy, MPEA representative in Paris from 1946 until 1949, had been General Marshall's former aide as well as an assistant Secretary of State.

Soon after the defeat of Germany, the United States War Department invited a team of Hollywood producers, including Harry Cohn, Jack Warner and Darryl Zanuck, to tour Europe. They visited various parts of Germany, including the concentration camp at Dachau, as well as France, Italy and the United Kingdom. On their return they issued a statement noting that the movies could help to 'cleanse the minds, change the attitudes and ultimately win the co-operation of the German people'. Films would enable American service personnel to act as 'front-line fighters in the first phase of psychological warfare', making them 'well armed intellectually for a war of ideas'.

As the trade barriers created by war came down, they were rapidly succeeded by new obstacles. To the Europeans' pre-war concern about the threat to their national cultural integrity was now added a more immediate and fundamental issue. The European economies, with their fragile currencies and acute foreign exchange problems, could not afford to ignore the huge flow of scarce dollars being consumed by nothing more significant than the demands of their own people for Saturday night entertainment. Wartime alliances had done little to stem the clamour about the corrosive effects of American movies. If anything, the massive American contribution to winning the war in Europe, which was on a quite different scale to their involvement in the Great War a quarter of a century earlier, had simply sharpened the awareness among the Allies of the extent to which they seemed to be, in every way, dependent on the Americans.

At any rate, within less than two years of Johnston's appointment, the American movie industry found itself embroiled in two ferocious transatlantic trade battles. The first involved France. Under orders from Germany, the Vichy government had banned Hollywood imports, but immediately after the liberation the US Army's Psychological Warfare Division brought over 400 prints of the latest American movies and handed them to American companies for distribution throughout the country. The films were tremendously popular and de Gaulle's government quickly moved to restore some of the import restrictions. While such moves may have commanded support among French producers, they were denounced by the exhibitors who had flourished as a direct result of the popularity of Hollywood movies. 'If you wish to stab America in the back, you shall not do it in our cinemas,' the president of the exhibitors' association told one government minister in August 1945. The cinema exhibitors were correct in their perception that wider issues were at stake. Once again, the economic interests of the film production community seemed to have converged with the interests of a political and cultural elite, resulting in a policy which paid scant heed to the tastes of the public at large, or the concerns of distributors and exhibitors.

In 1946 the USA negotiated a comprehensive aid agreement with the government, intended to help the French economy back on its feet. Aware of just how desperately the French needed their help, the Americans used the negotiations to extract valuable trade concessions in what they regarded as key industrial sectors, including film. The chief French negotiator, the former socialist prime minister Léon Blum, was regarded as a dangerous radical by some in the American press, and one American newspaper reported news of the aid package under the decidedly double-edged headline, 'When Karl Marx calls on Santa Claus'. In some respects, Santa Claus was getting at least as much as he was giving away. The agreement replaced fairly stringent import quotas with a far less punitive system which simply guaranteed that French films would play for a certain number of weeks per year at each cinema. The French had little choice but to give way. The Blum–Byrnes Agreement was signed on 28 May 1946. The French war debt was wiped out and they were granted $650 million in aid.

For much of the French film industry, the agreement was little short of a disaster. France was swamped with American films. By the end of 1947 it was estimated that over half the country's film studios had been forced to suspend production activities. According to some reports, more than 75 per cent of the workforce were unemployed. A Committee for the Defence of French Cinema was formed. Apparently unconcerned by these dire consequences, French audiences flocked to see Humphrey Bogart in *The Maltese Falcon*, Otto Preminger's classic thriller *Laura*, and dozens of other films shut out during the long years of war.

Thousands of cinema professionals and their supporters poured on to the streets of Paris in protest marches, although it is probably true that these had at least as much to do with a more widespread and resurgent anti-Americanism than they did with the immediate ramifications of the agreement itself. As had happened in many parts of Europe in the 1930s, cinema found itself entangled in a much broader cultural and political battle. The increasingly influential Communist Party, the PCF, played a vital role in orchestrating such antagonism. In April 1948, Maurice Thorez, the general secretary, told party militants that American films 'literally poison the souls of our children, young people, young girls, who are to be turned into the docile slaves of the American multi-millionaires, rather than French men and women attached to the moral and intellectual values which have been the grandeur and glory of our nation'. Only with the signing of a new accord between France and America – reintroducing a limited measure of import quotas – in September 1948 did the fury start to subside.

A similar storm erupted in France over another icon of the American way of life: Coca-Cola. Just as overseas sales of Hollywood movies were justified on the grounds that they helped to spread the gospel of liberal democracy and free enterprise, so it was claimed by the president of Coca-Cola that every bottle contained 'the essence of capitalism'. Both were stigmatized not so much for what they were, as for what they represented. Both were seen as symbols of a noisy and aggressively modern society which were foisted on an unwilling public through a barrage of advertising. *Le Monde* denounced the 'Red delivery trucks and walls covered with signs, placards and advertisements'. Eventually, in 1949, the National Assembly passed a bill authorizing the Ministry of Health to ban the drink.

The hostilities stirred up in France by the Blum–Byrnes Agreement helped spur the creation in October 1946 of the Centre National de la Cinématographie (CNC), a public body charged with overseeing the financial and regulatory affairs of the industry. Two years later, the government introduced the Loi d'aide temporaire à l'industrie cinématographique, which in essence used a tax on cinema admissions and on the distribution of films (whatever their nationality) to create a fund for backing future French productions.

Following in the wake of the earlier nationalization of companies such as Renault, Air France and La Banque de France, the government now took rather more modest steps to secure control of some aspects of the film industry. For the moment, that interest was driven almost entirely by economic rather than cultural concerns and the CNC was placed under the aegis of the Ministry of Industry and Commerce. Despite this clear emphasis, the creation of a centralized state body to police the film industry seemed, finally, like a logical and long overdue response to the perceived crisis in France's cultural identity brought about by Hollywood movies during the first half of the 1930s. The long arm of *dirigisme* – the familiar tool used by the French state to manage its key industries – had at last made itself felt in the movie business. In fact, the film industry was beginning to be treated as something like an official expression of French culture.

Meanwhile, the American movie industry moved swiftly to recapture other markets. In Italy, they experienced little resistance, for the government dismantled much of the protectionist legislation which had kept Hollywood at bay. Although the Italian neo-realist movement, led by directors like Roberto Rossellini, Vittorio de Sica and Luchino Visconti, achieved critical acclaim, for the most part their films flopped at the box office. In February 1949, hundreds of film industry employees thronged the streets of Rome calling for new legislation to protect the Italian industry. In response, the politician with responsibility for cinema (and a future prime minister), Guilio Andreotti, passed a law establishing import restrictions and providing loans for production companies. This had some success in rejuvenating the commercial fortunes of the local industry, but Andreotti loathed the neo-realist movies with what he saw as their harping on poverty and misery. '*Meno stracci, più gambe*' ('Fewer rags, more legs') became his crude and simple slogan as he manoeuvred to divert money from neo-realism into more mainstream, populist movies, such as those starring Totò, the phenomenally popular comic who was capable of turning out as many as six farces in a single year. In any case, the rightist Christian Democratic Party to which Andreotti belonged was far more in tune with the commercial opportunism of the Hollywood studios than were French politicians. Increasing co-operation with Hollywood cleared the way for a huge boom in American production in Italy during the early 1960s.

In Great Britain, the American movie industry found itself caught up in a struggle for control of the nation's screens, which was even more bitter than the battle in France. By 1947, $70 million a year was pouring out of Britain and into the coffers of the Hollywood studios, more than double its pre-war level. For a government facing a balance of payments crisis and obliged to slash the import of food and other essentials because of a shortage of hard currency, this was politically unacceptable. Summing up the sentiments of many politicians, the Scottish MP Robert Boothby announced: 'If I am compelled to choose between Bogart and bacon I am bound to choose bacon at the present time.' Although film accounted for only 4 per cent of the nation's dollar expenditure, the government decided, on 6 August 1947, to impose an *ad valorem* customs duty of 75 per cent on all imported films. This swingeing tax, known as the Dalton Duty after the Chancellor of the Exchequer who imposed it, meant that overseas distributors could retain only 25 per cent of their British earnings. The move was a devastating blow to Hollywood. It struck at the very heart of its largest export market, and retaliation was inevitable and swift. The day after the plans for the duty were unveiled, the American companies announced an indefinite boycott of the British market. A few days later posters appeared across London, apparently advertising a new Paramount film, but with no hint of where the film was to be shown; indeed, there was no explicit reference to a movie at all. It simply showed a picture of an eagle and, in bold letters, the title *Unconquered*. A full-scale trade war had erupted.

The British government was stunned by the reaction. With American films occupying 80 per cent of British screen time, they realized that the boycott would rapidly precipitate an acute product shortage and a major public outcry. Could the British exhibition industry survive in the absence of American movies? While some pinned their hopes on a domestic production boom to fill the void, others feared that the entire industry faced extinction.

The optimists assumed that their salvation lay with J. Arthur Rank who, newly buoyed by the huge success of Laurence Olivier's *Henry V* in the American market, now had a chance to seize control of the British market. Hoping to see off the Americans for good, Rank unveiled an astonishingly ambitious scheme to produce sixty features a year through his Odeon Theatres group. Although the company managed to make only half that number of pictures in 1948, even that was a remarkable achievement.

Rank may have calculated that the boycott would last long enough to give him an unassailable dominance over the nation's screens, but in March 1948 the boycott suddenly ended. Harold Wilson, the newly appointed President of the Board of Trade, had managed to hammer out a compromise with Eric Johnston and Allen Dulles (later head of the CIA) which allowed the studios to remit at least $17 million a year back home. The negotiations were acrimonious. At one point members of the MPAA proposed pasting extracts from Wilson's speeches all over cinemas in the United States as hard evidence that he was intending to create a nationalized, socialist film industry. Wilson had been desperate to reach an agreement because many cinemas had simply opted to re-run old American movies, thus incurring continuing dollar debts and exacerbating the currency crisis. As he put it: 'We were paying out not 17 million but 50 million dollars for the privilege of seeing *Hellzapoppin'* for the third time and *Ben Hur* for the twenty-third.' An avalanche of unreleased American movies now poured into the British market, completely burying Rank's films. Odeon chalked up losses of over £3 million on its recently expanded production activities.

In the wake of the catastrophe, British film studios became almost wholly reliant on American companies using their blocked currency to finance their own production activity in Britain. It was a situation that would become sadly familiar in the decades to come. It was as if nothing had been learned from the events of the late 1930's which had brought the British industry so close to collapse. Once again, the modest success of a handful of British movies in the United States had created the illusion that, if only it could start producing enough big movies, it might seize a significant slice of the American domestic market. The assumption was that somehow British films, many of them based on great literary classics (for example, *Henry V*, *Great Expectations* and *Hamlet*), were intrinsically superior to the output of Hollywood. If only the money was available to make them on a bigger scale, surely American audiences would flock to see them in preference to the dross churned out by the West Coast studios? This 'prestige experiment', as it came to be known, would continue to beguile some British producers right through until the 1980s.

What the dreamers failed to see was that a successful film industry, like that of America, was not built on the back of a few hit movies, but was dependent on a complex and long-established system in which consistent profits were generated by control of distribution and cinemas. The Americans saw their industry as a totality, in which the glamorous business of production was crucially underpinned by ownership of other aspects of the marketing chain. Even Rank, the most powerful figure in the British business, had no stake in an American cinema chain (since Universal did not own theatres) and his control over distribution in the United States was severely limited.

Moreover, for all the agitation of producers and politicians about American domination of the British market, the embargo revealed the extent to which the British industry was reliant on Hollywood merely to remain in business. Cinema-owners, and even some independent distributors, could not hope to survive without access to American films. Even the producers, who saw their single most feared competitor removed from the market at a stroke, could not ignore the fact that, left to themselves, they had no chance at all of satisfying their own audiences.

There were, however, some positive outcomes to the Dalton Duty and the subsequent boycott. In March 1949 Harold Wilson created the National Film Finance Corporation, capitalized at £5 million, to subsidize the production of British films. This was followed, in August 1950, by the Eady Levy, a tax on all cinema tickets named after Sir Wilfred Eady, the Treasury official who implemented the scheme. Under an arrangement which was initially voluntary, part of the proceeds of Eady were paid to a new British Film Production Fund, which provided finance to producers wanting to make British films (including American companies who backed films shot in the UK using British talent and technicians). Harold Wilson always claimed that this idea, which was to become the mainstay of British film production finance for almost forty years, had come to him while he was out walking on holiday in Cornwall. Payments were made to producers on 'a purely automatic and objective basis', linked to the box-office gross achieved by their previous film. Within a few years the Eady scheme had proved itself a huge success, resulting in a sustained production boom that lasted throughout the 1950s, and attracted scores of American producers to the UK.

There can be little doubt that, without the Eady Levy, the British production industry might have collapsed altogether, swamped by the sheer power of Hollywood. Because of its 'automatic' nature, the effect of Eady was quite different from that of an otherwise similar subsidy scheme introduced in France. Where the French scheme deliberately sought to promote films of artistic merit, Eady was simply a mechanism to get the industry back on its feet and its backers had no interest in aesthetic considerations. As much as anything, that underlined the essential difference between the British industry and those on the continent: the British had never developed the kind of fervent passion for 'art' films as was shown in France. British policy shared the French objective of preventing the Americans from seizing control of the local film industry, but whereas the French preoccupation was to nurture a distinctively national cinema, British producers always believed that if they could only get the formula right, they could best the Americans at their own game. In that sense the goal of British policy was to create something that looked and felt very much like Hollywood. This was reinforced by the obvious bond of a common language and by a long history of practical co-operation. Since the mid-1930s the American studios had been increasingly active in financing movie production in the United Kingdom. Together with the extensive interests that American companies held in British cinemas and film studios, this ultimately created something of a sense of an underlying affinity between the two industries, something which surfaced more and more once memories of the boycott began to fade. Even if they didn't much care to think about the cultural consequences of it all, many in the British film business in the post-war years would increasingly acknowledge that they had a lot more in common with the Americans than they did with their continental counterparts. That feeling was strengthened by periodic surges in American investment in Britain, particularly during the 1960s.

However unequal the relationship between Hollywood and the British industry, the benefits were, at least to some extent, mutual. Elsewhere in Europe, American policy after the Second World War tended to be brutally simple. In the mid-1940s, the newly installed Truman administration was well aware that, for all their rhetorical posturing about promoting the American way of life, the underlying concern of the studios was to regain their dominance of the international marketplace. The government therefore offered the industry a quid pro quo. '[I]n the post-war period, the Department desires to co-operate fully in the protection of American motion pictures abroad,' proclaimed a 1944 Department of State circular addressed to the industry. 'It expects in return that the industry will co-operate wholeheartedly with the government with a view to ensuring that the pictures distributed abroad will reflect credit on the good name and reputation of this country and its institutions.'

The American administration saw movies as a crucial weapon in the battle to re-educate the peoples of Germany, Italy and elsewhere in the virtues of democracy in general and American democracy in particular, a propaganda offensive which, in the words of one American senator, was simply 'a world-wide Marshall plan in the field of ideas'. A Hollywood producer put it even more plainly: 'Donald Duck as World Diplomat!'

From the point of view of the Hollywood majors, the informal pact suggested by the government was hardly an onerous one. American films had almost never engaged in social or political controversy, either explicitly or implicitly. After all, their strength was built precisely on their ability to play to apparently universal concerns rather than narrowly domestic issues.

In Germany and Italy especially, the ideological case made by the government for encouraging the distribution of Hollywood movies effectively allowed the American industry to re-establish its dominance. In Italy, Admiral Stone, the chairman of the Film Commission which oversaw the development of the industry, unambiguously stated that the country no longer needed a film industry and that it should not be allowed to create one. In Germany, the American film companies had found that their earnings were blocked by foreign exchange restrictions and could not be changed into dollars. The studios developed all sorts of extraordinary ruses in an effort to repatriate their revenues. In one case, a Hollywood studio acquired a sunken tanker off the coast of France, paid for its salvage in francs, and then sold it for dollars to an American oil company. It was hardly an efficient way of doing business.

In 1948, the Truman administration came to the rescue, creating the Informational Media Guaranty Program (IMG) under which the government paid dollars for soft foreign currencies earned by American media firms, providing that the material presented a favourable picture of American life. In effect, the United States Information Agency directly subsidized American distributors in countries such as Germany, Poland and Yugoslavia so long as the local currencies remained blocked. As a result, Germany remained saturated with Hollywood product throughout the 1950s and well into the 1960s. By 1957, the German market, which only twelve years earlier had been completely closed to the American industry, would be its third largest export market after Canada and the United Kingdom.

One national film industry that did expand after the war was that of Hong Kong. Many Chinese workers at Shanghai's Huaying Studios had moved to Hong Kong after the war, fearful of being denounced as traitors because they had worked at the studio during the Japanese occupation of the city. The civil war in China further fuelled this emigration. Hong Kong eventually found itself the centre of the Mandarin-language cinema. Soon a thriving, dynamic industry was operating, led by the Shaw brothers, members of a wealthy family who had originally started in films in Shanghai in 1920. With Run Run Shaw at its head, the firm operated a studio system even more streamlined than that of Hollywood in the 1930s, and many of its stars were 'eager young teenagers recruited from its own drama school . . . who are housed in the studio's own dormitories where they are lectured on the importance of moral rectitude'.

The foreign successes of the American industry became even more important as it found itself under new pressures at home. In 1947, as part of its search for 'subversives', the House Un-American Activities Committee (HUAC), now chaired by the Republican J. Parnell Thomas, a pudgy one-time insurance broker from New Jersey, turned its attention to Hollywood. Thomas led what writer Ben Hecht described as a band of 'mental hobgoblins' on a witch-hunt to root out supposed communist sympathizers, focusing initially on ten alleged radicals who became known as the Hollywood Ten. The MPAA's Eric Johnston joined this hunt with enthusiasm, ensuring that the Ten were duly sacked and that the studios agreed never to knowingly employ communists, but, overall, the HUAC hearings had little direct impact on the economic organization of the business. One of the underlying factors behind the investigation was almost certainly the fear that closet communists might effectively undermine the 'Marshall plan' of ideas.

However, there were also many reservations about the idea of Hollywood movies acting as ambassadors for the American way of life. Back in the late 1920s, some government officials had questioned the propriety of providing support for the export of movies, particularly given the somewhat tainted picture of American life which they presented. This debate was reignited after the war. In 1950, there was a stormy exchange in the *Saturday Review of Literature* when its editor Norman Cousins argued that 'the movies do not accurately reflect America and Americans ... we [are not] predominantly a nation of murderers, gangsters, idlers, deadbeats, touts, tarts, and swindlers, as Hollywood would have us appear ... And while we like to hold our own in discussion or debate, it isn't true that the only rebuttal is a sock on the jaw.' In reply, the MPAA's Eric Johnston ridiculed the idea that anyone might be influenced by the image of America peddled by the movies: 'Of course they don't. No more than Americans believe all Italians steal bicycles because they saw the picture *Bicycle Thieves*.'

Indeed, during the immediate post-war period, there was a degree of tension between the US government and Hollywood. Some officials felt that the film industry pursued its economic interests in a selfishly aggressive manner that was insufficiently sensitive to the real needs of reconstruction in Europe. While the Commerce Department was generally supportive of the industry, the State Department had reservations about the way that the industry was trying to wield its power abroad. In Germany in particular, there were disagreements between the MPEA and the military government which unsuccessfully pushed for the introduction of formal quotas to assist its objective of rebuilding the German movie industry. In the end, though, what was remarkable was how little such problems affected Hollywood's post-war drive to recapture foreign markets. For in truth, the industry's position in Europe was now more entrenched than ever.

13

The Star-spangled
Octopus

WHILE IT SURGED AHEAD in foreign markets, Hollywood suffered a shattering blow at home, one that struck at the very heart of the studio system, and seemed set to sweep away the entire edifice, radically transforming the shape of the industry. For the moguls it was a blow every bit as traumatic as those massive earth tremors which periodically rocked the foundations of their opulent mansions. On 3 May 1948, in a judgment handed down by Justice William O. Douglas, the 'Nine Old Men' of the Supreme Court finally ruled that the major studios must sell their cinema chains, bringing to an end eight years of bitter legal wrangling, punctuated by an apparently endless series of supplementary complaints, abortive compromises and even FBI investigations. It was a stunning decision. Justice Douglas found that the studios had conspired to fix cinema admission prices and had used block-booking as a means of forcing small exhibitors to take all of their produce: '[S]o far as the five majors are concerned . . . the conspiracy had monopoly in exhibition as one of its goals.' 'We've been hit by a baseball bat,' was the way one defence counsel saw it a few hours after the verdict was announced. Another opined that it heralded 'a revolution in the industry'.

The so-called 'Paramount decree' did indeed threaten the studios with dire economic consequences. While it may have been the star-laden business of production that stole the headlines, in 1948 investment in cinemas accounted for 93 per cent of *all* investment in the American movie industry, while production accounted for a mere 5 per cent. Looked at from that perspective, the studios were more akin to real-estate companies than creators of entertainment, with the cinemas serving as collateral which underwrote their activities in production and distribution. The Paramount decree not only effectively destroyed one of the pillars of the vertically integrated structure which had sustained the studios since the early 1920s, it also carried a powerful symbolic charge. By forcing them to sell their cinema chains, the decree cut them off physically and emotionally from the business in which moguls like Laemmle, Zukor and Mayer had started their careers forty years earlier. 'The day of the big studios is finished,' said one agent in the early 1950s. 'Their costs are too high and there isn't any way to get those costs down – really get them down – without tearing them apart and reorganizing from the ground up.' As had happened before (and was to happen again), it seemed that Hollywood itself might be about to pass into history. 'Hollywood's like Egypt,' said producer David Selznick a couple of years later, 'full of crumbling pyramids. It'll never come back. It'll just keep on crumbling until finally the wind blows the last studio prop across the sands.'

A journalist with *Life* magazine was not being entirely facetious when he observed in 1951: 'Looking ahead . . . it is easy to imagine the decaying hulks of the studios standing empty in the misty sun, the props scattered and broken, the swimming pools weed-grown . . . and here and there among the ruins, the bleaching bones of some former $4000 a week executive who, incredulous to the last, died miserably of malnutrition of body and ego.' Some exhibitors seeking compensation for past misdemeanours now filed suit against the studios for treble damages. At one point, total claims were alleged to amount to $600 million, enough to bankrupt all the studios.

It was the biggest shock to the industry since the collapse of Edison's Trust. In fact, it carried uncanny echoes of that earlier event. Once again, it signalled a shift of power within the industry, away from the entrenched values of the old guard towards a new style established by a group of feisty, entrepreneurial independents who would in their own way revolutionize the business. And it presaged another moment, still twenty-five years in the future, when the so-called Fin-Syn rules would transform the business once more, helping rejuvenate the studios, and ushering in a new era of powerful media conglomerates.

It was some time before all the studios had sold their cinemas. Warner Brothers did not sell its theatres until 1951, and the last of the studios to divest itself of its cinemas, Loews, did not do so until 1954. Even before these deals were completed, however, the studio system had begun to dissolve. Faced with the demand to sell their cinemas, the studios could no longer afford the high fixed cost of keeping a permanent roster of stars, directors, writers and other personnel on their payroll. In the late 1940s and early 1950s, contracts with talent were renegotiated, and many major stars and directors left the studios to set up their own independent production companies. As a result, the whole system began to unravel. The majors simply hired talent on a picture-by-picture basis, while the smaller studios such as Columbia and Universal, which had never owned cinemas, now began to challenge the pre-eminence of MGM and others.

In 1951, Warner Brothers signed a deal to finance and distribute films by an independent producer, Fidelity Pictures. What was startling about the deal was that it gave Warner no control over the development and production of the films. As for the pictures made by Warner Brothers itself, when a film had finished shooting, all those involved with it were off the payroll. One day during the 1950s, Jack Warner stormed into the dining hall at Warner Brothers and began jabbing his finger and screaming at his contract players as they sat eating their lunches. 'I can do without you! And you! And you! I can do without you!' Making his way round the room he eventually spied Jerry Wald, easily the most important producer on the lot and responsible for making at least half of the company's films. 'I can *almost* do without you,' he yelled. He wasn't joking. In March 1953, Warner announced plans to shut down studio production for ninety days. MGM was the last studio to lay off its contract personnel in the mid-1950s, the final signal that the era of the studio system was over.

The studios survived 'divorcement' (the obligatory separation of the cinema chains) because they continued to maintain control over distribution. Indeed, the leading distributors were forced to become far more aggressive in their negotiations with the cinema chains, several of which were now controlled by independent companies run by executives who had formerly performed the same role for the studios themselves. The amount remitted to them by the cinemas actually began to increase. Had the government ordered the studios to sell their distribution arms, the situation would have been far more serious. And because distribution was a more predictable and profitable business than production, it was inevitable that it was the distribution subsidiaries which would be expected to make up the shortfall in revenue. Since distribution operated on a worldwide basis, it became imperative to wring every last dime from a film's foreign release. At the same time, the newly independent cinema chains now had much greater freedom to choose where their films came from. This would eventually help to open the way for an influx of foreign films into the American market during the early 1960s.

The studios' difficulties were compounded by a sudden and totally unexpected drop in cinema attendances. Even the industry's natural predilection for hyperbole could not disguise the problems. As a *Variety* headline mockingly put it in April 1947: 'Film Biz Dips to Only Terrific From Used-To-Be Sensational'. By 1951, admissions had plummeted to the levels of twenty years earlier. And this despite a soaring population, and a national income which in the interim had tripled. Many young parents, it seemed, either did not want, or could not afford to go to the cinema, and the accelerating flight of middle-class America to the suburbs meant that city centre theatres became increasingly remote from their audiences. The nation's suburbs were growing fifteen times faster than the cities they encircled. The Lost Audience was seen as those between the ages of thirty and sixty, who had comprised 40 per cent of all cinema-goers a few years earlier. All this only served to make foreign earnings more important than ever. In the early 1940s, the foreign market accounted for only 20 to 25 per cent of film rentals received by distributors. By 1956, Arnold Picker, head of foreign distribution at United Artists, told the Senate Small Business Committee that the foreign market 'accounts for anywhere from 40 to 50 per cent of the total business done'.

Even before the Paramount decree, there were increasing signs of strain within the studio system. The stars, aware that *they* were the real draw of the movies, had begun to chafe against the onerous contract system which had made them little better than highly paid wage slaves throughout the 1930s. It was time for them to break free. With the help of a young agent, Lew Wasserman of MCA, they began to do so, ushering in a new era in the age of celebrity.

Born in Cleveland in 1913, Wasserman had become a cinema usher after leaving school. He rose to become manager of a nightclub and, at the age of twenty-three, was offered a job by MCA boss Jules Stein, handling the company's advertising and publicity. 'I think I'll take the job because there is a great future in it,' Wasserman said to his bride of six months. 'What's so great about it?' she asked. 'Stein is not a young man,' retorted Wasserman.

As with the lawyers and accountants, agents had been a feature of the Hollywood landscape since the early days of the studios but, under the onerous conditions of the contract system, they, along with virtually everyone else in Hollywood, had been obliged to dance to the tune of the studio chiefs. The most powerful agency in Hollywood was William Morris, headed by Abe Lastfogel who had worked for the company since he was fourteen, but it was increasingly challenged by MCA as Jules Stein and Lew Wasserman pushed ever harder to snap up stars all over Hollywood.

The role of the movie talent agent had originally been imported from the theatre business. Someone, after all, had to represent the stars in their negotiations with the studios, however unyielding the latter might appear. The first talent agent really to flourish by specializing in movies was Myron Selznick, brother of David and son of Lewis J., an early independent producer nicknamed 'C.O.D.' because of the straightforward way in which he was prepared to deliver roles to starlets in return for sessions on his casting couch. A pugnacious man at the best of times, Myron detested producers and was not averse to using his fists if he didn't like the way a deal was going, especially when he had had a drink or two. He was convinced his father had been forced into bankruptcy by the venom-ous behaviour of the studio bosses, and lost no opportunity to avenge the old man. Rumour had it that, returning home after closing a particularly tough and lucrative deal, he had yelled: 'Remember what those bastards did to Dad? They paid more than a million dollars for it today.'

In 1927 as Selznick closed his first deal – an extraordinarily lucrative one for Lewis Milestone at RKO – he spat out, 'It isn't enough.' That became his mantra, the phrase that was ritually invoked no matter how rich the deal, and for many of those who dealt with agents, that summed it all up. Agents were universally loathed as 'flesh-peddlers', and probably deserved the appellation. It was said that they always refused to drink tomato juice because they were so tired of hearing the quip, 'I see you're drinking your client's blood.'

MCA (the Music Corporation of America) became far and away the most powerful agency of all. The company had been created by Dr Jules Stein, a qualified eye specialist from South Bend, Indiana. While completing his internship at medical school in Chicago, he had teamed up with a friend, Billy Goodheart, to create a show band and to act as agents for fellow bandleaders. This subsidiary enterprise proved so successful that Stein stopped playing himself and was soon booking bands all over Chicago, while maintaining his day job as an eye surgeon. 'I had a young assistant, and he'd ring me up about bookings while I had a patient in the chair,' Stein recalled. 'I'd be saying "Can you read this, can you read this?" and all the while I'd be talking on the phone.' In the 1920s, jazz clubs were springing up everywhere, and MCA soon flourished.

For all Stein's shrewdness, and his fantastic capacity for hard work, much of MCA's magic could be imputed to the ruthlessness with which the company pursued both talent and venues. When Stein started out the band business was, at best, anarchic in its organization. He imposed order on the marketplace, partly through his obsession with what he called 'exclusives', and partly by 'packaging'. An exclusive meant that a venue agreed only to use talent booked through MCA. Packaging was an extension of the same concept: a hotel would be offered an all-in entertainment package for a whole year, everything from the band to the hat-check girl and swizzle-sticks, on condition that they dealt solely with MCA. In a variation on the same concept, the company offered entire radio shows – stars, producers, gag-men, musical directors and so on – to the broadcast networks. These were early precursors of the kind of packaging deal which would become commonplace in the movie industry some fifty years later.

While Stein's hard-headed business style helped propel MCA to the position of world's number one agency, Billy Goodheart's eccentric style of business helped to woo the talent. He sat in a raised chair looking down on his visitors, with a stopwatch on his desk. When a visitor arrived asking for 'just two minutes of your time', he would make a great point of setting the watch and, at the exact second, would gesture towards it and bark, 'Sorry, but you see your time is up.'

Stein's ferocity was probably a necessity in Chicago at a time when gangsters threatened to move in on every branch of the entertainment business. It also brought him rapid success. By the 1930s MCA was the largest band agency of them all and, towards the end of the decade, Stein decided to move into Hollywood. To spearhead the campaign he chose Lew R. Wasserman.

A tall, somewhat austere man, Wasserman weighed his words carefully, rarely gestured and almost never raised his voice. His insistence on discretion became the established house style at MCA. Nothing was set down on paper except when absolutely essential. Executives were instructed not to leave messages on their desks overnight, in case they were seen by rivals within the company. According to one source, recognizing that such qualities might be useful in a politician, President Johnson apparently offered him the post of commerce secretary but Wasserman declined.

MCA's first real coup in Hollywood came when Wasserman signed Bette Davis, who had specialized in playing feisty, resolutely independent women in a world dominated by men. Davis was married to long-time sweetheart Harman Nelson, whose best friend was a frail young man by the name of Eddie 'The Killer' Linsk. Learning that The Killer could use a job, MCA put him on the payroll. The Killer then helped them woo the volatile Davis. With Davis aboard, MCA was suddenly a company to be reckoned with. By the mid-1940s, it had over 700 clients including Gregory Peck, Ginger Rogers, Jimmy Stewart, Betty Grable and, some way down the list, Ronald Reagan. Armed with this galaxy of talent, its tentacles extended into virtually every aspect of showbusiness, so much so that one journalist dubbed it 'the star-spangled Octopus'.

Stein and Wasserman drove their staff hard. One journalist described a staff meeting as full of 'executives screaming at one another, pounding their fists and kicking chairs aside'. Stein meanwhile sat to one side, smiling and quietly making the final decisions. In return, MCA salaries were lavish and expense accounts were generous.

What distinguished Stein from almost everyone else in showbusiness was his singular distaste for personal publicity. Not for him the grandiloquent public gestures of a Mayer, a Zukor or a Korda. He rarely went to Hollywood's endless round of star-encrusted parties; that sort of disagreeable task was left to his clients. He filled his leisure time with work. 'I don't live on the golf course,' Stein curtly told one interviewer, 'I would rather deal with corporate tax problems and the intricacies of corporate structure. I relax that way.' An impenetrable veil of secrecy surrounded the company's business affairs. In 1946 estimates of its revenues ranged from $20 million to $100 million. The otherwise omniscient Wall Street handbook, Dun and Bradstreet, was utterly unable to come up with a credit rating for the Octopus. He was fiercely protective of his clients too. Stein, said Wasserman many years later, looked on his clients as a doctor would look on his patients.

In 1946 Stein, now aged fifty, decided to step back from the gruelling task of running MCA's daily operations, and appointed himself company chairman. Wasserman was named his successor as president. Aged just thirty-three, Wasserman instantly became one of the most powerful executives in showbusiness. The year before, MCA had taken another huge leap forward when it snapped up Leland Hayward's agency, Hayward Deverich, in a deal which brought into the fold a further slew of top-flight stars such as Fred Astaire, Joseph Cotten, Gene Kelly and Henry Fonda. Wasserman inherited his boss's dislike of publicity and much else besides. As Stein put it, he became 'the student who surpassed the teacher'. Or as Nick Schenck, the president of Loews, MGM's parent company, confessed: 'I never see him after twelve noon, I'm too slow to take him on after that.'

Most significantly, Wasserman was the bridge between the old Hollywood and the new. Like the moguls, he was ruthless in his drive to make MCA the biggest, most powerful player of them all. Unlike his predecessors, Wasserman brought a sense of order and financial discipline to a community that had long been ruled by mercurial showmen with little flair, and even less taste, for hard numbers. The moguls had operated principally on instinct, not to mention whim. Many of them proved disastrous at handling corporate finance. Wasserman had the instinct – it was said that he could guess how much a movie would gross just by looking at the first hour's receipts – but in him it was allied to a hard-nosed understanding of figures and corporate order. When MCA later bought Universal, he would spend hours poring over spreadsheets, checking payments of fees due to actors for repeat screenings of their work.

As with members, so too with sartorial discipline. MCA's employees were known to some as 'the black-suited Mafia', because of the company dress code, rigorously enforced by Wasserman, which deemed that all executives should wear black suits, narrow black ties and white shirts. 'Here come the penguins,' someone once joked when a squadron of MCA's agents arrived for a meeting. One day one of the employees working in the MCA mail-room wore a pink shirt into the office. He ran into Wasserman who told him, 'That's a nice shirt ... but I don't think it's fitting for an MCA employee.' Six months later, the mail boy took a chance and dared to wear the shirt once more. 'Didn't I tell you not to wear that shirt any more,' erupted Wasserman when the boy had the misfortune to run into him in the lift.

While MCA showed the way – itself becoming one of the first such conglomerates – none of those running these corporate empires would ever be able to match Wasserman's instincts. So it was that gradually the wire leading to Harry Cohn's ass came to be replaced by the humble slide-rule.

The power exercised by the studios over the stars had been waning for some time. As early as 1936 Bette Davis, weary of feeling like 'an assembly-line actress' declined one of many unattractive parts offered to her by Warner Brothers and fled to Great Britain, where she felt she would no longer be constrained by her contract. Warners successfully sued in the British courts to enforce the contract, but the fact that Davis had dared to challenge the studios encouraged others.

The next person to attempt to throw off her shackles was Olivia de Havilland, who had shone in *Gone with the Wind*. She was also under contract to Warners and had made *Gone with the Wind* only when Jack Warner had reluctantly agreed to loan her to David Selznick. Even after the huge success of the film, Warner insisted on her performing insubstantial roles in equally insubstantial movies, while her sister, Joan Fontaine, played the title role in Selznick's adaptation of *Jane Eyre*. De Havilland had been repeatedly suspended for refusing roles. Now her patience had run out. She refused the next film Warners offered her – which had the unpromising title of *The Animal Kingdom* – and was once again suspended. It was Wasserman who offered her the advice which helped her find a way out of her predicament. 'It was his opinion that the Hollywood custom of suspending actors and actresses ... and then adding the suspension time to their contracts was illegal,' observed Ronald Reagan. 'Fiery Olivia rose to this like a trout (a pretty trout) to a fly.' Worried that she could be tied up with Warners for the rest of her career, she sued to get out of her contract. After lengthy hearings, and an appeal by Jack Warner, de Havilland won her case in the California Supreme Court in autumn 1944. She was free, and the contract system had suffered a mortal blow.

The deal that finally broke the system apart was not consummated for another seven years, but once again Lew Wasserman was at the heart of it. This time it involved James Stewart. Stewart had been under contract to MGM before the Second World War. After military service he returned to Hollywood, only to find MGM determined to hold him for the remainder of his term. In 1950, released at last, he sought a way to avoid the astronomical tax rates – up to 90 per cent – levied on high earners which had been introduced by the Revenue Act of 1941. One way of avoiding such tax was to create profit-sharing deals in a system pioneered by Wasserman and William Paley, head of CBS, under which the salaries of entertainers were regarded as part of the film, and taxed as capital gains at a rate of just 25 per cent. Wasserman did something far more radical. He negotiated a deal for Stewart for a western entitled *Winchester 73*, to be made by Universal, whereby he would forgo a salary in return for a share of its profits, at a figure variously estimated to be anywhere between 10 and 50 per cent of the total. This income would be spread over the life of the film, and so would greatly ease Stewart's tax burden. This proved invaluable in the emerging age of television when a film might still be earning money on television years after it had been made. *Winchester 73* struck box-office gold, and Stewart's earnings reached $600,000, making him the highest paid star in Hollywood with an income way above the level commanded even by top earners like Clark Gable. Suddenly, stars all over town were clamouring for percentage deals.

By tying an actor's earnings to the actual value of the film, Wasserman created a mechanism which acknowledged the star as the real selling point of a movie. That, after all, was what the studios had been doing throughout the 1930s – using their top talent as brand names to sell movies to a public increasingly fascinated by celebrity and all the razzmatazz that went with it. The deal Wasserman engineered, and those that followed, had a momentous impact on the future of the business. It began to move the locus of power away from the studio to the star and, by natural extension, to the agent. All this was entirely fitting for the growing culture of celebrity in American life, something which would receive a terrific boost as the nation found itself swept by the new medium of television.

Buffeted by the combined impact of the Paramount decree and the decline in audiences, the studios were, in most cases, only too willing to embrace such deals. At the chintzy Hollywood restaurant Romanoff's, wrote one journalist in the 1950s, 'the straight talk about picture-making – who might star, who might script, who might direct – is laced with conversations from a different planet – conversations about charge-offs, depreciation situations, 27 and a half per cent depletion allowances, exploration expensing, spin-offs, Australian sheep ranches and Swiss corporations.'

In the days when the studio system had been at its zenith, lawyers and accountants had largely been studio functionaries, ensconced back East in New York, scrutinizing the fine print of deal-memos and endlessly crunching box-office numbers. The studio bosses were allowed to run their private fiefdoms out in Los Angeles largely on the basis of their own instincts. Now with the switch away from the studio system to independent production and profit participation, the 'suits' began to acquire an increasingly powerful voice in determining what films were made, how and at what cost. This trend would intensify throughout the 1960s and '70s, leading

Billy Wilder to reflect: 'In the old days we shot pictures, now 80 per cent of it is shooting deals.'

While the Paramount decree was instrumental in tearing apart the studio system, the deal between Stewart and Universal merely seemed like an inevitable consequence of the destruction of that system. But its impact was eventually greater than that. While the studios would eventually claw back an element of control over the exhibition business, they would never regain their hold over the stars. In the 1970s and throughout the 1980s and '90s, the stars, and their agents, became the undisputed sovereigns of the movie business. They alone determined the basis on which they were hired.

What Wasserman also brought to the table was a quite unparalleled grasp of the international structure of the business. Even while they aggressively expanded their empires around the world, almost none of Hollywood's founding fathers had shown any real enthusiasm for trying to understand the minutiae of foreign business. Wasserman was different. Quotas, tax incentives, currency restrictions; he had them all stored inside his head. That was one of the reasons why he, above all studio chiefs, would come to have the single greatest influence in determining the workings of the MPAA in Washington. That and his political connections; behind closed doors, Wasserman assiduously cultivated a network of political contacts second to none. He or one of his aides had direct access to just about every politician that mattered to Hollywood – Republican or Democratic – from the President downwards. For all his self-effacing manner and modesty, Wasserman gradually began to acquire a level of power and respect which exceeded that of the previous generation of moguls.

As the television era dawned, and many of his competitors took fright, it was Wasserman who led the fight back. It was a struggle which would finally determine whether Hollywood could be saved from the savagely destructive forces put in train by Thurman Arnold, and whether it could keep its grip on the world's movie industry in the face of a newly revitalized European industry. So began the battle to keep what David Selznick had described as the pyramids of Hollywood from crumbling into the sand.

14

Sleeping with the Enemy:
Television

ON 30 APRIL 1939, IMAGES of President Roosevelt's speech at the New York's World's Fair were simultaneously beamed out to a couple of hundred television sets in the city from NBC's transmitter on the Empire State Building. It marked the birth of commercial television in the United States. Over the next few decades, the medium would transform popular consciousness and the basic nature of American society. In Hollywood, the news was greeted with apprehension. Many believed that the reign of the movies as the most popular and influential mass medium in the country was over.

David Sarnoff, co-founder of RKO, was the father of commercial television in the United States. Like so many of the men who created the first Hollywood studios, he had arrived in America from Eastern Europe, and he shared their apparently limitless appetite for power. His first job was as a radio operator for American Marconi, the company created by the inventor of radio, Guglielmo Marconi. In 1912, aged twenty-one, he had picked up faint signals from far out in the Atlantic: 'S.S. Titanic ran into iceberg. Sinking fast.' For seventy-two hours he was the only link with the disaster, achieving an odd sort of fame throughout the world. As Marconi expanded, so did Sarnoff's ambition, and he rose through the executive ranks. In 1919, the company was absorbed by RCA and he became general manager of the merged enterprise. By 1930 he was president. Soon the firm not only controlled the nation's largest radio network – the National Broadcasting Company (NBC) – it has also become one of the biggest corporations in America. Sarnoff now embarked on a frantic struggle to beat off his rival, William Paley, head of the Columbia Broadcasting System (CBS), and to become the first man to launch a commercial television service in America. With its transmissions from the World's Fair in April 1939, NBC had won the battle.

By 1941 NBC and CBS were both running regular services. The schedule consisted mainly of comedies, plays and cookery shows – the latter confined almost exclusively to salad-mixing because the heat of the studio lights made serious cooking an unbearable prospect. By the end of that year, only a few thousand television sets had been sold, mostly in New York, but after the hiatus caused by the outbreak of war, sales rocketed. By 1948, they had passed the million mark; two years later the figure reached 12 million; and by 1954, as the price of sets tumbled from $600 to less than half that amount, the figure soared again to almost 38 million. The national networks controlled by NBC and CBS dominated the market. The smaller ABC radio network also diversified into television after the war, and the DuMont Television Network made a brief challenge before fading into obscurity.

To the Hollywood studios, television was a serious threat. At first they looked for ways to take control of it for themselves. In the mid-1940s, Warner Brothers, Twentieth Century-Fox and Paramount, determined to build networks of their own, attempted to start or acquire television stations across the country. The Federal Communications Commission, regulator of the American radio and television industry, alarmed by the Justice Department's allegations that the studios had violated anti-trust laws, refused to consider any such move until the case was resolved. When the Supreme Court came out against the studios in 1948, their ambition to create television networks of their own was effectively killed and a quarter of a century would pass before they dared to try again.

Meantime, the movies were in trouble. Some blamed the Paramount decree. Some blamed it on the quality of the movies themselves. As the writer Herman Mankiewicz acidly put it: 'if we show the pictures in the street, maybe it will drive the audience into the theaters.' Most blamed television. 'Television essentially is nothing but movies in the home,' wrote one journalist in 1948, and that was a prospect that struck fear into the hearts of even the toughest studio bosses. Jack Warner decreed that no television set should be shown in any movie made by his company. MGM went further and banned the use of the word 'television' in any of its scripts. Several studios refused to allow their contract players to appear in television productions. 'I wish for television only a tortured and miserable death,' growled one Washington cinema-owner in 1952. It was already a forlorn hope.

Television became a scapegoat, a convenient target for the studio bosses, shocked and bewildered that the empires to which they had devoted their lives were about to be destroyed. Aggressive, impetuous men like Harry Cohn, Jack Warner and Darryl Zanuck were utterly uninterested in any analysis of demographic and social change. They wanted a straightforward fight with an enemy they could see – and the enemy was television. 'The movies are in trouble?' snarled Fox production chief Zanuck in 1951. 'Television is in trouble ten times worse! They've got 25,000 separate productions a year to put on. They chew up talent, stories, people, ideas. They've already run out of material. They're already repeating themselves every night, every week. And actors hate it. It's torture for them. They'd infinitely rather work on film.' As it turned out, Zanuck was right. Television ended up needing film almost as badly as film needed television.

The major studios deployed every trick they could to persuade the public that the movies were bigger, more exciting and more colourful than television would ever be. They introduced Cinerama and CinemaScope, both of which used vast curved screens and stereophonic sound. They tried 3-D. Although some Scope films were popular, and widescreen is now standard, 3-D quickly flopped. Some of the studios were reduced to advertising movies 'You Can See Without Glasses', and found themselves stuck with a mountain of useless, unwanted spectacles.

The appeal of a cinema based purely on sensation seemed to have faded with the Lumière brothers. The audience wanted story and character, not gimmicks. The moguls had fundamentally mis-understood the forces which were threatening to tear their business apart. The troubles of the movie industry had begun well before sales of television sets took off. Attendances had started tumbling in 1947, when only a few thousand sets had been sold, and fell sharply over the next couple of years even though sales of televisions remained modest.

A series of social upheavals which transformed the shape of American society probably damaged the movies far more than tele-vision. The baby boom, which saw the population increase by almost 30 per cent between 1947 and 1960, meant that large numbers of parents preferred to stay home in the evenings looking after their young families. Many fled to the newly-built suburbs to escape run-down city centres and had little desire to make the long trek back to downtown cinemas for their evening's entertainment. They preferred to spend their money on increasingly affordable cars, furni-ture and washing machines rather than on movies. The leisure pur-suits which sprang into being as a result of the flight to the suburbs were largely oriented around the home and the family; the drop in cinema attendances had far more to do with mundane things like the growing popularity of gardening, suburban barbecues, bowling and the do-it-yourself movement than it did with television.

Still, as Darryl Zanuck had observed, television desperately needed more product. None of the networks could afford to put out all their programming live, and feature films seemed to provide the obvious solution. The major studios, terrified that they would be inviting their own destruction, refused to open their vaults to television. When ABC president Robert Kitner tried to persuade them to supply original programming to the networks, he was flatly refused. 'Harry Cohn was the rudest of them all,' recalled Kitner. 'I remember he said something like, "You dumb son of a bitch, you won't get any of my stars, you won't get any people – *you* can't make films! People want the companionship of the theater, they want their movies the way they *are* – not on TV!" The others were a little more polite, but just as negative.' Without any clear idea how to price material for television, many film executives believed that the networks, entirely reliant on advertising for their income, would never be able to afford feature films.

What really troubled the studio bosses was that television had developed outside their control. Since the early 1920s, they had grown accustomed to the idea that they were the undisputed kings of the moving picture industry. It was their instincts, their tastes, even their whims which determined the shape and the nature of the American movie industry, therefore helping to define the character of the overall entertainment business, not just in America but in many overseas countries, too. Now a group of upstarts, led by David Sarnoff and William Paley, had struck at the very roots of their authority by creating moving images which could be fed directly into people's homes. Men like Cohn, Mayer and Warner had devoted their lives to building up systems of control over the world they inhabited. The studio system was coherent, and there was no doubt as to who was in charge. As Harry Cohn put it when asked why he was so hard on those who worked for him: 'I am the king here. Whoever eats my bread sings my song.' The remorseless rise of television, following hard on the heels of the Paramount case and the disintegration of the contract system, only intensified the fear among the studio bosses that their days were numbered.

While the major studios refused to deal with television there were plenty of smaller players who had a much more positive, or possibly more pragmatic, view of the future. 'If the movies try to lick television, it's the movies that will catch the licking,' predicted long-time independent Samuel Goldwyn in 1949. 'The two industries can quite naturally join forces for their own profit . . . motion picture people now need to discuss how to fit movies into the new world made possible by television.'

For the independents, the prospect of doing business with the television networks came as a relief after years of unequal struggle against the arrogant complacency of the big studios. The great attraction of filmed drama was that it could make far more money for its producers than live programming ever could. Under a practice which came to be known as syndication, a producer would sell the re-run rights to the network and to groups of local stations. Films 'could be shown again, and again, and again in syndication', remembered one television director. 'After you saw a live television show, when it was over, it was over.'

From the late 1940s onwards, independent producers began setting up shop in Hollywood, all along the stretch of lower Sunset Boulevard known as Poverty Row, and began to crank out cut-price films for television, sticking mainly to a diet of westerns and crime pictures. Tempted by the huge profits which could be made, many superannuated or frustrated Hollywood performers also made the switch to independent television production. In the early 1950s two former RKO contract players, Lucille Ball and her husband Desi Arnaz, a Cuban band leader, formed Desilu Productions to make a show called *I Love Lucy* in which they would both star. They took the concept to CBS but the network wasn't interested in putting up any money. 'So we borrowed $5000,' recalled Ball, 'and became owners of our own idea.' It was a gamble which would have a fabulous pay-off. CBS eventually agreed to buy it, and when the show premièred on the network in September 1951 it became an instant hit. In the 1952–53 season, an average of 67 per cent of all those who owned television sets in the United States were watching every episode. By 1955, Desilu was turning out hundreds of hours of programming every year, far more than any Hollywood studio.

Just as the independents could see past the immediate threat of television to the possibility of a new kind of business opportunity, so too could another group of Hollywood players – the agents. In 1949 MCA executive Karl Kramer suggested creating a television show to be called *Stars Over Hollywood*. 'We all thought he was nuts,' recalled one MCA agent. But Lew Wasserman thought the concept well worth developing. Kramer persuaded the Armour meat-packing company to come in as a sponsor, and MCA formed a television subsidiary called Revue Productions. In 1952 the Screen Actors Guild, headed by Ronald Reagan, granted MCA a waiver, releasing it from the prohibition which prevented agents acting as producers. This rule had been put in place specifically to prevent agencies from packing productions with their own clients, but because Reagan himself was an MCA client, the deal inevitably aroused great suspicion. Reagan was later questioned about the matter before a grand jury but no proof of corrupt action ever emerged. In any case, in return for the waiver Reagan had secured a striking concession. MCA agreed to make additional payments – known as residuals – to actors whenever a television show in which they had appeared was repeated. 'Every writer, actor and director in this town ought to get down and kiss Ronald Reagan's feet,' one MCA agent later claimed, 'because the man got them television residuals. That has paid for most of the houses in the Valley.'

The man who did more than anyone else to revolutionize the relationship between the studios and television was Walt Disney. Like the men who had built the major studios, Disney had started from nothing. Unlike them, he was an Anglo-Saxon Protestant, raised in the Midwest, with a strong streak of prejudice concealed beneath his avuncular public persona. He had arrived in Hollywood in 1923 with $40, a suitcase full of pens and pencils, and not even a change of clothes. A decade later, he employed hundreds of people at his animation factory and was spending a million dollars a year turning out twenty short animated films which he called 'Silly Symphonies'. In 1937, he released his first feature-length film, *Snow White and the Seven Dwarfs*, which became a huge box-office hit.

Determined to protect himself against the vicissitudes of the movie business, he drew up a long-term plan to transform Walt

Disney Productions into a vast, diversified entertainment company that would sell all kinds of merchandise – everything from clothing to comic books and toys – based on Disney characters. Disney christened this approach 'total merchandising'. The cornerstone of his plan was to be a gigantic amusement park at Anaheim on the outskirts of Los Angeles, called Disneyland. It would feature spectacular rides and attractions, all modelled on Disney films and Disney characters. The park would promote the company's movies, and the movies would generate business for the park. As the plan evolved in the wake of the war, Disney was quick to realize that television could play an important part in this grand design. He struck a deal with Leonard Goldenson, head of the ABC network, to make an hour-long, weekly show called *Disneyland*. It was to be presented by Disney himself and would promote both the amusement park and his films. In October 1954, 'with a bang that blew Wednesday night to kingdom come for the two major networks', Disney burst into television. His show shot into the top ten, and instantly became the most successful series ABC had ever aired. One early episode featured a behind-the-scenes look at the making of Disney's own film 20,000 *Leagues Under the Sea*. A week later the film was released, and quickly became his highest-earning movie of all time, demonstrating beyond all doubt the effectiveness of his ambitious 'total merchandising' strategy.

The success of *Disneyland* fundamentally changed the relationship between Hollywood and television. Suddenly the studios realized that television could be made to work for them rather than against them. Television became a weapon in the battle for survival; it was a powerful new advertising tool with which they could promote their films and stars. Leonard Goldenson of ABC approached Jack Warner to suggest a programme-making deal. Warner demurred, telling Goldenson, 'I made those quickies thirty years ago, and I'm not going to make 'em again.' When Goldenson assured him that he would give him a slot in each show to promote his films, Warner finally changed his mind. The fees they would earn for making the shows were irrelevant. The explicit purpose of the deal was, in the words of Jack Warner, 'to secure advertisements through television'. Warner's decision had a certain inevitability about it. Increasing pressure had been put on him to reconsider his attitude to the new medium. His son-in-law William Orr, a Warner executive, had returned from a trip back east describing a forest of antennas running for miles across the roofs of Chicago's slums, and fretting that Warner Brothers might be left out in the cold.

So, in September 1955, the studio launched its first television series, *Warner Brothers Presents*, on the ABC network. The Warner series was built around adaptations of old Warner feature films such as *Kings Row* and *Cheyenne*, but it also included a section designed to promote forthcoming Warner movies. The shows were incredibly cheap; 'If you see more than two characters, it's stock footage,' as someone put it. Viewers switched off in droves. MGM and Twentieth Century-Fox had launched shows of their own. They too flopped.

The psychological barrier had been breached and the resistance of the studio chiefs to working with television had finally been broken. Warner and his peers knew that the good old days were gone for ever. Battered at the box office, worn down by their fight with the Justice Department, their battles with creative talent and haggling with agents, they threw caution to the wind, and finally embraced television.

Once again, Jack Warner led the way. In 1956, despite the failure of *Warner Brothers Presents*, he negotiated a new deal with ABC, under which the studio agreed to produce short 'telefilms' for the network. The other studio bosses gradually fell in behind him. Their programming met with mixed results, but by 1959 *Variety* reported that the major studios were making almost 40 per cent of the telefilms shown on the major networks.

As the studios launched into producing shows for television, their stubborn refusal to sell feature films to the networks began to look increasingly absurd. And the more their financial troubles intensified, the more absurd it seemed. In earlier years, some companies had sold the negatives of their films for as little as a dollar, simply to be able to write them out of the inventory. They were bought by small independent distributors, who hawked them round distant rural theatres or run-down urban cinemas, known as 'grind houses', usually located amid the slums where tickets sold for 10 cents. For the most part the studios had stored the negatives of films because they believed that at some future date they would be able to re-release them in the cinema. By the early 1950s, the more prescient members of the Hollywood community began to realize that, with the television networks desperate for programmes to fill their schedules, the studios were sitting on a potential goldmine. 'If I had millions to bet with in this business,' observed one such investment advisor in 1951, 'I wouldn't buy studios or contracts or stories or theaters. I'd buy negatives, just negatives.'

In the summer of 1955, RKO, which under the mercurial management of billionaire Howard Hughes had retreated from production altogether, sold its pre-1948 library to a company called General Teleradio. Now the floodgates burst. Within eighteen months, Warners, Paramount and Twentieth Century-Fox had cut deals for their pre-1948 catalogues generating millions of dollars in revenue. The unions representing creative talent were demanding additional payments, or 'residuals', for the television transmission of any films made since 1948, temporarily blocking any deals involving pictures made after that date. Once again, it was Warners that led the way among the major studios, selling a package of 750 films featuring such major stars as Bette Davis, Humphrey Bogart and Jimmy Cagney. The deal was done with a syndicate led by the Canadian financier Louis (Uncle Lou) Chesler. The deal involved an outright sale of the films, so that ownership of the negatives passed from the studio to the purchasing company. At an average price of $28,000 per picture, considered low even at the time, it soon came to seem like an extraordinary bargain.

The studios quickly realized that the outright sale of old movies, which meant losing control of the negatives, was not the best way to maximize the value of their assets. Television's voracious appetite for material meant that the value of TV rights to movies climbed steadily. Within three years of their sale to Chesler, the Warner accountants reckoned they had underpriced their films by about $35 million. Even the deals in which the studios licensed someone else to handle the rights on their behalf would, in time, seem extremely short-sighted. For as the studios should have known from long experience, it was in distribution that the real money was to be made.

Columbia and MGM made rather more intelligent arrangements than had Warners. They licensed their films directly to television stations, thus retaining all the profits as well as the underlying rights to the movies themselves. These deals were renewed every few years and, as television boomed, so the profits skyrocketed. As the television market continued to expand, and then spread out into video and cable television, these early licensing arrangements provided a useful and enduring model.

During their fight with the Justice Department over 'divorcement', the studios had argued that they would collapse without the income from theatres. Now the world had been turned upside down. It looked as if the income from television would rescue the studios, while the cinemas were left to pay the price. Even though they drastically increased the percentage of revenues they retained from the ticket sales in the first few weeks of release – up to 90 per cent in some cases – the exhibitors were struggling. By 1956 *Variety* was reporting: 'Wall Street, with its ears to the ground . . . is investing in production but it considers exhibition an increasingly poor risk.'

By 1958 almost 4000 movies had been either sold or leased to television, netting over $220 million for the major studios. Even so, the new alliance between Hollywood and the networks was far from being universally endorsed. Clark Gable complained bitterly that as a result of sales to television, 'When my current features go out to theaters I will find I am definitely in competition with myself.' Cinema exhibitors, too, were far from happy. They deluged the studios with angry letters and telegrams. When the Academy of Motion Picture Arts and Sciences sold the rights to the Oscar awards show to television, allowing it to be screened on a Saturday, the biggest movie-going night of the week, the editor of *Daily Variety* suggested that 'Hollywood return the art of hara-kiri to the Japanese'.

If anyone needed proof of the value of movies to television, it came in 1956 when MGM leased the rights to *The Wizard of Oz* to CBS, in a deal which enabled the network to provide the first complete screening of a feature film during peak viewing hours. When Dorothy and the Tin Man flickered into view on the evening of 3 November 1956, more than 40 million people tuned in to watch, only a few million less than the total weekly attendance at the nation's cinemas. No one in the film industry could ever again dismiss the significance of television. By 1958 it was estimated that 80 per cent of America's movie-viewing now took place not in the cinema but at home, in front of the TV.

By the end of the 1950s, Jack Warner, who barely a decade earlier had been a passionately sworn enemy of television, was prepared to admit that 'television has been a very healthy influence on the motion picture industry. It's the ninth wonder of the world'. Other former enemies had also done a volte-face. '[W]ithout our television sales (plus the income from the laboratory and from foreign theatres) we would be in the red,' confessed Fox boss Spyros Skouras in 1957. From 1960 onwards the studios began unloading their post-1948 libraries to television, after the Screen Actors Guild finally struck a deal with the studios which guaranteed healthy residual payments.

For the Hollywood studios, the income from television production and the television screenings of their films helped cushion the losses that arose from declining audiences and the enforced sale of cinema circuits. What made the television deals particularly attractive was that they represented almost pure profit. The films had been paid for in the 1930s and '40s, and the costs had long since been amortized. The cash that flowed in from television, therefore, was an entirely unexpected dividend.

It was yet another unanticipated benefit to stem from the decision of decades earlier to bring together production and distribution within one company, since it was control over distribution which had enabled and encouraged the studios to hang on to the rights of their films in the first place. In the decades that followed, as new technologies evolved and new means of delivering films to the viewers were developed, those dividends of ownership became greater and greater. By the mid-1990s, one library, owned by Turner Entertainment and incorporating classic titles from MGM, Warner Brothers and RKO, was generating $200 million a year in revenues. Hollywood's international television sales were worth $3 billion annually, growing at a rate of 25 per cent each year.

The men who ran Hollywood had learnt some valuable lessons from their brawl with television. 'We went into television when the movie business could have taken over the television business,' MCA's Jules Stein later admitted. 'But those men were too sure of themselves. They were too smug.' As a result, they let television get away from them and ended up having to sell to a market that they didn't entirely control. They would never make the same mistake again. When video and pay television appeared in the 1970s, they embraced them with enthusiasm from the start. Hollywood's attitude to television had been completely turned around in the space of a decade. In 1950 television was the hated enemy, the demon that would end up destroying the American movie industry; by 1960, it was being hailed by many as its saviour.

It took longer for television to become established in Europe. In most countries, sales of television sets did not really take off until the mid-1950s. 'There's little or no TV competition in outlying European communities,' observed one studio boss in 1956. 'People over there still love our stars and movies and are eager to see them above anything else.' As domestic cinema audiences plummeted, so the foreign market became ever more important. 'Without the more than 50 percent earnings which accrue in foreign markets, there could be no American motion picture industry,' admitted the vice-president of the MPAA in 1961.

Many of those foreign markets were in just as much turmoil as Hollywood itself. In America, the first instincts of most of the studio chiefs was to gain a foothold in television. They became hostile only when they were frustrated in their efforts. In Europe, on the other hand, antagonism prevailed from the outset. As far back as

1935, a year before the BBC even began television broadcasts, two British film trade associations banned their members from selling movies to television, convinced it 'might be regarded as a serious menace'.

In the early 1950s, the European Cinema Owners Union, representing members across the continent, passed a resolution urging film producers to hang on to the TV rights to their films, and so effectively block all sales to television. The call was taken up most enthusiastically in Britain. In 1958, at the instigation of Sidney Bernstein of Granada, the Film Industry Defence Organization (FIDO) was formed. Using funds raised by charging a small levy on box-office receipts, FIDO paid film-makers a modest sum to sign a covenant under which they agreed not to sell their films to television. Any such sales, they argued, would be 'injurious' to their members. It was hardly surprising that representatives of Britain's biggest cinema circuits, Rank and Associated British Picture Corporation, were among the most vocal supporters of FIDO. They had a lot to lose from television. What made this development even more surprising was that Sidney Bernstein's Granada, besides operating a chain of cinemas, was also the owner of one of Britain's first commercial television stations, which it had been running since 1955. Bernstein seemed to believe that his television station could survive on a diet of live programming and original drama.

Any producers who refused to bind themselves to one of FIDO's covenants were likely to find that their films had extreme difficulty in reaching the big screen. In the early 1960s, the Cinema Exhibitors Association told its members to refuse to book any pictures made by David Selznick's company after he sold a package of films to the BBC. There was even talk of blacklisting director Stanley Kramer when three of his films appeared on television, although the rights had long since passed out of his hands. Lew Grade, the driving force behind Associated TeleVision, the ITV company, bought a package of fifty movies from Samuel Goldwyn, and the latter was immediately blacklisted even though he had virtually gone out of business. Michael Balcon, head of Ealing Studios, whose plan to sell a hundred films to television had helped spark the creation of FIDO, was furious. He would later argue that the proceeds from television sales 'would have been·ploughed back into film production', and that in any case, 'it was wrong to set up barriers against any audience for a film'. As late as August 1963, defiant British cinema-owners were still insisting that 'FIDO has been the envy of the world', even though it also emerged that FIDO had laid out money on films for which the negatives had long since been lost. A few films would remain on the list for decades, because FIDO covenants to the film were due to last until the expiration of copyright.

FIDO eventually collapsed in the mid-1960s largely because many American independent producers, buffeted by years of declining cinema attendances, were desperate for cash. Admissions had plunged from an all-time annual high of 1.6 billion in 1946 to 288 million twenty years later. The offers from the British television networks became too tempting to resist, despite the threats from FIDO.

Similar stories of drastically declining audiences were told in Germany and Japan. Throughout the second half of the 1950s, the sales of television sets climbed and the box-office figures crumbled. In some European countries the rate of decline was somewhat slower, in part because sales of television sets took longer to take off. In 1960, for example, only 10 per cent of households in France owned a television set. In Italy, the fall was more modest, and in Spain the decline was not serious until the mid-1960s. It was clear that a fundamental change in the cinema audience was taking place. To many it seemed obvious that television was to blame and it was undeniably true that the growth of the television audience was a catalyst for the initial fall in audiences. The different rate of decline in admissions across Europe could be ascribed, to some extent at least, to the differing speed with which television was taken up in different countries. What aggravated the problem throughout Europe was the myopic response of the domestic cinema industries. In Germany, for example, there was an attempt by exhibitors to launch a scheme modelled on FIDO in late 1958. It was abandoned amid intense acrimony between producers, distributors and exhibitors, but the rancour of cinema-owners towards television lost none of its force. In Italy, cinemas put up ticket prices. This temporarily protected their revenues, but did nothing to reverse the decline in admissions. Exhibitors everywhere closed down cinemas, depressing attendance figures still further. One economist argued that 100 million admissions a year had been lost in Great Britain simply because of the premature closure of cinemas by jittery circuit-owners. Just as had happened in the United States, television became a convenient scapegoat for a variety of problems that were not necessarily connected to it at all.

All this had severe consequences, not just for Europe's cinema-owners, but for the entire European movie industry. A fall in admissions meant a fall in revenues, and thus a fall in production. What made things far worse was the way in which production companies throughout Europe were prevented from forming sensible alliances with television.

In the mid-1960s, a decade after television had first become really popular in Europe, most producers were only just starting to open up their vaults of old films to buyers from television stations. In any case, many European production companies, lacking the means to distribute films themselves, and chronically short of capital, had pre-sold the rights to their films in order to finance the original production. As a consequence, they had no library of films to offer to the broadcasters.

One man who did take advantage of the explosive growth of television was an assistant professor of business management at Munich University, Leo Kirch. In 1956 he left academic life and persuaded a bank to lend him $54,000 to buy the German distribution rights to Federico Fellini's *La Strada*. After it was a huge success at the cinema, Kirch sold it to television. Soon he was buying German-language rights to hundreds of Hollywood films and selling them on to German television. By the 1990s, he had acquired rights to a library of 15,000 feature films, with a value to television of hundreds of millions of dollars.

A particular feature of the situation in Europe was that most television stations were publicly funded and, unlike their commercial counterparts in America, had sufficient resources to produce most of their own programming. The few commercial stations that did exist, such as the companies which made up Britain's ITV network, usually had a monopoly on air-time and so were similarly well funded. Lord Thomson, who operated one of the ITV franchises, famously described such a monopoly as 'like having a licence to print your own money'. As a result, commercial broadcasters, too, had little need of production partnerships of any kind. In any case, if such broadcasters needed extra programmes they could buy them cheaply from the Americans. Salesmen from Hollywood began converging on Europe from the mid-1950s onwards, disposing of hundreds of telefilms to broadcasters across the continent. By the end of the 1950s, even publicly-owned stations in Denmark, the Netherlands and Sweden were gobbling up packages of American telefilms, and across the rest of the world, the pattern was much the same. In Australia, the dominance of American programming was so over-whelming that it provoked the federal government to show its first sign of interest in the movie industry for over three decades, setting up an enquiry into the production of national film and television programming. What made American television programming so attractive to foreign broadcasters was that it was astonishingly cheap. 'We gave them [the Australians] some series for as little as a thousand dollars for a one-hour programme,' admitted one American executive. What had made American movies so attractive to overseas distribu-tors, however, was not just their price, but their popularity and the consistent ability of the studios to deliver them in volume of films. With American television programming, things were different. Its popularity abroad had never been tested. Price alone was the spur.

American television programmes, many of them made by film companies, now flooded into overseas markets. This new wave of American images, styles and values often sparked the same hostile response that American movies had attracted in the 1920s. In Aus-tralia, Canada and Great Britain, quotas were introduced, limiting the amount of 'foreign' programming which could be shown on their country's television screens, whatever its source. Such blanket bans were really a smokescreen; the only real target was American productions.

The Americans had largely made their peace with television by the mid-1950s. The Europeans went on fighting for another decade. In part, that was because television became popular rather later in Europe than it had in the United States. But that was only part of the story. What remained indisputable was that the leaders of the American movie business had found a way of exploiting television that enabled them to start rebuilding their industry from the wreckage of the studio system. By the time the decline in cinema attendances in America finally flattened out in the early 1960s, the process of reconstruction was well under way. True, much had changed. Shorn of their stars and their cinema chains, the major studios no longer called the shots in the way they had been able to do fifteen years earlier. The agents, and a new generation of independent film-makers, jostled for power. The moguls were dead. 'As I see it today, the boss of the Studio is actually no longer a boss – he has a title but that is all,' observed director and screenwriter Philip Dunne in 1961. 'He is the slave of agents and actors with their own corporations and insane competition from independent operators and promoters.'

The networks controlled access to the television audience. Through it all the studios hung on to what had always been the real source of their power: their control of distribution. That lesson had been learned decades before when Carl Laemmle, William Fox and others had wrested control of the American industry from Edison and his allies. In the years that followed the Great War, the studio bosses used their power over distribution as a weapon with which to conquer and subdue foreign markets. Now it became the means by which they defused the threat from television, turning the rival medium to their own advantage and enabling them to strengthen their grip on a new international market for moving images. American television shows were being piped directly into living rooms the world over, massively reinforcing the economic, cultural and ideo-logical power wielded by the country that created them.

Those who ran the European film business, on the other hand remained intimidated by television, even after they had abandoned their fight against it in the mid-1960s and started buying films in bulk. The European film industry, so often cash-starved in the past, simply denied itself access to a new and rich source of funding which might have fuelled the creation of bigger, stronger companies capable of taking on the Americans. There had never been more than a handful of relatively large, securely funded film companies operating anywhere in the European film business; for the most part, it was an industry of minnows, surviving on the scraps left behind by the sharks of Hollywood. The sudden downturn in Euro-pean cinema attendances only made things worse, forcing even the larger companies to the wall.

Not until the 1970s, would the European movie companies begin to see television not as an enemy, but as a potential ally which might help them adjust to a marketplace that had been swept by so many radical changes in the decades that followed the war.

15

The Film-maker as Author:
The Arrival of
the Nouvelle Vague

WHILE THE FILM INDUSTRY worldwide struggled to come to terms with life in the television age, European cinema found itself in the midst of a very different kind of revolution, one which briefly seemed as if it might sweep away the sovereign power of Hollywood. In an essay published in the communist-backed magazine *Ecran français* in 1948, the director and critic Alexandre Astruc had argued:

> The cinema is quite simply becoming a means of expression, just as all the arts have been before it, and in particular painting and the novel. After having been successfully a fairground attraction, an amusement analogous to boulevard theatre, or a means of preserving the images of an era, it is gradually becoming a language. By language, I mean a form in which and by which an artist can express his thoughts, however abstract they may be, or translate his obsessions exactly as he does in the contemporary essay or novel. The filmmaker-author writes with his camera as a writer with his pen.

This modest essay, published in an industry trade paper, soon became a call to arms for a whole generation of French critics and film-makers. At first sight it was difficult to see why, since what Astruc was proposing hardly seemed new. The idea that cinema might be accorded a place alongside the more traditional forms of high culture had been a consistent motif in French thought ever since Edmond Benoît-Lévy had first articulated the idea in 1907. The idea that a film could be said to have an author had sprung into being at around the same time. In those early days, most critics had identified the scriptwriter as the author of the film. 'The scenario is the film itself . . . The author of the scenario must bear responsibility for the film,' observed one French critic in 1919. During the 1920s and '30s the author's mantle slowly came to be assumed by the director. This idea, though, seemed to have relatively little significance beyond the suggestion that the truly great directors, responsible for creating the finest films of the age, should in some way be fêted as artists.

What was new and striking about Astruc's essay was his contention that the director's thought was directly expressed, or 'written' into, each film he or she made. Astruc had taken the nineteenth-century romantic idea that art should be considered as the expression of individual personality and applied it to film-making. In doing so, he gave new impetus to the traditional French conception of cinema as, first and foremost, a form of cultural expression, rather than an industry dependent like any other on the right blend of capital and labour. From this perspective the producer, the cast, the writer, the composer, the crew – all were little more than tools to be manipulated by the director, the means by which he transferred his vision to celluloid. Astruc's idea of a personal cinema was subsequently taken up and extended by a group of critics associated with the magazine *Cahiers du cinéma*.

Founded by the journalist Jacques Doniol-Valcroze in 1951, *Cahiers du cinéma* rapidly became the most influential film publication in Europe. By 1953 a group of young writers including Jean-Luc Godard, François Truffaut, Jacques Rivette and Claude Chabrol had started contributing to the journal alongside more established commentators such as André Bazin. The following year Truffaut scandalized the cinematic establishment when he published an essay in *Cahiers* entitled 'Une Certaine Tendance du cinéma français'. In a trenchant attack on what he called the tradition of quality in French cinema, Truffaut argued that renowned directors such as Yves Allégret and Claude Autant-Lara, and the screenwriters who worked with them, failed to impose their personalities on their work. He compared the screenwriters to those French authors who adopted 'a distant, exterior attitude' in relation to their subject and claimed that as a result, 'the hundred-odd French films made each year tell the same story: it's always a question of a victim, generally a cuckold'. The directors, he claimed, were mere *'metteurs en scène'* who simply added the performers and the pictures to the work of the screen-writers. This type of film-making was derided as the *cinéma de papa*. He contrasted them to another group of directors whom he identified as genuine *'auteurs'*, men such as Jacques Tati, Jean Renoir and Robert Bresson, who worked from their own scripts. Many of these ideas were taken up in a more overtly political form in *Positif*, a rival journal founded in 1952.

Truffaut's polemic was like a declaration of war and the revolt against established cinema which it inspired became known as the *politique des auteurs*. The term was later translated into English as the 'auteur theory' but, as the original French term implied, what the group of critics around *Cahiers* were really engaged in was a crusade. It was a crusade that revolutionized French film criticism, inspired the creation of a radically new school of film-making across Europe, and determined the shape of European cinema for decades. Some supporters of the *politique des auteurs* developed the idea that a true *auteur* could take a poor screenplay or lame subject-matter and transform it into a great film. '[I]n the hands of a great director, even the most insignificant detective story can be transformed into a work of art,' as one of them put it. It was all a matter of the director's technique, or *mise en scène*. Not *what*, but *how*. Or, as one critic pro-vocatively put it, 'morality is a question of tracking shots'.

It was this conception of the director's sovereign power that enabled exponents of the *politique des auteurs* to champion the work of mainstream Hollywood directors such as Howard Hawks, Vincente Minnelli and Nicholas Ray. The *politique des auteurs* was an intellectual movement, and at first sight such enthusiasm seemed to run directly counter to the kind of contempt that the French intelligentsia had harboured towards Hollywood and all things American since the 1930s. In fact, the *politique des auteurs* was far less of a radical departure than it seemed. For what these critics were really saying was that, however deadening and impersonal the Hollywood studio system might have seemed, the truly great director could rise above it. Even in cases where they had virtually no control over the choice of subject, the script and the casting, they could still turn dross into gold.

On this view, the basic assumptions which had characterized the European conception of cinema for decades remained intact. Hollywood was run by tyrants, a place where everything and everyone was reduced to the demeaning status of a commodity. 'Hollywood is a microcosm which reproduces, magnified many times over, the defects of American society,' wrote one *Cahiers* contributor. 'It is capitalism to the "n"th degree, a monstrous excrescence of the "air-conditioned nightmare" which Henry Miller mentions when talking about America.' Many of the sentiments were wearily familiar. What was surprising was that in the early 1960s such arguments would be taken up and even extended by Andrew Sarris, an American exponent of the auteur theory, who became one of the most influential critics of his generation. 'All directors, and not just in Hollywood, are imprisoned by their craft and culture,' he wrote. The sterile opposition between art and commerce had reasserted itself once more. Important critics like André Bazin might still maintain that 'the cinema is an art which is both popular and industrial. These conditions, which are necessary to its existence, in no way constitute a collection of hindrances.' As the 1960s wore on, so in France such voices would be increasingly drowned out by the strident denunciation of all things American, epitomized by the Hollywood factories.

What made the *politique des auteurs* so influential was that, in the late 1950s, a group of its most enthusiastic proponents started directing their own films. In the two years following General de Gaulle's return to power in 1958, their first efforts hit the nation's cinema screens. The films included Claude Chabrol's *Le Beau Serge*, François Truffaut's *Les 400 Coups* and Jean-Luc Godard's *A Bout de Souffle*. They had a cataclysmic impact on audiences and film-makers alike. Most of them were shot on location, using little-known actors and small crews. The films made by the *Cahiers* critics, with their distinctive preoccupations with contemporary life, and their radical technique, clearly reflected their theoretical beliefs. They also owed much to the work of two cinematographers, Henri Decaë and Raoul Coutard, whose introduction of hand-held camera techniques and minimal lighting enabled them to shoot on location with relative ease. This new generation of directors was dubbed the *Nouvelle Vague* (New Wave), a term first coined by Françoise Giroud, editor of the French weekly *L'Express*. Many of the early films were spectacular successes in France and gave birth to a new generation of stars, including Jean-Paul Belmondo, Jean-Claude Brialy and Jeanne Moreau. The emergence of the *Nouvelle Vague* in France coincided with the rise of rock 'n' roll as a significant social force, as well as with such cultural innovations as the *Nouveau Roman* associated with writers like Alain Robbe-Grillet and Marguerite Duras. These developments all helped create an air of renewal and a spirit of excitement, especially among younger people living in the larger cities. The huge box-office success in 1956 of *Et Dieu créa la femme* starring Brigitte Bardot, directed by twenty-eight-year-old Roger Vadim, although hardly a *Nouvelle Vague* film, had convinced many younger film-makers that their time had come.

The excitement quickly spread abroad. Inspired by the French example, similar movements of new film-makers sprang up across Europe and as far afield as Japan. '[The] new film requires new freedoms. Freedom from the usual conventions of film-making. Freedom from commercial influences ... The old film is dead. We believe in the new film,' declared a group of West German film-makers in 1962, in a manifesto put together at meetings in the back room of a Chinese restaurant in Munich. The influence was just as strong in Scandinavia and Eastern European countries such as Czechoslovakia, Poland and Hungary. 'Everybody went to Paris to see Truffaut and Godard's films,' recalled a Hungarian film-maker. '[P]eople imitated them, but it was liberating.'

In 1959, de Gaulle's administration had created a Ministry of Culture and installed the writer André Malraux at its head. At the same time, in a powerfully symbolic act, the French state moved control of the Centre National de la Cinématographie away from the Ministry of Industry and Commerce and placed it under the aegis of the new Ministry of Culture. This marked official recognition of an assumption that had long prevailed among the French elite; namely, that cinema was a cultural, rather than industrial, form. Or as André Malraux put it on another occasion, cinema was essentially an art which also happened, as a contingent matter, to be an industry. Different aspects of French culture were exhibited in the *Maisons de la culture* which now sprang up in towns and cities across France. Somewhat ironically, in the light of the political radicalism adopted by its leading exponents, the film-makers of the *Nouvelle Vague* benefited from this increase in state support for the idea of culture, and in particular from the increased importance accorded to the CNC.

Still, for all the excitement it generated, and despite its enormous aesthetic and critical influence, the New Wave of film-making that swept Europe never had much real chance of displacing American cinema from its sovereign position. Most of the *Nouvelle Vague* films in France had been financed under a system of subsidy introduced in 1959 by the newly empowered CNC. The central element in the scheme, the *avance sur recettes* (advance on receipts), offered film-makers funding for their next project, based on the CNC's assessment of the artistic qualities of the script. Unlike the British Eady Levy, which returned a proportion of the tax levied on cinema tickets to every film released, projects did not automatically receive support. It was this mechanism, a form of direct state subsidy to film-makers, which provided the funding for most *Nouvelle Vague* films in France. It enabled film-makers to get genuinely innovative projects off the ground, thereby injecting new blood into the industry. It did little to encourage the development of keen commercial instincts, even though the subsidy was supposed to be repaid if the film achieved a certain level of box-office success. Despite the box-office success achieved by the early *Nouvelle Vague* films, audience interest began to decline, and by 1963 few such films received a full theatrical release. During and immediately after this period, many of the most popular French films at the national box office were mainstream comedies such as Yves Robert's *La Guerre des boutons* (1962). This, together with Jacques Demy's *La Parapluies de Cherbourg* (1964) and Gérard Oury's *Le Corniaud* (1965) were unique films which owed little or nothing to the New Wave. After all, a farce like *Allez France*, directed by Robert Dhéry in 1964, in which a French rugby fan nearly misses his wedding when he rushes to England for a vital match, didn't exactly chime with the crusading spirit of the *politique des auteurs*.

Throughout the 1950s, French cinema had proved far more resistant to the challenge from Hollywood than had most other countries around the world. In 1960, French films accounted for just over 50 per cent of box-office receipts in the national market, whereas the comparable figure in Britain was about 20 per cent. Attendances in France had always been far lower than those in other European countries, largely as a result of the lack of cinemas in rural districts. Even though their share of the box office improved, French films were hit by a sharp decline in overall admissions. The *Nouvelle Vague* was an aesthetic rather than economic phenomenon. Its film-makers had enormous creative influence, but did little to revive the overall financial fortunes of the industry. In fact, the success of French cinema became increasingly reliant on the state which would soon be pouring half a billion francs a year into the industry through its various support mechanisms.

Despite this unprecedented level of aid, the fastest-growing genre of the 1960s, in numerical terms, was not *Nouvelle Vague* 'art films' at all, but pornography, and that story was being repeated across the rest of Europe. In the light of all this, it is perhaps surprising that certain aspects of the critical ideology and conception of cinema which informed the *Nouvelle Vague* should still be wielding considerable influence more than thirty years later. This may be a testimony to the enduring appeal of the romantic myth of the artist – in this case the director – which shaped so many of the movement's ideas. In any case, throughout the 1960s, the film policies of many other European countries, including Germany and Italy, began to swing behind the French model, as the influence of the *Nouvelle Vague* swept through industries across continental Europe. A new pattern of film-making evolved, one that was increasingly dependent on subsidies.

The story in Great Britain was different. The Eady Levy, tied simply to box-office performance, remained far more significant than direct funding from government. The film industries of these two countries – Great Britain and France – gradually came to define the two poles of the European response to Hollywood's challenge. They were united in their desire to resist American domination, but in terms of ambition, funding and style they had almost no features in common, but this mattered little either way: in terms of popular appeal and market share they both steadily lost ground to the American industry.

Even before the *Nouvelle Vague* unleashed a generation of brash new film-makers on the world, American movie companies were more active in production in Europe than they had been for decades. As costs rose, the majors abandoned their studio lots in Hollywood and fled to Great Britain, Italy and France to shoot their films. By the early 1960s, the phenomenon known as 'runaway production' had become so serious that the American government launched an investigation into its impact on the domestic economy. In the early post-war years runaway production had been a convenient means of side-stepping European foreign exchange problems; since the studios couldn't take all their earnings out of certain countries, they invested in local production, and so repatriated their money in the form of celluloid. The studios soon came to realize a further and more significant advantage: productions could be made far more cheaply in Europe and with far less obstruction from the unions than was the case in Hollywood. Even better, since they qualified as national productions, the films were entitled to receive a proportion of the financial assistance which was now flowing in ever larger quantities from local subsidy schemes.

When the Kennedy administration launched its investigation into the impact of runaway production, the leaders of the American industry marshalled the usual battery of ideological arguments to defend their economic interests. In his evidence to the investigation, Eric Johnston even cited the testimony of three young Hungarians who had recently escaped from their country, claiming they had done so

> because of what they had seen in American motion pictures. They said that even if it was a gangster picture the policeman was always on the side of the people while he was not in their country; that a person could turn on the radio set without looking around to see whether somebody was spying on them; that a man could quit his job and look for another job. You could not do that in their country.

Such crude rhetoric could cut both ways. The exploitation of cheap European labour suggested to some that the studios had struck a kind of Faustian pact with 'communist-controlled unions abroad'. One Californian congressman attempted to introduce a bill demanding that all foreign-produced films should be labelled so that patriotic audiences could be made aware of their origin. Eric Johnston sought to lower the temperature of this debate by pointing out: 'We have in the neighborhood of $500 million invested in studios and facilities in Hollywood. I want to emphasize that Hollywood is still the motion picture capital of the world. We want to keep it that way.' After all, they still controlled distribution and, as Johnston explained, many runaway films, if they had not been made in Europe would not have been made at all. In any case, once made, they did 'produce revenue that comes back to provide additional income and jobs in the United States'. In effect, Johnston admitted that the economics of modern film-making meant that a significant element of overseas production was inevitable.

Others argued that the only way to maintain the competitiveness of the American industry was to follow the European lead and demand government subsidies. In 1964, the Association of Motion Picture and TV Producers, backed by labour and production representatives, began lobbying for a subsidy scheme modelled on Britain's Eady Levy which would use a modest surcharge on cinema tickets to offer producers financial incentives. Spyros Skouras, chairman of Twentieth Century-Fox, was reported to be an enthusiastic supporter. The scheme ran into an entirely predictable barrage of hostility from the cinema exhibitors, and three years after it had been floated it seemed as far away from implementation as ever. The problem, however, did not go away. Thomas H. Kuchel, the Republican senator for California who supported the measure, went so far as to claim that 'imported films have overtaken American production to the extent that, if the trend is not halted, the American film industry faces a challenge to its very existence'.

Runaway production, in a variety of forms, continued to gather pace. By the early 1960s, the Americans were so active in Italy that some took to calling it 'Hollywood on the Tiber', and one magazine referred to it as 'The Roman Orgy of Movie Making'. Carlo Ponti and Dino de Laurentiis, two expansive old-style producers, led the way in forging alliances with Hollywood. Ponti's partner was an entrepreneurial American called Joe Levine, founder of the independent Embassy Pictures, who had made a fortune by acquiring the American distribution rights to Japanese science fiction extravaganzas like *Godzilla*. Together they produced a number of Italian films, including Vittorio de Sica's *Two Women*, starring Ponti's wife Sophia Loren, Fellini's *Eight and a Half* and Pietro Germi's *Divorce Italian Style*, both with Marcello Mastroianni. Encouraged by the huge success of many of the films which Levine was producing, the majors followed in his wake; Twentieth Century-Fox, for example, backing de Sica's *The Condemned of Altona* and Luchino Visconti's masterpiece *The Leopard*.

In the mid-1960s, a new and even more successful form of transatlantic collaboration was born. With the financial backing of a former lawyer called Alberto Grimaldi, the Italian director Sergio Leone made *A Fistful of Dollars*, which became the most successful Italian film ever made and for which United Artists acquired world distribution rights outside Italy. The first of a long and hugely successful run of what came to be popularly known as 'spaghetti westerns', *A Fistful of Dollars* was deliberately styled to look like an American movie. Leone himself adopted the pseudonym of Bob Robertson, in an attempt to convince American audiences that the film was an authentic Hollywood production. For Grimaldi, the association with United Artists led to a series of prestigious films, including Fellini's *Satyricon* and Bernard Bertolucci's *Last Tango in Paris*, with Marlon Brando and Maria Schneider.

Much of the success of the Italian industry in attracting American productions could be attributed to the quality of the facilities at Rome's Cinecittà studios. Mussolini's pre-war investment had finally paid off, if not quite in the way he had intended. His goal had been to build an industry capable of competing with the technological sophistication of Hollywood. What had actually evolved was, indeed, a dynamic Italian industry, but it was effectively under the control of American investment. By the mid-1960s, the Italian market was by far the most valuable in Europe. The decline in attendances had slowed, and films of Italian nationality regained much of the ground which they had lost to Hollywood movies as a result of Guilio Andreotti's policies in the immediate aftermath of the Second World War.

Italian rules for film subsidy specified only that the director of the original Italian version of a film had to be Italian in order to qualify. A number of American companies saw that this gave them a loophole for access to state support. They began to appoint what came to be known as 'straw directors', people who were credited as director on the Italian version of a film, but were in reality nothing more than local assistants to American directors. This meant, for example, that the highly successful epic *El Cid*, directed by Anthony Mann, appeared with an entirely different director in Italy. However fictitious the credits, the subsidy money they generated was real enough.

It was perhaps inevitable that for all the welcome work and investment which the influx of American productions brought to Italian studios like Cinecittà, there was very little change in the underlying balance of power within the industry. After all, the American partners retained the distribution rights outside Italy for most of the pictures they co-produced with Italian partners. That meant the overwhelming bulk of any profits accrued directly to them, rather than being recycled back into the Italian industry. Even at the height of the boom, some of Italy's larger film companies, such as Titanus, were experiencing severe financial difficulties. Unable to get their hands on a significant slice of the profits from their own movies, the Italians were never able to build up companies with the capital resources and scale of operation to compete effectively with the Americans. Appearances to the contrary, there was never a chance that Cinecittà and the Via Veneto would displace Hollywood and Beverly Hills as the centre of the world's movie industry. The power of the Italian industry was an illusion, scarcely more substantial than the sets at Cinecittà. America remained sovereign.

In the 1960s the American studios, led by United Artists, became directly involved with European film-makers. United Artists' method was to make deals with film-makers, giving them the freedom to make the films they wanted, subject to the studio's acceptance of the subject, the script and the budget. The best European film-makers were naturally attracted to United Artists' working methods. They also knew that they were more likely to get their product distributed in America if they were financed by a US distributor, as opposed to making a film with a European company which would then have to do a deal with a US company.

In France the company funded films made by François Truffaut, Claude Lelouch, Louis Malle and Philippe de Broca and others, while in Sweden it financed films made by Ingmar Bergman. The latter had never made a film with an American company, but United Artists made four pictures with him, asking for approval only of the idea of the movie. Bergman's pictures included *The Passion of Anna* and *Shame*; Truffaut's included *Le Mariée était en noir* and *Baisers volés*. In this way, United Artists established a credibility with European film-makers. The company believed that if it was in business with the best film-makers in Europe and it had strong American product, each type of product would help the other.

United Artists benefited from a superb international distribution network run by Arnold Picker. As Jay Kantor, who headed operations for MCA in London, observed: 'If you are going to make films in Europe, make European films, using the best European talents. Otherwise, forget it.' MCA also financed foreign-language pictures, including Claude Chabrol's *Le Scandale*.

The Americans were increasingly active, too, in the United Kingdom. By 1967, it was estimated that as much as 90 per cent of the funding for films made in the United Kingdom came from the United States, and the tag 'Hollywood, England' became increasingly popular. United Artists were also at the forefront of activity in the UK, financing such films as *A Hard Day's Night*, the Beatles picture directed by Richard Lester, as well as the James Bond series of films, produced by Albert 'Cubby' Broccoli. In the mid-1960s, much of the attraction of the United Kingdom to the Americans stemmed from the energy and youthful vitality associated with 'Swinging' London. By contrast, many of the films being made in Hollywood seemed staid. Only with the emergence of films like *Bonnie and Clyde* and *The Graduate*, both made in 1967, would that start to change. At the end of the 1960s, however, the Americans suddenly withdrew from the UK, having burnt their fingers with a series of expensive flops such as *The Battle of Britain* and *Goodbye, Mr Chips*. They were also facing increasing financial pressures at home which contributed to the decision to cut back overseas. British producers found themselves facing a serious funding crisis.

Meanwhile, the American studios were wrestling with major

changes at home. By the mid-1960s, some studios were deriving as much as one-third of their income from television and movies were running on the television networks five or six nights a week in prime-time. In 1966 ABC astounded the industry by paying $2 million for the rights to *The Bridge on the River Kwai*. Their gamble paid off handsomely and they smashed the ratings records with 60 million viewers.

By 1968, the average price paid by the networks for a feature film had reached $800,000, an astonishing increase on the $28,000 price tag Warners had put on so many of their classic titles less than ten years before. 'It's strictly a seller's market,' observed *Newsweek* in 1967. 'Film vaults contain enough for only three more years, and current production won't meet future need.' The television networks were hungry for movies, but were deeply concerned at inflationary price increases and at the prospect that before long the studio vaults might run dry. Their response was to go into production for themselves. ABC and CBS created their own production companies and were joined by another new player, the cinema chain National General. The unsurprising response of the established studios was a flood of allegations about breaches of anti-trust laws, designed to prevent media companies from exercising excessive control over too many aspects of the American industry. The studios were taking on more than they had bargained for. William Paley, who had run CBS almost as a private fiefdom for four decades, had long cherished the idea of taking on the Hollywood studios. Towards the end of 1966, he made his move. 'I want to be in the feature film business,' he informed one of his senior executives. 'We ought to be there. Get us in.' There was no business plan other than a commitment to make ten films, at $3.5 million a film, through a newly created subsidiary called Cinema Center Films. One of CBS's first films was an adaptation of a controversial Broadway play, *The Boys in the Band*. As one gleeful CBS executive put it: 'What better way to get their attention in Hollywood than to have a movie that begins "Who do you have to fuck around here to get a drink?"'

Such excited optimism proved to be more than a little premature.

The networks had not bargained for the fact that there was a limit to the number of movies their audiences wanted to see and as a consequence they stopped buying. A string of dismal flops produced by ABC and CBS led to mounting losses. Without the ability to distribute its own pictures, CBS was unlikely to get much financial benefit from its new production company, unless one of its films became a really big hit. That seemed less and less likely. By the time the company closed down Cinema Center Films in the early 1970s, it had lost $30 million on its film-making venture. ABC and National General suffered a similar fate.

These new players in production had been forced to pay extravagant prices for scripts and creative talent, leading to skyrocketing budgets. This affected all the majors. As long as television was paying huge prices for movies, the studios reaped rich dividends. When the networks stopped buying, the majors were hit hard. Almost all of them were rocked by losses running into hundreds of millions of dollars. Suddenly Hollywood was in crisis, and once again some feared it might never recover.

Earth to Hollywood –
You Win!

VARIETY, 1995

BY THE BEGINNING OF THE 1970S, Hollywood was in crisis. Five of the seven major studios were in the red, with collective losses of well over $100 million. MGM auctioned off hundreds of props and costumes, including the shoes Judy Garland had worn in *The Wizard of Oz* which raised $15,000. Twentieth Century-Fox and Columbia faced bankruptcy. With a suitably grotesque sense of the appropriate, Gulf and Western, the owners of Paramount, contemplated selling the studio for use as a cemetery. The movies, that craze which had first swept the inner-city slums sixty-five years earlier and whose imminent demise had been frequently predicted, seemed finally to have burnt itself out. Perhaps it was time to bury Hollywood and along with it the film business itself.

The failure of many Hollywood films had less to do with their astronomic costs and stratospheric star salaries than with their sub-ject-matter and treatment. A new popular culture had emerged, driven by rock bands such as the Beatles, the Doors and the Rolling

Stones, and quasi-mystics such as Timothy Leary. For a new generation, raised during the Vietnam War, the traditional Hollywood diet
of musicals, westerns and historical epics seemed increasingly stale
and irrelevant.

Television, too, had become a dominant force, fostering an entertainment culture more immediately responsive to current styles and
values. Perhaps most significantly, a yawning gap had opened up
between the men who ran the studios and their audience. The
executives were for the most part in their fifties and sixties, while
the bulk of their audiences were in their teens or early twenties.
The American film industry, which for so long had prided itself on
its capacity to respond to, and even anticipate, popular taste, had
perhaps for the first time lost touch with its public.

Throughout the late 1960s, the studios had suffered a string of
hugely expensive flops: *Doctor Dolittle*, a musical fantasy aimed
principally at children and starring Rex Harrison as a man who had
learned almost 500 languages from his pet parrot; *Star!* in which
Julie Andrews tried and failed to re-create the magic that had made
The Sound of Music such a success; *Hello Dolly* in which Barbra
Streisand did much the same – with much the same result; and
Paint Your Wagon, yet another musical disaster, this time with Lee
Marvin. 'The worst thing that ever happened to this business was
The Sound of Music,' claimed Alfred Hitchcock. 'That film stimulated
everybody into making expensive films.'

There were other reasons for this unhappy state of affairs. The
American economy was in recession and, as an editorial in the *Los
Angeles Times* in March 1971 ruefully pointed out: 'If the economy
is in a recession, the motion picture production business – in terms
of films produced here rather than abroad – is in out-and-out
depression.' The paper reported that more than half the members
of film unions in Hollywood were out of work, and that in some
crafts unemployment had reached 90 per cent. Blaming the ills of
the industry on fiscal incentives created by foreign governments, the
paper called for an import duty on 'films made abroad under conditions of unfair, subsidised competition'. These sentiments were

familiar enough. It was a message that industry lobbyists had been trumpeting for decades. What made things different this time was that the call was being taken up by an increasing number of people both inside and outside the industry, for reasons that were not difficult to understand.

With mounting panic the industry's most senior executives began to sense disaster. '[There is] a probability that the product shortage will be filled largely with pictures from abroad,' predicted Al Howe, a pivotal figure in film financing with Bank of America. Such pictures might well be distributed by American companies but they constituted a different kind of nightmare, an end to decades of US dominance of the world market.

The conglomerates and banks which now controlled the studios moved to reduce their losses. They enforced massive cuts in overhead, merged production facilities and amalgamated some of their overseas distribution operations. Entire layers of management were stripped out. Old studio hands were unceremoniously dumped and a new breed of aggressive young managers was installed in their place. Just as had happened during the depression of the 1930s, these tended to be the more buttoned-down corporate types with a formal business training but no sentimental attachment to the idiosyncratic and expensive traditions of movie production.

The changes at Warner Brothers typified what was happening all over Hollywood. In 1966, Jack Warner had sold out to Seven Arts, a company which had grown rich and complacent from the revenues of the Warner Brothers films it had purchased back in the 1950s. Within three years Warner Brothers was back on the market, to be acquired this time by Kinney National Services, a New York-based company headed by Steven Ross. Ross had started his career in his father-in-law's funeral business, then expanded into car-parking and cleaning services. He hungered for something more in keeping with his own taste and lifestyle, and in 1967 he bought the talent agency, Ashley Famous. On acquiring Warners in 1969, he installed the agency's founder, Ted Ashley, as head of the studio. Ashley got rid of large numbers of employees in California and New

York and merged the company's production facilities at Burbank with those of Columbia.

Ross set out to re-create Warner Brothers as an international entertainment conglomerate. He expanded its music interests, snapped up publishing companies, moved into the cable business in a joint venture with American Express, and created a London-based company to make television programmes for the international market.

Not all of his ventures were successful. The collapse of Atari, Warner's video games subsidiary, almost brought the company to its knees, but Ross's underlying strategy was sound. It was the same strategy of diversification that had enabled both Disney and MCA to weather one of the worst recessions the movie business had ever known. Instead of the traditional Hollywood policy of vertical integration, it represented a new form of horizontal integration as pioneered by Walt Disney, fitting the high-risk activity of film production into a broader spectrum of leisure businesses. The benefit was obvious. Instead of seeking to recoup escalating production costs from box-office alone, it allowed these costs to be defrayed across a variety of related activities, with spin-offs into soundtracks, books, toys and merchandising. A large, diversified entertainment group could insulate itself, at least to some extent, from the worst effects of periodic box-office flops, while at the same time capitalizing on marketing opportunities in other growing leisure sectors such as tourism.

Such internal reorganizations of the industry were not, in themselves, enough to turn the tide. Not for the first time, Hollywood now looked to Washington for a helping hand. In 1971, California senator Thomas H. Kuchel put forward the Domestic Film Production Incentive Act, under whose terms 20 per cent of gross income from the distribution and export of any film made in the United States would be exempt from tax. The industry lobbied hard in support, enthusiastically assisted by Ronald Reagan, then Governor of California. In the same year a series of hearings was held in Congress on 'Unemployment Problems in the American Film

Industry'. Stars, directors, producers, technicians – all were suffering. According to Charlton Heston, president of the Screen Actors Guild, the American film industry was 'in desperate need of federal assistance'.

The Incentive Act never reached the Statute Book. In a sense it had already become redundant, for, after intensive lobbying elsewhere in Washington, Hollywood had already secured invaluable assistance from another piece of domestic legislation, one that had originally been framed without any thought of providing help for the American movie industry. Investment tax credits had originally been introduced in the United States in 1962 as a means of creating jobs and promoting economic growth. The credit allowed American companies to write off against tax 7 per cent of any investment made in equipment and machinery within the United States. It was eliminated in 1969, but reintroduced in the 1971 Revenue Act. After fierce lobbying, which included a meeting between industry leaders and President Nixon, the Internal Revenue Service was persuaded to allow investment in films and television programmes to qualify for the credit, so long as they were produced in the United States. As was so often the case, rumour had it that more than anyone else in the business it was Lew Wasserman who helped to secure the victory.

The new measures helped bring about a dramatic upswing in the fortunes of the American movie business, with significant benefits, particularly in the job market. The requirement that films be shot in the United States helped cut the levels of runaway production. In March 1972, *Variety*, reporting vastly improved profits at MCA, observed: 'ninety seven per cent of the company's profit increase last year is directly attributable to the new tax rules.' Walt Disney immediately sued the government for retrospective tax credits dating back to 1963. They were quickly joined by the other studios which together won almost $400 million in back credits. In the 1971 hearings on unemployment, Charlton Heston had observed that the tax credits had been 'of inestimable help in our desperate predicament'. When the credit was raised to 10 per cent, the benefits multiplied. In particular, it helped to boost the studios' activities in the increasingly lucrative field of the production and distribution of television programmes.

Hollywood's legislative triumph was not without a touch of irony. For years the studios had fulminated against the preferential tax incentives for film production offered by foreign governments. Now they had successfully lobbied their own legislature to introduce just such a programme. In the past, government support had mostly taken the form of political lobbying or information-gathering carried out by US government envoys on behalf of the industry, as with the statistical information gathered in the late 1920s and early '30s. What was new this time around was that the support was offered directly in the form of protective tax waivers.

When the French consul in Washington learned of the tax credit, he claimed it was discriminatory and promised retaliatory action against American movies distributed in France. Although the threat came to nothing, it demonstrated that traditional animosities still seethed as strongly as ever.

Buried deep in the new tax legislation was another, less publicized, clause which provided Hollywood with a direct stimulus to increase movie exports. The Revenue Act enabled the studios to create subsidiaries known as Domestic International Sales Corporations (DISCs), which could indefinitely defer tax on half the profits earned from exports. Another equally significant tax change had been introduced in 1969, though its real impact was not immediately felt. It allowed individuals who invested directly in movies to claim 100 per cent tax exemption. This made it much easier for small independent production companies to finance some genuinely innovative films, as the irresistibly attractive tax terms, coupled with the enduring glamour of the industry, led swarms of investors to come forward with their money. *One Flew Over the Cuckoo's Nest*, Milos Forman's Oscar-winning picture starring Jack Nicholson, Bob Rafelson's *Five Easy Pieces* also starring Nicholson, and Martin Scorsese's *Taxi Driver* all epitomized the bold and adventurous independent spirit that helped to revitalize Hollywood film-making. All were financed using tax shelter money. Some studios, such as Columbia, used tax shelters as a means of raising additional, outside finance and so spread risk across a larger slate of films. Without this money, raised through tax shelters, 'Columbia Pictures would have been bankrupt,' the studio's president and chief executive officer Alan Hirschfield told a Senate committee in 1976.

The shelters were routinely abused. Many investors would 'leverage' up the amount they appeared to be investing in a film, pretending to be responsible for a much higher degree of risk than was really the case. Some films were put together solely as an exercise in tax avoidance. In one case, investors acquired American rights to a Japanese film about the man who masterminded the raid on Pearl Harbor. 'Only three copies of that film ever existed anywhere in the United States,' the tax authorities observed, 'and the only income they ever reported was $13 negative income from Seattle.' It was tax fraud pure and simple. Some even blamed the shelters for a surge in the output of pornographic films produced in the 1970s.

The tax shelters were abolished by the government in 1976. At the same time, Senator Edward Kennedy introduced an amendment under which the investment tax credit for films would also be abolished. 'It is just an outright tax subsidy for a service industry,' argued Kennedy in the Senate. But the industry lobbied hard against Kennedy's proposal using some old and familiar arguments when doing so. One senator, for example, argued that the industry was nothing less than an 'American institution' and that the credits were essential to making American movies 'more competitive in the world market'. They were a necessary response to the 'substantial, direct subsidies to film production' offered by foreign governments. Kennedy's amendment was eventually defeated. The credit was retained until the mid-1980s, by which time it was no longer really needed since Hollywood had returned to financial health. Even as the legislation was being renewed, MGM reported its highest ever profits, which one trade paper ascribed to the immediate 'fiscal impact . . . of the recently affirmed investment tax credit'.

At the same time the studios benefited from money generated by tax shelters overseas. One British financier, John Heyman, generated around $2.5 billion of new money for the studios, much of it from Japan. Walt Disney and Columbia Pictures also raised significant new amounts of capital from these same Japanese tax shelters. Throughout the 1980s, Hollywood became ever more dependent on foreign capital.

Without question, the investment tax credit provided significant help in enabling the Hollywood studios to recover from the doldrums of the late 1960s. But Washington had still more and better assistance to offer. In 1970, the Federal Communications Commission (FCC) had introduced rules designed to regulate the way in which the three main television networks – ABC, CBS and NBC – acquired programming. At the time, these three networks accounted for around 90 per cent of both the television audience and the advertising revenues. In the wake of a series of investigations stretching back to 1958, the FCC concluded that the networks had used their dominant position artificially to depress prices paid for programming from outside producers. The FCC also found that the networks had used their power to impose their programming on hundreds of local stations across the country during peak viewing hours. These charges bore a striking resemblance to those that had been made against the studios by the Department of Justice three decades before. In a judgment which echoed the Justice Department's earlier investigation of the film industry, the FCC concluded: 'The three national television networks for all practical purposes control the entire network television program production process from idea through exhibition.'

When the FCC legislation finally emerged in 1970, it differed from that earlier legislation introduced by the Justice Department in one crucial respect; by moving to curb the networks' control over the distribution of programming, both at home and overseas, it struck at the very heart of the mechanism by which the networks kept the independents at bay. In its attempt to rein in the power of the Hollywood studios, the Justice Department had mistakenly targeted the studios' control of cinemas, believing that this alone would give independents freedom to determine the terms on which their films were shown. Since control of distribution was allowed to remain in the hands of the studios, very little had really changed. The FCC's assault, by contrast, was a well-targeted, three-pronged strike on the combined power of the networks. They were to be prevented by law from selling their programming to independent stations in the United States, a practice known as 'syndication'. They were also prohibited from selling any programming abroad which they had not produced themselves. And they were no longer allowed to acquire any financial interest in any programming which they had not made themselves. Known as the financial interest and syndication rules, or 'fin-syn' as it was quickly dubbed, the legislation reshaped the landscape of American television and, in doing so, enormously strengthened the position of the Hollywood studios in production and sales, not just at home but overseas too.

The networks fought desperately to get the legislation reversed. NBC claimed that it would suffer 'irreparable damage' as a result of the ban on syndicating programmes at home and overseas. The measures provided a huge and to an extent unexpected bonanza for the Hollywood studios, which quickly stepped up their production of television programming and strengthened their distribution networks at home and overseas. As a result they quickly came to dominate the market for mini-series, movies of the week and half-hour situation comedies, the three types of shows which drove the TV market both in the United States and around the world.

In addition, by giving the studios the opportunity to expand their output of television programming, the fin-syn rules allowed them to underwrite the endlessly risky business of producing and distributing movies. Although the earning power of TV programming was far more limited than the massive sums which could be made from a hit movie, television had the advantage of offering an infinitely more stable and consistent source of revenue.

In overseas markets, the legislation benefited both the studios and the television industry. The studios had by now been selling feature films around the world for decades. They were far more experienced than the relatively new TV networks, and knew how to exploit overseas markets far more aggressively. In 1959, the studios had created a television division within the MPAA to fight for their interests abroad. Now, as a result of government legislation, they and other independent distribution companies had been effectively handed exclusive rights to sell American shows overseas. By maximizing the sale of television programmes around the world, the studios did themselves the further favour of expanding the television market for movies which had been sitting gathering dust, sometimes for years, in studio vaults.

It was the regulator, the FCC, rather than the studios which had been the driving force behind the introduction of this far-reaching legislation. Nevertheless, it suited the studios perfectly. Whatever its merits, and despite the furious opposition of the TV networks, it was without doubt a significant factor in helping the American film industry to survive one of the most tense and difficult chapters in its history. It also played a crucial role in not just sustaining but encouraging the creation of large, diversified American entertainment companies, which had interests spanning film, television and other related media.

It is tempting to speculate on what might have happened if similar legislation had been introduced in Europe in the late 1950s or 1960s. In the UK, Ealing Studios, Rank or British Lion would have been able to supply both the BBC and the commercial networks with thousands of hours of programming every year. This revenue would have enabled them to survive the slump in admissions and would have created a platform for significant expansion into other media.

Both the investment tax credits and the fin-syn rules played a significant role in enabling the Hollywood studios to recover from the recession of the late 1960s and early '70s, though in fairness neither had been framed with that intention in mind. As soon as they realized the level of financial benefits they could reap from such measures, the studios lobbied long and hard against any attempt to repeal them. It was the same mixture of good fortune and aggressive opportunism that had allowed them to turn contingent political events to their advantage during the Great War, and which had enabled them to embark on a new phase of economic expansion in the aftermath of 1945.

The structural reorganization of the studios and the legislative revolution in Washington were now complemented by a cultural revolution in Hollywood more radical than anything since the introduction of sound. In an increasingly young and liberal America, traumatized by the war in Vietnam, urban race riots and a rising drug culture, established moral certainties had begun to crumble. The old Production Code, with its restrictions on nudity, language and violence seemed at once outmoded and irrelevant. This changing mood was symbolized by the release, in 1966, of *Who's Afraid of Virginia Woolf?* The film featured Richard Burton and Elizabeth Taylor locked in a vicious and destructive on-screen relationship which in some respects at least seemed to mirror their much-publicized off-screen marriage. The film's torrent of abusive and sexually explicit language outraged many traditional movie-goers, but to younger audiences such a frank exploration of human emotions was a breath of fresh air after the tedious and anodyne predictability of most Hollywood romances. At first the MPAA refused to grant the film a certificate under the terms of its Production Code. After relentless pressure from Jack Warner – who himself had always had something of a predilection for foul language – they caved in. Soon afterwards, the MPAA liberalized the code, introducing a new certification category, 'Suggested for Mature Audiences', as a tentative step towards catching the mood of the times.

A spate of new films continued to test the Production Code to its limits. Nineteen sixty-seven saw the release of *Bonnie and Clyde*, Arthur Penn's graphic, gruesome tale of a pair of bank-robbers, starring Warren Beatty and Faye Dunaway. After a faltering start it became a runaway success, grossing almost $23 million.

The Production Code was all but finished. In 1968, after intensive negotiations, Jack Valenti, Eric Johnston's recent successor at the MPAA, successfully persuaded the studios to adopt the age-based ratings system of classification which continues to this day. The collapse of the old Production Code fuelled the cultural revolution which was already well underway in Hollywood. It gave a new, young group of film-makers the courage and freedom to tackle stories which reflected their experience of contemporary America. Their ambitions were encouraged by the success of *Easy Rider*, a counter-cultural odyssey starring Dennis Hopper and Peter Fonda which was released in 1969. Having cost less than half a million dollars to make, it grossed $19 million in North America alone. It proved that movies addressing a new popular culture, which sceptical middle-aged studio executives might regard as being on the fringes of society, could in fact attract mainstream audiences and, more importantly, box-office figures to match. In some ways, though, unlikely as it may have seemed, *Easy Rider* was a *Sound of Music* for the counter-cultural generation of younger film-makers, an overwhelming box-office success that inspired a host of poorly-made imitations which almost bankrupted their makers.

The new film-makers, soon described collectively as the 'movie brats', included the directors Francis Ford Coppola, Brian de Palma, George Lucas, Martin Scorsese and Steven Spielberg. Most of them had emerged from film schools, in Los Angeles and New York, which had begun to make an impact on the creative culture of film-making in the USA during the 1960s. All of them shared an abiding love for European cinema. Films like Coppola's *The Godfather* and its sequel, Scorsese's *Mean Streets* (1973) and Lucas's *American Graffiti* (1973) betrayed European influences that ran all the way from Sergei Eisenstein to Michael Powell, Bernardo Bertolucci and Jean-Luc Godard. 'He's an extraordinary talent,' Francis Coppola said of Bertolucci in remarks which seemed to define this fresh interest in European cinema. 'I look at two reels of *The Conformist* every day. He's my freedom therapy.' As had happened so often before, Europe once again found itself providing the creative stimulus for American cinema.

At first sight, the movie brats looked like classic exemplars of the auteur theory as defined by critic Andrew Sarris; artists struggling

It's all in the script – Darryl
Zanuck one of Hollywood's most
powerful production chiefs – first
at Warner Bros then at Fox –
hunts for the next box office hit

Louis B. Mayer, whose
management style veered
between savage attack and
shows of sentiment

Just sign on the dotted line – Harry Cohn cuts a deal with Stanley Kramer

Will Hays, first head of the MPPDA, enjoys a leisurely breakfast before going into battle on behalf of the moguls

J. Arthur Rank
and Carol Marsh
– a European
mogul with one
of his starlets

Alexander Korda
and Vivien Leigh
share a moment
of affectionate
humour

Alfred Hitchcock and James Stewart – Hitchcock became one of the most successful
European talents in Hollywood. Stewart was the first star to receive a significant share of a
film's earnings thanks to a deal engineered for him by Lew Wasserman on *Winchester '73*

Sophia Loren, one of the stars who brought a new-found glamour
to a resurgent European industry during the 1960s

Jean-Luc Godard, one of the architects of the French Nouvelle Vague. He eventually retreated from mainstream filmmaking altogether, undermining the commercial fortunes of the French industry he had helped to rejuvenate

During the 1959 Cannes Film Festival an informal meeting of 17 young directors was organized by UNIFRANCE FILM to allow them to exchange ideas. (left to right) François Truffaut, Raymond Vogel, Louis Félix, Edmond Séchan (1st row) Eduoard Molinaro, Jacques Baratier, Jean Valère (2nd row) François Reichenbach, Robert Hossein, Jean Daniel Pollet, Roger Vadim, Marcel Camus (3rd row) Claude Chabrol, Jacques Doniol-Valcroze, Jean-Luc Godard, Jacques Rozier (4th row)

Lew Wasserman and his wife Edie. For more than five decades MCA's Wasserman would be one of the most powerful figures in Hollywood, first as an agent then as a studio boss

**Earth to Hollywood –
You Win!**

To Jack Valenti
    With thanks, *Bill Clinton*

The special relationship between Hollywood and the White House that began with
President Woodrow Wilson in 1917 continues today. As head of the MPA for more than
thirty years, Jack Valenti has battled strenuously for the interests of the American industry
all over the globe

to maintain the purity of their vision in the face of industrial imperial-ism. '[W]e are the guys who dig out the gold,' claimed George Lucas. 'The man in the executive tower cannot do that. The studios are corporations now, and the men who run them are bureaucrats. They know as much about making movies as a banker does ... [T]he power lies with us – the ones who actually know how to *make* movies.'

The notion that the movie brats exercised real power was a seductive one, but it was essentially a myth created by the media. In truth, the relationship between the movie brats and the studios revealed the fundamental flaws of the auteur theory as preached by Sarris and practised by so many European directors. The strength and creative influence of these new American film-makers came not from their ability to defy the corporate system, but from their willingness to work with it, even though they knew that this at times meant sacrificing some aspects of their personal vision. When Francis Coppola was asked by Paramount to make a film of Mario Puzo's novel *The Godfather* in the early 1970s, he told his father: 'They want me to direct this hunk of trash. I don't want to do it. I want to do art films.' Understandably, Robert Evans, Paramount's production chief, was less than sympathetic: 'He couldn't get a cartoon made in town, yet he didn't want to make *The Godfather*.'

Faced with mounting financial pressures, Coppola finally agreed to do the film. When he finished shooting, after endless fights with the studio, he told an assistant that there were three golden rules for directing a film: to arrive with a completed script, to work with people you trust, and to ensure that no studio can order or veto changes. 'I have failed on all three,' he confessed. Yet *The Godfather* was an extraordinary commercial and critical success. When it opened it became the biggest grossing film of all time, transforming Paramount's fortunes and winning plaudits throughout the world. The first blockbuster of the 1970s, it was the catalyst for yet another series of changes that transformed the American movie business. With a budget of $6 million and a virtually unknown director, it represented an expensive gamble for Paramount. The studio played the risk for all it was worth, turning the film into a popular national event. It spent heavily on advertising and booked the film to open into an unprecedented number of cinemas across the country, with ticket prices fixed at the unusually high level of $4. The gamble paid off. By the end of the year, *The Godfather* had grossed $43 million in the United States, way ahead of its nearest competitor. Its success helped convince the new, younger breed of studio bosses that the movie business had changed for ever. Gone were the days when Hollywood could pump out hundreds of movies a year and assume that audiences would flock to see them simply out of a routine desire to be entertained. Television, which offered consumers entertainment around the clock, now very effectively performed that function. If cinema was to remain competitive, it would have to offer audiences a far more distinctive experience, something which television could never hope to emulate.

The success of *The Godfather* made it clear that if a studio had enough confidence and could back it with marketing expertise it could turn certain movies into 'events' that audiences would feel they simply could not afford to miss, even if they had to pay slightly more for the privilege. This approach meant spending heavily not only on production, but also on advertising and marketing. It followed that in order to extract the maximum value from the marketing campaign, the studio had to open the film in as many cinemas as possible and as quickly as possible. In theory, at least, this strategy was relatively fool-proof for, even if the film turned out to be a dud, simultaneous release would entice a large number of people to go and see it during the opening weekend, before the bad news had a chance to spread. As production and marketing budgets shot upwards, it was inevitable that the number of films being made began to decline. During the 1940s, the major studios had released about 450 pictures a year. By 1977 that had been cut by two-thirds, to around 150, the lowest figure since the introduction of sound. However, average productions costs jumped from around $1 million in the early 1970s, to over $11 million a decade later. A small number of blockbusters began to account for an ever-increasing share of the marketplace. Advertising costs likewise spiralled. At the same time, the conglomerates which owned the studios used the release of their 'event movies' to promote a slew of other products ranging from toys and games to books, records, T-shirts and baseball caps. This formula was applied with overwhelming success to films such as *Jaws*, *Star Wars* and *Close Encounters of the Third Kind*. The rewards that might be reaped from a hit film grew ever greater.

As costs soared, so too did the risks. The studios sought to minimize the latter in whatever way they could. One obvious way of doing this was to repeat a formula which had already proved to be successful, as was the case with *Nightmare on Elm Street* and *Police Academy*. Just as, during the 1930s, the studios had learned to use genres and stars as recognized 'brands', so in the 1970s and '80s sequels were designed to attract audiences by exploiting familiar ingredients.

The extent to which Hollywood movies appeared to have become little more than gigantic exercises in corporate merchandizing gave rise to understandable unease among those concerned with the vitality of the art of cinema. In an influential essay published in 1974 in *The New Yorker*, entitled 'Onward and Upward with the Arts – on the Future of the Movies', the critic Pauline Kael averred: 'There's a natural war in Hollywood between the businessmen and the artists. It's based on drives that may go deeper than politics and religion: on the need for status, and warring dreams.' She lamented that the businessmen seemed to have got the upper hand since it had become 'tough for a movie that isn't a big media-created event to find an audience, no matter how good it is'. She deplored the 'event strategy', arguing that 'the businessmen have always been in control of film production; now advertising puts them, finally, on top of public reaction as well'. Kael argued that America's finest directors could escape sterility only by getting together to create their own distribution outfit.

Kael's anxieties were understandable, and yet the 1970s came to represent one of the most richly creative periods in Hollywood's history. Movies like *The Godfather* and, especially, *The Godfather II*,

Scorsese's *Taxi Driver*, and Spielberg's *Close Encounters of the Third Kind*, all showed American film-making at its boldest and most inventive. They delighted critics and audiences alike, and in doing so made handsome returns for the studios which financed them. Far from undermining the creativity of the nation's film-makers, the cultural revolution in Hollywood had allowed a new generation to reinvent the grammar of American cinema. For all Kael's hostility to Andrew Sarris and an aesthetic theory founded on the mystique of the director's personality, she shared many of the assumptions that underpinned Sarris's work. Both of them believed that the business of film and the art of film were somehow in fundamental conflict. It was, in many ways, a thoroughly European way of looking at things and revealed just how much the culture of criticism, even in America, owed to concepts forged on the other side of the Atlantic.

In fact, the 1970s demonstrated that, at its best, American film-making was founded on a dynamic relationship between commerce and art. The antipathy that existed between the movie brats and the studios that hired them resolved itself through a synthesis in which creative brilliance was matched with commercial flair. The result was a string of hit movies that breathed new life into American cinema.

At the same time, star salaries began to soar. As with so many elements of the Hollywood story, the never-ending need to reduce the cost of film production seemed to run in a depressingly familiar cycle and, for studio accountants with long memories, the issue of star salaries was like a recurring nightmare. During the Great War the fees commanded by Mary Pickford, Charles Chaplin and a handful of others had rocketed as a result of their new-found fame. This runaway inflation was only brought under control as the studio system became more effective and dominant in the 1920s and '30s. As costs again spiralled crazily in the 1990s, it seemed as if the only thing that might put a stop to it would be the creation of a modern-day version of that same system.

In the 1960s, a new generation of superstars had made another unhelpful contribution to movie costs when Elizabeth Taylor was reputedly paid a million dollars for her role in *Cleopatra*, a film which, despite some success, never really came close to recouping its original cost. Not only did such fantastic deals raise expectations elsewhere in the industry, thereby contributing to a more general inflation of costs, what really frustrated the studio chiefs was that there was no apparent logic to it. The supply of talent in Hollywood had always been relatively inelastic. It could not be suddenly and conveniently expanded or contracted in response to audience demand or available capital. The reason for these occasional surges in salary costs lay not in any mechanism of the labour market but rather in commercial distrust and its effect on the changing patterns of deal-making between studios and talent.

MCA, the most powerful agency in the film and television business, had been obliged to pull out of representing talent when it acquired Universal in 1962. That cleared the way for new companies to enter the business. Among them was Creative Management Associates (CMA), founded by Freddie Fields and David Begelman, former agents with MCA. They took with them a number of stars including Henry Fonda, Paul Newman and Joanne Woodward. In 1975, CMA was acquired by Marvin Josephson's International Famous Agency to create International Creative Management (ICM).

ICM was led by a new breed of aggressive, high profile 'super-agents', very different from the self-effacing Lew Wasserman, or the rather more staid executives who continued to run William Morris. Sue Mengers, ICM's best-known agent of the period, typified the breed. In her early days at CMA, she had been driving down Sunset Boulevard when Burt Lancaster pulled alongside her. 'Oh, Mr Lancaster, who represents you?' 'IFA,' he replied. 'Not for long,' she riposted. On another occasion she cornered Ryan O'Neal and said, 'When are you going to get rid of your dumb asshole of an agent?' Lancaster wasn't persuaded, but O'Neal eventually joined CMA.

'Packaging' was now very much a constituent part of the business. The idea had begun much earlier when MCA offered a comprehensive service for major events – everything from bands and swizzle sticks to hotels. By the 1970s, packaging had become an infinitely more sophisticated process whereby an agent, or more rarely a producer, would bring together a project in the form of novel, play or a screenplay, attach to it a specified director and stars, and then seek to sell the combined package for an all-in fee. This took control of the development process away from the studio, and placed it in the hands of the agents and their clients. Packaging increasingly became a symbol of the way in which the balance of power had shifted in favour of the agents and the talent. Agents were no longer mere salesmen peddling their client's wares to the studios; they had become key brokers in the industry, instrumental in getting pictures off the ground.

Although it didn't seem like it at the time, perhaps the most significant upheaval occurred in January 1975 when a small group of agents broke away from William Morris, traditionally the most conservative company, to found Creative Artists Agency (CAA). Under the leadership of Michael Ovitz, CAA went on to become far and away the most powerful agency in the film business. Ovitz was undoubtedly one of the most powerful men in Hollywood. His discreet, low-key style epitomized the way in which the men who controlled the modern American movie business differed from the brash, outspoken moguls who had created and run the industry in an earlier epoch.

Growing up in the San Fernando Valley, Ovitz had originally planned to be a doctor. Then after he picked up a summer job as a tour guide at Universal Studios he determined to make his career in films and got a job in the mailroom of the William Morris Agency, working alongside Barry Diller who later headed Paramount and Twentieth Century-Fox. 'I was scared of them even then,' recalled one producer. 'Ovitz, he was so mysterious.' When the boss's secretary called in sick one day, Ovitz was asked to fill in, and began booking clients for TV shows.

In 1975, Ovitz left with four partners to start a new firm, Creative Artists Agency, with $100,000 funded by second mortgages. Hiring their wives as secretaries, they used card tables as makeshift furniture and began chasing potential clients. After working frantically, by summer 1980 they counted Robert Redford, Paul Newman and Dustin Hoffman among their clients.

A black belt in karate, with apparently Zen-like powers of concentration, Ovitz claimed to be a student of Japanese business practices, and conducted his own business in an austere, rigorously disciplined way. He often spoke in a half-whisper on the telephone, and might initiate even trivial conversations by asking, 'Are you on a hard line?' He could be every bit as ruthless as the moguls of old when required, apparently telling *Basic Instinct* screenwriter Joe Eszterhas, 'My foot soldiers who go up and down Wilshire Boulevard will blow your brains out,' though in fairness Ovitz has denied making the remark. He acted as a broker when Japanese electronic giants Sony and Matsushita were looking to buy a Hollywood studio, introducing them to potential vendors. His new role signalled the central place that agents had acquired in the Hollywood of the 1980s and early '90s. After a brief and unhappy spell as number two to Michael Eisner at Walt Disney, he left the company at the end of 1996, seeking new challenges.

This was the new corporate face of Hollywood, building on the buttoned-down discipline pioneered by Lew Wasserman's MCA. CAA, with its headquarters designed by I. M. Pei, epitomized an order, loyalty and rhythm that would have been entirely alien to the mercurial bosses who presided over Hollywood from the 1920s until the mid-1950s.

The agency business had certainly matured. Agents had become far more individually entrepreneurial as they sought to capitalize on the changes occurring in the business. As budgets had grown, so too had the rewards that could be reaped from a really successful film. This led to demands for ever higher fees for their clients since the number of truly popular 'bankable' stars remained relatively stable. The stars themselves became brand names which were used to sell the film, just as they had been during the 1930s and even earlier. But this time there was one crucial difference: it was no longer the studios that dictated this process, it was the stars themselves or more accurately their proxies, the agents.

Top stars had long been able to demand contractually a percentage of a film's box-office profits. A number of stars, and a handful of directors, now radically changed the established rules by demanding a percentage not of the profit but of box-office gross – the cash generated by a film before the deduction of any expenses. In part, this was because of the way in which the studios skilfully assigned overheads to films so that even hugely successful pictures appeared to show a loss on the company books. In 1992, writer Art Buchwald took Paramount Pictures to court in a case which centred on the studio's contention that *Coming to America* starring Eddie Murphy, a film which had grossed $350 million worldwide, had failed to generate net profits. The court upheld Buchwald's position, but the decision is still on appeal.

While deals tied to the gross remained relatively rare, they had a wider impact on star salaries in general. In the past, residual income had, in one way or another, always been tied to performance at the box office. Now the studios were competing so desperately for the services of leading stars that they began offering huge upfront salaries, as well as a gross percentage of the subsequent box-office performance of the film, paid from the first dollar the film generated at the box office, and sometimes as high as 20 per cent. This system was known as 'gross plus'. There were even rumours that stars were being guaranteed millions of dollars against future revenues from merchandizing. It was all analogous to the kind of rampant inflation which had gripped the salaries of American sports stars. In the 1930s, after the exhibitor had taken its share, the studio took virtually the entire box-office gross for itself. Today, as much as a third of that gross is being drawn-off upfront by stars, directors and other creative talent, so the studio has to work that much harder to show a profit.

What also drove the price of stars up was the entry of some new players into the Hollywood business. A group of independent companies including Cannon, run by two brash Israelis, Menaham Golan and Yoram Globus, DEG, headed by Italy's Dino de Laurentiis, and Carolco, entered the industry in the hope that they could exploit the burgeoning video market. Many of these companies were backed by credit from an obscure branch of Crédit Lyonnais in Rotterdam, where a banker called Frans Afman had begun specializing in loans to the American movie business. Eventually some $4 billion was pumped into these companies. It was appropriate that Crédit Lyonnais should be the principal supplier of capital; after all, it was that same bank which had been the first financial institution to take a serious interest in the film industry when it invested in Charles Pathé's fledgling company in the late 1890s. Even more ironically, Crédit Lyonnais supplied the finance which enabled a former ship's waiter from Italy called Giancarlo Parretti to mount a successful $1.3 billion takeover bid for MGM, the most venerable Hollywood studio and the vehicle which Parretti used for his takeover was none other than Pathé, descendant of the original company. As a result of the funds which poured in from Rotterdam and elsewhere to these companies, Carolco in particular became an instant 'major' by offering the stars more money than the studios offered. Since they did not control the distribution of their own movies – the really profitable part of the business – the new companies soon collapsed, leaving huge debts. The stars, however, were reluctant to forgo extravagant salaries.

Profit margins in Hollywood seemed modest. In 1996 Harold Vogel, a veteran industry analyst, estimated that the business of making movies carried a profit margin of only 5 per cent. Just a few years previously, it had been double that. 'The studios' financial managers would be better off putting their money into mutual funds or other securities,' observed *The Economist*. Perhaps this was hardly surprising. In the five years previous to that, cinema audiences in America had declined by 10 per cent, while costs had soared by 66 per cent. Much of that was down to the increasing cost of stars. Some, like Tom Cruise, Sylvester Stallone and Jim Carrey, started commanding salaries of $20 million per picture. Still the potentially unlimited profits that could be made from a huge hit such as *Jurassic Park*, *The Lion King* or *Independence Day*, together with the revenues from merchandising an endless array of products, made the film industry an irresistible lure. An ever smaller number of films captured ever increasing proportions of the box office and ancillary markets. This was a cause as well as a consequence of the significantly increased expenditure on advertising and publicity. A handful of highly profitable pictures were, at least for the time being, sufficient to pay for a larger number of losers.

Worldwide earnings from video now easily exceeded theatrical revenues. However, the percentage of consumer spending flowing back to the studios from these media such as video and pay-television was less than half the level that followed back from the sale of tickets at the box office. Overall growth in the video market therefore needed to be correspondingly greater for the studios to secure real benefits. This also gave the studios added incentive to press for the introduction of new technologies such as video-on-demand, a means of screening a large number of films across scores of television channels, which would provide them with a higher level of income.

Some saw dangers ahead. 'There's been a polarisation of performance at the box-office,' observed entertainment attorney Peter Dekom. 'The big movies perform well and everything else dies, so you get a lot of studio executives trying to package something so that it becomes a hit. That's when you get star-heavy deals with too much money thrown into them.' Some studios seemed to be attempting to drive down the costs of talent and engineer a return to a modified form of the old studio system, in which the moguls, rather than the stars and agents, called the shots. Walt Disney and Universal began striking deals in which key stars and directors were contracted for lengthy periods, rather than for a single movie, giving the companies a better chance to recoup their outlay. With an increasing number of films heavily reliant on special effects, some believed that the power of stars and agents would start to be eroded, as the special effects themselves increasingly became the stars. There were also signs that stars were attaching themselves to particular agents, rather than to an agency per se.

The studios, however, also had something of an interest in

keeping the cost of stars relatively high, since it acted as an effective deterrent to ambitious corporations like Polygram and Bertelsmann, companies keen to make star-driven movies which compete directly with the majors. 'The studios are basically distributors, banks and owners of intellectual copyrights, contracting out creative and production activities to others,' observed Richard Fox, executive vice-president at Warner Brothers. They also believe that the new markets provided by technologies such as digital and interactive television, as well as growth in the Far East, Eastern Europe and elsewhere, will eventually provide significant new revenues, in relation to which the cost of individual stars is a relatively minor issue.

The conglomerates controlling the studios grew ever larger, and nowhere was this more true than at Walt Disney. In 1984, Michael Eisner, the head of Paramount who had started as a clerk at NBC, was appointed chief executive at Walt Disney at a time when the moribund company was largely surviving on its library of animated classics. Together with Jeffrey Katzenberg, chairman of the company's film studio, Eisner revitalized Disney with a series of hugely successful animated films such as *The Lion King*, selling films like *Bambi* and *Aladdin* into the video market and opening a worldwide chain of Disney stores. One important advantage of animated films was that the company kept the box-office gross exclusively for itself, since the films had no stars with whom to share it. In 1994, Disney became the first studio to gross over $1 billion a year at the box office. Although films accounted for only a little over a third of the company's income, they formed the locomotive that drove the company, providing rides for theme parks and concepts for an endless stream of merchandising activities. When Disney acquired the ABC television network in 1995, it marked one more move in the consolidation of the American media industry into a handful of players. It also marked another stage in the alliance between the movie industry and television which had been gathering pace since the mid-1950s. No longer was it enough for a film company simply to sell its products to a network, now there was felt to be a strategic advantage in spending $19 billion to own the network. 'By the year

2000 we'll probably see ten or twelve companies controlling every-thing we see, hear and convey in entertainment, voice and data,' noted Andrew Barrett, head of the Federal Communications Commission.

The potential for international expansion was cited as a major factor driving the Disney/ABC deal. 'More and more I have noticed that our company's expansion is outside the US,' observed Eisner at the time the deal was unveiled. 'We think the combination of ABC and its assets, particularly outside the US ... gives us the ability to grow.' As the cost of making and marketing films rises, the studios need to keep expanding their audience and that is why markets like India, China and the 'Tiger Economies' of South-East Asia are becoming ever more important to them. The expansion of commercial television in Europe also promises to provide rich dividends; according to one estimate the Hollywood studios will make over $7.5 billion during the next decade from film deals they have recently made with German television stations alone.

The most consistently successful modern Hollywood studio, Warner Brothers, having travelled far from the days when its biggest star was Rin Tin Tin, now maintains relationships with a galaxy of stars including Clint Eastwood, Mel Gibson and Kevin Costner. In large part, that is down to the quality and longevity of its manage-ment; co-chairmen Terry Semel and Bob Daly have been in place since 1980, a continuity of management unparalleled in the volatile world of modern Hollywood. It was the success of *Batman* in 1989, grossing $250 million and generating a billion-dollar merchandising industry, which transformed the studio. They also increasingly specialized in star-driven vehicles, partly because, as Terry Semel put it: 'In the mid-'80s we realized that the really potent market for big-star movies was international, at times grossing two or three times the domestic rate.' In a move to diversify its interests further, Warner Brothers also successfully entered retailing and began making animated films.

In 1994, in perhaps the biggest gamble in Hollywood for decades, Steven Spielberg, together with former Disney executive Jeffrey

Katzenberg and billionaire record mogul David Geffen, unveiled plans to create the first major new studio in Hollywood since the formation of United Artists in 1919. Like the original United Artists, the company hoped to provide an environment in which creativity would flourish and in which 'distribution serves production, not the other way round'. It is positioning itself as a multi-media company for the new millennium by becoming a 'digital studio' with a strong emphasis on the production of animated material using the latest computer technology.

In the meantime, the core audience for movie-going had also fundamentally changed. The generation of baby-boomers born in the wake of the Second World War had become avid consumers of popular culture. During the 1960s and '70s, Americans invested significant amounts of capital in the construction of new cinemas, designed to meet the changing demographics of the nation. Had these cinemas not been built, it is questionable whether the rejuvenation of Hollywood would have been possible. Without these new suburban screens, it would have been much more difficult for the studios to attract younger audiences into the cinema, certainly in such large numbers as for films like *Ghostbusters*, *ET* and *Jurassic Park*.

The new investors in exhibition recognized that city-centre cinemas with just one or two screens were hopelessly unsuited to coping with the new suburban audiences. Three companies in particular – American Multi-Cinema, led by Stan Durwood; General Cinema, headed by Richard Smith; and National Amusements, under Sumner Redstone – revitalized the whole concept of the cinema by building entirely new complexes, often situated in suburban shopping malls.

These new cinemas, often with as many as six or eight screens, were easily accessible by car, incorporated other facilities such as restaurants, and were consciously designed to be attractive to family audiences. The success of the early multiplex cinemas led the companies to construct thousands of new screens across the United States and ensured that the teenage children of those baby-boomers who had moved to the suburbs now had easy access to the cinema. It was not just the number of screens, but the density of the screens across the country which played an important role in helping to boost the indigenous industry. The fact that the US had a much higher level of screen density than any major European country meant, all other things being equal, that a film had to play for a much shorter time to reach the same number of people. Spurred by the emergence of these new suburban screens across the United States, by 1973, almost 75 per cent of total cinema admissions in the United States were accounted for by twelve- to twenty-nine-year-olds (even though they represented only some 40 per cent of the total population).

In particular, the studios focused on marketing pictures to American teenagers. They were the easiest segment of the audience to reach. Every weekend, millions of them would queue at their local cinema, often regardless of what films were on offer. For a studio marketing department, the task was simply to try and ensure that these young movie-goers went to see *their* film, in preference to that of the competition. The most enthusiastic cinema-goers of all, known in the trade as 'avids', who went to see movies two or three times a week, were usually in their teens or early twenties. It became crucial to target these avids, since their opinions on a film would weigh heavily with their peers, and such 'word of mouth' could play a crucial role in determining the commercial fortunes of a film.

The key target audience for Hollywood movies became that group of American teenagers described by the producer and distributor Samuel Arkoff as 'gum-chewing, hamburger-munching adolescents dying to get out of the house on a Friday or Saturday night'. As a result of this ever-narrowing focus of marketing effort, the tastes of sixteen- to twenty-four-year-old American males began to exercise an increasingly decisive and utterly disproportionate influence over the kinds of films made and the way in which they were marketed. The studios would spend millions on previewing movies to selected audiences, just as Doc Giannini had screened films to teenage girls back in the 1920s. If the film scored badly with the preview audience, the studio would spend a great deal of time and money reworking it, just as Thalberg and Selznick had in the 1930s. The studios were now set up principally to market and distribute films to this audience, with a simultaneous release on 2500-plus screens, supported by expensive television campaigns and extensive media coverage. The economics of this policy were, in essence, very sound, since the distribution and promotion of a film at the cinema was the major factor in creating a market for that film on video and television. It was much harder, and far more labour-intensive, for these same studios to orchestrate a release on a few screens with enough advertising to create awareness, and then to go on to 'platform' the film in, say, 200 screens. If a film did not bite by the second week, they were in serious trouble, with little chance of recouping print and advertising costs, let alone making a profit.

Because the studios were geared to promote most major releases on the basis of the stars of the films, it was even more expensive to market a film that featured relative 'unknowns'. A studio had to work harder to promote such a movie to a public accustomed to making their decision about seeing a film primarily on the basis of 'who's in it'. In many ways the economics of modern studios militated against them handling more specialized pictures aimed at a specific strand of the audience. Some of the studios sought to address this problem by creating 'classics' divisions which distributed specialist, art-house releases. This gap in the market also created opportunities for independent distributors, such as New Line and Miramax, which concentrated on handling pictures aimed at a particular but profitable niche, rather than at the broad, mainstream audience.

If they were to have any chance of recovering their costs, American movies had to succeed in their home market, still by far the largest in the developed world. The fate of a movie in the United States also tended to determine how well it performed in the increasingly lucrative overseas markets. The giant promotional campaigns conducted by the studios in their home market, featuring stars, spin-off merchandise and a host of related gimmicks, often also made headlines around the world. The overwhelming importance of the American market in determining the worldwide fortunes of a film convinced many foreign film-makers to use the country as a launch-pad for their own productions. In 1994, the distributors of the British film *Four Weddings and a Funeral* adopted exactly this approach with the ironic result that the most successful box-office hit in the history of British cinema was advertised in its home market as 'America's No. 1 Smash Hit Comedy!'

Not only did American firms control the worldwide movie business, but such was the power of the American marketing machine that even foreign films could be successfully portrayed as American movies. In 1994, the net receipts of studio pictures from overseas theatres exceeded for the first time the amount earned from cinemas in the United States, with countries such as Germany, Japan, France and the United Kingdom generating the largest proportion. As well as action movies such as *Lethal Weapon* and *Speed* which had always performed well overseas, there were increasing signs that such quintessentially American comedies as *Forrest Gump* and *Wayne's World* were performing increasingly well outside the United States. At a creative level there was a greatly enhanced awareness of what kinds of films and stars worked overseas. 'We're seeing the Hollywood decision-making process increasingly focus on this phenomenon,' observed Michael Williams-Jones, former president and chief executive officer of United International Pictures, which handles overseas distribution for three major Hollywood studios. There was more than a grain of truth in *Variety*'s front-page headline of March 1995: 'Earth to Hollywood – You Win!'

17

'Films are made
for one or maybe two
people . . .'

JEAN-LUC GODARD, 1993

AS IN THE USA, the ethos of film-making in much of Europe underwent radical changes during the 1970s. But while the changes were very bit as far-reaching as those which shook Hollywood, there could hardly have been a greater contrast in terms of the nature and impact of the changes themselves.

The catalyst for this, as for so many other events that shaped the history of European cinema, was to be found in France. In May 1968 the French Republic had been shaken to its foundations when huge student protests and factory occupations led to the biggest general strike in European history, involving 9 million workers. For a few weeks it looked as if the government might be toppled by an unlikely alliance of students and workers. These events, which sent shockwaves throughout Europe, had their roots in a widespread contempt for the authoritarian regime of General de Gaulle which, combined with resurgent anti-Americanism, created an explosive cocktail of anger and resentment, particularly among students. Their virulent opposition to the Vietnam War, together with an unalloyed admiration for such iconic revolutionaries as Chairman Mao, Fidel Castro and Che Guevara, fanned their sense of injustice. Residual anger over the ill-fated military intervention in Algeria a few years earlier helped fuel this resentment. This was reinforced by a conviction that pursuit of academic knowledge in many universities and colleges was being undermined by the crude demands of Western capitalist economies, effectively turning these institutions into little more than 'brain factories'. Throughout May students and workers alike fought pitched street battles with the French police.

All this had serious consequences for the French film industry, since many of its leading practitioners, especially those who had been associated with the *Nouvelle Vague*, were closely identified with the events of May '68. The film-making community had already fought a political battle with the French authorities earlier that year. In February, the Minister of Culture, André Malraux, had sparked huge protests when he removed Henry Langlois, founder and director of the Cinématheque Français, from his post. Langlois who had been involved in collecting and preserving films since the 1930s had become a potent national symbol of cinema as an art-form. Although his management style had been under attack for some time, the government's decision to intervene in the operation of an independent institution provoked immediate outrage. A few days later, 3000 people, including virtually every French director of note, as well as stars such as Jean-Paul Belmondo, Simone Signoret and Michel Piccoli, gathered outside the Palais de Challiot for a public show of solidarity for Langlois. After a vociferous campaign that attracted support from individuals as diverse as Roland Barthes and Gloria Swanson, Langlois was reinstated. The clash served to underline the fractious relationship between the political establishment and many prominent members of the French industry.

The Cinématheque reopened in the rue d'Ulm in Paris on Thursday 2 May, with a triumphant Henry Langlois returning to a rapturous ovation. The following day, just 100 metres further down the street, the first students started their protest against the government amid a hail of missiles and tear-gas canisters. The events that became known simply as 'May '68' were underway.

That same month, largely at the instigation of the film technicians' union, a body calling itself Les Etats Généraux du Cinéma was formed with the aim of placing the cinema industry at the service of the working class. The name was a reference to the radical assembly which had championed the representation of ordinary citizens during the French Revolution of 1789. The organization's intention was to create a public sector of the film industry in competition with the private, 'based on the total absence of profit-making as a goal'. Among other things, it called for the 'reactionary structures of the Centre National de la Cinématographie (CNC) to be abolished'.

It was at the Cannes Film Festival that the most dramatic impact was felt. The genteel resort on the French Riviera had played host to a film festival since 1939. During that time, Cannes had become not only the world's most famous and prestigious film festival, but an event that was synonymous with images of opulent excess. Nothing better symbolized this than those aspiring starlets who would ritually fling off their bikinis to the delight of the packs of predatory photographers who stalked the beaches urging them on.

It was difficult to imagine anything more antithetical to the crusading spirit of May '68. For a few days most of those attending the festival seemed too absorbed in the usual round of cocktail parties and lavish gala dinners to comprehend the events that were shaking the rest of the country to its foundations. On the morning of 18 May, François Truffaut, Jean-Luc Godard and two other French directors gathered on the rostrum of a small room in the Palais des Festivals for a press conference on the Langlois affair. Truffaut called for an end to the festival, while Godard wanted all the screenings thrown open to the public, free of charge. Chaos ensued. An attempt to screen *Peppermint frappé*, a film by the Spanish director Carlos Saura, led to Truffaut, Godard and other directors hanging themselves from the curtains of the auditorium as the lights went down, in a rather theatrical bid to prevent the screening. While one half of the audience chanted, '*Projection! Projection!*', the other yelled, *'Pas de projection, révolution!'* Amid the uproar, the auditorium lights were switched back on and a heated debate ensued, lasting until well past midnight. The following day the organizers announced that all screenings were to be halted. With the festival shut, the cinéastes headed for Paris to join forces with the Etats Généraux. 'Many were convinced that the Cannes Festival was finished for ever,' one French critic later observed. Then on 30 May, just when it seemed he had finally conceded defeat, de Gaulle made a radio broadcast in which he dissolved the National Assembly, called elections for the following month and threatened military intervention to quell any further unrest. This, together with offers of increased salaries for the striking workers, helped to turn the tide in his favour. What had briefly seemed to be the dawn of a new social and political era evaporated. The Gaullist administration triumphantly swept back into power and the Etats Généraux collapsed when it became clear that the broader struggle of May '68 to overthrow de Gaulle and his authoritarian policies had ended in failure.

Even if the creative revolutionary fervour of many film-makers turned to bitterness and recrimination, the spirit of '68 remained alive. *Cahiers du cinéma*, despite its strident opposition to many of the traditions of French cinema, had always been relatively apolitical. After May '68, all that changed. In August, an editorial called for a 'Revolution in and through the cinema', adding that creating revolution in the cinema also meant 'fermenting revolution everywhere else at the same time'.

Those associated with *Cahiers* – which had remained a hugely influential publication – focused their energies on the need for a far more radical system of production and distribution based on a militant cinema, and for the creation of a far more radical school of film criticism. They remained implacably hostile to the entire conception of film as a profit-making activity. The political rhetoric of the journal was studded with references to Marxist-Leninism and, more particularly, to Maoism. The work of such celebrated contemporary French intellectuals as Louis Althusser, Roland Barthes and Jacques Lacan was also frequently invoked. During the

1970s, in France, the United States and elsewhere this rather chaotic combination of Marxism, semiotics and psychoanalysis played a defining role in shaping the study of cinema in universities, in specialized film journalism and in the actual practice of avant-garde film-making. Such theories left little room for the idea of cinema as a form of commerce, and sat uneasily with the cult of the director that was being promoted equally vigorously by many of the same film-makers whose work was critically dissected. After all, many of the theories associated with Barthes and his colleagues, based on concepts of language derived from the work of the linguist Ferdinand de Saussure, focused on the alleged 'death of the author' and the way in which the meanings generated by any 'text' – be it a book, a film or a painting – were not reducible to the intentions of any single individual or artist. The work of many *auteurs*, on the other hand, still seemed to owe a significant debt to that romantic idea of the individual artist struggling to express himself in the face of oppressive circumstances. In the case of the films of Jean-Luc Godard, much of their fame seemed to rest not on the 'death of the author' so much as the fact that he had transformed himself into a media celebrity, albeit an avowedly radical one. Indeed, it would be certain elements of the French media, notably the critics of the more prestigious newspapers and journals, who would do most to perpetuate the mythology of the *Nouvelle Vague* long after it had ceased to serve any useful purpose.

At a political level, too, the intellectual posturing of those associated with the movement had created something of a political paradox. Godard claimed that his struggle against the commercial imperialism of Hollywood was analogous to the eternal struggles of the working class against monopoly capitalism, yet he was forced to acknowledge that 'workers don't come to see my films'. The editors of *Cahiers* and the film-makers about whom they wrote faced the classic dilemma of a revolutionary intellectual elite: they spoke on behalf of people who, with few exceptions, remained utterly indifferent to the ideology that was being elaborated in their name. Having failed to win the masses over, Godard and his followers now turned their backs on them. Far from being egalitarian, the prevailing spirit among some of these film-makers evoked the very authoritarianism they claimed to be fighting. When Iain Quarrier, the producer of Godard's *One Plus One*, added some explanatory material for a London Film Festival screening without seeking Godard's agreement, the director physically assaulted him on stage. In 1969 Godard, together with the political militant Jean-Pierre Gorin, created the Dziga Vertov group (named after the Soviet film-maker of the 1920s) which proclaimed its intention as nothing less than revolutionizing the language of film: 'to make . . . a political cinema . . . to make concrete analysis of a concrete situation . . . to understand the laws of the objective world in order to actively transform that world . . . to know one's place in the process of production in order then to change it.'

In many ways, Godard was simply following the well-worn trajectory of the bourgeois revolutionary. Born in 1930 in Paris, his father was a Swiss physician and his mother came from a wealthy Parisian banking family. He grew up in Switzerland, and at the age of nineteen enrolled at the Sorbonne ostensibly to study ethnology, though he dedicated most of his energy to the self-consciously eclectic lifestyle typical of a young bohemian. He devoured films and books in huge quantities, and by 1949 had formed productive friendships with a wide variety of kindred spirits including Jacques Rivette, Eric Rohmer and François Truffaut. Together they were to become the nucleus of the *Nouvelle Vague*. Rohmer later recalled that the group would sometimes watch four films a day, amounting to about a thousand a year, at various cinemas around Paris.

Godard's family eventually cut off his income, to make ends meet he began to steal from those around him; these thefts allegedly included a raid on the cash-box at *Cahiers du cinéma*. He even spent a brief spell in a Swiss gaol. After securing a job in the local publicity department of Twentieth Century-Fox, Godard went to work for his friend, the producer Georges de Beauregard. Godard's early films were packed with thematic and stylistic references to American cinema, most notably *A bout de souffle* in which the protagonist, played by Jean-Paul Belmondo, quite consciously models himself on Humphrey Bogart. The film achieved great critical and box-office success. By the time of *Le Mépris*, Godard had grown far more sceptical of the film industry as an economic institution, and the crass character Prokosch was apparently modelled on one of the film's producers, Joseph Levine. The Godard of this period seemed in reality far more of an intellectual fashion plate than a committed radical. 'I was always taken aback by the glum look and the brown shoes that went with his black suits,' recalled the producer Anatole Dauman. 'Adding to his paradoxical dandyism, he usually wore a tatty, ill-fitting raincoat . . . But the miscreant was at heart, friendly and charming; a good companion rather than a Marxist comrade.' Over time Godard came to prefer the role of the strident militant to that of dandy. With *Made in U.S.A.* and *Deux ou trois choses que je sais d'elle*, Godard embraced increasingly explicit political statements, criticizing the entire panoply of capitalism, together with the dehumanizing social and personal relations which he now believed it engendered. For Godard, as for so many French and European intellectuals, the commercialism of Hollywood epitomized everything he despised about the West. In France, other militants formed collectives to undertake film production but, as was the case with Godard, despite an overt commitment to collaborative work, most of these bodies were dominated by particularly strong-willed individuals. Of these, only Marin Karmitz, a Romanian-born member of a proletarian Maoist group, would eventually succeed in significantly influencing French cinema. Karmitz, through his company MK Productions, later expanded into distribution and exhibition helping promote the early work of young directors like Wim Wenders.

By now, the concept of the director as king had become firmly enshrined among serious film-makers and critics right across Europe. For a while it served as an invaluable catalyst for change. During the 1950s and early '60s, the *auteur* theory had reinvigorated the study of Hollywood directors like Raoul Walsh, Howard Hawks and Alfred Hitchcock. It encouraged an entire generation of French film-makers to overthrow the more staid traditions of their national cinema, but it left a legacy that eventually proved every bit as dangerous artistically as it was damaging commercially. The cult of the director, taken to its extreme by Godard and his acolytes, only served to accentuate the increasing self-absorption of many European directors. After the shattered dreams of May '68 some of them seemed to want little to do with producers, screenwriters or even, for that matter, the audience. Jean-Claude Carrière, one of France's leading screenwriters, later observed that the notion of the *auteur* as espoused by such directors was no longer that 'a film must bear the mark of its director', but that 'an author's film is one in which the director principally talks about himself'. As a result, the French screenwriter became something of an endangered species.

Despite all evidence to the contrary, the more insular and self-regarding the movies, the more they were likely to be greeted by a few influential critics as evidence that art had triumphed over the robber-barons of capitalism, some of whom just happened to run the movie industry. The critics fed the vanity of the directors every bit as much as the directors played to the critics. The real tragedy was that, by and large, the audiences simply left them to it, going off in their thousands to see *Jaws* and *Star Wars*. And so it went on, in France, Germany, Italy and elsewhere in Europe, throughout the 1970s.

In France, media attention remained targeted on the audiences who had flocked to the *Nouvelle Vague* films of the late 1950s and very early 1960s. The legacy of *Cahiers* and the culture of ideas it inspired was still apparent in the mid-1990s, even if it was based on something of an exaggeration of the actual impact of the original *Nouvelle Vague*. With each succeeding year, the exponents of these ideas saw themselves as increasingly beleaguered. Klaus Eder, secretary general of the Fédération Internationale de la Press Cinématographique (FIPRESCI) wrote in 1994:

> Of all the different obligations that film criticism finds itself exposed to, the worst is the maelstrom of the mainstream. In the 60s, a new film from Jean-Luc Godard was an event. Today,

a critic who wants to discuss a new film from Godard would, more often than not, get the laconic, indifferent reply 'Do we have to?' . . . Today, films are a form of entertainment, and at best, the critics are just expected to say whether it was good or boring entertainment.

Perhaps because so many directors had started their lives as critics, a symbiotic relationship developed between the culture of criticism and that of film-making throughout much of Europe. Both betrayed an overwhelming nostalgia for the heyday of the *Nouvelle Vague*, a nostalgia which ultimately became crippling. In France it was almost as if time itself stood still: in 1960 the average age of film directors was twenty-eight; by 1993 it was fifty-five, with 85 per cent of them over fifty.

Meantime, pornographic films became increasingly popular. Since the late 1960s there had been a notable increase in the number of pornographic films securing international distribution, most of which originated in Scandinavia. In France, a more relaxed regime of censorship under the presidency of Giscard d'Estaing, encouraged the production of similar films which secured distribution in mainstream cinemas. Among these was Just Jaeckin's *Emmanuelle*, a soft-core picture which became a phenomenal success, becoming the top grossing film of 1974 in France, and one of the most popular French pictures of all time. Unsurprisingly, harder material followed in its wake. During the period 1975–79, pornographic films accounted for an average of 50 per cent of all productions. Left and right alike denounced what one newspaper called the 'Macs du Porno', but to little avail and it was not until the emergence of video in the early 1980s that the popularity of pornography at the cinema began to die out.

In some parts of Europe during the 1970s, film-making did appear to have been genuinely refreshed. In Germany, a new wave of film-makers rose to prominence, led by directors such as Rainer Werner Fassbinder and Wim Wenders, whose films were financed substantially by the television companies. Much their work was truly innovative and popular. As with the French *Nouvelle Vague* fifteen years earlier, one of the most striking ironies about the rise of the New German Cinema was that many of its champions were heavily influenced by Hollywood directors such as Douglas Sirk and Samuel Fuller. That they in turn had been influenced by a galaxy of talented German film-makers such as Billy Wilder, Fritz Lang and F. W. Murnau who had moved to Hollywood in the 1920s was a wonderful irony. Now some forty years later the influence of those early German directors was being refracted back to contemporary German film-makers through the prism of Hollywood. Even so, neither the money nor the ideas were sufficiently broad-based to make a significant or lasting change to the general trend in European cinema, and the vitality and energy which had once characterized the new wave slowly evaporated, for the most part to be replaced by an increasingly sterile mediocrity.

German cinema, too, had its share of film-makers who, like their counterparts in other countries, appeared to harbour something approaching contempt for their audience. They included directors like Vlado Kristl, originally from Yugoslavia, who, after making a series of innovative shorts for Bavarian television in the 1960s, became increasingly hostile to the mainstream cinema of the 1980s. Having made films with provocative (if honest) titles like *Death to the Audience* (1983) Kristl went on to proclaim 'that 'A full movie house entails low motivations' and 'Kill off the spectator and then we'll have culture'.

Traditions of radical film-making had always functioned alongside the mainstream commercial cinema in Europe, but for much of the 1970s and '80s those traditions were debased to the extent that they seemed to function simply as an excuse for failure. Indeed, by demonizing the mainstream industry as part of a global capitalist conspiracy, and by dismissing reluctant audiences as victims of 'false consciousness', some European film-makers managed to contort themselves into a position from which commercial failure seemed a badge of artistic success, and any form of commercial success somehow carried the stigma of artistic betrayal. So while the Hollywood industry of the early 1970s reinvented itself in the image of its audience – young, inventive, self-confident – Europe's film industry succeeded only in mirroring the disillusion of those who worked in it – tired, rancorous and increasingly inward-looking.

The great French director François Truffaut eloquently described the problem in 1975:

> When I was a critic, films were often more alive though less 'intelligent' and 'personal' than today. I put the words in quotes precisely because I hold that there was no lack of intelligent directors at that time, but that they were induced to mask their personalities so as to preserve a universality in their films . . .
>
> All that is changed; not only has cinema caught up with life in the past fifteen years, sometimes it seems to have gone beyond it. Films have become more intelligent – or rather, intellectual – than those who look at them. Often we need instructions to tell whether the images on the screen are intended as reality or fantasy, past or future; whether it is question of real action or imagination.

During the 1970s and '80s, this strident insistence on the primacy of the director's vision, no matter what the cost, became the unquestioned orthodoxy throughout much of Europe. The power and privilege of the *auteur* was also inscribed within the legal and institutional framework governing film production. With the acquiescence of state bureaucrats, in some countries subsidies were assigned specifically to the director, without any reference to the production company, the distributor or anyone else. With a little help from subsidy systems and television, it was relatively easy for even unproven directors to fund their films, regardless of whether or not they had any interest in capturing an audience. By the early 1990s, it was estimated that almost half the films produced in Germany never received any type of theatrical release, forming instead the staple diet of television in the early hours of the morning.

The generation of May '68 did much to perpetuate this state of affairs. It became hard to judge whether or not Godard was joking when in an interview published in the French newspaper *Libération* in 1993 he asked: 'Do you know the definition that Jules Renard gave of the critic? "The critic is a soldier in an army put to rout, who deserts and goes over to the enemy." And who is that enemy? The audience . . . I think that films are made for one or maybe two people.'

Directors had, of course, played a vital role in revitalizing production in Hollywood, but their power was to some extent circumscribed. In the system used in the United States and Great Britain it was, on the whole, the producer who controlled the copyright, with the work of the director being the subject of a commercial contract. The *droit moral* (moral right), which forms the linchpin of the legal system for film production in France and other parts of Europe, gives the author of the work the sole right to perform or publish it, or to withdraw it from the marketplace. In theory at least, it gave the director, conceived as the author of the film, ultimate control over the version of a picture that was released.

The concept of the moral right first appeared in France during the late nineteenth century. It was not until 1957, however, – coincidentally just before the appearance of the *Nouvelle Vague* – that it was inscribed within the framework of French law. In point of fact, the *droit moral* is almost never invoked, partly because it has always been hedged about with qualifications which made it difficult to exercise; both the director and the producer have to agree that the work is complete before the *droit moral* can become operative. Directors also have practical issues to consider, knowing that it will be that much harder to finance their next films if they decide to exercise their moral rights and withdraw works from distribution. 'If we were to cling to the notion of moral rights we wouldn't work at all,' admitted French director Marcel Ophuls. Its importance is more symbolic than actual; it seems to legitimize the idea that the director as *auteur* in the supreme power in the film-making process. '[M]oral rights are the link between an author and his work,' explained a French lawyer, 'the work itself is an extension of the individual.'

In the United States, by contrast, there is no moral right. Moreover, copyright law does not make a distinction between ownership and authorship – the owner is defined as the author. So the producer, in effect the studio or independent production company, is considered to be the 'author' of a film and exercises ultimate power over its finished form, having the right to determine final cut, unless contractually agreed otherwise. Only in the late 1980s did the US sign the Berne Convention, which gives an author the right to object to any unauthorized changes to the work. But since the US definition of authorship equates to ownership, this had no practical implications for American directors.

Although the *droit moral* was almost never invoked, it became a symbol of the way in which a group of cinéastes deified the role of the director at the expense of just about everyone else involved in film production. The *auteur* theory had begun as a polemical movement, based on a quintessentially romantic conception of the beleaguered artist, and was designed in part to salvage the neglected reputations of certain Hollywood directors. It was in continental Europe, however, that its impact was most strongly felt. It rapidly mutated into a political ideology which played a key role in shaping both the aesthetics and the economics of European film-making for twenty-five years or more. In doing so, it seems as if it has condemned much of Europe's cinema to a cultural ghetto from which it may never have the will to escape.

18

A Bridge Too Far?

IN FILM-MAKING, as in so much else, the British had always felt closer to the Americans than to their European neighbours. This was reflected in the fact that the *auteur* tradition never exercised the same kind of influence in the United Kingdom. The renewal of British film-making in the mid-1970s and early '80s was driven by a somewhat different set of imperatives. To a large extent, the changes were instigated by a group of people who had started their careers in the advertising industry. As well as myself, this group included Alan Parker, Hugh Hudson, Adrian Lyne and Ridley Scott.

Perhaps this was because in the early 1970s the UK was less prone to the radical political disillusion which seemed to permeate France, Italy and even Germany. In Britain, much of the excitement that had been generated by the 1960s was seen as relatively superficial, having more to do with fashion and, especially, popular music. Politics was something of a sub-text to all this. In France, the legacy of the country's colonial interests in the Far East fuelled the spirit of anti-Americanism which was so widespread in the wake of the Vietnam War. No such emotional ties existed in the UK. As a consequence, in the 1970s the political fall-out was far less severe. Not only that, but the UK had a tradition of 'creative' producers such as Alexander Korda and Michael Balcon. Although it had produced some very influential directors, the industry had never really been held hostage to the notion of director-as-king, as was increasingly the case in France.

In many ways, what I and others were doing with films like *That'll be the Day* and *Stardust* was not dissimilar to what film-makers like George Lucas were doing in America with pictures like *American Graffiti*. The work of both groups addressed itself directly to a younger audience, and was frequently tinged with similar elements of recent nostalgia. Because many of us had come from advertising, we knew that films, like any other product, really had to be *sold* to their audience. The American studios were simultaneously coming to recognize the increasing value of sophisticated marketing and distribution. Until the mid-1970s, a rule of thumb for British producers was that an average of 10 per cent of the budget of a film was spent on its marketing. When we released *Midnight Express* in 1978 it represented a significant new departure, being the first picture on which expenditure on prints and advertising significantly *exceeded* the negative cost. Sadly, the lesson of its success was largely lost on British distributors.

The greater problem facing the British industry, and one which was making production financing increasingly difficult, was that the overall national market for feature films was severely contracting. Admissions had started falling during the late 1960s and now seemed inextricably locked into a downward spiral.

In 1970, looking for opportunities to break out of that spiral, together with my partner producer Sandy Lieberson, I formed a company called Visual Programmes Systems (VPS). The decline in cinema admissions, brought about by television and the social changes which had rocked post-war Britain, had led us to believe that the future of the audio-visual industry lay in video cassettes.

VPS could at that time have acquired the video cassette rights to every film ever made in Britain – from Korda's London Films to Rank and Ealing – for not much more than £1 million. Sadly, our backers eventually decided that such a purchase was simply too risky. Twenty-five years later, it would have cost billions of pounds to have acquired those same rights.

Other opportunities were also missed. Whenever the British developed a really strong skills base it seemed that they failed to capitalize on it. In the late 1960s, with Stanley Kubrick's decision to make *2001: A Space Odyssey* in Britain, the UK industry was handed the chance to develop a unique talent base in an increasingly important and highly profitable branch of the industry. Most of the effects in the early parts of the film – which involved intricate work with models – was done by British members of a hastily constructed special-effects team. As a result of this, and their work on the James Bond movies, British technicians developed an international reputation for their skills with physical and mechanical effects. It was, after all, the British who had pioneered the images of exploding policemen and flying automobiles during the earliest days of cinema, and who had been responsible for more sophisticated techniques during the 1930s when Alexander Korda made his adaptation of H. G. Wells's *Things To Come* as well as *The Ghost Goes West*, both of which relied heavily on special effects.

Britain's skills in this department were further boosted in 1975 when George Lucas and Gary Kurtz decided to use many of the team that had worked on *2001* to shoot *Star Wars* at Britain's Elstree Studios. A British team was also recruited to handle the physical effects, including the creation of R2-D2 and the other androids. They won the trust of Lucas who, demonstrating his loyalty, returned to Britain to make a whole string of high-budget, special-effects pictures including *The Empire Strikes Back*, the *Indiana Jones* series and *Who Framed Roger Rabbit?* As a result, a host of model-making and optical-effects companies were established in London as well as at Elstree and Pinewood studios, with the latter playing host to the Bond, Superman and Batman pictures.

The British industry, and its government, did little or nothing to encourage or invest in this pool of by now unique and highly-skilled talent. As a result, the cream of Britain's special-effects industry left to join other enormously valued British technicians who found Hollywood more receptive and appreciative of their gifts.

Still, even those producers with access to significant amounts of capital struggled to find a place on the world stage. Several attempts to make films for the international market ended in abject failure. At the end of the 1970s, Lord Lew Grade, a man of expansive tastes, rolled the dice on *Raise the Titanic*, a film self-consciously designed to appeal to audiences on either side of the ocean. The movie was plagued by logistical problems during its production – the tank designed to hold the model *Titanic* constantly leaked water and a large team were kept on standby to fill it – and it all turned out to be a vastly expensive flop. 'It would have been cheaper to lower the Atlantic,' Grade ruefully remarked in the wake of the débâcle.

In 1981 the worldwide success of *Chariots of Fire*, plus Richard Attenborough's *Gandhi* of the following year, at last seemed to herald the transformation of the British industry into a dynamic and internationally competitive business. *Chariots* took over $30 million in the United States, while picking up four Oscars, including that for Best Picture. *Gandhi* likewise made handsome profits at the worldwide box office, in the process winning an even larger clutch of Oscars.

Chariots of Fire, the story of athletes Eric Liddell and Harold Abrahams, had actually been privately financed by Allied Stars, controlled by Mohammed Fayed, in partnership with Twentieth Century-Fox. But it was a small independent British company, Goldcrest, run by Jake Eberts, a self-effacing, former banker, which, having put up £17,000 to pay for the original screenplay, reaped the richest rewards, attracting new investors in the company. When Goldcrest came up with *Gandhi* the following year, the firm's reputation was sealed; in the eyes of the British media, and by extension the British public, Goldcrest was the company which single-handedly was about to revive the fortunes of the British film industry. The very name Goldcrest was evocative of those values of quality embodied in its films. It had a string of critical and commercial successes with films like *Room with a View* and my own productions such as *Local Hero* and *The Killing Fields*. At the 1982 Oscar ceremony Colin Welland made his exultant announcement that 'The British are coming!' and despite having been an ironic reference to Paul Revere, the call was taken up as a rallying cry for all those who fondly believed that the long-cherished dream of an all-conquering British film industry was finally about to be realized.

One of the most remarkable things about Goldcrest's success was that it attracted significant investment into the film industry from the City of London for the first time for decades. Much of this was due to the financial acuity of Jake Eberts, but Goldcrest was not alone in building strong links with the City. Helped by a system of tax incentives (known as capital allowances) which encouraged outside investors to pour money into features, a significant amount of institutional finance began pouring into the production of British movies. An insanely complicated arrangement known as sale and leaseback allowed an outside firm to acquire a film from a producer and lease it back to them, with the cost of purchase being set-off against tax. A host of firms ranging from the high-street banks to Marks and Spencer began investing in the film industry on this basis, as a means of reducing their own tax burden.

It was Goldcrest, above all, which symbolized the new link between the film industry and the City. The company had used a leasing deal to help finance *Gandhi*, but a number of City institutions such as the Electra Investment Trust and the National Coal Board Pension Fund were shareholders. In addition, one of Goldcrest's original backers was Pearson Longman, a firm which epitomized the patrician culture of much of British business and whose other interests included the *Financial Times* and Penguin Books.

To those with a taste for history, this apparently magical success story had ominous echoes of the mid-1930s, when the astonishing worldwide success of Alexander Korda's *The Private Life of Henry*

VIII prompted many to believe that the British film industry was about to throw off the shackles of American domination. Then too the City, led by the Prudential, had clamoured to invest in the British film industry, although the boom quickly turned to burst when it became apparent that Korda had over-reached himself.

Goldcrest, too, eventually fell prey to the same mistakes that Korda had made, mistakes which had similarly almost destroyed Rank during the late 1940s. In 1985 Goldcrest embarked on the simultaneous production of three major movies: *Revolution*, a histori-cal drama starring Al Pacino and budgeted at $15 million; *Absolute Beginners*, a musical set during the 1950s, directed by Julien Temple and budgeted at around $8 million; and one of my own productions, *The Mission*, a period film starring Robert De Niro and Jeremy Irons, budgeted at $17 million. Although all three films were partly financed by international distributors, Goldcrest, eager to reap the rewards of success, had been ready to shoulder a significant element of the risk. At these prices the films would have to succeed in the United States if they were to have any real chance of covering their costs. The fact that *The Killing Fields* had not performed as well as expected in the United States had led me to conclude that the American market for this kind of prestige, quality picture was soften-ing. Goldcrest wanted to make the film, but for less. I knew that couldn't be done, and suggested that if they had reservations they would be far better off pulling out of *The Mission* completely. Set against the knowledge that Goldcrest would have to shoulder some of the risk for this group of fairly costly films was the fact that two of them films featured 'A' list Hollywood stars – De Niro and Pacino – and a raft of Oscar-winning talent behind the camera. The third, *Absolute Beginners*, was admittedly a greater risk but featured appear-ances by international pop stars including David Bowie and Ray Davies. It had a smaller budget and was backed by two adventurous British production companies, Palace Pictures and Virgin, both of whom had built a reputation for their ability to produce and market self-consciously hip movies aimed at the burgeoning youth market.

It was only when two of the films, *Revolution* and *Absolute Beginners*, ran into difficulties and their production costs started to soar that it become apparent how much of a gamble Goldcrest had taken on. Both films were bedevilled by creative and logistical problems, some of which were clearly beyond the control of the producers. There was no similar excuse for the furious rows which erupted over the scripts of both films, and which would continue raging even as they were being edited. *The Mission* suffered its own logistical problems but managed to come in within budget. In truth, there are *always* crises; it's the ability to deal with the crises that is the making of a good or bad producer. Once a film starts, producing is, for the most part, crisis management; you have no other real function. In many respects, you are probably in the way.

What made matters worse was the fact that as the budgets of *Absolute Beginners* and *Revolution* began to climb, so did the value of the dollar against the pound. The sales to the American distributors had been calculated in dollars. When the original American deal for *Absolute Beginners* had been struck with Orion, the pound was valued at $1.56. While the movie was being shot, the exchange rate went to approximately $1.06, but all the costs remained in sterling. Orion's payment for the US rights, which would not be made until the film was completed, was originally intended to cover 90 per cent of the budget. By the time the cheque was paid it covered barely 60 per cent.

Revolution was a critical and box-office disaster and *Absolute Beginners* fared little better. One of the problems with *Revolution* was that Goldcrest went into it too fast. The company could have saved itself a fortune had it had the courage to insist that the whole thing be delayed by four or five months. An important new investor who had signalled his willingness to put up finance failed to materialize. These events, together with the massive cost over-runs, spelled disaster for Goldcrest, and for everything it represented. Although it won the Palme d'Or at Cannes and, following an Oscar nomination as Best Film, showed some initial promise at the box office, *The Mission* compounded the company's problems by also failing to recoup its costs. Before long everything was in tatters as management desperately sought a buyer for the company. In October 1987, at a meeting lasting about three minutes, Goldcrest, which just a couple of years earlier had been the blue-chip symbol of the British film industry, was sold at a knock-down price to Masterman, a company controlled by Brent Walker whose interests ranged from betting shops to pubs.

Like Korda and Rank before it, it seemed that Goldcrest was fatally seduced by the idea that British films could conquer the American market. Its real mistake was one of timing; had it not embarked on three expensive films at one time, had any two of them been better, had the value of the pound remained constant, or had the promised re-financing been achieved, then the company might have pulled off its daring coup.

As the critics and commentators sat down once again to write their obituaries for the British film industry, they conveniently chose to overlook the fact that the Golden Age of the British film industry, whose revival Goldcrest was supposed to herald, was an entirely mythical notion. Ever since the introduction of sound in the late 1920s, British producers and politicians alike had been engaged in a futile battle to wrest control of a market from an industry which was overwhelmingly better financed and far more sophisticated on the other side of the Atlantic.

The difficulties of British producers were made more acute by their own failure to build up interests in distribution and cinema exhibition which might have given them the capital to mount a serious domestic challenge to the Hollywood studios. In that sense at least, Goldcrest was little different. Although the company retained the notional copyright to its projects, the rights to distribute its films were licensed to others and most of the profits from its successful films therefore returned to those companies. Unlike its two larger rivals, Rank and EMI, the company had no interests in exhibition.

In many respects, the real problem was the burden of expectation. It was absurd to believe that one, relatively small independent production company could relaunch the British film industry, especially at a time when admissions had fallen to their lowest level since before the Great War. For, as was later to become clear, the catastrophic decline in box-office admissions had little to do with the quality of the films on offer, and everything to do with the parlous state of British cinemas, most of which richly deserved the epithet 'flea pit' that was routinely applied to them.

The collapse of Goldcrest had a disastrous impact on the relationship between the British film industry and the City. More than a decade later it would still be virtually impossible for independent British film and television producers to raise money from City investors. The bankers' aversion to film was exacerbated by the ideological obsessions of Margaret Thatcher's Conservative government which, attached to its simplistic free-market dogmas, gradually phased out capital allowances which eventually disappeared in 1986. The Eady Levy, the mechanism which recycled money from the box office back into production, was abolished by the 1985 Films Act. The White Paper which proposed abolition argued that it represented 'an unreasonable burden on the cinema exhibition industry', and that it did not provide 'an efficient way of encouraging an economic activity that should be essentially oriented towards the market'. But like the system of automatic aid in France, the Eady Levy was based on the operation of market forces. It was an industrial instrument for promoting cultural objectives; the more commercially successful the film, the larger the amount remitted to the producer, and the more money was available to stimulate the production of more British films.

The problem with Eady was that, by the mid-1980s, cinema admissions had fallen so sharply that the amounts of money it generated were becoming relatively insignificant. Nevertheless, that did not invalidate the principle of recycled revenues. What was required was not the abolition of the levy, but its intelligent extension to other outlets which depended heavily on the supply of feature films, such as video. In this way, the huge ancillary sums generated by the distribution of films on video in the 1980s could have been recycled into new production. After all, the effect of video was to promote a renewed interest in feature films which eventually may have helped push up cinema admissions. This process worked both ways; there was some evidence that films that were screened in multiplexes were subsequently rented more frequently on video, to the further benefit of the American studios who owned or controlled many of the multiplexes and the video distribution companies. This in turn spurred them to build further screens.

The role of the Eady fund was partially replaced by British Screen Finance, a private organization aided by government grant. Despite relatively meagre resources, throughout the late 1980s and the '90s British Screen would play an extremely valuable role in nurturing new talent, fostering links with Europe and helping to finance projects which might have had difficulty in attracting funding on a purely commercial basis. Among the films it supported were *Scandal*, *The Crying Game* and *Orlando*, all of which achieved box-office success. Despite such successes, by the second half of the 1980s, any British producer with serious ambitions to make sizeable mainstream movies was almost entirely dependent on American investment.

In 1985, fifty-four films were produced in the UK. By 1989, that number had shrunk to just thirty. Just as damaging as the overall decline in investment was the fact that in real terms average budgets fell sharply from £5.1 million in 1984 to just £3.4 million in 1993. Similar patterns were recorded in many other European countries. During the same period, the average budget of movies made by the Hollywood studios more than doubled, from $14.4 million in 1984 to $29.9 million in 1994, and the average amount spent by the Hollywood studios on prints (copies) and advertising for their films rose from $6.6 million to $16 million. The Americans were investing more money and expertise than ever in marketing and distribution. While there are no comparable figures for the changes in European print and advertising costs, any rise is likely to have been minuscule; indeed, it is perhaps doubtful if, prior to the mid-1990s, there was any increase at all in real terms.

Certainly, the anecdotal evidence from individual films reveals a bleak picture. In the summer of 1993, Universal Pictures budgeted $68 million on marketing *Jurassic Park* – possibly more than the cost of actually making the film. Their confidence was handsomely rewarded. At the other end of the scale there was the example of *The Crying Game*. Its UK promotion budget was a paltry £50,000 and, sadly, it paid the price at the box office. It was not until the film was shown in America and began to be promoted lavishly as a thriller with a twist in its tail that it suddenly took off and became a major box-office success. As always, the American distributors understood that having a first-rate film on your hands does not guarantee success – you have to realize its potential by going out and selling it. Incredibly, in many European countries, the attitude still exists that a good film shouldn't really *have* to be marketed at all, that the public will somehow instinctively find and appreciate artistic quality without the assistance of a vulgar marketing campaign.

While Goldcrest acted as standard-bearer for the British industry, other companies including Thorn-EMI, Virgin, HandMade and others marched along behind. With the collapse of Goldcrest, and its adverse impact on the financing climate and levels of confidence in the industry, many of these companies, large and small, began scaling back their own activities. The British film production industry returned once more to the doldrums.

While the climate for making films deteriorated, a revolution was sweeping another previously neglected sector of the British industry, one which would eventually transform the face of cinema-going across much of Europe. Before November 1985, few in Britain had ever heard the name of American Multi-Cinema (AMC), one of America's largest cinema-owners. AMC was a family-owned firm based not in smog-encrusted Los Angeles but in Kansas City, a Midwestern metropolis that with its well-scrubbed streets, pristine shopping malls and young, upwardly mobile population seems emblematic of the suburban dream.

AMC introduced the concept of the multiplex cinema to Britain.

The company had been created in the early 1920s by 'Handsome' Ed Durwood, who had shown films on the travelling tent circuit throughout the Midwest. By the early 1960s, it had become the leading cinema exhibitor in the region. Just like the nickelodeon created by Harry Davis in Pittsburgh almost six decades earlier, the first multiplex came about through a mix of chance and opportunism, rather than by any kind of design. Stanley Durwood, son of the company's founder, had originally wanted to create a 700-seat cinema in two spaces in a shopping mall in Kansas City. When it proved impossible to combine the two spaces, Durwood simply opened two cinemas side by side, one with 400 seats and the other with 300. The site opened by playing two prints of *The Great Escape*, starring Steve McQueen. The Parkway II, as it was known, soon proved a resounding success. Durwood decided to experiment with larger sites opening three- and four-screen complexes, eventually opening his first six-screen multiplex in Omaha in 1969.

By the mid-1980s, Durwood was ready to take his concept abroad. Meanwhile, across much of Europe – with the notable exception of France, where the exhibition sector had long been subsidized by the state – thousands of movie houses had fallen into a wretched state of decay. The situation was especially bad in the UK where the owners of two leading chains, Rank and ABC, had consistently refused to make any serious investment in the upgrading of their existing sites, let alone build new venues. Instead, they had sub-divided many of their large cinemas – some of which were capable of seating 1000 people – into three- or four-screen complexes in a desperate attempt to milk more money from what they saw as a declining business. True, the large cinemas were no longer economic. Many screens, however, were so cheaply partitioned that the soundtrack from one film was audible in adjoining auditoria. The screens were often so small and with such appalling projection, that the audience were probably better off staying at home to watch television, which is precisely what they increasingly chose to do.

The roots of this decline went back a number of years. Much of the blame can reasonably be laid at the door of the Rank Organization

which, during the late 1930s and '40s, had been one of the more
dynamic forces in the British industry. As early as 1958, John Davis, a
former accountant who had become deputy chairman and managing
director of Rank, had advocated the closure of 1000 cinemas (a
quarter of the nation's total), admitting that 'because so far we have
not persuaded the industry to tackle rationalization, we in the Rank
Organization have, in effect, been quietly carrying out our own'.
That same year, Rank merged its Odeon and Gaumont circuits,
forcing the closure of a great many excellent cinemas. Closures
continued during the 1960s and '70s, doing little to alleviate the
widely-held view of Davis as a brutal and irrational tyrant. 'Sir John
controls a regime for which it is difficult to find an analogy except
in the Byzantine court of Josef Stalin,' concluded one profile writer.
Davis could be as ruthless as the most savage Hollywood mogul of
old, yet without any of their redeeming passion for movies. In fact,
as one British producer recalled, 'He thoroughly disliked the film
business. It was against his training and all his attitude towards life
. . . the whole process seemed to him very inefficient.' The movie
interests of Britain's largest film concern declined while the company
sat on an ever-growing mountain of cash generated by its stake
in Rank Xerox which had the right to manufacture and market
photocopying equipment under a deal cleverly struck by Davis in
the mid-1950s. Nor was it much of a surprise that the interests of
British producers generally should languish when the main trade
body, the British Film Producers Association, was headed by Davis.

While the growing popularity of television could be blamed for
the decline in cinema attendances, there is little doubt that the
closure of cinemas meant that the drop in admissions became a
self-fulfilling prophecy. In 1962, John Spraos, an economist, published a book-length study on the decline of British cinema suggesting that as many as 100 million visits a year were lost merely as
a result of the programme of cinema closures initiated by Davis and
later imitated by rival chain ABC. ABC diversified into bowling,
squash clubs and pubs in a move to protect itself. To Spraos it
seemed obvious that if cinema-going was to survive it would have

to become a special occasion enjoyed in genuine comfort. Sadly, it was a lesson completely lost on Davis and the vast majority of those responsible for steering the fortunes of the film industry in Britain and, for that matter, throughout Europe.

The consequences of all this for European cinemas, and by extension for European producers and distributors, was catastrophic. In 1946 Britain had the highest per capita rate of cinema-going of any major nation in the world, with the number of annual admissions soaring to 1.6 billion. By 1984 that figure had tumbled to just 54 million, well behind most of its European neighbours as well as a number of far poorer countries such as Bulgaria, Romania and Malaysia. Almost everywhere in Europe the pattern was much the same, with a precipitous drop in admissions being followed by the closure of cinemas, creating a vicious cycle of decline, with no one apparently having the will or the confidence to try and arrest it.

Across the Atlantic, the Americans, who since the very earliest days of the nickelodeon had led the way in making cinemas popular and accessible, had already spotted an opportunity to revitalize Europe's exhibition sector. They had argued from the mid-1970s for new investment in the sector. It was, after all, in no one's interest, least of all the Hollywood studios whose films dominated cinema screens across most of Europe, that the decline should be allowed to continue unabated. Local companies in European countries such as Belgium and Sweden had already embarked on a modest pro-gramme of multiplex construction, but nobody of substance had dared to take on the much bigger task of transforming the cinema sector in the larger European markets. The American studios had already seen what a sustained programme of investment by AMC and other big exhibitors like General Cinema could do to bolster admissions. In fact, it hardly seemed a coincidence that the overall decline had begun to level out in the early 1960s at precisely the time that AMC and others began to introduce new concepts of cinema-going. In the early 1980s, Jack Valenti, head of the Motion Picture Association of America, privately approached Rank and other British cinema chains in an attempt to persuade them to invest in building new cinemas. The management at some of these chains were already thinking about getting into the multiplex business, but they were unable to persuade their owners to commit the necessary cash. The majors were reluctant to build their own cinemas as most of them no longer had expertise in the exhibition business, having been forced out of it by the Paramount decree in the late 1940s. 'We couldn't get any national chains or City investors to commit money,' Valenti later recalled. The British firms had good reason to be unenthusiastic about the idea of newcomers entering the market-place. Between them Rank and ABC effectively controlled the British exhibition market, operating what many, including myself, felt to be an over-cosy duopoly which denied the public real choice. This was mirrored by another purchasing duopoly operated by the BBC and ITV, distorting the value of UK television rights to feature films. Small wonder the domestic industry languished. The development of multiplexes in the UK also proceeded slowly because would-be cinema operators had to buy the sites or take very long leases. In the United States, on the other hand, cinema-owners took very short leases from real-estate developers who helped them leverage the financing.

In the meantime, Stan Durwood's AMC had teamed up with Bass Leisure and in November 1985 I opened its first British multiplex cinema comprising ten screens in Milton Keynes. The location was appropriate. Milton Keynes was one of the new towns which for some represented yet another symbol of the 'Americanization' which had permeated post-war Britain. Indeed, it was hardly surprising that the multiplex, emanating as it did from the suburban shopping malls of the Midwest, should be viewed in this light. The cinemas were housed in low-slung buildings resembling glamorized discount warehouses, invariably located on the edge of local conurbations to facilitate access by car. With their brightly-lit café areas serving cokes and hamburgers they more closely resembled a supermarket for fast food. Despite predictions of disaster from most of the established operators, the cinema was an immediate success, and soon AMC together with other American companies like National

Amusements, United Cinemas International (a joint venture between Paramount and Universal) and Warner Brothers were building
multiplex cinemas all over the United Kingdom. Even as AMC was
opening its first multiplex, the ABC chain, under control of new
management at Thorn-EMI, was drawing up its own plans for multiplexes. As a direct result of this investment in new screens, the
vast majority of it driven by American capital, in the ten years to
1994, annual cinema admissions in the UK more than doubled to
123 million.

It helped that Hollywood was now pumping out films capable
of appealing to very broad swathes of the audience. The first really
successful example was *Ghostbusters* released in the UK in 1985,
the same year as the AMC complex opened in Milton Keynes. The
film was undoubtedly responsible for assisting the significant upturn
in admissions in that year. This growth in admissions even out-
stripped that in the number of screens (which rose by 54 per cent
to 1969 during the same period), indicating that the influence of the
multiplexes had as much to do with the way in which they created
an image of modernity and confidence for Britain's once ailing exhibition sector. Where the Americans had led, the British chains
eventually followed. Soon the concept had been exported to Germany, Spain and Italy, helping to push up cinema admissions in
those countries, although not as dramatically as they had in the
United Kingdom. In France, the national cinema chains such as
Gaumont and Pathé, which had long provided standards of comfort
and luxury unmatched in other countries in Europe, eventually began
building their own multiplexes. Traditional French cinemas were
by now looking very tired and run-down despite continuing state
support.

It was hardly surprising that multiplexes, yet another American
import, should provoke anxiety among the French political establishment. In 1996 the French government indicated that it would move
to prevent the spread of the multiplex by introducing legislation
designed to curb construction of new venues. Ostensibly, this was
a late and somewhat clumsy response to fears that the growth of

multiplexes might have a detrimental impact both on European films – since the complexes were dominated by American product – and on the smaller, traditional exhibitors, many of whom were in danger of being put out of business by this unwanted competition. Yet at root it seemed to owe at least as much to that same suspicion of American cultural exports that had united and energized so many French intellectuals and politicians since the early 1930s.

However, it is not just the number of screens, it is also screen density which is a factor in determining the strength of an indigenous industry. The US has a far more highly developed screen density than that of any major European country, with 100 cinema screens for every million people, a figure far in advance of any other European country except Sweden. In France, a comparatively well-screened European nation, there are eighty screens per million people, while in Germany the figure is sixty-two screens, and in the UK the figure is still only around thirty-four. This means that, all other things being equal, a film has to play for far fewer weeks in the United States to reach the same number of potential spectators.

For those exhibitors with the necessary imagination and confidence, opportunities began beckoning all over the world. Despite their impressive rates of economic growth and growing consumer affluence, the countries of South-East Asia and the Pacific Rim still suffer from a desperate shortage of good cinemas. A leading Australian company, Village Roadshow (of which I am a board member), is busily engaged in building screens throughout the region, with plans to create some 3000 profitable screens from Bangkok to Buenos Aires well before the end of this decade.

Even before the advent of the multiplex, Hollywood's share of the European market had been dramatically expanding. By 1995 American movies accounted for 73.5 per cent of total cinema revenues in the European Union. But even that figure was a distortion of the true picture in many European nations, largely because in the French market domestic films had retained a relatively robust 35 per cent, thanks in part to the sophisticated system of national subsidies.

In the latter half of the 1980s, in an effort to compete by becoming more cost-effective than the expensive, star-laden Hollywood productions, many European producers once again turned to the idea of co-producing films with their neighbours, just as they had during the late 1950s and '60s. To an extent, this reflected the spirit of increased European co-operation in the wake of the signing of the Treaty of Rome in 1957, which had cleared the way for the creation of the Common Market. It also provided producers with a way of defraying costs. Between 1955 and 1965, co-productions leaped from 10 per cent to 40 per cent of all films made in Europe. The French film industry remained the linchpin of most significant co-productions, which usually involved partners from Italy or Germany, so much so that by 1965, over two-thirds of French films were co-productions. British producers, bolstered by the success of the Eady Levy, and terrified by the complexity of foreign languages, largely remained aloof. In just about every sense, they felt closer to Hollywood than they did to Europe. But from the late 1980s onwards, as British producers became more aware of the potential of working with Europe, partly as a result of the increasing influence of the EC, the British began to play a far more active role. By the mid-1990s it was estimated that around one in three films in Europe was a co-production of some kind, although this was still somewhat lower than the comparable figure for the 1960s.

Co-production had significant financial attractions. The decline in national cinema admissions often meant that it was impossible to raise much beyond a relatively modest budget from a single territory. In some cases, co-production enabled a producer to raise more money than would have been possible had he been forced to rely on investors from a single country. Reflecting this, co-produced films invariably had higher budgets than purely national films. In other instances, the decision to co-produce flowed from the nature of the story which happened to traverse more than one European country, or involved themes which had specific appeal in more than one culture. But unlike many of the classic French–Italian co-productions of the 1960s, such as *The Leopard* and *Belle du Jour*, very few European co-productions achieved significant box-office success. In the case of many so-called 'Euro-puddings', it seemed as if the logic of the narrative was driven solely by the desire to provide each participating financier with a sufficient rationale, national or financial, for investing in the project. This would usually involve the inclusion of an appropriate number of scenes set in their own country, or the use of stars from that same territory however inappropriate they might seem for the role – none of this was a recipe for box-office success.

One notable exception to the litany of creative and commercial failures among European co-productions was *The Name of the Rose*, a $30 million German/French/Italian co-production based on Umberto Eco's novel and starring Sean Connery. Despite a poor box-office performance in the United States it eventually achieved a worldwide gross of over $120 million. Unlike many smaller European co-productions, *The Name of the Rose* was shot in English, which may help to account for its outstanding success in some territories. Since the 1970s and '80s the increasing influence of American cinema has meant that audiences in most English-speaking countries have become ever more resistant to deciphering sub-titles. In the 1960s, foreign-language European films accounted for 5 per cent of the American box office, yet by the mid-1990s that figure had fallen to just 0.5 per cent. The audience which had once followed these films grew older and just drifted away from that type of cinema experience. At the same time, the succeeding generation of aspiring *auteurs*, many of whom would only bother to make one relatively unsuccessful film before giving up on cinema, failed to provide anything like the same degree of creative excitement and audience loyalty. In effect, an entire segment of the audience, the one that sustained an important strand of ambitious films shot in languages other than English, had been lost to the cinema. Repertory venues which relied on showing classic works from the great *auteurs* found it ever harder to make ends meet. In any case, many of the spectators who had once flocked to these cinemas were now able to buy their favourite works on video, and watch them as often as they liked in the comfort of their own homes. The hegemony of Hollywood movies in most parts of the world meant that, for many audiences, the English language had become synonymous with the very idea of cinema itself. Indeed, while the worldwide popularity of Hollywood films was boosted by the increasing ubiquity of English as the language of international commerce and diplomacy, the saturation of many markets by American movies may itself have played a part in promulgating the ever-increasing use of English in so many corners of the globe. If silent movies had once seemed like an 'Esperanto of the eye', then there were times when the prevalence of English-language films and English-speaking stars seemed as if it were helping to create its aural equivalent.

In the case of American pictures seeking to penetrate foreign markets, the majors have preferred to dub their films, simply because they know that in the overwhelming majority of cases this will enable them to reach a far larger number of people. They have been helped by the fact that in many countries television stations buy dubbed films, and the audience is therefore accustomed to what for many is an uncomfortable cultural experience. In India, the lifting of restrictions on dubbing films into Hindi has given a significant boost to films such as *Jurassic Park* and *GoldenEye*.

Even if very few European films are seen by American audiences, contemporary Hollywood still draws on European ideas, as it has done since the days of Edwin Porter and Adolph Zukor. Yet at the same time, the audience's resistance to sub-titling, the lack of interest in European stars and the different pace and style of European storytelling has meant that American producers have become increasingly drawn to the idea of remaking European films. Notable among these have been the French pictures, *Trois hommes et un couffin*, which was transformed into *Three Men and a Baby* with Tom Selleck, Steve Guttenberg and Ted Danson, and *Le Retour de Martin Guerre*, starring Gérard Depardieu, remade as *Sommersby*, with Richard Gere and Jodie Foster.

The developing tendency for producers in Europe to rely on financing from other parts of the continent pointed to a more general blurring of the cultural and economic lines which had traditionally divided the national industries. Throughout the last two decades, European cinema has become increasingly international both in its financing structure and its choice of subject-matter. Leading European producers increasingly financed their films not just from neighbouring countries but from sources all over the world. At the same time, many were happy to tackle stories rooted in far distant cultures. *The Last Emperor*, for example, released in 1987, an epic drama based on the life of Chinese Emperor Pi Yu, was put together by a British producer, Jeremy Thomas, was directed by the Italian Bernardo Bertolucci, and was financed with the help of a British bank, a Japanese movie company, an American studio, and individual distributors around the world. It is virtually impossible to define such films as the product of a particular nation, in either economic or cultural terms.

At the same time, European and Japanese media companies showed an increasing propensity to invest in the production and distribution of American movies, most usually by purchasing equity stakes in independent Hollywood companies. Canal+, the hugely successful French pay-television channel took an equity stake in Carolco, the American company which produced such films as *Terminator 2* the $90 million hi-tech special-effects picture starring Arnold Schwarzenegger, and *Cliffhanger*, an action thriller starring Sylvester Stallone. Another French company, Chargeurs, part of a combine whose interests range from textiles to pay-television, was a backer of the film *Showgirls* about the exploits of a group of female strippers in Las Vegas. JVC, the Japanese electronics company, was another investor in independent production companies in Hollywood, as were German, Italian and British films.

In part, this move towards international financing reflected the globalization of capital which resulted from the deregulation of financial markets around the world. Corporate investors, unhampered by currency controls and devoid of the cultural anxieties which had in the past plagued some of their more traditionally-minded countrymen, simply sought to put their money where they thought it would gain the maximum return. Some of these companies argued that their investment in Hollywood also brought direct benefits for their core businesses, since they ensured a consistent supply of product for their film, television and video operations in Europe or Japan. During the 1980s and '90s, European companies alone poured several hundred million dollars into Hollywood production.

Few of these financial justifications really stood up to closer analysis. Many of these foreign companies seemed inextricably drawn, like moths to the flame, to invest in American production companies famed for profligate salaries, the lavish use of corporate jets and extravagant party-giving. Carolco in particular became noted for its annual parties at the Cannes Film Festival. It would fly in stars like Sylvester Stallone and Arnold Schwarzenegger by private jet from Los Angeles, whisk them to the nearby Hotel du Cap in a fleet of limousines accompanied by a police motorcade, then hold a gala party aboard some palatial rented yacht. At one party, the company turned part of a restaurant into a casino and handed out chips of $1000 for games of blackjack. From a purely financial point of view, it looked as if Carolco's European backers were themselves engaged in a high stakes gamble. In reality they did not need to acquire equity stakes in these companies to ensure consistent access to the movies made by those same firms – that could have been achieved simply by striking long-term agreements known as output deals, which gave them the rights to distribute the movies in specified overseas territories.

It seemed as if many of these investors had been seduced by the idea of purchasing a seat at the table of some of Hollywood's most powerful independent companies. What appeared most sur-prising was that companies from France, still widely regarded as the country in Europe most aggressively neurotic with regard to the economic and cultural incursions of American movies, should be at the head of those lining up to invest in Hollywood. What this sug-gested was that the clash of values was no longer being played out simply between Europe and America, but between different groups within the same countries. The liberalization of international trade and finance, together with the ease with which American cultural exports of all kinds crossed borders, had helped to dissolve traditional cultural allegiances. The management of conglomerates in the French film industry, as well as elsewhere, no longer felt obliged to defend those established values of high culture so long espoused by their intellectual compatriots. Whatever the underlying rationale may have been, companies like Canal+ and Chargeurs had no compunction about investing in Hollywood at the same time as the majority of French producers and policy-makers were engaged in a strenuous battle to prevent American movies from flowing unimpeded on to Europe's cinema and television screens.

In June 1977, Dimitri Balachoff, president of a European film association, proposed a scheme to encourage the Europeans to act as one in an effort to rebuild their film industry. Among his proposals was that all films originating in the Common Market should benefit from the imposition of a levy on box-office receipts and television sales which would be applied in every member nation. At root, the 'Balachoff Plan', as it became known, was based on the same philosophy which had informed European thinking and the Film Europe movement half a century earlier. Since most individual markets were too small to support a fully competitive film industry, Balachoff argued that the only way forward was for the Europeans to operate collectively. This particular proposal came to nothing, but his ideas were eventually taken up by others, notably within the European Commission.

In the late 1980s, the Commission created MEDIA (Measures to Encourage the Development of the Audio-visual Industry), a programme designed to encourage collaboration between film and television professionals at all levels across Europe. The first stage of the programme, MEDIA 1, comprised of around twenty schemes, known by a bewildering array of acronyms such as EFDO and SOURCES. In many ways, the ultimate objectives of the scheme were the same as those initiated some sixty years earlier by Erich Pommer. By conceiving of Europe as a single market comprised of 320 million consumers, European producers and distributors had an opportunity to create more ambitious films and television programmes which might eventually compete with those of the Americans.

The MEDIA programme, by helping to foster a spirit of collaboration in Europe, was seen as the first stage along the way towards creating such a market. The European Commission set aside ECU250 million to fund an initial five-year programme. MEDIA played a valuable role in nurturing many new voices in Europe's film industry, and did much to improve the level of script development and the training of producers. But the decision to create twenty separate initiatives, scattered throughout the Community, to provide a sense of inclusiveness for each individual nation, meant that the programme remained too fragmented to have any significant impact. on the way in which the industry in Europe is organized. Because the programme was run from Brussels, it seemed to some excessively bureaucratic, with complaints that too much time was spent on gatherings in expensive hotels, and too little time focusing on the actual needs of the market. The number of initiatives was cut back in the second phase of the programme, MEDIA II. But it was arguable that MEDIA remained overwhelmingly focused on the needs of producers, and not sufficiently on the expressed desires of the audience. To that extent, it mirrored that historic tendency of the European industry to focus on production rather than distribution, which for so long has prevented the possibility of serious competition with the Americans.

By the mid-1990s, the film industry in Europe had still failed to tackle the problems which had dogged it since before the outbreak of the Great War. It remained hopelessly fragmented, an industry in which there was little consistent connection between the production and distribution of films. As a result, the production sector remained severely under-capitalized. At the same time the obsession with making films, rather than marketing and distributing them, meant that there was, if anything, an over-supply of production. Four hundred films a year were being made in Europe, with many of them never finding an audience. Where films did receive adequate distribution, it was largely carried out on a national basis, since there were almost no companies in Europe – other than the American studios – capable of distributing films in a cost-effective manner to cinemas in more than one country. Only around one in five European films was ever seen at the cinema outside the country in which it was made, and even then it was difficult to find an audience; even in France where cinema-goers had always been sympathetic to the kind of art-house films made by the Europeans, only 4 per cent of the annual box office was accounted for by films from other European countries.

The Europeans had invented cinema and they could rightly claim to have industrialized it. Europe still supplied much of the talent responsible for some of Hollywood's finest movies. Yet with few exceptions the European film business remained no more than a cottage industry, and European audiences still acted out of choice as they flocked to see Hollywood pictures.

By the mid-1990s, many feared that the battle waged by Charles Pathé, Ole Olsen, Erich Pommer, J. Arthur Rank and a host of others had been conclusively lost.

19

Films without Frontiers

WHEN LOUIS LUMIÈRE, inventor of the Cinématographe, hired Félix Mesguich as a cameraman and projectionist, he had warned him: 'You know, Mesguich, we're not offering anything with prospects, it's more of a fairground job ... It may last six months, a year, perhaps more, probably less.' As it turned out, Lumière was right about Mesguich's job prospects, but spectacularly wrong about cinema. He certainly would have been surprised to know that 100 years later the 'fairground' job has become one of the most powerful and important industries in the world.

I entered the film industry in 1970, some three-quarters of the way through the story told in these pages, after a spell working in the photographic and advertising industries. Long before that the movies had left indelible traces on my psyche. For, of all the influences which shaped my life, cinema had far and away the most powerful cultural, social and ethical impact. The first movies I watched were those of the 1950s, and, for the most part, they were

American. I was just one among millions of young people around the world who basked in the seemingly benign, positive and powerful aura of post-war America. I quickly became an ardent fan of Hollywood and all that it stood for, an entirely willing recipient of that 'Marshall Plan of ideas' that I referred to earlier. Cinema allows us to sit in the darkness, watching people something like five times real size on the screen, and it enables us to borrow, as it were, their identities. Such magnification of the self is unique to cinema. As a boy I would sit in the darkness and soak up the images and ideas of films like Fred Zinnemann's *The Search*, Elia Kazan's *On the Waterfront* and Stanley Kramer's *Inherit the Wind*. Those films were my education. I wanted to express the humanism of Montgomery Clift caring for that boy in *The Search*; I allowed James Dean to work out my adolescent complexities and frustration in *East of Eden*. It was from films like these that almost every tenet by which I have tried to live somehow evolved. Many of them were critical of American society, but they also demonstrated that capacity of the Americans for a kind of infinite hopefulness, that pursuit of happiness enshrined in the American constitution, and entirely commensurate with those values of 'vision, initiative, enterprise and progress', so theatrically promulgated by Will Hays, the first real lobbyist for the overseas interests of the American movie industry.

For many years I have owned a signed Norman Rockwell print which encapsulates many of the values of American cinema embodied in the films of that era. It's the one of a runaway kid sitting at a lunch counter, next to a policeman. The cop has a gun, but you're pretty sure he's not going to use it; there is a man looking at the child from behind the counter, but it never crosses your mind that he wishes him any harm; you know that sooner or later the kid, having made his protest, is going home and everything will be all right. That is the image of America I was brought up with.

As a result of the intoxicating impact of those movies, the first day that I went to America, in 1963, was, in many ways, the most exciting of my life. Part of me was coming home. That's how powerful the impact of American cinema had been on me. Far more than any other influence, more even than school, my family, my attitudes, dreams, preconceptions and pre-conditions for life had been irreversibly shaped five and a half thousand miles away in a balmy suburb of Los Angeles called Hollywood. It wasn't until my late teens that I found myself slipping off to London's National Film Theatre to catch a rare screening of seminal European films like *Battleship Potemkin*.

My experience is hardly unique. Many must have felt it, even those who didn't spend much of their childhood in the darkness of the local cinema avoiding real life. For in the end, the impact of Hollywood went far beyond the movies themselves. As President Woodrow Wilson had been among the first to recognize, American movies served to disseminate both American goods and American ideals. In doing so they dramatically accelerated the Americanization of the world, and helped to fulfil Henry Luce's prophecy that this would, after all, be known as 'The American Century'. Popular music, popular literature, television, fast food, soft drinks, automobiles, even architecture and fashion, but most of all through movies from the 'Roaring Twenties' onwards, the United States of America has left its imprint on so many aspects of our lives. And while the movie industry could hardly be held responsible for all that America did (although there were many like Jean-Luc Godard and his disciples who violently denounced it precisely on that account), still we could all recognize the underlying truth expressed in that slogan adopted by the political champions of the American industry: 'Trade follows the film.' In Europe on the other hand, too often we have tried jealously to guard the purity of the creative process from what we have ignorantly parodied as the crude commercialism of the Hollywood studios. In the 1920s, European politicians vainly tried to use quotas to protect their industries and audiences alike from what they saw as the corrosive impact of a far stronger competitor across the Atlantic. In the decades that followed, film-makers, executives and politicians across Europe were either ignorant of or chose to ignore, the obvious lessons which Hollywood offered to other, less consistently successful film industries.

Cinema, like television, architecture, newspaper publishing, commercial theatre and much of today's literature, is a costly undertaking, and a collaborative one; more and more it falls only within the financial means of global baronies. In such a system, artistic freedom finds itself limited by, and frequently colliding with, primarily economic demands. So it was that two conceptions of cinema, fundamentally opposed at just about every conceivable level – culturally, economically, politically – went to war in a struggle for the hearts, the minds and the money of audiences around the world.

Perhaps movie producers are particularly caught up in that battle since their task is, in essence, to mediate between the two underlying forces – one creative, the other commercial – which animate and inform the whole activity of film-making. In Europe, from the early 1920s through to the present, the way in which movies have been produced and financed has tended to offer individual film-makers a high degree of creative freedom and autonomy sufficient to make some intensely personal films. This nurturing of creative talent helps explain why almost half of all post-wars Oscars have been won by Europeans. At the same time, European film-makers have on occasion, most notably in the late 1960s and '70s, displayed varying degrees of irresponsibility towards their financial backers, and something approaching a contempt for the audience.

In the mid-1960s an average 35 per cent of box-office revenues in continental Europe was earned by American films. Thirty years later, American movies account for at least 80 per cent of the box office in most European countries, and in some places that figure is well over 90 per cent. American movies have not suddenly achieved greater popularity; it is simply that the audience has all but fled from European films. During the last fifteen years, the audience for American films in Europe has remained fairly constant, while at the same time admissions for European movies have slumped dramatically. Renewing the market for European films need not therefore be at the expense of American movies. In any case, Hollywood benefits enormously from a healthy European market, not only because the American majors have a significant financial interest in exhibition through their multiplex chains but also because, historically, Hollywood has badly needed the vigour offered by European creative talent. The crisis in European cinema has steadily eroded the opportunity to renew this talent base, and many of the traditional skills associated with the art of cinema are slowly being lost.

It is in France, more than in any other country, that the conception of cinema as a means of articulating cultural identity has been most forcefully expressed and most vigorously defended. For many of its practitioners, such a view of cinema is intimately tied to their ability to articulate a deeply felt psychological, cultural and even political sense of identity. While recognizing that the best individual films are almost always firmly rooted within the particularities of a specific culture, it is also true that within Europe's film industry there has, on the whole, been a broadly shared vision of the function and purpose of cinema.

On the other side of the Atlantic is a conception of cinema fundamentally driven by the imperatives of the marketplace, by the acknowledgement that, as the title of Adolph Zukor's autobiography had it, 'The public is never wrong'. This view holds that the creative dimension of film-making is just one of a series of connected activities – the distribution, marketing and exhibition of films – all of which are entirely mutually interdependent, and all of which are predicted on one fundamental principle: the maximization of profit. Hollywood has created a sophisticated industry requiring people with highly specialized skills, ranging from script executives to market researchers and marketing executives, to mediate between the different creative talents and to act as the eyes and the ears of the audiences. While the danger of such a system is that at times it can be formulaic and stifle risk, at its best it is invaluable in gauging how effectively a writer is communicating with the potential audience. Such a system hasn't developed to anything like the same degree in Europe, partly because the director (often doubling as the writer) can often secure funding from public subsidies without having to worry about the likely audience for the finished work. In such a climate, there is little appetite or inclination to listen to script editors. It has been estimated that in Hollywood something like 15 per cent of the money spent on production is spent on developing scripts, while in Europe the equivalent figure is 2–3 per cent.

Hollywood sees itself as being at the heart of the entertainment industry, the very essence of a mass culture which can reach out and touch audiences anywhere. The duty to entertain has been raised to the status of an ethical imperative. No rules or obligations, no canons of art can displace that fundamental obligation to entertain, to be accessible, to succeed with the audience. The deification of movie stars, the ceaseless exaltation of emotional uplift, the relentless exploitation of every conceivable weapon of advertising and publicity, all these are vital components of a truly popular global culture which has become virtually synonymous with Hollywood and, by extension, America itself.

Although the Lumière Brothers invented cinema, and Charles Pathé industrialized it, it was the American moguls like Laemmle, Zukor and Mayer who made the movies into a product which could be exported around the world, and which eventually became one of that country's biggest overseas earners with a current annual export value of almost $5 billion. In doing so they created a revolutionary cultural form which, embraced from the start by lower-class immigrants, and overtly championing values of 'vision, initiative, enterprise and progress', successfully synthesized the American Dream to become a universal language.

Of course, at the human level, the divisions have not been so stark. The underlying ethos of Europe and Hollywood may seem irreconcilable but from the very beginning there has been an exchange of people, ideas and capital. Like other film-makers, I have striven throughout my career to combine those qualities which for me typify the best of both traditions: the narrative drive, energy and accessibility of American cinema, and that subtlety and sophistication of the best European cinema which mainstream Hollywood only rarely seems to achieve. From the early idealism of Goodtimes, my first film partnership, through the hand-to-mouth existence of Enigma's early years; throughout the ups and downs of Goldcrest (where I sat on the board), and the cold blast of reality experienced during my spell heading Columbia Pictures, I have constantly attempted to formulate a way of working that allows financial prudence to co-exist with artistic ambition, so as to lay the foundations for original, unusual and, I hope, sometimes even triumphant ventures. I am hardly unique in aspiring to do so. Any serious film-maker knows that the desire to create enduring work must be balanced against the need to make a living, and an honest attempt to reward the film's investors.

These tensions have been unremittingly evident to me throughout my career, all the more so because I am a British producer who for much of the time has been lucky enough to have the support and encouragement of an American studio; in my case, Warner Brothers. One example of the type of creative dilemma I have had to face came after we finished shooting *Local Hero*. The ending is not entirely happy. The American protagonist goes back to his apartment in Houston, having completed his task in Scotland. But he feels somehow hollow and unfulfilled. Warner Brothers offered us additional funding to reshoot the ending, so that the American, Mac, remained in Scotland, removing the lingering ambiguity. Were we to do so, they felt, we would have a film more 'sympathetic' to the expectations of the audience. This they believed could add 10 or even $20 million to its eventual box-office performance. The studio regarded any additional expenses incurred in reshooting the ending as an entirely worthwhile investment.

I have absolutely no doubt that they were right; had we reshot the ending, *Local Hero* may well have grossed an additional $20 million in the international marketplace. But in accepting their offer, both myself and the director, Bill Forsyth, felt that we would have been betraying the spirit of the film. After all, the movie itself dramatizes an unresolved conflict between a pastoral view of the world and a more hard-edged commercial ideology. I still think that, given its impact on those who came to love the film and the integrity of its long-term reputation, we were right to decline. That is not a criticism of the studio, just an acknowledgement that they were locked into a very particular and entirely justifiable set of imperatives. They were responding to the sum total of the movies they had made, how they performed at the box office, and their assessment of how possible audiences for this particular movie might respond.

At no time in my career was the conflict between the two conceptions of cinema so sharply dramatized as during the fifteen-month period from June 1986 to September 1987 when I was chairman and chief executive of Columbia Pictures. In part, I was hired because the owners of the studio, Coca-Cola, were hoping that they could increase the amount of revenue that Columbia's films earned overseas, and they believed that a European with extensive experience of the international market might be ideally placed to achieve this goal. Because the company had been so successful in expanding its exports during the post-war period, some 65 per cent of Coca-Cola's entire revenues now came from abroad, compared with only 30 per cent of Columbia's revenues.

It was clear from the beginning that my conception of cinema differed from that of most traditional studio bosses. Before I went to the Coke headquarters in Atlanta to discuss the job, I wrote a long screed about what cinema represents to me, about what I saw as the responsibilities and duties of the film-maker. In the course of the meeting, I handed this document, which really amounted to my personal film-making manifesto, to the Coke chairman Roberto Goizueta and the then president Don Keough. In it I argued: 'The medium is too powerful and too important an influence on the way we live, the way we see ourselves, to be left solely to the "tyranny of the box office" or reduced to the sum of the lowest denominator of public taste.' I went on to say:

> Movies are powerful. Good or bad, they tinker around inside your brain. They steal up on you in the darkness of the cinema to inform or confirm social attitudes. They can help to create a healthy, informed, concerned, and inquisitive society or, alternatively, a negative, apathetic, ignorant one – merely a short step away from nihilism ... Accepting this fact, there are only two personal madnesses that film-makers must guard

against. One is the belief that they can do everything, and the other is the belief that they can do nothing. The former is arrogant in the extreme. But the latter is plainly irresponsible and unacceptable.

Naturally, I wanted Columbia to concentrate on making films which reflected the concept of cinema to which I was committed. Many of these were films aimed at a somewhat older audience than was being targeted by Hollywood at the time. At the end of the 1960s the studios had effectively lost touch with the teenage market. Having won it back in the 1970s and '80s they had become almost obsessed with this core segment of their audience, churning out second-rate action pictures for teenage boys while almost ignoring the larger, more sophisticated and varied audience elsewhere. As the baby boom generations of the late 1940s and '50s grew older, they were establishing new patterns of cinema-going. Satisfying them clearly required new stories, new marketing strategies, but simply to ignore them seemed to me absolute folly.

I wanted to bring a more sophisticated boutique mentality to what was in essence a department-store operation. That was probably a reflection of my European roots. The mistake I made was to believe I could concentrate my energies on the production of perhaps four films a year, while simultaneously overseeing another twelve to sixteen. I was torn between wanting to be an executive producer with a significant level of control over individual movies, and the growing knowledge that a studio boss simply does not have time to give all the productions the level of attention they deserve. But this is another story for another time.

Although there were many factors which contributed to my eventual departure from Columbia in September 1987, it was this irreconcilable conflict of demands which, for me, made the job impossibly frustrating and ultimately unsatisfying; it daily became a conflict between two differing ideas of cinema which, in some ways, seemed to be at the heart of everything. So it was that I returned to Europe, only to find myself embroiled in a very different kind of battle, one in which the stakes were in an altogether different league.

In the mid-1980s the explosion in the number of commercial television stations in Europe as a result of a combination of political deregulation and new technology, had created something of a political dilemma. The problem was that in the early stages of their existence these new commercial broadcasters had very little guaranteed revenue from advertising. As a result, there was a natural tendency for stations to seek out the cheapest possible programming. In most cases, that meant buying programmes from Hollywood. Such programming, particularly in the field of drama, can be bought for a tenth, or even a twentieth, of the cost of domestic production. The Europeans could not hope to compete with these prices. Although they had manifestly failed to work for the film industry, it was clear that some system of television quotas across Europe was urgently required, if only on a temporary basis, to ensure the long-term future of what had been a thriving production industry.

This led to the introduction in 1989 of a European Union directive entitled *Television Without Frontiers*, which stipulated that within each European country at least 50 per cent of television programmes broadcast (excluding news and certain other types of non-fiction shows) should be of European origin, 'where practicable'. A key figure in the adoption of the directive was Jack Lang, the French minister of culture. A former theatrical entrepreneur, Lang had launched an outspoken attack on the cultural aggression of the United States as early as 1982 when he denounced the American television industry during a conference in Mexico City.

The MPAA (now the MPA), had already signalled its hostility to the quotas, and a fierce war of words broke out. By the autumn of 1989, it seemed to me that there was a real need for bridge-building on both sides of the Atlantic. In a letter to MPA president Jack Valenti I observed: 'There's so much misinformation, so much misunderstanding and so much mutual suspicion you almost sense World War Three is about to break out! It's even possible that the sheer weight of lobbying by the State Department could have become counter-productive, the issue of quotas has been raised so far up the political agenda that the counter-arguments are now being taken seriously by those who previously showed little interest.'

The MPA was increasingly seen by many European film-makers as a pressure group whose sole interest was to maximize the market share of its member companies, if necessary by mobilizing Washington to its cause. Certainly, there was a fair amount of historic evidence to suggest the existence of a knee-jerk reaction within the American film industry which required that it drive home every possible advantage when dominant, but was equally quick to seek the political support of Congress whenever it felt threatened. The intensive lobbying for the retention of essentially protectionist tax breaks in the mid-1970s was only the most recent example of this well-honed instinct. The reaction of the American automobile and steel industries to foreign competition seemed to provide further evidence to Europeans that across the Atlantic a deep strain of protectionism still lurked beneath the surface. In the cultural arena, actors, musicians and even entire orchestras were unable to work in the United States without strict reciprocity.

By 1990, film had once again emerged as a contentious issue on the broader political stage. It had become one of the disputed sectors in the Uruguay Round of the GATT negotiations. As far back as the initial post-war GATT negotiations in Geneva and Havana, the status of film within the agreement had been a major source of contention. The United States had wanted films to be covered by the Treaty so that they could be traded freely around the world like any other form of manufactured goods. Many European countries, notably Britain, objected. They believed that without the system of tariffs and quotas with which they had protected their respective film industries, national movie production would quickly collapse, overwhelmed by a barrage of American product. The British pushed for films to be excluded from GATT altogether. The Americans refused. In the end a compromise was reached and as a result the treaty included special provisions for the treatment of film. This allowed individual countries to retain quotas. What looked like a modest victory for Europe was in fact only the first skirmish in a battle that would flare up periodically during the subsequent negoti- ating rounds of the GATT. Now it had emerged once again but this time the stakes were higher.

The so-called Uruguay Round of negotiations began in 1986 and was scheduled to conclude at the end of 1993. Its primary purpose was to extend the scope of GATT from goods to services. The Americans argued that films and television programmes were a ser- vice and that they should therefore be included in GATT. This would mean that, in principle at least, it would no longer be possible for the Europeans to maintain special measures to protect their industry. The Europeans, largely at the instigation of the French, wanted the GATT agreement to include a 'cultural exception'; a recognition that films and television programmes could not be treated as openly as any other service, allowing them to keep appro- priate protective measures in place. Underpinning the debate on both sides of the Atlantic was the recognition that new transmission technologies from video-on-demand to on-line services were about to open up a vast new market for the audio-visual sector. The Ameri- cans were anxious to clear the ground of obstacles. 'The US majors were opposed to any deal which included acceptance by them of TV quotas, unless in return they could get a firm standstill on the application of EU policy to new technologies,' was the view of one senior European Commission Official.

The early stages of the Uruguay Round were dominated by dis- agreement over agricultural issues which tended to overshadow everything else. The election of Bill Clinton in November 1992, and the nomination of Mickey Kantor, with his strong links to California, as US Special Trade Representative, brought the issue into the public eye as never before. At the same time, once agriculture had been sorted out – with the French making significant concessions – the Europeans felt able to press more aggressively for the 'cultural exception'. The Spanish and the Italians lined up behind France; the British and the Germans initially took a more sceptical position.

The Americans remained unremittingly hostile. 'Why this EC quota?' asked Jack Valenti. 'Is a thousand, two thousand years of an individual nation's culture to collapse because of the exhibition of American TV programs?' As he denounced the apocalyptic visions of the Europeans, his own rhetoric became more heated: 'The Quota is there, it hangs with Damoclean ferocity over the future. And it will in time, as its velocity increases, bite, wound, and bleed the American TV industry.' Meanwhile, the Americans also argued that they should have equal access to any European subsidy raised through levies on video and audio cassettes.

As one of those engaged in seeking a position which might be acceptable to both sides, in early December 1993 I prepared a briefing note for the Club of European Producers in which I warned: 'the danger for us, as Europeans, is that we retreat into a corner, seeking to protect our ailing production base by the use of quotas . . . Politically, it casts us in the unattractive role of defending our own interests as producers, rather than the interests of European consumers.' I proposed instead that a levy be placed on a portion of box-office receipts, video sales and, most importantly, new technologies. The proceeds of this levy would be used as capital to fund future production. Such a system would work by rewarding success; the greater the revenue generated, the greater the availability of capital for investment in future production. I very deliberately (and, in the view of some interests, controversially) followed the suggestion by stating my belief that investors of all nationalities should be able to exploit the benefits which would flow from these proposals. The idea was to create a pool of capital to which US companies would have access on equal terms. By promoting the production of an increased number of films in Europe, it would provide a significant boost for both the industrial and the cultural interests of the European industry.

In the autumn of 1993, the GATT negotiators in Geneva were frantically seeking to reach agreement on a host of outstanding issues before the self-imposed deadline of 15 December. One by one a series of contentious matters, ranging from rice imports to aircraft subsidies, were settled or set aside for the future. With neither side prepared to budge on the audio-visual issue, the disagreement was threatening to derail the entire GATT round. Tempers became increasingly frayed on both sides. Bill Clinton made a series of direct personal interventions with European leaders in an attempt to get the issue resolved. If GATT failed, the Americans were apparently happy to arrange their own trading pact with the countries of the Pacific Rim. Agreement seemed further away than ever.

On 13 December Leon Brittan and Mickey Kantor met at the offices of the United States Trade Representative in one last attempt to thrash out an agreement over film and television. The meeting dragged on into the small hours. 'Blow up the deal,' urged one studio representative. 'Have the President go to the American people, explain what happened. Tell him to blame it on the French!' As dawn approached, and the mood grew increasingly desperate, Mickey Kantor finally picked up the phone and called the President. Should the Americans bring the entire edifice of GATT crashing down over the failure to conclude a deal on the film and television industry? Clinton hesitated. The United States had already been accused of intransigence in other trade sectors during the talks. The last thing he wanted was for the Americans to get the blame for the breakdown of the entire negotiating round. He reportedly instructed Kantor to call Lew Wasserman, chairman of entertainment giant MCA which owned Universal Studios. For over thirty years, Wasserman, austere and inscrutable, had been the principal architect of the relationship between Hollywood and the White House. A supreme realist, he understood that it was impossible to allow the whole GATT agreement to fail solely on the issue of film and television. Clinton, he argued, should do whatever he felt was best.

A few minutes later in Geneva, a weary Jack Valenti broke the news to his colleagues. The issue of the cultural exception was side-stepped. The GATT was saved and the threat of an international trade war was averted, at least for the time being.

Jack Valenti was stunned by the failure to secure victory. The Hollywood studios genuinely believed they had a commitment from Clinton that failure to reach agreement on the audio-visual industry would be regarded as a 'deal-breaker'. Politically, the Clinton administration could not afford to fail in securing an overall agreement. Valenti now launched a ferocious attack on the EC: 'In a global treaty supposed to reduce trade barriers, the EC erected a great wall to keep out the works of non-European creative men and women . . . This negotiation had nothing to do with culture, unless European soap operas and game shows are the equivalent of Molière. This is all about the hard business of money.' Mickey Kantor was equally furious: 'You can't sustain a functioning democracy and at the same time control what people see and hear. We are going to fight this one for ever.' In his official statement, Bill Clinton was more restrained, noting that 'we were unable to overcome our differences with our major trading partners, and we agreed to disagree'.

The Europeans, and especially the French, were jubilant. 'It's not a victory of one country over another,' said Jack Lang. 'It is a victory for art and artists over the commercialization of culture.' In fact, the real battle was simply put off for another day. The result was a stalemate. The Americans were unsuccessful in their attempt to secure commitments from the EC to 'liberalize' the film and television industries. For their part, the Europeans failed to win any kind of lasting 'cultural exception'.

The audio-visual sector (an ugly term but, for the present, there is no adequate alternative) is covered within the overall scope of the General Agreement for Trade in Services (GATS). It has no special status, culturally or otherwise. On the other hand, the Europeans have not committed themselves to particular liberalization measures and can retain their systems of subsidies, levies and quotas. The industry is subject to Article XIX of the Agreement, which notes, somewhat laconically in view of the battles that have gone on over the audio-visual sector, that 'Members shall enter into successive rounds of negotiations [within five years of the Agreement] with a view to achieving a progressively higher level of liberalization'.

In the wake of the negotiations, there was something of an attempt to rebuild bridges between Hollywood and Europe. There seemed to be a realization that a constructive dialogue between the industries might enable future legislation to stimulate the sector without creating barriers to international competition in the new technologies. Jack Valenti was probably a key figure in securing the last-minute renewal of the US offer on the audio-visual industry. The move was made partly to lay the basis for returning to the issue in future negotiations and partly because the American industry was genuinely keen to create a dialogue, since the mood of acrimony and aggressive protectionism generated in Europe was regarded as running counter to the long-term interests of the United States.

In early 1994, the Club of European Producers and the MPAA were invited to create a 'Roundtable' to discuss ways in which to help build energetic and thriving cinema and TV industries throughout Europe. After the acrimonious end to the GATT negotiations, the Roundtable convened under the auspices of the European Parliament jointly chaired by the Irish MEP Mary Banotti and the British MEP Alan Donnelly. It sought to create a dialogue between the industries on either side of the Atlantic. Small but potentially significant gestures emerged and, in 1995, the MPAA and its member companies agreed to contribute to professional training in Europe and helped to organize a system of internships enabling European producers to spend time working within the framework of the Hollywood studios.

The struggle for control of the industry had assumed the shape of a battle between national cultures, between Europe – and France in particular – and America; and to an extent between the values of the old world and those of the new. As far as the Americans were concerned it was primarily a battle for the future. With its long dominance of the movie business, and its reliance on Hollywood as a means of winning friends and influencing people around the world, the US was determined to clear the ground of any protectionist obstacles in advance of the arrival of a whole new array of multimedia services and delivery systems. The Europeans, by contrast, were fighting a romantic battle, one rooted primarily in the past and driven by a sense that the rich diversity of European culture was in danger of being finally extinguished by the overwhelming might of Hollywood's distribution and marketing machine.

Europe has traditionally concentrated nearly all of its energies on one part of the industry – production – and largely ignored changes to the marketing, distribution and exhibition networks which could possibly have put more indigenous films on the screens, and achieved a higher level of box-office popularity.

The problem is that in a truly competitive sense we have almost lost the ability to market our movies, because our industry has been unable to deliver the right kind of product in sufficient volume, and on a consistent basis. The Americans, by contrast, have developed a marketing machine which is capable of successfully turning its hand to delivering virtually any kind of entertainment.

As a producer, I can make the most thrilling or challenging movie imaginable, with the best crew and the most talented cast, but unless I have a well-thought-out arrangement with an effective worldwide distribution resource, one which understands how to market a film in different countries and when necessary to different audiences, I am, to a great extent, wasting my time.

Public policy throughout Europe has focused too much on questions of supply and not enough on demand, too much on the financial needs of film-makers and not enough on the changing patterns of consumer demand. After all, the problem is not necessarily a shortage of European capital. There are large media conglomerates in Europe, such as the Dutch-based group Polygram, the French firm Chargeurs, and Germany's Bertelsmann, all of them able and sometimes eager to invest in the film business. Companies like these are anxious to build up the kind of software libraries which have paid such rich dividends for the Hollywood majors. To build a significant library, however, means that a company has to generate a substantial amount of product for ten to fifteen years, so these firms will need a steady nerve and deep pockets if they are to succeed. One way of speeding the process up is to buy existing companies, a strategy already pursued by Polygram which now owns the rights to films like *Return of the Pink Panther* and the *Thunderbirds* series.

The roots of our strength in Europe go back a long way. One hundred years ago France was the acknowledged birthplace of cinema. Throughout the last century virtually every country in Europe has, in some way, fed the moving image with artistic experimentation, creative talent and wonderful stories. Europe was the birthplace of Alfred Hitchcock, Billy Wilder, Marlene Dietrich and Greta Garbo. More recently we've exported stars like Gérard Depardieu, Daniel Day Lewis and Anthony Hopkins, and directors like Paul Verhoeven, Jan De Bont, Alan Parker and Ridley Scott. It was a European company, Pathé, which first pioneered the idea of vertical integration, the fundamental basis for the organization of the American film industry for the last eighty years.

The opportunities still beckon. Potentially, we possess a huge, if fragmented, domestic market right here on our doorstep. With over three hundred million consumers, the European Union has the largest fully developed audio-visual market in the world in terms of customers, and easily the second-largest in terms of value. It is a market which, it is predicted, will treble in value, to some $130 billion, over the next twenty years. Yet, throughout Europe, the feature film industry faces a crisis of confidence that in some respects is probably more severe than any in its history.

Meanwhile, with every passing decade, Hollywood movies increasingly appear to represent a truly universal experience. Cinema has played a major role in helping to blur the distinction between national and global cultures. In many ways, the norms and values embodied in Hollywood films have come to be absorbed as universal. The genealogy of its value system has been forgotten, so that its films no longer appear as the products of any particular society.

As if by a kind of osmosis, the particular lexicon of Hollywood starts to feel like our very own. An animated film like *The Lion King* is not seen by its audiences as a specifically 'American' product at all. In the same way, it is no longer certain that Demi Moore or Arnold Schwarzenegger are perceived as having any particular nationality, especially when dubbed into a foreign language, since the same voice will be used to dub them in film after film.

If the value system that pertains to Hollywood has succeeded in acquiring a universal validity, this is partly because American films have always been consciously tailored to a multi-cultural audience; in the early days they had to be simply because of the high proportion and diverse mix of the immigrant population in America. In defining itself in acceptable national terms, the US domestic industry quite naturally tended to be international. Hollywood has also retained a global outlook in relation to creative talent. As far back as the 1920s, the studios were sending talent scouts to Germany and elsewhere to ensure that they attracted the best creative talent from every corner of the globe.

Nor has Hollywood ever saddled itself with any allegiance to the United States as a production base, to American directors or even to American stars. The studios' strength has always been their utter flexibility, driven solely by an economic imperative based primarily on the taste and interests of the global audience. It is in this sense that Hollywood really is a state of mind, a concept of a particular form of entertainment rather than any specific place. Hollywood will set up shop wherever it needs to, and seek the best possible production values for the best possible price. Given a stable exchange rate, Europe has consistently offered something like a 30 per cent cost advantage over the United States, so all other things being equal there is a considerable incentive to shoot offshore. Its studios and technicians as well as its actors have been essential ingredients of many of the movies which seem to encapsulate the very essence of Hollywood.

At the same time, the flow of international capital has also rendered the concept of any truly 'national' film industry increasingly fragile. Polygram, for example, is a Dutch-owned company, operating a filmed entertainment division through a London-based subsidiary that in turn frequently finances films through US-based production companies using directors, actors and crew from all over the world, and with stories that may be set anywhere. Who is to say what nationality those films have?

347

'A permanent war, vital . . .
An economic war'

PRESIDENT FRANÇOIS MITTERRAND, 1994

WITH FILM PRODUCTION and distribution an increasingly global business, with national boundaries of diminishing significance, and with American domination already so overwhelming, it is tempting to ask 'Why bother with a European film industry at all?' Why don't we simply accept that the Americans understand, better than any-one else, how to produce and market films, just as the Germans make cars, the French make perfume and the Scots make whisky? Why don't we just accept that there are certain manufacturing and marketing skills peculiar to certain countries?

It's an option we should not even consider. A hundred years after its invention cinema has established itself as one of the most powerful and effective means of communication we have, not just to entertain ourselves, but to express ourselves. The appeal of the movies is universal. Its stars provide a mirror in which we can see a heightened reflection of our own lives and dreams. Its stories can open a window through which we see and understand the lives of others. Cinema has become part of our sense of identity, as individuals and as nations. And, located as it is at the heart of a rapidly expanding range of moving-image media, it has now acquired an economic importance which we cannot afford to ignore.

In these circumstances, it is frankly dangerous to allow Hollywood's extraordinary dominance in the field of filmed entertainment to go on intensifying. It raises the very real prospect of a fundamental dislocation between the world of the imagination, created by the moving image, and the everyday lives of people around the globe. We have no idea what the consequences of such a dislocation might be, for it is genuinely without precedent. But it is surely no exaggeration to say that it has the potential to be one of the social time-bombs of the twenty-first century. Already the governments of China, India and the Middle East are being confronted with this problem in embryonic form as a direct result of the growth of satellite television. Some have sought to ban satellite dishes, a desperate remedy which is unlikely to succeed in anything but the very short term. The process of what we call 'modernization' appears to be unstoppable but, as Professor Sam Huntington of Harvard University has pointed out, 'modernization and economic development neither require nor produce cultural westernization. On the contrary, they tend to promote a resurgence of, and renewed commitment to, indigenous cultures.' Indeed, he argued, 'much of the world is becoming more modern but less western'. In a widely praised analysis he has predicted that international conflict may soon be traced along cultural rather than economic fault-lines. The same theme has been pursued by the former United States ambassador to Britain, Raymond Seitz, who has studied the rise of Islamic fundamentalism in terms of its reaction against Western influences: 'Telecommunications can harden cultural differences just as much as soften them, and I suspect in the years ahead, we will see a lot of cultural reaffirmation.'

The complex relationship between the cultural and commercial power of cinema which has been such a prominent feature throughout its history, looks set to continue, and even grow in importance in the decades ahead. To pretend that such a sensitive and explosive issue can be neutralized by the alchemy of 'free trade' or by a theory of 'globalization' is an illusion, especially in the context of a highly competitive struggle for jobs and security. Nations that lose their confidence, and therefore their sense of identity, become destabilized and, in the long run, make bad neighbours and even worse customers.

We call Hollywood 'Tinseltown' as if it somehow didn't matter. Some try to persuade us that films and television are a business just like any other. They are not. Films and television shape attitudes, create conventions of style and behaviour, reinforce or undermine the wider values of society. At a time when the most highly developed nations (which, incidentally, also have the most highly developed and pervasive media industries) are, almost without exception, going through a crisis of social disintegration, it is inconceivable that we should pretend that film and television do not have a major impact on our lives. Creative artists, and those who work with them, have a heavy moral responsibility to challenge, inspire, question and affirm, as well as to entertain. Movies are more than fun, and more than big business. They are power.

That is certainly as true economically as it is culturally. In 1995, the European Community ran an audio-visual trade deficit with the United States of some $6.3 billion, a 15 per cent increase on the previous year. On present trends it could grow to $10 billion by the turn of the century. That figure would, I believe, be unacceptable to just about any government, European or otherwise.

Despite the global movement of capital, most businesses remain anchored in a particular culture. As one analyst has recently concluded: 'Only a very few multinationals . . . have become genuinely detached from a national interest.' The enduring relationship between Hollywood and Washington is an eloquent testimony to this. On all the key trade issues relating to the future, the various companies which make up the MPAA – despite the enormous tensions created by their divergent interests – are likely to maintain their unity. There have been ferocious battles between the studios for control of the American home market, and even more ferocious battles between Hollywood and Washington over aspects of legislative control of the industry. But in overseas markets there has been a close and consistent harmony between government and industry which has helped to make movies and television into one of the nation's most significant export earners. Even more importantly, it has created something resembling a 'brand image' for America, one which is as stunningly effective as it is instantly recognizable; an image of affluence, of opportunity, excitement, technological progress and, at least for most of the time, of an open liberal democracy. It is an image which has, with equal success, sold both American values and American goods.

There is a further dimension to the economic power of the movie business. Almost by definition, films and television are labour-intensive. They depend upon talented and creative people and generate a demand for specialized goods and services that ripples out into the wider economy. In the European Union, with almost 18 million of its citizens out of work, this job-generating power is a factor of real significance, not least because many of these jobs are better paid and more personally fulfilling than much employment in traditional manufacturing and services. According to the European Commission's White Paper *Growth, Competitivity and Jobs*, published in December 1993 in the name of the Commission's President Jacques Delors:

> In line with the increased growth predicted for the [audio-visual] sector, on the condition that this growth is translated into jobs in Europe and not into financial transfers from Europe to other parts of the world, job creation could be of the order of two million by the year 2000, if current conditions prevail ... [I]t is not unrealistic to estimate the audio-visual sector could provide jobs, directly or indirectly to four million Europeans.

While Delors may have been optimistic in his numbers, subsequent events have done nothing but reinforce his central argument that this sector has a vital contribution to make to the economy as well as to the cultural vitality of Europe. Of course, we need to be pragmatic about what can be achieved. For the foreseeable future, national film industries within Europe are not in any position to compete head to head with the Americans. In the UK, for example, a realistic target might be to increase the share of box office earned by British movies from its present derisory 7–8 per cent to around 15 per cent over the course of a decade. What is certain is that it will remain vitally important to be able to go on telling ourselves stories that draw their inspiration from our own culture. The experience of television broadcasters across Europe shows that, given the choice, audiences overwhelmingly prefer to watch home-grown drama on the small screen rather than American imports. For all the alarmist talk during the 1980s about wall-to-wall *Dallas* and *Dynasty*, the threat failed to materialize and the popularity of American programming has, if anything, declined over the last decade. This may reflect the fact that, historically, the Europeans have always excelled at the type of intimate drama best suited to the small screen, but it also demonstrates that there remains an underlying appetite for dramatic material rooted in our own cultures. The ownership of Europe's television broadcasters, spread as it is across a wide range of public service and commercial operators, has preserved a genuine diversity of choice for viewers which is no longer available to the majority of Europe's cinema audiences.

The links between film and television are of critical importance, for there is a growing paradox at the heart of the modern movie business. In the 1950s, earnings at the cinema box office represented more than 90 per cent of the industry's revenues. The proportion coming from television or merchandising was practically irrelevant. In 1995, despite the fact that the overall volume of theatrical revenues is still increasing worldwide, the proportion of the industry's revenue earned at the box office fell below 30 per cent. With the introduction of digital television, which will allow a single satellite to transmit scores of channels, and other new methods of distributing films, it has been predicted that by 2010 that proportion may drop to as little as 5 per cent. The widespread hostility with which film-makers on both sides of the Atlantic greeted the introduction of television seems a little ironic in view of the clear evidence that television and other media outlets now generate the bulk of the revenues that keep film production buoyant.

It would be wrong to assume that the film industry is therefore dependent on television, however. Although cinema box office is, in itself, of declining commercial significance, the big screen remains the shop-window for the moving-image industries as a whole. The best and most ambitious creative talents of the age – both in front of the camera and behind it – still see the cinema as the true focus of their energies, and, to that extent, they set the agenda for much of the overall communications business. In a very real sense, movies are a locomotive pulling much of television and multi-media in its wake.

Hollywood may have proclaimed victory in the battle for control of the world's film industry, but now entirely new areas of opportunity and struggle are opening up. As the distinctions between film, television, video, telecommunications and computer software evaporate in the face of the digital revolution, whole new industries are being created. Forty years ago the symbols of national wealth and progress were steel and shipbuilding, or companies producing consumer durables. Now the rising and dominant corporate symbols of success are, almost without exception, related to information: media companies, telcos, entertainment companies, software houses. The initial convergence between the film industry and the interests of telephone and electrical giants that occurred when the Warner Brothers screened the first talkies, is now being repeated, but on an infinitely bigger scale. The dominance of the written word as our primary means of interpreting the world is giving way to a more diffuse, visual culture whose shape is, as yet, impossible to foresee accurately. What is clear is that as money and commodities are able to move around the globe with ever-greater ease and speed, the distinguishing characteristics of any nation or community today lie in the quality of its intellectual property; in other words, the ability of its people to use information and intelligence creatively to add substance and value to global economic activity, rather than just quantity. We are on the threshold of what has come to be called the Information Society. As Professor Charles Handy of the London Business School has put it: 'Intelligence is the new form of property.' It has been frequently asserted that the audio-visual industry is America's second greatest export. In fact, it would be more accurate to say that position is occupied by intellectual property, of which films, television programming and other audio-visual software represent a massive and still-growing share.

The new hybrid, multi-media sectors contain a potential for growth which already makes them far more important than the traditional feature film industry. Perhaps the most significant development in the Information Society is the increasing convergence between entertainment and education. When resources that have traditionally been associated with the best in entertainment are applied to education and training, surprising results begin to flow. Anyone who has tried to learn a foreign language will know that to be able to see and hear people speak with the help of an imaginatively constructed piece of software is significantly more effective than sitting alone with a textbook. The educational potential of the medium has long been recognized – if not realized. In the early days of cinema, Thomas Edison predicted its primary and most valuable use would be as an educational tool. The British Film Institute was originally created with the simple aim of encouraging teachers to realize the educational potential of film and thereby bring about closer co-operation between the education system and the film industry. It may be that these early dreams are finally on the way to being fulfilled. As information technology becomes more and more essential to the functioning of our education system, the need for software and support materials is going to grow at a prodigious rate. If we are ever to harness the multi-media revolution to the needs of our education systems we cannot treat it as just another teaching aid.

We need to develop new approaches to learning and teaching

which will be relevant to, and can flourish in, an age of interactive technology which gives ready access to ever-greater quantities of information. Interactivity now offers the prospect of personally tailored teaching by means of on-line and off-line services, to any student, at home as well as at school, however remote their geographical location, and however advanced or obscure their interest. The possibilities this creates to revolutionize learning and teaching are almost incalculable.

Whether we like it or not, education is, in every respect, a fast-growing global business. Together with training it accounts for about 15 per cent of the European Union's total GDP. Not only does this proportion look certain to continue rising across the developed world, the demand for education in the developing countries is also increasing at an exponential rate. The United Nations Development Agency estimates that over the next thirty years as many people will be seeking some kind of formal educational qualification as have done since the dawn of civilization. If Europe's disparate education systems decide to take on board the possibilities of audio-visual technology, they would, almost overnight, create the potential to establish a world lead in one of the most valuable growth industries of all.

One senior Hollywood executive recently told me that in his opinion the best-known names and the highest earning stars of 2005 and 2010 would not be traditional movie stars at all, but a still-to-emerge generation of teachers and educational presenters who would dominate the TV channels, the CD-ROM market and the cable systems of the world.

Looked at in this light, the balance of resources between Europe and the USA is very unlike the imbalance that exists in the traditional entertainment movie business. In Britain, for example, we are lucky enough to have some of the world's finest talent in television and film production, in educational publishing, in animation and even in the authoring of electronic games. We have a unique range of relevant institutions, including the BBC, the world's premier public service broadcasting organization, and the Open

University, the world's most experienced distance-learning organization. Perhaps most important of all, we enjoy cultural ownership of the language which much of that world uses and wants to learn, the language in which 80 per cent of all electronic information happens to be stored. As a senior executive of one of Britain's leading computer companies has put it, Britain has the potential to become the 'Hollywood of Education'.

Where does this leave us? If you accept that it was the enormous size of its domestic market that generated growth and uniquely benefited the US entertainment industry over the last 100 years, and if you accept that technology-based learning as a global reality is almost inevitable, then we are left with a very simple choice: do we in Europe manufacture our own multi-media resources for education at all levels or do we sit back, wait and eventually import them from the US and the Pacific Rim? Are we going to be foolish enough to hand over this new, potentially massive business, with all of its likely cultural, let alone commercial, implications to the US in exactly the same way as we have handed over control of our movie industry? It seems to me that to be thinking in these terms is sobering but not unreasonably alarmist; 1995 was the first year on record in which Britain ran a deficit on its international trade in learning materials.

Different though these technologies and services may seem to be from the traditional film industry, the key issues that affect the way they are traded in world markets will be remarkably similar to those which lay at the heart of the most recent GATT negotiations. They are issues of control of distribution and access to markets. Already the Americans have managed to secure a free trade agreement on information technology and, once again, the Hollywood studios will be key players in the debate. They are broadening their spheres of activities, keenly aware that a video game can gross more than a blockbuster movie. Once again, they are likely to put aside their narrow commercial differences to maintain unity on key issues, arguing free access to international markets and an end to any unilateral taxes and subsidies. Such unity is likely to be maintained even though the owners of at least half the major studios are no longer American corporations. For despite all the talk of globaliz-ation, the political interests of those studios remain irreducibly iden-tified with those of America as a whole. The fact that the American industry speaks with one voice on such matters, through the MPAA, has been a key factor in its success on the international stage over the last few decades. So has the stability of the MPAA itself. Since its creation in 1922, the organization has had just three leaders: Will Hays, Eric Johnston and Jack Valenti.

For many Europeans, this has momentous implications for the future of both our economy and our culture. If the largest and most influential element of our entertainment business has inexorably shifted abroad, and then the same happens with our education and information resources, what will become of our, or for that matter any other nation's, cultural identity?

Stories and images are among the principal means by which human society has always transmitted its values and beliefs, from generation to generation and community to community. Movies, along with all the other activities driven by stories and the images and characters that flow from them, are now at the very heart of the way we run our economies and live our lives. If we fail to use them responsibly and creatively, if we treat them simply as so many consumer industries rather than as complex cultural phenomena, then we are likely to damage irreversibly the health and vitality of our own society.

Like it or not, these crucial social outcomes will be won or lost in the arena of global commerce. It is thirty years since the French media entrepreneur Jean-Jacques Servan Schreiber published his seminal book *The American Challenge*, which analyzed Europe's economic decline in the face of the overwhelming penetration of American goods and ideas. '[T]he confrontation of civilisations will now take place in the battlefield of technology, science and manage-ment,' he concluded. 'The war we face will be an industrial one.' As far as the European audio-visual industry is concerned, we may have lost an important battle – for control of mainstream cinema –

but we still have the opportunity to create a programming, software and information-based industry capable of competing at the leading edge of what may well turn out to be the twenty-first century's most exciting, profitable and influential industrial and cultural sector. We have, in the European Union, the largest market in the developed world, intellectual and technical resources of enormous depth, and a cultural inheritance of almost incalculable richness. Surely we should be developing strategies which will encourage the intelligent exploitation of these vast assets, both for own benefit and for the benefit of the world as a whole.

A new round of international trade negotiations, convened under the auspices of GATT's successor body, the World Trade Organiz-ation, is scheduled to commence, at the very latest, by 1 January, 2000. Talks will probably begin before then. Trade in cultural prod-ucts, including film, will once again form an essential part of those negotiations, as will the new technologies. This time everything must be done to ensure that the accusations, denunciations and evasions which have dogged the debate for the last 100 years are put aside in pursuit of what should be everyone's goal: a market in entertainment, information and education which is thoroughly inclusive at a cultural as well as an economic level.

What is at stake is too complex, too important, to be reduced once again to the crudely adversarial struggle which has unfolded over the last century. Sooner or later it must become clear that both filmmakers and the corporations who finance their work have a considerable responsibility to attune themselves to the needs of their audience, to select projects which at the very least offer a clear sense of values.

Our planet is now too small and too crowded to afford either the arrogance of the very rich or the ignorance of the very poor. H. G. Wells memorably described civilization as 'a race between education and catastrophe'. I have no doubt at all that the electronic audio-visual media, with all the wealth of skills and resources that they command, can help us tilt the balance decisively towards edu-cation and away from catastrophe. And that is only the beginning.

These media give us the power to communicate more effectively, to inspire, delight and entertain each other more readily and with ever greater variety.

At its best cinema has always been universal, always accessible, always at the cutting edge of popular concerns. But, from its earliest beginnings, its real magic has been its ability to conjure up and sustain the dreams of ordinary men and women. At the turn of a new millennium the human race needs those dreams as much as at any time in its history. The question is, do we have the ambition to seek a new and most sustainable dream, and do we have the determination to achieve it?

I believe that the acrimonious conclusion of the GATT Round in Geneva in 1993 should not be seen as an end but as a beginning. We can allow the undeclared war to rumble on, or we can work together to turn it into something altogether different; a battle to win a better, more fulfilling future for us all.

NOTES

CHAPTER ONE — PROLOGUE

page   3.   On espionage and GATT see *Le Monde*, 23, 24, 25 February 1995; *New York Times*, 23, 24 February 1995, 15 October 1995 and *Newsweek*, 29 April 1996.

6.   'the American audio-visual industry is everywhere. . .' quoted in Annemoon van Hemel, Hans Mommaas and Cas Smithuijsen (eds) *Trading Culture: GATT, European Cultural Policies and the Transatlantic Market* (Amsterdam, Boekman Foundation, 1996), p. 30.

6.   . . . more than $3.5 billion. . . US Congress Senate, *Review of the Uruguay Round: Commitments to Open Markets. Hearings before the Committee on Finance*, 102nd Congress, 1st Session, 17–18 April 1991 (Washington US Government Printing Office), p. 60.

6.   . . . Clinton telephoned Helmut Kohl. . . *Le Monde*, 13 December 1993.

7.   'Creations of the spirit. . .' quoted in Jean-Pierre Jeancolas, *From the Blum-Byrnes Agreement to the GATT affair* from Geoffrey Nowell-Smith and Steven Ricci (eds), *Hollywood and Europe: Economic and Cultural Interchanges 1945–1995* (London, British Film Institute, forthcoming).

CHAPTER TWO

10.   'The old nations of the earth. . .' T. Jackson Leas, *No Place of Grace* (Chicago, University of Chicago Press, 1994), p. 8.

11.   Authoritative information on Edison's life is difficult to secure. Among the sources used here are F.L. Dyer and T.C. Martin, *Edison: His Life and Inventions* (2 vols, New York, Harper & Row, 1910) and Matthew Josephson, *Thomas Edison* (McGraw Hill, New York, 1959). Wyn Wachorst, *Thomas Alva Edison: An American Myth* (Cambridge, Mass., MIT Press, 1981) provides a comprehensive overview of differing reports and stories concerning Edison's life.

11.   'a maze of wires and gadgets. . .' Albert Smith with Phil A. Koury, *Two Reels and a Crank* (Garden City, NY, Doubleday, 1952, republished 1985), p. 78.

13.   'great flapping sail-like roof. . .' W.K.L. Dickson and Antonia Dickson,

History of the Kinetograph, Kinetoscope and Kinetophonograph (New York, Albert Bunn, 1895), p. 19.

13. 'It may seem curious. . .' Ezra Goodman, *The Fifty Year Decline and Fall of Hollywood* (New York, Simon & Schuster, 1961).

14. For information on Antoine Lumière's life see Bernard Chardère, *Le Roman des Lumières* (Paris, Éditions Gallimard, 1995), Chapter One.

15. 'It is not an entrance duty which hits. . . ibid., p. 29.

16. 'He took out of his pocket. . .' trans. from Auguste et Louis Lumière, *Correspondances*, (Paris, Cahiers du Cinéma, 1994), p. 48.

16. For an account of the origin of the name Domitor see 'Founding Father Louis Lumière in conversation with Georges Sadoul', in John Boorman, Tom Luddy, David Thomson and Walter Donohue (eds) *Projections 4: Film-makers on Film-making*, (London, Faber & Faber, 1995), p. 6–7.

17. 'You who amaze everyone. . .' trans. from Georges Coissac, *Histoire du cinematographe, des origines jusqu'a nos jours* (Paris, Editions du Cinéopse, 1925) p. 192.

19. 'We left enchanted. . .' ibid., p. 193.

20. 'The cinema is an invention without. . .' trans. from Paul Vigne, *La Vie laboriuese et féconde d'Auguste Lumière* (Lyons, Durand-Girard, 1942), p. 91.

20. 'You know we're not offering anything with prospects. . .' trans. from Félix Mesguich, *Tours de Manivelle* (Paris, Bernard Grasset, 1933), p. 2.

20. 'Had I been able to foresee. . .' trans. from René Jeanne, *Cinéma 1900* (Paris, Flammarion, 1965) p. 26.

21. As early as October, 1895 one of his subordinates . . . See Auguste et Louis Lumière, *Correspondances*, op. cit., p. 50.

21. Edison fired off another letter, ibid., p. 113.

21. 'If there had been a pavilion for Marey. . .' ibid., p. 50.

22. 'The Sensation of Europe. . .' Robert Allen, *Vaudeville and Film 1895–1915: A study in media interaction*, (New York, Arno Press, 1980, n.p.).

22. 'America's greatest sensation. . .' Advertisement quoted in Charles Musser, *History of the American Cinema: Vol. 1. The Emergence of Cinema: The American Screen to 1907* (New York, Charles Scribner's Sons, 1990), p. 140.

22. 'Never in all our experience. . .' ibid., p. 139.

22. 'It has the additional advantage. . .' *New Haven Morning News*, 4 December 1896, cited in Kemp R. Niver (ed.) *Biograph Bulletins, 1896–1908* (Locare Research Group, Los Angeles, 1971), p. 11.

23. There were also darker whisperings. . . See Mesguich, op. cit. p. 14 ff.

23. 'Gaslit Barbary. . .' Denis Lacorne, Jacques Rupnik, Marie-France Toinet (eds) *The Rise and Fall of Anti-Americanism: A Century of French Perception*, translated by Gerald Turner, (Basingstoke and London, Macmillan, 1990), p. 214.

25. Friese-Greene's death. See Ray Allister, *Friese Greene: Close Up of an Inventor* (London, Marsland Publications, 1948), p. 181.

25. The Greeks had installed the machines. 'Before 1910: Kinematograph Experiences', R.W. Paul, C.M. Hepworth and W.G. Barker in *Proceedings of the British Kinematograph Society*, No. 38, February, 1936.

25. 'His work room was at the very top of a tall building...' Cecil Hepworth *Came the Dawn: Memoirs of a Film Pioneer* (Phoenix House, London 1951), p. 29.

26. 'A gentleman from Spain...' Paul et al, *Proceedings of the British Kinematograph Society*, op. cit.

26. 'the audience thought the pictures great...' Carl Hertz, *A Modern Mystery Merchant*, (London, Hutchinson, 1924), p. 145.

26. 'the theatre was packed to suffocation...' ibid., p. 158.

26. Paul apparently attempted to sell shares... see W.H. Eccles, Robert W. Paul, 'Pioneer Instrument Maker and Cinematographer', *Electronic Engineering*, August 1943.

27. 'Kindly friends...' Albert Smith, *Two Reels and a Crank*, op. cit., p. 52.

27. 'From Russia to England...' trans. from Charles Pathé, *De Pathé Frères à Pathé Cinema*, (Lyons, Premier Plan, 1970), p. 38.

28. 'sideline', *Electronic Engineering*, op. cit.

28. 'Animated photography is quite in its infancy...' Cecil Hepworth, *The ABC of the Cinematograph* (London, Hazell, Watson and Viney, 1897), p. 105.

CHAPTER THREE

29. For Pathe's own account of his life see Charles Pathé, *De Pathé Frères à Pathé Cinema*, op. cit. and Charles Pathé, *Souvenirs et conseils d'un parvenu* (Paris, 1926). See also the information in Jacques Kermabon (ed.), *Pathé: Premier Empire du Cinéma* (Paris, Editions du Centre Georges Pompidou, 1994).

30. the only business associates he ever allowed. See the memoir by his daughters in Jacques Kermabon (ed.), *Pathé Premier Empire du Cinéma*, op. cit., p. 400.

31. 'I decided to leave...' trans. from Charles Pathé, *De Pathé Frères à Pathé Cinema*, op. cit., p. 31.

31. For information on Grivolas see Richard Abel, *The Cine Goes to Town: French Cinema, 1896–1914* (Los Angeles, Univesity of California Press, 1993) p. 14.

32. Pathé was a punctilious man. See the memoir by his daughters in Jacques Kermabon (ed.), *Pathé Premier Empire du Cinéma*, op. cit., p. 400.

32. 'At that time, I'd hardly even thought...' trans. from Marcel Lapierre (ed.), *Cinéma*, (Paris, La Nouvelle Edition, 1946), p. 51.

32. 'le plus petit grand homme du...' Sacha Guitry quoted in René Jeanne, op. cit., p. 126.

33. For biographical information on Gaumont see Richard Abel, *The Cine Goes To Town: French Cinema, 1896–1914*, op. cit. p. 10.

35. 'All you needed was fifty dollars, a broad and a camera. . .' anonymous observer quoted in Jesse L. Lasky Jr., *Whatever Happened to Hollywood* (London, W.H. Allen, 1973), p. 46.

36. 'A variegated collection of. . .' Carl Laemmle, 'This Business of Motion Pictures', *Film History*, Vol. 3, No. 1., 1989.

37. Story of Harry Davis' nickelodeon. See Charles Musser, *The Emergence of Cinema: The American Screen to 1907*, op. cit., pp. 418–28.

37. 'The nickelodeon is usually. . .' *Saturday Evening Post*, 23 November 1907.

37. 'nickel delirium. . .' *Harpers Weekly*, 24 August 1907.

38. 'As one early historian put it. . .' Benjamin Hampton, *History of the American Film Industry: From its beginnings to 1931*, (New York, Dover Publications, 1970), p. 14.

38. 'Esperanto of the Eye' Edward S. Van Zile, *The Marvel, The Movie: A Glance at its Reckless Past, its Promising Present, and its Significant Future* (New York and London, G.P. Putnam's Sons, 1923), p. 10.

38. 'The newly arrived immigrant. . .' *Harpers Weekly*, op. cit..

39. 'In opening a factory and office in New York. . .' *Complete Catalogue of Genuine and Original Star Films*, (New York, Star Films, n.d.), n.p.

39. 'Suddenly he jumped up. . .' recounted in Fred J. Bolshofer and Arthur C. Miller, *One Reel A Week* (Berkeley and Los Angeles, University of California Press, 1967), p. 8–9.

40. 'For more than a year. . .' Kristin Thompson, *Exporting Entertainment, America in the World Film Market* (London, BFI Publishing, 1985), pp. 6.

41. In an episode that . . . See Charles Musser, *Before the Nickelodeon: Edwin S. Porter and the Edison Manufacturing Company*, (Berkeley, Calif., University of California Press, 1991), p. 265.

42. 'Not realizing the importance of prompt delivery . . .' Carl Laemmle, *The Business of Motion Pictures*, op. cit., p. 66.

42. A French trade paper was soon boasting that . . . Richard Abel, *The Cine Goes To Town: French Cinema, 1896–1914*, op. cit., p. 25.

43. 'Monsieur Charles Pathé. . .' Jacques Kermabon (ed.), *Pathé: Premier Empire du Cinéma*, op. cit., p. 407.

43. 'I didn't invent cinema but I did industrialize it. . .' trans from Charles Pathé, *De Pathé Frères à Pathé Cinema*, op. cit., p. 36.

45. 'where pickpockets could go through you. . .' quoted in Benjamin Hampton, *History of the American Film Industry: From its beginning to 1931*, op. cit., p. 12.

45. 'The fact that these amusement places. . .' *Chicago Daily Tribune*, 13 April 1907.

45. 'the people who go to five-cent theaters. . .' ibid..

46. For information on the term 'movie' see Anthony Slide, *The American Film Industry: A Historical Dictionary* (New York, Greenwood Press, 1986), p. 221–3.

46. 'It became rather like a game of hide-and-seek...' Fred J. Bolshofer and Arthur C. Miller, *One Reel A Week*, op. cit., p. 9.

47. 'Kennedy was a sort of...' Albert Smith with Phil A. Koury, *Two Reels and a Crank*, op. cit., p. 238.

47. 'So far as we concerned...' Cecil Hepworth, *Came the Dawn*, op. cit., p. 94.

48. 'We are troubled with neither...' *Moving Picture Weekly*, 11 February 1911.

48. 'American, French and Italian films...' ibid.

48. 'the Americans will soon conquer...' *Moving Picture Weekly*, 5 February 1910.

48. 'the importation of foreign stuff...' Kristin Thompson, *Exporting Entertainment, America in the World Film Market*, op. cit., p. 12.

48. 'The French are somewhat...' *Variety*, 20 June 1908.

49. 'to be spent in a campaign in the American field...' *Variety*, 23 March 1908.

49. Allegation that James Williamson forced out of business. See Rachel Low, *History of the British Film*, Vol. II, (London, Allen and Unwin, 1949), p. 136.

49. In November 1908... See Kristin Thompson, op. cit., p. 213.

49. For Olsen's own account of his life see Ole Olsen, *Filmens Eventyr Og Mit Eget* (Jespersen, Copenhagen, 1940). See also translations from that text in Ebbe Neergaard, *The Story of the Danish Film*, trans. Elsa Gress, (Copenhagen, Den Danske Selskab, 1963) and Ron Mottram, *The Danish Cinema Before Dreyer* (Metuchen, N.J., Scarecrow, 1988). See also Bebe Bergsten, *The Great Dane and The Great Northern Film Company* (Locare Research Group, Los Angeles, 1973).

CHAPTER FOUR

53. 'full of fight...' Adolph Zukor, *The Public is Never Wrong* (London, Cassell and Company, 1954), p. 41.

53. 'never sacrificed a principle...' John Drinkwater, *The Life and Adventures of Carl Laemmle*, (London, William Heinemann, 1931), p. 229.

53. For information on Laemmle's life see John Drinkwater, op. cit., and also Neal Gabler, *An Empire of Their Own: How the Jews Invented Hollywood* (London, W.H. Allen, 1989), pp. 47–64.

53. 'I was approaching forty...' trans. from memoir in Marcel Lapierre (ed.) *Cinéma*, op. cit., p. 103.

53. 'It was evident that...' Carl Laemmle, 'This Business of Motion Pictures', *Film History*, op. cit., p. 49.

54. 'There was a flavor...' ibid., p. 53.

54. 'You paid your money...' ibid., p. 56.

54. 'seemed to see humour...' Garson Kanin, *Hollywood: Stars and Starlets, Tycoons and Flesh-Peddlers, Movie-makers and Moneymakers, Frauds and Genuises, Hopefuls and Has-Beens, Great Lovers and Sex Symbols*, (London, Hart-Davis, MacGibbon, 1975), p. 72.

54. 'I'm Not Running a Bargain Counter. . .' Advertisement in Charles Musser, *The Emergence of Cinema: The American Screen to 1907*, op. cit., p. 437.

55. 'Each morning found me. . .' Carl Laemmle, 'This Business of Motion Pictures', *Film History*, op. cit., p. 62.

56. 'I have quit the Patents Company. . .' Advertisement reproduced in *Film Daily*, 28 February 1926.

57. Charles Inslee received. . . Fred J. Bolshofer and Arthur C. Miller, *One Reel A Week*, op. cit., p. 40.

57. 'We Nail a Lie. . .' cited in Eileen Bowser, *History of the American Cinema: Vol. 2. The Transformation of Cinema*, (New York, Charles Scribner's Sons, 1990), p. 112.

57. 'a poor, half-witted ruse. . .' Drinkwater, op. cit., p. 133.

58. 'no personal exploitation. . .' Carl Laemmle, 'The Business of Motion Picture', *Film History*, op. cit., p. 59.

58. 'If far-sighted opinion. . .' See Rachel Low, *History of the British Film*, Vol. III, (London, Allen and Unwin, 1950), pp. 59–60.

59. 'Please don't try to. . .' Geoffrey Nowell-Smith (ed.), *Oxford History of World Cinema* (Oxford, Oxford University Press, 1996), p. 45.

60. 'How can an ex-huckster. . .' *Moving Picture World* quoted in Eileen Bowser, *History of the American Cinema: Vol. 2. The Transformation of Cinema*, (New York, Charles Scribner's Sons, 1990), p. 112.

61. 'Hundreds of little rental. . .' Albert Smith with Phil A. Koury, *Two Reels and a Crank*, op. cit. p. 238.

62. 'up and down of the stairs. . .' Upton Sinclair, *Upton Sinclair Presents William Fox* (Los Angeles, published by the author, 1933), p. 15.

62. 'I can get you a sword. . .' quoted in Joseph P. Kennedy (ed.) *The Story of the Films* (Chicago, A.W. Shaw Company, 1927), p. 310.

62. 'We needed no more. . .' ibid., p. 311.

63. 'In our moving picture business. . .' Charles Musser, *Before the Nickelodeon: Edwin S. Porter and the Edison Manufacturing Company*, op. cit. p. 449–50.

63. On Fox's battle with the Trust see also Gabler, op. cit., p. 68.

64. 'The arts symbolize. . . quoted in Michael Palmer, 'GATT and culture: a view from France', in Annemoon van Hemel, Hans Mommaas and Cas Smithuijsen (eds) *Trading Culture: GATT, European Cultural Policies and the Transatlantic Market*, op. cit., p. 27.

65. 'What is a film. . .' trans. from citation in Georges Coissac, *Histoire du Cinématographe, des origines jusqu'a nos jours*, op. cit., p. 348.

65. 'a mechanical profession. . .' trans. from Charles Havermans, *Le Droit d'auteur*, address to Premier Congrès International du Cinématographe, Bruxelles, 1910, reprinted in Marcel L'Herbier, *Intelligence du cinématographe*, (Paris, Editions Corréa 1946), p. 189.

65. 'The great competition. . .' *Times Educational Supplement*, 6 August 1912.

68. 'Our house always smelled. . .' Eugene Zukor quoted in Will Irwin, *The House That Shadows Built* (Garden City, NY, Doubleday and Doran, 1928), p. 84.

69. 'Everything was ripped out. . .' Adolph Zukor, *The Public is Never Wrong*, op. cit., p. 25.

69. 'It was my custom. . .' ibid., p. 27.

69. 'I felt the impact of. . .' ibid., p. 28.

69. 'The novelty wore off. . .' Zukor in Bernard Rosenberg and Harry Silverstein (eds), *The Real Tinsel*, (New York, The Macmillan Company, 1970), p. 70.

70. 'quiet almost timid-looking. . .' William De Mille, *Hollywood Saga* (New York, E.P. Dutton, 1939), (p. 83).

70. 'cross between Christopher Columbus. . .' Allene Talmay, *Doug and Mary and Others*, (New York, Macy-Masius, 1927), p. 49.

70. 'There would come a time. . .' Cecil B. De Mille, *Autobiography*, edited by Donald Hayne, (W.H. Allen, London 1960), p. 139.

70. 'They were making. . .' Zukor quoted in Joseph P. Kennedy (ed.) *The Story of the Films*, op. cit., p. 58.

70. 'When I saw. . .' ibid., p. 58.

70. 'The exchanges at that time. . .' quoted in Eileen Bowser, *History of the American Cinema: Vol. 2. The Transformation of Cinema*, op. cit., p. 197.

71. Riding home on the subway. . . Adolph Zukor, *The Public is Never Wrong*, op. cit., p. 40.

71. 'a visionary of the fillums. . .' Allene Talmay, op. cit., p. 50.

72. 'In those early days. . .' Zukor quoted in *Variety*, 4 January 1956.

72. 'kill the slum tradition. . .' Will Irwin, *The House That Shadows Built*, op. cit., p. 151.

73. 'Victory! Victory!' Drinkwater, op. cit., p. 97.

CHAPTER FIVE

75. 'Without doubt from 1910. . .' trans. from Charles Pathé, *De Pathé Frères à Pathé Cinema*, op. cit., p. 61.

75. 'My intention is to. . .' interview in *Moving Picture World*, 14 November 1914.

76. 'Those of us who are. . .' *Moving Picture World*, 11 February 1991.

77. 'One day we saw hanging. . .' quoted in Victoria de Grazia, 'Mass Culture and Sovereignty: The American Challenge to European Cinemas, 1920–1960'. *Journal of Modern History*, Vol. 61, No. 1, March 1989, p. 53.

78. 'We are ready to go. . .' Cecil B. De Mille, op. cit., p. 66.

78. 'Flagstaff no good. . .' Jesse Lasky Sr., *I Blow My Own Horn*, (London, Victor Gollanz, 1957), p. 93.

78. 'was largely peopled by folks. . .' William de Mille, op. cit., p. 83.

79. 'heat waves you could actually see' Jesse L. Lasky Jr., *Whatever Happened to Hollywood*, op. cit., p. 8.

79. 'No dogs or actors. . .' Carey McWilliams, *Southern California Country*, (New York, Duell, Sloan and Pearce, 1946), p. 232.

79. 'coming out of an inferno. . .' Pola Negri, *Memoirs of a Star*, (New York, Doubleday, 1970), p. 204.

80. 'they merely camped. . .' McWilliams, op. cit., p. 331.

81. 'I've got the name. . .' *Film Daily*, 28 February 1926.

81. 'I was looking. . .' ibid.

81. 'cheering Universalites' ibid.

81. 'a city that had. . .' Drinkwater, op. cit., p. 171.

83. 'I didn't think it suggested. . .' Lasky, Sr., op. cit., p. 121.

83. 'The distributors seemed to be in the driving seat. . .' Zukor, op. cit., p. 86.

84. 'He was learning golf. . .' Lasky, Sr., op. cit., p. 122.

84. 'Lasky, we are being throttled. . .' ibid., p. 124.

84. Removal of Hodkinson. See Gabler, op. cit., p. 37.

84. 'the United States steel. . .' Richard Koszarki, *History of the American Cinema: Vol. 3: An Evening's Entertainment* (New York, Charles Scribner's Sons, 1990), p. 69.

84. 'You don't work for Sam. . .' Allene Talmay, op. cit., p. 80.

84. 'claiming anything from fraud. . .' ibid.

85. 'The hell with the cost. . .' Garson Kanin, op. cit., p. 306.

85. 'My God, whatever will they. . .' ibid.

85. 'I've never had a harder decision. . .' Lasky, Sr., op. cit., p. 123.

85. 'a broader and bigger grasp. . .' Cecil B. De Mille, op. cit., p. 161.

85. 'an unremitting state. . .' Lasky, Sr., op. cit., p. 143.

86. 'Not a foot. . .' quoted in Larry Wayne Ward, *The Motion Picture Goes to War*, (Ann Arbor, Michigan, UMI Research), p. 6.

87. 'There was a time. . .' *Bioscope*, 1 January 1920.

87. 'This war was made. . .' quoted in Kristin Thompson, *Exporting Entertainment*, op. cit., p. 61.

87. 'I believe America's domination. . .' Lasky Sr., op. cit., p. 110.

87. 'We express our unshakeable. . .' quoted in Thompson, op. cit., p. 70.

88. 'The real problem in Europe. . .' quoted in ibid., p. 49.

88. 'miles of motion pictures. . .' Hal Reid to Joseph Tumulty, 22 April 1915, Series 4, Film 72, *Woodrow Wilson Papers* (Library of Congress Microfilm), Reel 199.

88. 'It is like writing. . .' quoted in Ward, op. cit., p. 7.

89. Uncle wrote his own version. . . Ward, op. cit., p. 15.

90. 'Western ideas go. . .' Wilson quoted in William Diamond, 'Economic Thought of Woodrow Wilson' in *Johns Hopkins University Studies in Historical and Political Science*, (Baltimore, Johns Hopkins University Press, 1943), p. 137.

90. 'Go out and sell. . .' ibid., p. 139.

90. As early as 1918. . . See Ian Jarvie, *Hollywood's Overseas Campaign, The North Atlantic Movie Trade, 1920–1950* (Cambridge, Cambridge University Press, 1992), p. 280.

90. 'probably the most important market. . .' ibid., p. 280.

90. 'eyes for the whole business community. . .' Diamond, op. cit., p. 136.

90. For George Creel's account of his own life see *How We Advertised America* (New York, Harper and Brothers, 1920). For information on Creel

see James R. Mock and Cedric Larson, *Words That Won the War: The Story of The Committee on Public Information 1917–1919* (Princeton, Princeton University Press, 1939).

90. 'The motion picture can be. . .' William Brady to Joseph Tumulty, Series 4, File 72, Woodrow Wilson Papers, op. cit., Reel 199.

91. 'The film has come to rank. . .' Woodrow Wilson to William Brady, 28 June 1917, Series 4, File 72, Woodrow Wilson Papers, op. cit., Reel 199.

91. 'We did not call it. . .' Creel, *How We Advertised America*, op. cit., p. 4.

91. 'are eager–it is not too much. . .' *Moving Picture World*, 5 April 1919.

92. Each Thursday evening. . . See Paul Virilo, *War and Cinema* (London, Verso, 1989), p. 52.

92. 'it was agreed by leading. . .' Creel, op. cit., p. 276.

92. 'It was not only. . .' Creel quoted in Ward, op. cit., p. 121.

93. 'the government, while it cannot. . .' quoted in Emily Rosenberg, *Spreading the American Dream, American Economic and Cultural Expansion 1890–1945* (New York, Hill and Wang, 1982).

94. 'to show its patriotism. . .' Zukor quoted in Gabler, op. cit., p. 40.

CHAPTER SIX

96. For information on the birth of Ufa see Klaus Kreimeier, *The Ufa Story: A History of Germany's Greatest Film Company 1918–1945*, (New York, Hill and Wang, 1996), pp. 29–48.

96. 'Lord of the Press. . .' See John A. Leopold, *Alfred Hugenberg* (London, Yale University Press, 1977), p. 20.

96. 'A small man. . .' quoted in Kreimeier, op. cit., p. 159.

97. 'Precisely because of. . .' quoted in Gary D. Stark, 'Policing the Film Industry in Imperial Germany', in Gary D. Stark and Bede Karl Lackner, *Essays on Culture and Society in Modern Germany* (Arlington, Texas A&M University Press, 1982), p. 162.

97. 'a further unification. . .' quoted in M.S. Phillips, 'The Nazi Control of the German Film Industry', *Journal of European Studies* (1971), 1, p. 39.

97. 'the German empire go under. . .' D.J. Goodspeed, *Ludendorff: Soldier, Dictator, Revolutionary*, (London, Rupert Hart Davis, 1966).

98. 'There was no choice. . .' quoted in Neergaard, op. cit., p. 48.

99. 'it maintains complete. . .' cited in Lothar Gall, Gerald D. Feldman, Harold James, Carl-Ludwig Holtfrerich, Hans E. Büschgen, *The Deutsche Bank*, (London, Weidenfeld & Nicolson, 1995), p. 153.

100. 'The cinemas are a dangerous. . .' Stark and Lackner, op. cit., p. 149.

102. 'European producers must. . .' quoted in Thompson, *Exporting Entertainment*, op. cit., p. 113.

103. 'European unity that was. . .' Edmund H. Stinnes, *A Genius in Chaotic Times* (Bern, OFDAG, 1979), p. 30. On Hugo Stinnes see also Gaston Raphaél, *La roi de la Ruhr*, (Paris, Payot, 1924).

103. Information on Pathé-Westi. . . See Thompson, op. cit., p. 113. See also

Richard Abel, *French Cinema: The First Wave, 1915–1929*, (Princeton, Princeton University Press, 1984), pp. 29–31.

104. 'A European film cartel. . .' quoted in *New York Times*, 22 June 1928.

104. 'America's dominant. . .' Department of Commerce, *Trade Information Bulletin No. 617: The European Motion Picture Industry in 1928*. (Washington, United States Government Printing Office, 1929), p. 12.

105. 'We are short. . .' *Kines* quoted in David Forgacs *Italian Culture in the Industrial Era*, (Manchester, Manchester University Press, 1990), p. 51.

105. 'Of all the arts. . .' quoted in Kristin Thompson and David Bordwell, *Film History: An Introduction* (New York, McGraw-Hill, 1994), p. 132.

106. 'amazed before the gigantic. . .' George Pearson, *Flashback*, (London, Allen and Unwin), p. 134.

106. 'indisputably second. . .' *New York Times*, 2 October 1921.

107. 'they construct whole. . .' Siegfried Kracauer quoted in Kreimeier, op. cit., p. 100.

108. 'This German invasion. . .' Zukor in *Photoplay* cited in Kevin Brownlow, *The Parade's Gone By* (London, Abacus, 1973), p. 586.

109. 'He simply didn't know. . .' quoted in Herbert G. Luft, Erich Pommer, *Films in Review*, October, 1959.

109. 'The mass of non-stylized. . .' quoted in George A. Huaco, *The Sociology of Film Art*, (New York, Basic Books, 1965), p. 51–2.

109. 'Each producer has. . .' *The Graphic*, 25 April 1925.

110. 'America is currently in style. . .' quoted in Thomas J. Saunders *Hollywood in Berlin: American Cinema and Weimar Germany*, (Berkeley, University of California Press, 1994), p. 89.

110. Lang sent a memorandum. . . See Lothar Gall et al, *The Deutsche Bank*, op. cit., p. 211.

111. By the end of 1924, according to one estimate. . . Thompson, op. cit., p. 107.

111. 'Ufa sucked money the way. . .' See Gall et al, op. cit., p. 210.

112. Fierce competition between Paramount and MGM. See Thompson, op. cit., p. 109.

114. 'Film is not merchandise. . .' *Film-Kurier*, 26 November 1926 quoted in Saunders, op. cit., p. 290.

CHAPTER SEVEN

115. For biographical information on the Gianninis see Felice A. Bandio. *A.P. Giannini, Banker of America* (Berkeley, University of California Press, 1994), Gerald D. Nash, *A.P. Giannini and the Bank of America* (Norman, University of Oklahoma Press, 1992) and Julian Dana, *A.P. Giannini, Giant in the West*, (Englewood Cliffs, New Jersey, Prentice-Hall, 1947).

115. Spying a short cut. . . See Nash, op. cit., p. 14.

115. 'I don't think he ever. . .' Dana, op. cit., p. 30.

116. 'The idea of the crates worked. . .' *Saturday Evening Post*, 20 September 1947.

116. Giannini and Sol Lesser. . . Sol Lesser's version of this story in which A.P. Giannini makes the loan is recounted in Bernard Rosenberg and Harry Silverstein (eds), *The Real Tinsel*, op. cit., and also by Gabler, op. cit., p. 134. See *Los Angeles Times*, 21 April 1935 for the version of the story which claims A.H. Giannini was responsible for deal with Lesser. The latter version claims the loan was for $500.

117. 'Who cares if they smell of cheese and garlic. . .' *Saturday Evening Post*, 14 January 1939.

117. 'The moving picture is sharing. . .' *Moving Picture World*, 7 November 1912.

117. 'in many cases. . .' *Photoplay*, March 1916.

118. 'If a film is offered me. . .' *Los Angeles Times*, 21 April 1935.

118. 'If the girls reacted favourably. . .' ibid.

119. 'let out a roar. . .' Cecil B. De Mille, *Autobiography*, edited by Donald Hayne, op. cit., p. 224.

119. 'The Giannini's have so much power. . .' *Saturday Evening Post*, 13 September 1947.

119. By the end of the 1930s . . . *Saturday Evening Post*, 14 January 1939.

120. 'a town frequently mentioned. . .' quoted in Mary Jane Matz, *The Many Lives of Otto Kahn* (New York, Macmillan, 1963), p. 3.

121. 'The visitor who pays. . .' ibid., p. 77.

121. 'held that the request. . .' Zukor, *The Public Is Never Wrong*, op. cit., p. 129.

121. 'We were in the habit of writing. . .' Lasky Sr., op. cit., p. 144–5.

122. 'It has produced untold millions. . .' Otto Kahn, *Of Many Things*, (London, Jonathan Cape, 1926) p. 34.

122. 'I never worry about your debts. . .' Jack Warner quoted in Gabler, op. cit., p. 134.

123. Motley Flint death. . . See Gabler, op. cit., p. 147.

123. 'Don't give the people. . .' quoted in Robert Sklar, *Movie-Made America, A Cultural History of American Movies*, (rev. ed., New York, Vintage Books, 1994), p. 45.

124. Grauman and Lubitsch. . . See Gabler, p. 101.

124. 'Henry Ford of Showbusiness,' *Variety*, 19 October 1927.

125. They included Rosenwald and Wrigley. . . See Douglas Gomery, *Shared Pleasures, A History of Movie Presentation in the United States*, (London, BFI Publishing, 1992), p. 42.

126. The Public Health Commissioner. . . See ibid., p. 54.

126. 'We sell tickets to theaters. . .' Loew quoted in Richard Koszarki, *History of the American Cinema: Vol. 3:. An Evening's Entertainment*, op. cit., p. 9.

126. 'You don't need to know. . .' quoted in Gomery, op. cit., p. 58.

127. Invested about $1.5 billion. . . See *Film Daily Yearbook*, 1927, p. 3.

128. 'considering the establishment of a small. . .' Jarvie, *Hollywood's Overseas*

Campaign, The North Atlantic Movie Trade, 1920–1950, op. cit., p. 283. Jarvie provides valuable information on Hoover's corporatism, see ibid., p. 17 and *passim*.

128. 'gave the press its opportunity. . .' Cecil B. De Mille, *Autobiography*, edited by Donald Hayne, op. cit., p. 217.

129. 'Our home had the kind of. . .' Will Hays, *The Memoirs of Will H. Hays*, (Garden City, NY, Doubleday, 1955), p. 1. For a profile of Hays, see *New Yorker*, 10 June 1933 and 17 June 1933. For another account of Hays' life see Will Hays Jr., *Come Home With Me Now* (Indianapolis, Guild Press of Indiana, 1993).

129. 'a 100 per cent American. . .' Hays, *The Memoirs of Will H. Hays*, p. 370.

129. 'to a great university. . .' ibid., p. 341.

129. atmosphere was tense. . . See Jarvie, op. cit., p. 291.

129. 'The folks had bought the goods. . .' Hays, op. cit., p. 350.

130. 'a case of inherited American standards. . .' ibid., p. 370.

130. 'There is a special reason. . .' Hays speech 'What's Right With America', delivered to the Poor Richard Club, Philadelphia, 18 January 1938 quoted in Jarvie, op. cit., p. 296.

131. 'We are becoming more and more. . .' quoted in ibid., p. 304.

132. 'The Motion Picture Section. . .' *Film Daily Yearbook*, 1927, p. 925.

132. 'Steps have been taken. . .' Hays quoted in Jarvie, op. cit., p. 305.

133. 'The organized industry plunged. . .' Hays, op. cit., pp. 333–4.

133. 'the movie industry is the only. . .' quoted in *Guardian*, 12 May 1995.

CHAPTER EIGHT

135. 'the mortgage lifter. . .' Norman Zierold, *The Moguls: Hollywood's Merchants of Myth* (Los Angeles, Silman James, 1991), p. 239.

136. 'Accepting an award in New York. . .' See ibid.

136. 'Well, professor, I have. . .' See ibid., p. 235.

136. 'a man who would. . .' Warner with Jennings, op. cit., p. 214.

136. 'Jack's not a bad guy. . .' in Stephen Vaughn, *Ronald Reagan in Hollywood: Movies and Politics* (Cambridge, Cambridge University Press, 1994), p. 33.

136. 'Jack L. Warner, President. . .' Warner with Jennings, op. cit., p. 143. See also Bob Thomas, *Clown Prince of Hollywood: The Antic Life and Times of Jack L. Warner*, (New York, McGraw Hill, 1990).

137. Harry wardrobe story as related by Robert Altman, *Guardian*, 21 November 1996.

137. 'a small, strong swarthy man. . .' *Fortune*, December 1937.

137. 'was icy cool. . .' Warner with Jennings, op. cit., p. 167.

138. 'Now that is something. . .' ibid. pp. 167–8.

138. 'adding sound to movies. . .' A. Scott Berg, *Goldwyn*, (London, Hamish Hamilton, 1989), p. 173.

141. 'beyond comparison. . .' quoted in Robert Sklar, *Movie-Made America, A Cultural History of American Movies*, op. cit., p. 153.

142. 'Noise yes. . .' quoted in Victoria de Grazia, 'Mass Culture and Sovereignty: The American Challenge to European Cinemas, 1920–1960', *Journalism of Modern History*, op. cit., p. 69.

143. For background on Tobis-Klangfilm see Douglas Gomery, 'Economic Struggle and Hollywood Impeialism: Europe Converts to Sound', *Yale French Studies*, 60, (1980).

145. 'Gimme a shot of red-eye. . .' Michael Balcon, *Michael Balcon Presents . . . A Lifetime in Films*, (London, Hutchinson, 1969), p. 34.

146. In 1930 Sir Gordon Craig. . . See Margaret Dickinson and Sarah Street, *Cinema and State: The Film Industry and the Government 1927–84* (London, BFI Publishing, 1985), p. 46.

146. memorandum. . . See Memorandum, *With regard to British Film Production and the Cinematograph Industry*, April 1931, Public Record Office (PRO, FO 395/452).

146. In a letter. . . See A. Willert to Lord Tyrrell, PRO FO 395/452.

147. 'John Bull. . .' *Saturday Evening Post*, 29 July 1933.

147. 'It is safe to say. . .' Dalton Trumbo, 'The Fall of Hollywood', *North American Review*, August 1933, p. 146.

CHAPTER NINE

148. 'The bulk of picture-goers. . .' quoted in Victoria de Grazia, 'Mass Culture and Sovereignty: The American Challenge to European Cinemas, 1920–1960', *Journal of Modern History*, op. cit., p. 53.

149. 'sense of costliness. . .' quoted in Leo C. Rosten, *Hollywood: The Movie Colony*, (New York, Harcourt Brace and Co., 1941), p. 71.

150. 'the institution of a percentage. . .' quoted in Abel, *French Cinema: The First Wave, 1915–1929*, op. cit., p. 12.

151. 'high national. . .' quoted in Jarvie, op. cit., p. 106.

151. 'the enormous power. . .' quoted in Dickinson and Street, op. cit., p. 19.

152. Universal and the Army. . . See Willert to Gregory, PRO FO 371/10651. See also Dickinson and Street, op. cit., p. 19.

152. 'deplorable that the Army. . .' ibid.

153. 'It is clearer than most. . .' quoted in Ian Jarvie and Robert L. Macmillan, 'John Grierson on Hollywood's Success 1927', *Historical Journal of Film, Radio and Television*, Vol. 9, No. 3, 1989.

154. 'a nation of ignorant shopkeepers. . .' quoted in Jean-Phillipe Mathy, *Extrême Occident: French Intellectuals and America* (Chicago and London, University of Chicago Press, 1993), p. 33.

154. 'I will try to glorify. . .' quoted in Wilton S. Dillon and Neil G. Kotler (eds) *The Statue of Liberty Revisited: Making a Universal Symbol*, (Smithsonian Institute, 1994), pp. 6.

154. 'No true art. . .' Georges Duhamel, *America: The Menace*, trans. Charles Miner Thompson, (London, George Allen and Unwin, 1931), p. 39.

155. 'a deliberate plan...' translated from René Jeanne, 'L'Invasion Cinématographique Américaine', Revue des Deux Mondes, February, 1930.

155. 'only 7 per cent...' Colin Crisp, The Classical Cinema, 1930–1960 (Bloomington and Indianapolis, Indiana University Press, 1993), p. 213.

155. 'A collection of enterprises...' quoted in Richard Maltby and Ruth Vasey. 'The International Language Problem: European Reactions to Hollywood's Conversion to Sound' in R. Kroes and D. Ellwood (eds) Hollywood in Europe: Experiences of Cultural Hegemony (Amsterdam, VU University Press, 1994), p. 75.

157. 'Details of the system...' 'War In the Film World', North American Review, March 1930, p. 351.

157. 'If the United States...' quoted in Sklar, Movie-Made America, op. cit., p. 219.

158. During the early 1930s, figures taken from Tino Balio, History of the American Cinema: Vol. 5: Grand Design (New York, Charles Scribner's Sons, 1990), p. 32. For further information see also William Victor Strauss, 'Foreign Distribution of American Motion Pictures', Harvard Business Review, April 1930, pp. 307–15.

158. On Korda's early life see Karol Kulik, Alexander Korda: The Man Who Could Work Miracles (London, Allen and Unwin, 1975).

159. 'British producers are denied access...' William Marston Seabury, The Public and The Motion Picture Industry (New York, Macmillan, 1926), p. 195.

160. 'more like a professor...' Lord Grantley, Silver Spoon, edited by Mary and Alan Wood (London, Hutchinson, 1954), p. 166.

160. 'You think I know fuck nothing...' Kulik, op. cit., p. 211.

161. 'to be truly international...' Cinema Quarterly, Vol. 2. No. 1, Autumn 1933, p. 13.

162. 'American pictures are...' Australian Parliamentary Debates (Senate), 3 May 1928, p. 4569.

162. 'The portrayal of...' ibid., p. 4579.

163. 'Last year alone we made...' quoted in Randal Johnson, The Film Industry in Brazil – Culture and State, (University of Pittsburgh Press, 1987), p. 39.

163. 'The photographs...' Department of Commerce, Trade Information Bulletin No. 630: Motion Pictures in Argentina and Brazil, (Washington, United States Government Printing Office, 1929), p. 14.

163. 'There is a feeling...' ibid.

164. 'the booking office...' Cinema-owner Shri Abdulally quoted in Indian Talkie 1931–56: Silver Jubilee Souvenir, (Bombay, Film Federation of India, 1956), p. 121.

164. For information on the benshi's reaction to sound see Joseph L. Anderson and Donald Richie, The Japanese Film: Art and Industry, (Princeton, Princeton University Press, 1982, rev. ed.), p. 74 ff.

CHAPTER TEN

166. 'I am the king here. . .' quoted as epigraph to Bob Thomas, *King Cohn: The Life and Times of Harry Cohn*, (London, Barrie and Rockcliffe, 1967).

166. On John Otterson's plan to merge the studios see N.R. Danielan, *AT&T: The Story of Industrial Conquest*, (New York, The Vanguard Press, 1939), p. 161.

166. 'When we operated on movie money. . .' Cecil B. De Mille, *Autobiography*, op. cit., p. 265.

168. 'It is hard to explain. . .' 'Why Motion Pictures Cost So Much', *Saturday Evening Post*, 4 November 1933.

168. 'friendly and generous. . .' Howard Dietz, *Dancing in the Dark*, (New York, Quadrangle Press, 1974), p. 110.

169. 'he strode. . .' D. Schary, *Heyday* (Boston, Little, Brown, 1979), p. 178.

169. 'was lifted a foot. . .' Jack Warner with Dean Jennings, op. cit., p. 136.

170. 'two faces. . .' Schary, op. cit., p. 282.

170. Mayer simply adopted. . . See Gabler, op. cit., p. 79.

170. 'private grammar. . .' quoted in Thomas Schatz, *The Genius of the System: Hollywood Filmmaking in the Studio Era*, (New York, Pantheon Books, 1988), p. 47.

171. 'the ideas we have. . .' Henry Ford in collaboration with Samuel Crowther, *My Life and Work* (London, William Heinemann, 1922).

171. 'We will accept. . .' quoted in Thomas Schatz, *The Genius of the System: Hollywood Filmmaking in the Studio Era*, op. cit., p. 138.

171. 'A man should control. . .' quoted in Richard Schickel, *His Picture in the Papers: A Speculation on Celebrity in America, Based on the Life of Douglas Fairbanks, Sr.* (New York, Charterhouse, 1973), p. 5.

172. For Harry Reichenbach stories see Richard Koszarki, *History of the American Cinema: Vol. 3: An Evening's Entertainment*, op. cit., p. 38.

173. On merchandizing tie-ins see Tino Balio, *History of the American Cinema: Vol. 5: Grand Design*, op. cit., p. 170–1.

175. 'very sedentary persons. . .' quoted in Laurence Bergreen, *Look Now, Pay Later: The Rise of Network Broadcasting* (Garden City, N.Y., Doubleday and Company, 1980), p. 4.

174. 'any woman under thirty. . .' Ben Hecht, *A Child of the Century*, op. cit., p. 462.

174. 'Which would you. . .' *Fortune*, December 1937.

175. 'Working for Warner Brothers. . .' Max Wilk, *The Wit and Wisdom of Hollywood: From the Squaw Man to the Hatchet Man*. (New York, Atheneum, 1971), p. 80.

175. 'wall-eyed. . .' critics quoted in Samuel Marx, *Mayer and Thalberg: The Make-Believe Saints* (New York, Warner Books, 1980), p. 44.

176. 'writers did not. . .' Philip Dunne quoted in Mel Gussow, *Don't Say Yes Until I Finish Talking: A Biography of Darryl F. Zanuck*, (Garden City, NY, 1971), p. 142.

176. 'He declaimed. . .' Philip Dunne, *Take Two: A Life in Politics and Movies* (New York, McGraw-Hill, 1980), p. 55.

177. 'horrifiers' Paul Macnamara, *Those Were the Days My Friend: My Life in Hollywood with David O. Selznick and Others*, (Metuchen, N.J., The Scarecrow Press, 1993), p. 32.

177. 'I have just received. . .' ibid.

177. For Mankiewicz story see Bob Thomas, *King Cohn: The Life and Times of Harry Cohn*, op. cit., pp. 141–2.

178. 'What the hell do you know. . .' ibid., p. 243.

178. 'Well, it only proves. . .' ibid. pp. xxi–xxii.

178. 'I was struck. . .' George Oppenheimer, *The View from the 60s*, (New York, David McKay, 1966), p. 122.

178. 'I never had a conversation. . .' Howard Dietz, *Dancing in the Dark*, op. cit., p. 157.

179. On *Foolish Wives* see Thomas Schatz, *The Genius of the System: Hollywood Filmmaking in the Studio Era*, op. cit., p. 25.

179. 'The age of the director was over. . .' Lewis Milestone quoted in Richard Koszarki, *History of the American Cinema: Vol. 3: An Evening's Entertainment*, op. cit., p. 253.

180. 'The writer was very important. . .' quoted in Bernard Rosenberg and Harry Silverstein (eds), *The Real Tinsel*, op. cit..

181. For details of the Thalberg and Schoenberg encounter see Salka Viertel, *The Kindness of Strangers*, (New York, Holt, Rhinehart and Winston, 1969), p. 207 ff. See also Gabler, op. cit., p. 227–8.

182. 'While everyone else. . .' Anita Loos, *Kiss Hollywood Goodbye*, (London, Penguin Books, 1979) p. 178.

182. 'Credit you give. . .' quoted in Schatz, op. cit., p. 24.

182. 'For a thousand a week. . .' quoted in Leo C. Rostén, *Hollywood: The Movie Colony*, op. cit., p. 310.

182. 'There are grave difficulties. . .' quoted in Nick Roddick, 'Movies, Moguls & Money', *Stills*, May–June, 1983.

183. 'Don't buy anything. . .' Dore Schary, *Heyday*, op. cit., p. 55.

183. 'Movies were seldom. . .' Hecht, op. cit., p. 446.

183. 'Forget it Louis. . .' Thalberg, *The Last Tycoon and the World of MGM* (New York, Crown Publishers, 1994), p. 1.

183. 'About six producers. . .' quoted in Rosten, op. cit., pp. 302–3.

184. 'He was a very poor man. . .' Irene Mayer Selznick, *A Private View* (New York, Alfred A. Knopf, 1983), p. 148.

184. 'This is the only way. . .' quoted in Rosten, op. cit., p. 215.

CHAPTER ELEVEN

187. 'the first real offensive. . .' quoted in Thomas Greer, *What Roosevelt Thought: The Political and Social Ideas of Franklin D. Roosevelt*, (Michigan, Michigan State University Press, 1958), p. 64.

187. 'looks like a small town. . .' quoted in Ellis W. Hawley, *The New Deal and the Problem of Monopoly: A Study in Economic Ambivalence* (Princeton, Princeton University Press, 1966), p. 423. For an account of Arnold's life see Edward N. Kearney, *Thurman Arnold: Social Critic: The Satirical Challenge to Orthodoxy* (Albuquerque, University of New Mexico Press, 1970).

187. 'combined and conspired. . .' quoted from Amended and Supplemental Complaint, United States of America v Paramount Pictures Inc. et al, Equity No. 87–273, 14 November 1940 reprinted in *Film History*, Vol. 4., No 1, 1990. See Michael Conant, *Antitrust in the Motion Picture Industry*, (Berkeley and Los Angeles, University of California Press, 1960) for a comprehensive account of the government's anti-trust suit and Hollywood's response to it.

188. *Variety* estimated that. . . *Variety*, 27 July 1938.

188. 'in response to numerous. . .' Raymond Moley, *The Hays Office* Indianapolis, Bobbs-Merrill, 1945), p. 208.

188. 'if we are to maintain an industrial. . .' Arnold quoted in Otto Friedrich, *City of Nets: A Portrait of Hollywood in the 1940s* (New York, Harper & Row, 1986) p. 197.

189. 'dynamite gang' and the 'wrecking crew' quoted in Tino Balio (ed.), *The American Film Industry*, (Wisconsin and London, Univesity of Wisconsin Press, 1985 rev. ed.), p. 450.

189. Some 80 per cent. . . US Temporary National Economic Committee. *Investigation of Concentration of Economic Power. Monograph No. 43: The Motion Picture Industry: A Pattern of Concentration* (Washington US Government Printing Office, 1941), p. 11.

190. In March 1939. . . Harry Warner quoted in *Ronald Reagan in Hollywood: Movies and Politics*, op. cit., p. 99.

190. He wrote to the President. . . See ibid., p. 34.

190. 'administrative officers high in Government. . .' *Variety*, 14 August 1940.

190. 'the film industry is co-operating. . .' ibid.

191. 'Will this picture help us win. . .' quoted in Clayton R. Koppes and Gregory D. Black, *Hollywood Goes to War: How Politics, Profits and Propaganda Shaped World War II Movies*, (London, I.B. Tauris and Co., 1988), p. 84.

192. 'ahead of us in wanting. . .' See Richard W. Steele, *Propaganda in an Open Society, The Roosevelt Administration and the Media 1933–1941* (Westport, CT, Greenwood Press, 1985), p. 157.

192. Barney Balaban told Harry Hopkins. . . ibid.

193. 'In many cases. . .' report by Goodbody and Co., cited in US Congress, Senate, *Propaganda in Motion Pictures*, Hearings Before a Subcommittee of the Committee On Interstate Commerce, Seventy-Seventh Congress, First Session, (Washington US Government Printing Office, 1941) p. 38.

193. 'almost insurmountable transportation. . .' *Film Daily Yearbook*, 1942, p. 71.

194. 'Yes. Italy just banned. . .' Leo Rosten, op. cit., p. 35.

194. Creation of Filmkreditbank. . . See *Film History*, Vol. 3, No. 4., 1989.

196. 'Films constitute one of the most modern . . . quoted in Gordon Craig, *Germany 1866–1945* (Oxford, Oxford University Press, 1981 rev. ed.), p. 654.

196. 'in 1943 when. . . 'Quoted in Moley, op. cit., p. 185–6.

196. posing before a giant slogan. . . See David Forgacs, *Italian Culture in the Industrial Era*, op. cit., p. 71.

196. Mussolini's son Vittorio. . . Victoria de Grazia, 'Mass Culture and Sovereignty: The American Challenge to European Cinemas 1920–1960', *Journal of Modern History*, op. cit., p. 85.

197. 'By the time. . .' See Bob Thomas, *King Cohn*, op. cit., p. 102.

197. 'a burly grandfather clock. . .' quoted in Geoffrey Macnab, *J. Arthur Rank and the British Film Industry*, (London and New York, Routledge, 1993), p. 3.

198. 'his large face. . .' ibid.

198. habit of jiggling coins. . . See Michael Powell, *A Life in Movies* (London, William Heinemann, 1986), p. 387.

198. even confided to Michael Balcon. . . Michael Balcon, *Michael Balcon Presents . . . a Lifetime in Films*, op. cit., p. 186.

198. 'there's Methodism in his madness. . .' See Alan Wood, *Mr Rank*, (London, Hodder and Stoughton, 1952), p. 192.

198. 'Arthur Rank is the worst. . .' quoted in ibid.

199. On Oscar Deutsch see Macnab, op. cit., pp. 27–9.

199. partial to quoting from Juvenal. . . Wood, op. cit., p. 129.

199. By 1944. . . See Robert Murphy, 'Rank's attempt on the American market, 1944–1949' in James Curran and Vincent Porter (eds) *British Cinema History* (London, Weidenfeld and Nicolson, 1983), p. 166.

199. 'before long . . . Britain would be. . .' Wood, op. cit., p. 218.

200. 'Quality tells in the end. . .' quoted in Powell, op. cit., p. 647.

CHAPTER TWELVE

203. 'sail(ing) the financial. . .' *Business Week*, 11 May 1946.

203. Already by 1946. . . See ibid.

203. 'lean voluble man. . .' Schary, *Heyday*, op. cit., p. 160.

203. 'to wash the Red stain. . .' quoted in Vaughn, *Ronald Reagan in Hollywood: Movies and Politics*, op. cit., p. 199.

203. Frank McCarthy. See Jarvie, op. cit., p. 245.

204. 'cleanse the minds. . .' Vaughn, op. cit., p. 195.

204. 'front-line fighters. . .' ibid.

205. 'If you wish to stab. . .' quoted in Frank Costigliola, *France and the United States: The Cold War Alliance Since World War II*, (New York, Twayne Publishers, 1992), p. 56.

205. 'When Karl Marx calls on. . .' Irwin Wall, *Wall Street Journal* quoted in *The United States and the Making of Post-War France, 1945–1954*,

(Cambridge, Cambridge University Press, 1991) p. 52.

205. Blum–Byrnes agreement was signed... See Pierre Billard, *L'Âge classique du cinéma français: Du cinéma parlant à la Nouvelle Vague* (Paris, Flammarion, 1995), p. 517–8. See also Thomas H. Guback, *The International Film Industry: Western Europe and America Since 1945* (Bloomington, Indiana University Press, 1969), p. 21–2.

206. 'literally poison the souls...' quoted in Jean-Pierre Jeancolas, *From the Blum–Byrnes Agreement to the GATT affair* from Geoffrey Nowell-Smith and Steven Ricci (eds), *Hollywood and Europe: Economic and Cultural Interchanges 1945–1995* op. cit..

206. 'essence of capitalism' Costigliola, op. cit., p. 77.

206. 'Red delivery trucks...' quoted in ibid., p. 77.

207. creation of the CNC... See Billard, op. cit., pp. 503 ff.

208. '*Meno stracci, più gambe...*' quoted in Victoria de Grazia, op. cit., p. 83.

208. By 1947 $70 million... 'Political and Economic Planning', *The British Film Industry*, (London, Political and Economic Planning, 1952), p. 98.

208. 'If I am compelled to choose...' quoted in Margaret Dickinson and Sarah Street, *Cinema and State*, op. cit., p. 180.

209. *Unconquered*... see 'Political and Economic Planning', *The British Film Industry*, op. cit., p. 99.

209. 'We were not...' quoted in Ben Pimlott, *Harold Wilson*, (London, HarperCollins, 1992), p. 118.

212. '(I)n the post-war period...' 1944 departmental circular quoted in Arthur W. Macmahon, *Memorandum on The Postwar International Information Program of the United States*, (Washington, Department of State, 1945), p. 76.

213. 'a worldwide Marshall plan...' Walter Wanger, 'Donald Duck and Diplomacy', *Public Opinon Quarterly*, Fall, 1950, p. 452.

213. Admiral Stone... See Lorenzo Quaglietti, *Storia economico-politica del cinema italiano 1945—1980*, Rome, Editori Riuniti, 1980).

213. In one case... *Life* magazine, 13 August 1951.

213. Creation of IMG... See Richard D. McCann, 'Hollywood Faces the World', *Yale Review*, Vol. LI, No. 4 June, 1962, pp. 593–608. See also Thomas Guback, 'Shaping the film business in postwar Germany; the role of the US film industry and the US state' in Paul Kerr (ed.) *The Hollywood Film Industry: A Reader*, (London, Routledge & Kegan Paul in association with the BFI, 1986), pp. 245–276.

214. By 1957... See Guback in Kerr, op. cit., p. 266.

214. For information on Hong Kong industry... See I.C. Jarvie, *Window on Hong Kong: A Sociological Study of the Hong Kong Film Industry and its Audience*, (Hong Kong, University of Hong Kong, 1977).

215. 'the movies do not...' quoted in Richard D. McCann, *Hollywood Faces the World*, op. cit., p. 601.

215. 'Of course, they don't...' ibid.

215. while the Commerce Department. . . for more information see Jarvie, op. cit., p. 375 ff.

215. disagreements between the MPEA and the Military Government. . . See Guback in Kerr, op. cit.

CHAPTER THIRTEEN

217. 'We've been hit. . .' *Variety*, 5 May 1948.

217. 'a revolution in the industry' ibid..

217. '93 per cent of all investment', *Film Daily Yearbook*, 1949, p. 65.

217. 'The day of the big studios. . .' *Life* magazine, op. cit..

217. 'Hollywood's like Egypt. . .' quoted in Ben Hecht, *A Child of the Century*, op. cit., p. 436.

217. 'Looking ahead. . .' *Life* magazine, op. cit..

219. 'I can do without you. . .' quoted in Erik Barnouw, *A History of Broadcasting in the United States Vol. II: The Golden Web 1933–53*, (New York, Oxford University Press, 1968), p. 291.

219. 'Film Biz Dips to Only. . .' *Variety*, 9 April 1947, cited in Hortense Powdermaker, *Hollywood: The Dream Factory* (London, Secker & Warburg, 1951), p. 35.

220. The Lost Audience. . . See Richard Griffith, 'Where are the Dollars?' Part Two in *Sight and Sound*, January, 1950.

220. 'accounts for anywhere. . .' US Congress, Senate Select Committee on Small Business, *Motion Picture Distribution Trade Practices – 1956*, Report, 84th Congress, 2nd Session.

220. For background information on MCA and Lew Wasserman, see 'Star-Spangled Octopus', *Saturday Evening Post*, 10, 17, 24 and 31 August 1946, *Fortune*, July 1960, *Time*, 1 January 1965 and Michael Pye, *Moguls Inside the Business of Showbusiness* (New York, Holt, Rhinehart and Winston, 1980), Chapter One.

220. 'I think I'll take the job. . .' *Time*, op cit..

221. nicknamed C.O.D., Hedda Hopper and James Brough, *The Whole Truth and Nothing But* (New York, Pyramid Books, 1963), p. 108.

221. 'Remember what those bastards. . .' quoted in Allen Rivkin and Laura Kerr, *Hello, Hollywood!* (Garden City, N.Y., Doubleday & Co., 1962), p. 197.

221. 'it isn't enough,' quoted in Frank Rose, *The Agency: William Morris and the Hidden History of Showbusiness*, (New York, HarperCollins, 1995), p. 57.

222. 'I had a young assistant. . .' quoted in Pye, op. cit..

222. 'just two minutes of your time. . .' *Saturday Evening Post*, 17 August 1946.

223. Nothing was set down. . . See Pye, op. cit., p. 47.

223. Eddie 'the Killer' Linsk see *Saturday Evening Post*, 31 August 1946.

223. 'the star-spangled Octopus' title of article in *Saturday Evening Post*, op. cit..

223. 'I don't live on the. . .' interview in *New York Times*, 20 July 1963.

224. In 1946 estimates... *Saturday Evening Post*, 10 August 1946.
224. Stein, said Wasserman ... quoted in *Variety*, 28 August 1995.
224. 'the student who...' quoted in Pye, p. 46.
224. 'I never see him after...' quoted in Schary, *Heyday*, op. cit., p. 132.
224. it was said that he could guess... See *Variety*, 28 August 1995.
225. 'Here come the Penguins...' quoted in *Wall Street Journal*, 10 July 1973.
225. 'That's a nice shirt...' story told in *Fortune*, July 1960.
225. 'like an assembly line actress' Bette Davis, *The Lonely Life*, (London, Macdonald, 1963) p. 157.
226. 'It was his opinion that...' Ronald Reagan with Richard G. Hubler, *My Early Life or Where's the Rest of Me?* (London, Sidgwick & Jackson, 1981), p. 105–6.
226. profit-sharing deals in a system pioneered ... See William Paley, *As It Happened*, (Garden City, N.Y., Doubleday and Company, 1979), p. 193.
226. Wasserman deal for Stewart... See Pye, op. cit., p. 45 and Schatz, *The Genius of the System: Hollywood Filmmaking in the Studio Era*, op. cit., pp. 470–1.
227. 'the straight talk...' Irving Bernstein, *Hollywood at the Crossroads: An Economic Study of the Motion Picture Industry*, (Hollywood, by the author, 1957), p. 68.

CHAPTER FOURTEEN

229. On 30 April... Erik Barnouw, *Tube of Plenty: The Evolution of American Television* (New York, Oxford University Press, 1975), pp. 89–90.
230. 'S.S. *Titanic* ran into...' ibid., p. 17.
230. The schedule consisted of... ibid., p. 90.
230. By the end of that year... Michael Conant, *Antitrust in the Motion Picture Industry*, op. cit., p. 13.
231. 'if we show the pictures...' quoted in Ben Hecht, article in *Playboy*, 1962.
231. MGM went further and banned... See Christopher Anderson, *Hollywood TV: The Studio System in the Fifties*, (Austin, University of Texas Press, 1994), p. 293.
231. 'I wish for television only a tortured...' 'The Big Brawl: Hollywood versus Television', Part II, *Saturday Evening Post*, 26 January 1952.
231. 'The movies are in trouble...' quoted in *Life*, op. cit..
232. 'You Can See Without Glasses...' Schary, op. cit., p. 264.
233. 'Harry Cohn was the rudest of them...' Kitner quoted in Max Wilk, *The Golden Age of Television: Notes from the Survivors*, (New York, Delacorte Press, 1976), p. 258.
233. 'I am the king here. Whoever eats my bread...' for source see note to Chapter 10 epigraph.
233. 'If the movies try to lick television...' *New York Times*, 13 February 1949.
234. 'could be shown again, and again...' in Gorham Kindem, *The Live Television Generation of Film Directors: Interviews with Seven Directors*

(Jefferson, North Carolina and London, McFarland & Company, 1994) p. 47.

234. 'So we borrowed. . .' quoted in Wilk, op. cit., p. 251.

234. In the 1952–3 season. . . See William Paley, op. cit., p. 238.

235. 'We all thought he was nuts. . .' quoted in Fortune, July 1960.

235. 'Every writer, actor and director. . .' quoted in Ronald Brownstein, The Power and The Glitter: The Hollywood-Washington Connection (Vintage Books, New York, 1992), p. 183.

235. For biographical information on the history of Walt Disney and the company he created see Fortune, November 1934, Richard Schickel, The Disney Version (New York, Simon and Schuster, 1958) and Bob Thomas, Walt Disney (London, W.H. Allen, 1981).

236. 'total merchandising' Anderson, op. cit., p. 134.

236. 'With a bang that blew. . .' quoted in James L. Baughman, The Weakest Chain and the Strongest Link: The American Broadcasting Company and the Motion Picture Industry in Tino Balio (ed.) Hollywood in the Age of Television (London, Unwin Hyman, 1990).

236. 'I made those quickies thirty years. . .' quoted in Leonard Goldenson, Beating the Odds: The Untold Story behind the Rise of ABC (New York, Scribner's, 1991), p. 124.

237. 'to secure advertisements. . .' quoted in Anderson, op. cit., p. 157.

237. His son-in-law, William Orr. . . See Erik Barnouw, Tube of Plenty: The Evolution of American Television, op. cit., p. 193.

237. 'If you see more than two. . .' ibid., p. 194.

237. . . . major studios making almost. . . Variety, 1 July 1959.

238. 'If I had millions. . .' Life, op. cit..

238. Once again, it was Warners. . . See Billboard, 12 February 1955. Hollywood Reporter, 13 February 1956.

238. . . . considered low even at the time. . . Wall Street Journal, 2 March 1956.

239. 'Wall Street, with its ears. . .' Variety, 16 May 1956.

239. By 1958 almost four thousand movies. . . Tino Balio (ed.), op. cit., Hollywood in the Age of Television.

239. 'When my current features go out. . .' quote from Washington Star, in US Congress, Senate Select Committee on Small Business. Motion Picture Distribution Trade Practices – 1956. Report, 84th Congress, 2nd Session.

240. 'Hollywood return the art. . .' quoted in Valley Times, 29 February 1956.

240. By 1958 it was estimated that. . . Sindlinger & Company, An Analysis of the Dollar Impact of Movies on Television, (Ridley Park, Pennsylvania, Sindlinger & Company, 1958), p. 30.

240. 'television has been a very healthy. . .' Variety, 17 June 1959.

240. '(W)ithout our television sales. . .' quoted in Penelope Houston, Hollywood in the Age of Television, Sight and Sound, Spring 1957.

241. By the mid-1990s. . . See interview with Roger Mayer of Turner Entertainment, Screen International, 1 December 1995.

241. 'We went into the television business. . .' New York Times, 20 July 1963.

241. 'There's little or no. . .' *Valley Times*, 29 February 1956.
241. 'Without the more than. . .' Griffith Johnson, Vice-President, MPAA in US Congress, House, *Hearings Before the Subcommittee on the Impact of Imports and Exports on American Employment of the Committee on Education and Labor*, 87th Congress, 1st and 2nd Sessions, (Washington, US Government Printing Office, 1962) Part 8, p. 479.
242. 'might be regarded as. . .' Michael Jackson, 'Cinema versus Television', *Sight and Sound*, (Summer 1980).
242. In the early 1950s, the European Cinema Owners Union. . . See Martin Blaney, *Symbiosis or Confrontation?: The Relationship Between the Film Industry and Television in the Federal Republic of Germany from 1950 to 1985* (Berlin, Edition Sigma, 1992), p. 24.
242. On FIDO see. . . Jackson, op. cit., and Blaney, op. cit., p. 59.
243. 'would have been ploughed back. . .' Michael Balcon, *Michael Balcon Presents . . . A Lifetime in Films*, op. cit..
243. 'FIDO has been the envy. . .' Jackson, op. cit..
243. Admissions had plunged. . . See *British Film Institute Handbook 1996* (London, British Film Institute, 1995), p. 62, for list of British cinema admission figures from 1993–94.
243. In Germany, for example, there was an attempt. . . See Blaney, op. cit., p. 59.
244. One economist argued. . . See John Spraos, *The Decline of the Cinema* (London, Allen & Unwin, 1962).
245. 'We gave them. . .' John McCarthy of the Television Program Export Association quoted in *Tube of Plenty: The Evolution of American Television*, op. cit., p. 234.

CHAPTER FIFTEEN

248. 'the cinema is quite simply. . .' Alexandre Astruc, 'The birth of a new avant-garde: Le caméra-stylo', in Peter Graham (ed.), *The New Wave* (London, Secker & Warburg, 1968), pp. 17–8.
249. 'The scenario is the film itself. . .' Henri Diamant-Berger in Richard Abel, *French Film Theory and Criticism, Vol. 1, 1907–1929*, (Princeton, Princeton University Press, 1988).
250. 'a distant, exterior attitude' B. Nicols (ed.) *Movies and Methods* (Berkeley and London, University of California Press, 1976), p. 232.
250. 'the hundred-odd French films. . .' ibid..
250. Translated into English as 'auteur theory'.
250. 'In the hands of a great director. . .' translation of a quote from Fereydoun Hoveyda, 'Les Taches du soleil' in Jim Hillier (ed.) *Cahiers du Cinéma: The 1950s – Neo-Realism, Hollywood, New Wave* (Cambridge, Mass., Harvard University Press, 1985), p. 10.
251. 'Hollywood is a microcosm. . .' Jean Domarchi, 'Knife in the Wound' in ibid., p. 244.

251. 'All directors and not just. . .' Andrew Sarris, *The American Cinema,
      Directors and Directors, 1929–1968*, (New York, E.P. Dutton, 1968),
      p. 36.
251. 'the cinema is an art which is both. . .' André Bazin, 'On the *politique des
      auteurs*' in Hillier (ed.), op. cit., p. 251.
252. 'The new film requires. . .' The so-called 'Oberhausen Manifesto' quoted
      in Hans Günther Pflaum and Hans Helmut Prinzler, *Cinema in the
      Federal Republic of Germany*, trans. Timothy Nevill, (Bonn, Inter
      Nationes, 1993).
253. 'Everybody went to Paris. . .' quoted in Kristin Thompson and David
      Bordwell, *Film History: An Introduction*, op. cit., p. 545.
254. After all, a farce like. . . See Susan Hayward, *French National Cinema*,
      (London, Routledge, 1993), p. 275.
254. In 1960 French films. . . See Colin Crisp, *The Classical French Cinema,
      1930–1960*, op. cit., p. 82.
256. 'because of what they had seen. . .' US Congress, House, *Hearing
      Before the Subcommittee on the Impact of Imports and Exports*, op. cit.,
      p. 470.
256. 'communist-controlled unions abroad. . .' ibid., p. 499.
256. 'We have in the neighbourhood. . .' ibid., pp. 470–1.
257. 'produce revenue that comes back. . .' ibid..
257. In 1964, the Association of Motion Picture. . .' *Daily Variety*, 9 April 1964.
257. 'imported films have overtaken. . .' *Film Daily*, 13 July 1967.
257. 'The Roman Orgy of Movie-Making' US Congress, House, *Hearings Before
      the Subcommittee on the Impact of Imports and Exports*, op. cit., p. 508.
258. Origins of spaghetti westerns. . . See Peter Bondanella, *Italian Cinema:
      From Neorealism to the Present* (New York, Continuum, 1994),
      pp. 253–75.
260. 'If you are going. . .' *SR*, 20 August 1966.
261. In 1966 ABC astounded. . . Tino Balio (ed.), *The American Film Industry*,
      op. cit., p. 435.
261. By 1968, the average price . . . ibid..
261. 'It's strictly a seller's market. . .' *Newsweek*, 6 November 1967.
261. 'I want to be in the feature film. . .' Paley quoted in Sally Bedell Smith, *In
      All His Glory: The Life of William S. Paley*, (New York, Simon and
      Schuster, 1990).
261. 'What better way. . .' ibid., p. 467.

CHAPTER SIXTEEN

264. 'The worst thing that ever. . .' quoted in Michael Pye and Lynda Myles,
      The Movie Brats: How the Film Generation Took Over Hollywood,
      (London, Faber & Faber, 1979), p. 37.
264. 'If the economy is in a recession. . .' *Los Angeles Times*, 17 March 1971.
264. 'films made abroad. . .' ibid..

265. 'There is a probability. . .' *Journal of the Producers Guild of America*, March 1970.
266. In 1971, Thomas Kuchel. . . Bill No. HR6060.
267. 'in desperate need of. . .' 'Unemployment Problems in the American Film Industry', in US Congress, House, *Hearings Before the General Sub-committee on Labor of the Committee on Education and Labor*, 92nd Congress, 1st Session, (Washington, US Government Printing Office, 1972), p. 76.
267. For a brief history of the origins of the Investment Tax Credit see US Congress, Senate, *Hearings Before the Committee on Finance*, 92nd Congress, 1st Session, (Washington US Government Printing Office, 1971), p. 196. For details of the revised credit introduced in 1971 see *United States Statutes at Large* (1971), Volume 85 (Washington, US Government Printing Office, 1972). For a broad consideration of the investment credits and tax breaks for the American film industry see Richard Warren Lewis, 'Gimme Shelter', *New West*, 7 June 1976.
267. including a meeting with President Nixon . . . see comments by Charles Boren, Vice-President, MPAA, op. cit., *Unemployment Problems in the American Film Industry*, op. cit., p. 89.
267. '97 per cent. . .' *Variety*, 29 March 1972.
267. 'of inestimable help. . .' Heston, *Unemployment Problems in the American Film Industry*, op. cit., p. 76.
268. When the French consul learned. . . *Hollywood Reporter*, 17 September 1976.
268. On the legislation relating to DISCs see *United States Statutes at Large* (1971) Volume 85, (Washington, US Government Printing Office, 1972), pp. 535 ff.
268. Another equally significant tax change. . . For an account of the use of tax shelters in relation to films in the US see *Tax Revision Issues 1976 (HR10612) 1 – Tax Shelter Investments: Prepared for the Use of the Committee on Finance by the Staff of the Joint Committee on Internal Revenue Taxation* (Washington, US Government Printing Office, 1976), especially 'Movie Films', pp. 67–81. See also *Tax Shelters: Movie Films: Prepared for the Use of the Committee on Ways and Means By the Staff of the Joint Committee on Internal Revenue Taxation* (Washington, US Government Printing Office, 1975). See also Richard Warren Lewis, op. cit..
269. 'Columbia Pictures would have been bankrupt. . .' US Congress, Senate, *Tax Reform Act of 1975, Part 2, Senate Committee on Finance Hearing*, 94th Congress, 2nd Session, (Washington, US Government Printing Office, 1976), p. 671.
269. 'Only three copies of that film. . .' quoted in Michael Pye and Lynda Myles, op. cit., p. 52.
269. 'It is just an outright tax subsidy. . .' US Congress, *Congressional Record: Senate*, 94th Congress, 2nd Session, Volume 122 – Part 20, 30 July 1976 to 5 August 1976, p. 25608 ff.

269. 'an American institution' Senator John V. Tunney, ibid., p. 25614.
269. 'fiscal impact. . .' *Hollywood Reporter*, 4 November 1976.
270. FCC legislation on network financial syndication and network financial interest; 47 CFR 73.658 (j)s. For an useful explanation of the origins of the Fin-Syn regulations, particularly with regard to the international implications of the legislation, see Bill Grantham, 'Finsyn's Foreign Flaw', *Television Business International*, June 1991.
270. 'The three national television networks. . .' Federal Communications Commission, Radio Broadcast Services, 'Competition and Responsibility in Network Programming', *Federal Register*, (Washington US Government Printing Office, 1970), Vol. 35, No. 93, 13 May 1970, p. 7420.
271. 'irreparable damage' Federal Communications Commission Reports, *Network Television Broadcasting*, Docket No. 12782, Memorandum Opinion and Order, 26 FCC 2d, (Washington US Government Printing Office, 1970), p. 29.
274. 'He's an extraordinary talent. . .' quoted in Peter Lev, *The Euro-American Cinema*, (Austin, University of Texas Press, 1993), p. 70.
275. 'We are the guys who dig out. . .' Michael Pye and Lynda Myles, op. cit., p. 9.
275. 'They want me to direct. . .' quoted in Kristin Thompson and David Bordwell, *Film History: An Introduction*, op. cit., p. 707.
275. 'He couldn't get a cartoon. . .' Robert Evans, *The Kid Stays In the Picture* (London, Aurum Press, 1994).
275. 'I have failed on all three. . .' quoted in Michael Pye and Lynda Myles, op. cit., p. 93–4.
276. average production costs jumped. . . MPAA figures.
277. 'There's a natural war. . .' Pauline Kael, 'Onward and Upward with the Arts', *New Yorker*, 5 August 1974.
279. 'Oh Mr Lancaster, who represents you?. . .' quoted in Frank Rose, *The Agency*, op. cit., p. 340.
279. 'When are you going to get rid. . .' ibid..
280. 'I was scared of them. . .' Bryan Burroughs and Kim Masters, 'The Mouse Trap', *Vanity Fair*, December 1996, p. 190.
280. In 1975, he left with four partners. . . Rose, op. cit., p. 336.
281. 'Are you on a hard line?' *Vanity Fair*, op. cit., p. 194.
283. In 1996 Harold Vogel. . . See *Screen International*, 3 May 1996.
283. 'The studios' financial managers. . .' *Economist*, 24 December 1994.
284. 'There's been a polarisation. . .' *Screen International*, 3 May 1996.
286. 'By the year 2000. . .' *Wall Street Journal*, 2 August 1995.
286. 'More and more I have noticed. . .' *Wall Street Journal*, 3 August 1995.
286. according to one estimate, the Hollywood studios. . . *Variety*, 5 August 1996.
286. 'In the mid-'80s. . .' *Premiere*, January 1996, p. 79.
287. 'distribution serves production not the other way round' *Variety*, 30 October 1995.

288. by 1973 almost seventy five per cent... American Film Institute report quoted in Chris Hugo, 'American Cinema in the 70s – The Economic Background', *Movie*, (Winter 1980/Spring 1980).

288. 'gum-chewing, hamburger-munching adolescents', Kristin Thompson and David Bordwell, *Film History: An Introduction*, op. cit., p. 381.

290. In 1994, the net receipts... *Variety*, 15 January 1996.

290. 'We're seeing the Hollywood decision-making process...' *Variety*, ibid..

290. 'Earth to Hollywood: You Win!'

CHAPTER SEVENTEEN

292. On the Langlois affair, see Michel Frodon, *L'Âge moderne du cinéma français: De la Nouvelle Vague à nos jours*, (Paris, Flammarion, 1995), p. 220 ff.

293. 'based on the total absence...' quoted in Sylvia Harvey, *May '68 and Film Culture*, (London, BFI Publishing, 1980), p. 22.

293. On the morning of 18 May...' See Frodon, op. cit., p. 231 ff.

294. 'Many were convinced that...' ibid., p. 233.

294. 'Revolution in and through...' Harvey, op. cit., p. 18.

295. 'workers don't come to see my films' James Monaco, *The New Wave*, (New York, Oxford University Press, 1976), p. 214.

296. 'to make ... a political cinema...' Harvey, op. cit., p. 30.

296. For biographical information on Jean-Luc Godard... See Julia Lesage, *Jean-Luc Godard: A Guide to References and Resources*. (Boston, Mass., G.K. Hall & Co., 1979), pp. 1–9.

297. 'I was always taken aback...' in Jacques Gerber, *Anatole Dauman: Pictures of Producer*, trans. Paul Willemen, (London, BFI Publishing, 1992).

298. 'a film must bear the mark...' Jean-Claude Carrière, *The Secret Language of Film*, trans. Jeremy Leggatt, (New York, Pantheon Books, 1994), p. 42.

298. 'Of all the different obligations...' *Felix*, European Film Academy, November 1994.

299. During the period 1975–9... Hayward, *French National Cinema*, p. 244.

299. 'Macs du Porno...' Frodon, op. cit., p. 407.

300. 'A full movie house entails low motivations...' Hans Günther Pflaum and Hans Helmut Prinzler, *Cinema in the Federal Republic of Germany*, p. 58.

301. 'When I was a critic...' quoted in Alan Williams, *Republic of Images: A History of French Filmmaking*, (Cambridge, Mass., Harvard University Press, 1992), p. 354.

301. 'Do you know the definition...' quoted in *Report: By the Think-Tank On the Audio-Visual Policy in the European Union* (Office for Official Publications of the European Communities, Luxembourg 1994), p. 34.

302. 'If we were to cling to the...' quoted in *European Media Business and Finance*, 28 October 1991.

302. 'Moral rights are the link. . .' ibid..

CHAPTER EIGHTEEN

313. In 1985, fifty-four films . . . figures quoted in *British Film Institute Handbook*, op. cit., p. 23.
313. By 1989 . . . ibid..
313. During the same period. . . Official MPA data.
314. Early history of AMC see *Variety*, 8 March 1993.
316. 'because so far we have not persuaded. . .' John Davis, 'Intermission: The British Film Industry', *National Provincial Bank Review*, (August 1958).
316. 'Sir John controls. . .' quoted in Macnab, J. *Arthur Rank and the British Film Industry*, p. 229.
316. 'He thoroughly disliked the film business. . .' Anthony Havelock-Allan quoted in Macnab, op. cit., p. 218.
316. In 1962, John Spaos, *The Decline of the Cinema*, op. cit.
320. Figures on screen density. . . *Screen Digest*, September 1996.
320. By 1995 the American movies . . . ibid..
321. By 1965. . . See Martin Dale, *Awaiting The Phoenix – The Challenge for the European Film Industry*, p. 11. Unpublished English version of text available in Spanish in *Situacion* No. 3, 1994 (Bilbao, Banco Bilbao Vizcaya, 1994).
322. In the 1960s, foreign-language. . . See ibid., p. 15 based on *Variety* figures.
325. On Carolco see *Wall Street Journal*, 16 July 1991.

CHAPTER NINETEEN

330. 'vision . . . enterprise and progress. . .' Jarvie, op. cit., p. 296.
332. In the mid-1960s. . . See *Report: By the Think-Tank On the Audio-Visual Policy in the European Union*, op. cit., p. 20.
340. 'The US majors were. . .' Confidential source.
340. 'Why this EC quota. . .' US Congress, Senate, *Review of the Uruguay Round: Commitments to Open Markets. Hearings before the Committee on Finance*, 102nd Congress, 1st Session, 17–18 April 1991, op. cit., p. 150.
342. 'Blow up the deal. . .' Jeffrey Goodell, 'The French Revolution', *Premiere*, May 1994.
342. Lew Wasserman's apparent involvement . . . ibid..
343. 'In a global treaty. . .' Official statement issued by MPAA.
343. 'You can't sustain. . .' Remarks made at press conference on GATT in Geneva.
343. 'We were unable to overcome. . .' *Memorandum for the United States Trade Representative*, The White House, Washington, 15 December 1993. Subsequently published in the Federal Register.
343. 'It's not a victory of. . .' *Premiere*, op. cit..
344. The Club of European Producers was launched in 1993 to address the

circumstances surrounding the GATT negotiations. The Club serves both as a permanent think-tank and a lobby at national and European level. Its president is René Cleitman, French producer of *Cyrano de Bergerac*. Other members include Andrés Vicente Gómez, the Spanish producer of Oscar-winning *Belle Époque*, German producer Dieter Geissler who made *The Neverending Story* and myself.

CHAPTER TWENTY

350. In 1995, the European Community. . . Figures from the European Audio-visual Obsevatory, published in *Screen International*, 29 November 1996. The Observatory predicted a sharp increase in the figure for 1996.

350. 'only a very few multinationals. . .' Anthony Sampson, *Company Man*, (London, HarperCollins, 1995), p. 306.

351. 'In line with the increased growth. . .' See *Growth, Competitiveness and Employment* – White Paper, COM (93) 700 final of 5 December 1993 – Part B, II, Chapter V, Sections A and C, (Luxembourg, European Commission, 1993).

357. 'The confrontation of civilizations. . .' Jean-Jacques Servan-Schreiber, *The American Challenge*, trans. Ronald Steel, (London, Hamish Hamilton, 1968), p. 199.

SELECT BIBLIOGRAPHY

This bibliography offers a guide to those books which were found to be among the most valuable in the course of researching the text. The footnotes contain the bibliographical details of all periodicals, government documents and other primary sources used, as well as references to further books on particular aspects of the film industry.

Abel, Richard. *The Ciné Goes To Town: Cinema, 1896–1914*. (Los Angeles, University of California Press, 1993).

Abel, Richard. *French Cinema: The First Wave, 1915–1929*. (Princeton, N.J., Princeton University Press, 1984).

Abel, Richard. *French Film Theory and Criticism, Vol. 1., 1907–1929*. (Princeton, N.J. Princeton University Press, 1988).

Anderson, Christopher. *Hollywood TV: The Studio System in the Fifties*. (Austin, University of Texas Press, 1994).

Anderson, Joseph L. and Richie, Donald. *The Japanese Film: Art and Industry*. (rev. ed., Princeton, N.J., Princeton University Press, 1982).

Armes, Roy. *A Critical History of the British Cinema*. (London, Secker & Warburg, 1978 f).

Bächlin, Peter. *Histoire économique du cinéma* (La Nouvelle Edition, 1947).

Balcon, Michael. *Michael Balcon Presents . . . A Lifetime in Films*. (London, Hutchinson, 1969).

Balio, Tino (ed.). *The American Film Industry*. (Rev. ed., Wisconsin and London, University of Wisconsin Press, 1985).

Balio, Tino (ed.) *Hollywood in the Age of Television*. (London, Unwin Hyman, 1990).

Bandio, Felice A. *A.P. Giannini: Banker of America*. (Berkeley, University of California Press, 1994).

Barnes, John. *The Beginnings of the Cinema in England*. (London, David & Charles, 1976).

Barnouw, Erik. *Tube of Plenty: The Evolution of American Television*. (New York, Oxford University Press, 1975).

Barnouw, Erik and Krishnaswamy, S. *Indian Film*. (Rev. ed., New Delhi, Oxford University Press, 1980).

Berg, A. Scott. *Goldwyn*. (London, Hamish Hamilton, 1989).

Bernstein, Irving. *Hollywood at the Crossroads: An Economic Study of the Motion Picture Industry*. (Hollywood, by the author, 1957).

Billard, Pierre. *L'Ârge classique du cinéma français: Du cinéma parlant à la Nouvelle Vague*. (Paris, Flammarion, 1995).

Blaney, Martin. *Symbiosis or Confrontation?: The Relationship Between the Film Industry and Television in the Federal Republic of Germany from 1950 to 1985*. (Berlin, Edition Sigma, 1992).

Bolshofer, Fred J. and Miller, Arthur C. *One Reel A Week*. (Berkeley and Los Angeles, University of California Press, 1967).

Bondanella, Peter. *Italian Cinema: From Neorealism To the Present* (New York, Continuum, 1994).

British Film Institute. *British Film Institute Handbook 1996*. (London, British Film Institute, 1995).

Brownlow, Kevin. *The Parade's Gone By*. (London, Abacus, 1973).

Brownstein, Ronald. *The Power and The Glitter: The Hollywood-Washington Connection* (Vintage Books, New York, 1992).

Capra, Frank. *The Name Above the Title*. (New York, Macmillan Co., 1971).

Carey, Gary. *All the Stars in Heaven: Louis B. Mayer's MGM* (New York, E.P. Dutton, 1981).

Carrière, Jean-Claude, *The Secret Language of Film*. trans. Jeremy Leggatt, (New York, Pantheon Books, 1994).

Caughie, John (ed.). *Theories of Authorship: A Reader* (London and New York, Routledge & Kegan Paul, 1981).

Chaplin, Charles. *My Autobiography*. (London, The Bodley Head, 1964).

Chardère, Bernard. *Le Roman des Lumières*. (Éditions Gallimard, 1995).

Coissac, Georges. *Histoire du cinématographe, des origines jusqu'a nos jours*. (Paris, Editions du Cinéopse 1925).

Conant, Michael. *Antitrust in the Motion Picture Industry*. (Berkeley and Los Angeles, University of California Press, 1960).

Costigliola, Frank. *France and the United States: The Cold War Alliance Since World War II*. (New York, Twayne Publishers, 1992).

Creel, George. *How We Advertised America*. (New York, Harper and Brothers, 1920).

Crisp, Colin. *The Classical French Cinema, 1930–1960*. (Bloomington and Indianapolis, Indiana University Press, 1993).

Curran, James and Porter, Vincent (eds). *British Cinema History*. (London, Weidenfeld & Nicolson, 1983).

Dale, Martin. *Awaiting The Phoenix – The Challenge for the European Film Industry*. Unpublished English version of text available in Spanish in *Situacion* No. 3, 1994 (Bilbao, Banco Bilbao Vizcaya, 1994).

Dale, Martin. *Europa, Europa*. (Académie Carat and Media Business School, 1992).

Dana, Julian. *A.P. Giannini,: Giant in the West*. (Englewood Cliffs, N.J., Prentice-Hall, 1947).

Davis, Bette. *The Lonely Life*. (London, Macdonald, 1963).

De Mille, Cecil B. *Autobiography*. Edited by Donald Hayne. (W.H. Allen, London, 1960).

de Mille, William. *Hollywood Saga* (New York, E.P. Dutton, 1939).

Deslandes, Jacques and Richard, Jacques. *Histoire comparée du cinéma. Vol. 2. 1896–1906* (Paris, Casterman, 1968).

Dickinson, Margaret and Street, Sarah. *Cinema and State: The Film Industry and the Government 1927–84.* (London, BFI Publishing, 1985).

Dietz, Howard. *Dancing in the Dark*. (New York, Quadrangle Press, 1974).

Drinkwater, John. *The Life and Adventures of Carl Laemmle*. (London, William Heinemann, 1931).

Duhamel, Georges. *America: The Menace*, trans. Charles Miner Thompson, (London, George Allen and Unwin, 1931).

Dunne, Philip. *Take Two: A Life in Politics and Movies*. (New York, McGraw-Hill, 1980).

Eberts, Jake and Ilott, Terry. *My Indecision is Final: The Rise and Fall of Goldcrest Films*. (London, Faber and Faber, 1990).

Elsaesser, Thomas. *Early Cinema: Space, Frame, Narrative* (London, BFI, 1990).

European Commission. *Strategy Options to Strengthen the European Programme Industry in the context of the Audiovisual Policy of the European Union*. (Luxembourg, Office for Offical Publications of the European Communities, 1994).

The Film Daily Yearbook of Motion Pictures. (New York, Film Daily, 1928–1969)

Finney, Angus. *A Dose of Reality: The State of European Cinema*. (Berlin, The European Film Academy and Screen International, 1993).

Fitzgerald, F. Scott. *The Last Tycoon*. (London, Penguin 1965).

Forgacs, David. *Italian Culture in the Industrial Era*. (Manchester, Manchester University Press, 1990).

Friedrich, Otto. *City of Nets: A Portrait of Hollywood in the 1940s*. (New York, Harper & Row, 1986).

Frodon, Michel, *L'Âge moderne du cinéma français: De la Nouvelle Vague à nos jours*. (Flammarion, 1995).

Gabler, Neal. *An Empire of Their Own: How the Jews Invented Hollywood*. (London, W.H. Allen, 1989).

Gall, Lothar, Feldman, Gerald D., James, Harold, Holtfrerich, Carl-Ludwig, Büschgen, Hans E. *The Deutsche Bank*. (London, Weidenfeld & Nicolson, 1995).

Goldenson, Leonard. *Beating the Odds: The Untold Story behind the Rise of ABC. (New York, Scribner's 1991)*.

Gomery, Douglas. *Shared Pleasures, A History of Movie Presentation in the United States*. (London, BFI Publishing, 1992).

Grantham, Bill. *A Big Bourgeois Brothel: France's Culture Wars with America*. (forthcoming).

Grau, Robert. *The Theatre of Science*. (New York, 1941; reprint, New York, B. Blom, 1969).

Guback, Thomas H. *The International Film Industry: Western Europe and America Since 1945*. (Bloomington, Indiana University Press, 1969).

Gussow, Mel. *Don't Say Yes Until I Finish Talking: A Biography of Darryl F. Zanuck*, (Garden City, N.Y., 1971).

Hampton, Benjamin. *History of the American Film Industry: From its beginnings to 1931*. (reprint, New York, Dover Publications, 1970).

Harpole, Charles (ed.). *History of the American Cinema* (New York, Charles Scribner's Sons, 1990-present):

– Vol. 1. Musser, Charles. *The Emergence of Cinema: The American Screen to 1907*. (1990).

– Vol. 2. Bowser, Eileen. *The Transformation of Cinema*. (1990).

– Vol. 3. Koszarki, Richard. *History of the American Cinema: Vol. 3: An Evening's Entertainment*. (1990).

– Vol. 5. Balio, Tino. *History of the American Cinema: Grand Design*. (1993).

Harvey, Sylvia. *May '68 and Film Culture*. (London, BFI Publishing, 1980).

Hays, Will. *The Memoirs of Will H. Hays*. (Garden City, N.Y., Doubleday, 1955).

Hayward, Susan. *French National Cinema*. (London, Routledge, 1993).

Hecht, Ben. *A Child of the Century*. (New York, New American Library, 1955).

Hemel, Annemoon van, Mommaas, Hans and Smithuijsen, Cas (eds.) *Trading Culture: GATT, European Cultural Policies and the Transatlantic Market*. (Amsterdam, Boekman Foundation, 1996).

Hepworth, Cecil. *Came the Dawn: Memoirs of a Film Pioneer*. (Phoenix House, London, 1951).

Hill, John, McLoone, Martin and Hainsworth, Paul (eds), *Border Crossing: Film in Ireland, Britain and Europe*. (Belfast, The Institute of Irish Studies in association with the University of Ulster and the British Film Institute).

Hillier, Jim (ed.). *Cahiers du Cinéma: The 1950s – Neo-Realism, Hollywood, New Wave*. (Cambridge, Mass., Harvard University Press, 1985).

Irwin, Will. *The House That Shadows Built*. (Garden City, N.Y., Doubleday and Doran, 1928).

Jarvie, Ian. *Hollywood's Overseas Campaign, The North Atlantic Movie Trade, 1920–1950*. (Cambridge, Cambridge University Press, 1992).

Jeanne, René. *Cinema 1900*. (Paris, Flammarion, 1965).

Jeanne, René and Ford, Charles. *Histoire encyclopédique du cinéma. Vol. 1. Le cinéma français 1895–1929*. (Paris, Robert Laffont, 1947).

Jowett, Garth. *Film: The Democratic Art*. (Boston, Little, Brown & Co., 1976).

Kanin, Garson. *Hollywood: Stars and Starlets, Tycoons and Flesh-Peddlers, Movie-makers and Moneymakers, Frauds and Genuises, Hopefuls and Has-Beens, Great Lovers and Sex Symbols*. (London, Hart-Davis, MacGibbon, 1975).

Katz, Ephraim. *The Macmillan International Film Encyclopaedia*. (London and Basingstoke, Macmillan, 1994).

Kennedy, Joseph P. (ed.). *The Story of the Films* (Chicago, A.W. Shaw Company, 1927).

Kermabon, Jacques (ed.). *Pathé: Premier Empire du Cinéma* (Paris, Editions du Centre Georges Pompidou, 1994).

Kerr, Paul. (ed.). *The Hollywood Film Industry: A Reader*. (London, Routledge & Kegan Paul in association with the BFI, 1986).

Kindem, Gorham (ed.). *The American Movie Industry*. (Carbondale Ill., Southern Illinois University Press, 1982).

Kreimeier, Klaus. *The Ufa Story: A History of Germany's Greatest Film Company 1918:1945*. (New York, Hill and Wang, 1996).

Kroes, R. and Ellwood, D. (eds.) *Hollywood in Europe: Experiences of Cultural Hegemony*. (Amsterdam, VU University Press, 1994).

Kulik, Karol. *Alexander Korda: The Man Who Could Work Miracles*. (London, Allen and Unwin, 1975).

Lasky Jr., Jesse L. *Whatever Happened to Hollywood*. (London, W.H. Allen, 1973).

Lasky, Jesse with Don Weldon. *I Blow My Own Horn*. (London, Victor Gollanz 1957).

Lent, John A. *The Asian Film Industry*. (Austin, University of Texas Press, 1990).

Lesage, Julia. *Jean-Luc Godard: A Guide to References and Resources*. (Boston, Mass, G.K. Hall & Co., 1979).

L'Herbier, Marcel. *Intelligence du cinématographe*. (Paris, Editions Corréa, 1946).

Lev, Peter. *The Euro-American Cinema*. (Austin, University of Texas Press, 1993).

Low, Rachel. *History of the British Film: Vols. II–IV. (London, Allen and Unwin, 1949, 1951 and 1971)*.

Low, Rachel and Manvell, Roger. History of the British Film: Vol. I. (London, Allen and Unwin, 1948).

Lumière, Auguste et Louis. *Correspondences*. (Paris, Cahiers Du Cinéma, 1994).

MacCann, Richard Dyer and Perry, Edward S. *The New Film Index: A Bibliography of Magazine Articles in English*. (New York, Dutton, 1975).

Macnab, Geoffrey. *J. Arthur Rank and the British Film Industry*. (London and New York, Routledge, 1993).

Macnamara, Paul. *Those Were the Days My Friend: My Life in Hollywood with David O. Selznick and Others*. (Metuchen, N.J., The Scarecrow Press, 1993).

Matz, Mary Jane. *The Many Lives of Otto Kahn*. (New York, Macmillan, 1963).

McWilliams, Carey. *Southern California Country: An Island on the Land*. (New York, Duell, Sloan and Pearce, 1946).

Mesguich, Félix. *Tours de Manivelle*. (Paris, Bernard Grasset, 1933).

Mock, James R. and Larson, Cedric. *Words That Won the War: The Story of the Committee on Public Information 1917–1919*. (Princeton, Princeton University Press, 1939).

Moley, Raymond. *The Hays Office*. (Indianapolis, Bobbs-Merrill, 1945).

Moran, Albert (ed.). *Film Policy: International, National and Regional Perspectives*. (London, Routledge, 1996).

Mottram, Ron. *The Danish Cinema Before Dreyer*. (Metuchen, N.J., Scarecrow, 1988).

Musser, Charles. *Before the Nickelodeon; Edwin S. Porter and the Edison Manufacturing Company*. (Berkeley, Calif., University of California Press, 1991).

Nash, Gerald D. *A.P. Giannini and the Bank of America*. (Norman, University of Oklahoma Press, 1992).

Neergaard, Ebbe. *The Story of the Danish Film*. trans. Elsa Gress, (Copenhagen, Den Danske Selskab, 1963).

Nichols, Bill (ed.). *Movies and Methods: An Anthology*. (Berkeley, Calif., University of California Press, 1980).

Nowell-Smith, Geoffrey (ed.). *Oxford History of World Cinema*. (Oxford, Oxford University Press, 1996).

Olsen, Ole. *Filmens Eventyr Og Mit Eget*. (Copenhagen, Jespersen, 1940).

Paley, William. *As It Happened*. (Garden City, N.Y., Doubleday and Company, 1979).

Pathé, Charles. *De Pathé Frères á Pathé Cinema*. (Lyons, Premier Plan, 1970).

Pathé, Charles. *Souvenirs et conseils d'un parvenu*. (Paris, 1926).

Pearson, George. *Flashback*. (London, Allen and Unwin).

Pflaum, Hans Günther and Prinzler, Hans Helmut. *Cinema in the Federal Republic of Germany*. trans. Timothy Nevill, (Bonn, Inter Nationes, 1993).

Political and Economic Planning, *The British Film Industry*, (London, Political and Economic Planning, 1952).

Powdermaker, Hortense. *Hollywood: The Dream Factory*. (London, Secker & Warburg, 1951).

Puttnam, David. *A Submission to the European Commission Think-Tank on Audio-Visual Policy* (London, Enigma Products, 1994).

Pye, Michael. *Moguls: Inside the Business of Showbusiness*. (New York, Holt, Rhinehart and Winston, 1980).

Pye, Michael and Myles, Lynda. *The Movie Brats: How the Film Generation Took Over Hollywood*, (London, Faber and Faber, 1979).

Quaglietti, Lorenzo. *Storia economico-politica del cinema italiano 1945–1980*, (Rome, Editori Riuniti, 1980).

Ramsaye, Terry. *A Million and One Nights: A History of the Motion Picture*. (London, Frank Cass & Co, 1926).

Report By the Think-Tank On the Audio-Visual Policy in the European Union (Luxembourg, Office for Official Publications of the European Communities, 1994).

Robinson, David. *The History of World Cinema*. (New York, Stein and Day, 1981).

Rose, Frank. *The Agency: William Morris and the Hidden History of Showbusiness*. (New York, HarperCollins, 1995).

Rosenberg, Bernard and Silverstein, Harry (eds). *The Real Tinsel*. (New York, The Macmillan Company, 1970).

Rosten, Leo C. *Hollywood: The Movie Colony*. (New York, Harcourt Brace and Co., 1941).

Sadoul, Georges. *Histoire générale du cinéma*. Vols. 1–6. (Paris, Denoël, 1946–1975).

Saunders, Thomas J. *Hollywood in Berlin: American Cinema and Weimar Germany*. (Berkeley, University of California Press, 1994).

Schary, Dore. *Heyday*. (Boston, Little, Brown, 1979).

Schatz, Thomas. *The Genius of the System: Hollywood Filmmaking in the Studio Era*. (New York, Pantheon Books, 1988).

Selznick, Irene Mayer. *A Private View*. (New York, Alfred A. Knopf, 1983).

Servan-Schreiber, Jean-Jacques. *The American Challenge*. trans. Ronald Steel, (London, Hamish Hamilton, 1968).

Sinclair, Upton. *Upton Sinclair Presents William Fox*. (Los Angeles, Published by the Author, 1933).

Sklar, Robert. *Movie-Made America, A Cultural History of American Movies*, (rev. ed., New York, Vintage Books, 1994).

Smith, Albert with Phil A. Koury. *Two Reels and a Crank*. (Garden City, N.Y., Doubleday 1952, republished 1985).

Spraos, John. *The Decline of the Cinema*. (London, Allen & Unwin, 1962).

Steele, Richard W. *Propaganda is An Open Society, The Roosevelt Administration and the Media 1933–1941*. (Westport, CT, Greenwood Press, 1985).

Talmey, Allene. *Doug and Mary and Others*. (New York, Macy-Masius 1927).

Thomas, Bob. *Clown Prince of Hollywood: The Antic Life and Times of Jack L. Warner*. (New York, McGraw Hill, 1990).

Thomas, Bob. *King Cohn: The Life and Times of Harry Cohn*. (London, Barrie and Rockcliffe, 1967).

Thomas, Bob. *Walt Disney*. (London, W.H. Allen, 1981).

Thompson, Kristin. *Exporting Entertainment. America in the World Film Market 1907–34* (London, BFI Publishing, 1985).

Thompson, Kristin and Bordwell, David. *Film History: An Introduction*. (New York, McGraw-Hill, 1994).

Thomson, David. *A Biographical Dictionary of Film*. (London, Andre Deutsch, 1994).

Vaughn, Stephen. *Ronald Reagan in Hollywood: Movies and Politics*. (Cambridge, Cambridge University Press, 1994).

Viertel, Salka. *The Kindness of Strangers*. (New York, Holt, Rhinehart and Winston, 1969).

Vigne, Paul. *La Vie laboriuese et féconde d'Auguste Lumière*. (Lyons, Durand-Girard, 1942).

Virilio, Paul. *War and Cinema*. (London, Verso, 1989).

Wachorst, Wyn. *Thomas Alva Edison: An American Myth*. (Cambridge, Mass., MIT Press, 1981).

Walker, Alexander. *Hollywood England: The British Film Industry in the Sixties* (London, Harrap, 1986).

Walker, Alexander. *National Heroes: British Cinema in the Seventies and Eighties*. (London, Harrap, 1985).

Ward, Larry Wayne. *The Motion Picture Goes to War*. (Ann Arbor, Mich: UMI, Research, 1985).

Warner, Jack L. with Dean Jennings. *My First Hundred Years in Hollywood*. (New York, Random House, 1965).

Wilk, Max. *The Golden Age of Television: Notes from the Survivors*. (New York, Delacorte Press, 1976).

Wilk, Max. *The Wit and Wisdom of Hollywood: From the Squaw Man to the Hatchet Man*. (New York, Atheneum, 1971).

Williams, Alan. *Republic of Images: A History of French Filmmaking*. (Cambridge Mass., Harvard University Press, 1992).

Wood, Alan. *Mr. Rank*. (London, Hodder & Stoughton, 1952).

Workers of the Writers' Program of the Work Projects Administration in the City of New York. *The Film Index: A Bibliography. Vol. II. The Film as Industry*. (White Plains, N.Y., Kraus, 1985).

Zierold, Norman. *The Moguls: Hollywood's Merchants of Myth*. (Los Angeles, Silman James, 1991).

Zukor, Adolph. *The Public is Never Wrong*. (Cassell and Company, London, 1954).

INDEX

A bout de souffle 252, 297
ABC (Associated British Cinemas) 145,
230, 233, 236–7, 261–2, 270, 285–6,
315, 316–19
Abrams, Hiram 84
Absolute Beginners 309–10
Academy awards 239
Acres, Birt 25
Actors' Equity 107
advertising, *see* marketing
AEG 143
Afman, Frans 283
agents 220–8, 234–5, 246, 279–82, 284
Alberini, Baron Alberto 67
Allégret, Yves 250
Allez France 254
Allgemeine Elektrizitäts AG 98
Alliance Cinématographique Européen
(ACE) 104
Allied Stars 307
Almodóvar, Pedro 5, 161
Althusser, Louis 294
Altman, Robert 171
Ambrosio 68
America - The Menace (Duhamel) 154
The American Challenge (Servan
Schreiber) 358
American Chamber of Commerce 90
The American Cinematic Invasion
(Jeanne) 155
American Express 266
American film industry, *see* Hollywood
American Graffiti 274, 305
American Legion 107
American Madness 119
American Multi-Cinema (AMC) 287,
314–15, 317–19

American Mutoscope and Biograph
Company (AM & B) 47–8
American Mutoscope Company
22–4
American Telephone and Telegraph
(AT&T) 141, 166
The Americanisation of the World (Stead)
148
Andreotti, Giulio 207–8, 258
animation 285, 286–7
Animatograph 25–6
Arbuckle, Roscoe 'Fatty' 59, 128
Arkoff, Samuel 288
Armat, Thomas 22, 47
Arnaz, Desi 234
Arnold, Thurman 187–9, 191, 228
art films 65–6, 68, 71, 100, 108, 212, 289
see also New Wave
Ashley, Ted 265
L'Assassinat du Duc de Guise 66
Associated British Picture Corporation
242
Associated TeleVision 242
Association of Motion Picture and TV
Producers 257
Astruc, Alexandre 248–9
Atari 266
Aubert 103
audio-visual industry 5–7, 185, 342–4,
346, 351–9
Australia 67, 86, 162, 193, 199, 202, 245–6
Autant-Lara, Claude 250
authorship:
auteur theory 100, 181, 249–52, 274–5,
297–8; death of the author 295; and
droit moral 302–3; of screenwriter 65,
100, 249

Balaban, Barney 125–6, 192
Balachoff, Dimitri 326
Balcon, Michael 243, 305
Baldwin, Stanley 151
Ball, Lucille 234
Banca Commerciale 104
Banca Italiana di Sconto 104–5
Bank of America 119–20
Banotti, Mary 344
Barrett, Andrew 286
Barthes, Roland 292, 294–5
Bartholdi, Frédéric-Auguste 23, 154
Barton Fink 171
Baruch, Bernard 91
Bass Leisure 318
Basserman, Albert 100
Batman 286
The Battleship Potemkin 105–6, 331
Baudelaire, Charles 23
Bazin, André 250, 251
BBC 242, 318, 356
Beauregard, Georges de 296
Begelman, David 279
Belgium 317
Bell Laboratories 137–8
Belmondo, Jean-Paul 252, 292, 297
Ben Hur (1923) 105
Benny, Jack 136
Benoît-Lévy, Edmond 64–6, 114, 249
Bergman, Ingmar 161, 260
Berlin 101, 143
Berne Convention 303
Bernstein, Sidney 197, 242
Berst, Jacques 70
Bertelsmann 285, 345
Bertolucci, Bernardo 5, 258, 274, 324
Biograph 22, 34, 46–7, 56–7, 59, 118
Bioscope 87
The Birth of a Nation 88–9, 169
Blum–Byrnes Agreement 205, 207
Bogart, Humphrey 136, 206, 238
Bonnie and Clyde 260, 273
Boothby, Robert 208
bootlegging 35, 39–40
Borelli, Lyda 68
Bosch, Robert 98
The Boys in the Band 261
Brady, William 69, 90, 128
Brandt, Joe 118

Bratz, Karl 99
Brazil 163
Brecht, Bertolt 110
Bresson, Robert 250
Brialy, Jean-Claude 252
The Bridge over the River Kwai 261
British Council 147
British film industry:
  and American boycott 208–9; assault
    on Hollywood 146–7, 158–61, 197,
    208–10; co-productions 321; decline
    of 314; and culture 99, 151;
    distribution 311; early technology
    24–6; and Edison's Trust 47; export
    markets 49, 146–7, 197, 307; finance
    145–6, 159–60, 211–12, 253, 255, 257,
    305, 307–9, 312–13; and
    International Film Chamber 195;
    market share 353; narrative films 33;
    1970s/1980s 304–19; prestige
    experiment 210; protectionism 90,
    145, 151, 153, 158, 162; Rank's role in
    197–200; relations with Hollywood
    208–12, 311; resurgence of 158–61,
    197; special effects 306–7; studios
    160, 198, 306; subsidies 211; talkies
    145–6; and television 242–3, 245–7,
    272; and World War I 86
British Film Institute 355
British Film Producers Association 316
British Film Production Fund 211
British Lion 272
British Screen Finance 313
Brittan, Sir Leon 8, 342
Broca, Philippe de 259
Broccoli, Albert 'Cubby' 260
Buchwald, Art 282
BUFA (Office of Photography and Film)
  97
Business Week 203

The Cabinet of Dr Caligari 107, 109
Cabiria 68, 87
Cahiers du cinéma 249–52, 294–6, 298
Canada 162–3, 193, 199, 214, 246
Canal+ 324, 326
Cannes Film Festival 293–4, 310, 325
Cannon 282

Capra, Frank 119, 178, 183
Carnegie, Andrew 10
Carolco 283, 324–5
Carrey, Jim 283
Carrière, Jean-Claude 298
Casler, Herman 22
Catchings, Waddill 122–3
CBC Sales Company 118
CBS 230, 234, 240, 261–2, 270
censorship 67, 101, 128, 299
Centre National de la Cinématographie
    (CNC) 207, 253, 293
Chabrol, Claude 249, 252, 260
Chandler, Raymond 182
Chaplin, Charlie 59, 61, 92, 94, 140, 149,
    169, 171, 278
Chargeurs 324, 326, 345
Chariots of Fire 307
Chase National Bank 166
Chesler, Louis 238
Chicago 15, 54, 126, 130
China 214, 286, 350
CICCE 326
Cinecittà 196, 258
Cinema Center Films 261–2
Cinema Exhibitors Association 242
Cinema Fashions Shops 173
cinemas:
    audiences 287–9, 337; block-booking
      50, 189, 216; box-office admissions
      203, 219–20, 227, 232, 243–4, 246–7,
      283, 305, 312, 316–17, 319, 332,
      353–4; closures 316–17; consent
      decrees 191; divorcement 218–19,
      239; finance 123–6, 317; first-run
      houses 85, 189–90; grind houses 238;
      independents 219; multiplex 72,
      287–8, 313, 315, 317–20, 332;
      nickelodeons 36–8, 45, 52–5, 117,
      136, 169, 315; permanent 33–6, 67–8;
      picture palaces 72, 123; repertory
      venues 322; screen density 320;
      simultaneous release 276; storefront
      36–8, 52; and talkies 141–2; taxation
      207, 211; and television 239, 243; see
      also exhibitors and under specific
      countries
Cinémathèque Français 292
Cinématographe 16–17, 20–2, 138

Cinés 47, 67
Clarke, Harley 167
classification system 274
Cleitman, René 344n
Cleopatra 279
Cliffhanger 324
Clinton, Bill 6–7, 340, 342–3
Close Encounters of the Third Kind 277,
    278, 287
Club of European Producers 341, 344
Coca-Cola 336
Cochrane, Robert 57, 60
Coen brothers 171
Cohn, Harry 118–19, 177–8, 194, 197, 204,
    231, 233
Cohn, Jack 118, 178
Columbia Broadcasting System, see CBS
Columbia Pictures 118–19, 170, 177–8,
    197, 218, 239, 263, 266, 269–70,
    335–7
Columbus Savings and Loan Society 116
Comédie Française 66, 80
Coming to America 282
Commercial National Trust and Savings
    Bank 119
Committee for the Defence of French
    Cinema 206
communism 206, 214–15, 256, 294–5
Coppola, Francis Ford 274–5
copyright 65, 302–3
Cousins, Norman 215
Coutard, Raoul 252
Coward, Noël 197
Craig, Sir Gordon 146
Creative Artists Agency (CAA) 280–1
Creative Management Associates (CMA)
    279
Crédit Commercial de France 33
Crédit Lyonnais 31–2, 167, 283
Creel, George 90–1, 96
Creel Committee on Public Information
    90–2
critics 294–5, 298–9, 302
The Crying Game 313–14
culture 5, 19, 350, 353, 358
    cultural colonization 148; global 326,
      334, 346–7; mass 8, 37–8, 44–5, 61,
      65, 99, 108, 121, 194, 334; and sound
      140, 142; and trade 147

Cuno, Wilhelm 98, 101
Czechoslovakia 253

Daily Express 148
Daily Variety 239
Daly, Bob 286
Dauman, Anatole 297
Davis, Bette 223, 225
Davis, Harry 36–7, 315
Davis, John 316–17
Dawes Plan 111
Death to the Audience 300
De Bont, Jan 346
Decaë, Henri 252
Decla-Bioskop 109
DEG 282
De Havilland, Olivia 225–6
Dekom, Peter 284
De Laurentiis, Dino 257, 282
Del Giudice, Filippo 199
Delors. Jacques 352
De Mille, Cecil B. 70, 77–8, 85, 119, 128, 166
De Mille, William 70, 78
Demy, Jacques 254
Denham Studios 160, 198
Denmark 47, 49–50, 87, 100, 245
De Palma, Brian 274
Depardieu, Gérard 346
De Sica, Vittorio 207, 257–8
Desilu Productions 234
Deutsch, Oscar 199
Deutsche Bank 98, 101, 111, 194
Deutsche Lichtbild Gesellschaft (DLG, Deulig) 96–7
Deux ou trois choses que je sais d'elle 297
Dhéry, Robert 254
Dickson, William 12–13, 22
Dietrich, Marlene 346
Diller, Barry 280
director 176, 180–1, 183, 218
  as author 100, 249–52, 255, 274, 302–3; cult of 295, 297–8, 301, 305; movie brats 274–5, 278; straw 258–9
Disney, Walt 196, 235–6
distribution 42, 239
  film exchanges 34, 54–5, 61–2, 70, 82; finance 118; independent 289;

Paramount and 82–3; rental system 34–6, 54, 66; states rights system 34, 82–3; and television 238, 240, 270–1
Doctor Dolittle 264
Domestic Film Production Incentive Act 266–7
Domestic International Sales Corporations (DISCs) 268
Don Juan 138
Doniol-Valcroze, Jacques 249
Donnelly, Alan 344
Douglas, Justice William O. 216
Dresdner Bank 98
Dreyer, Carl Theodor 109
dubbing 144–5, 323
Duhamel, Georges 154
Dulac, Germaine 103–4
Dulles, Allen 209
Dumont Television Network 230
Dunne, Philip 176, 246
Dupont, E.A. 112
Durwood, Ed 315
Durwood, Stanley 287, 315
Dyer, Frank 63, 70
Dziga Vertov group 296

Eady Levy 211, 253, 255, 257, 312–13
Eagle Lion 199
Ealing Studios 243, 272, 306
East of Eden 330
Eastern Europe 99, 193, 253
Easy Rider 274
Eberts, Jake 307–8
The Economist 283
Ecran français 248
Eder, Klaus 298
Edison, Thomas Alva 9–14, 69, 81, 137, 355
  and foreign competition 21, 24, 40–1, 43, 46, 48, 51; as inventor 9, 11–14; as litigant 11, 24, 40, 46, 55–6; and MPPC 47, 51, 53, 56, 63; as plagiarist 11, 12, 22, 40
Edison's Trust, see Motion Picture Patents Company
education 13–14, 91–2, 355–9
Eiffel, Gustave 33
Eisenstein, Sergei 105–6, 274

Eisner, Michael 281, 285–6
El Cid 259
Elgar, Edward 151
Elstree Studios 306
Embassy Pictures 257
EMI 311
Emmanuelle 299
employment 352
L'Enfant prodigue 64
Enigma 335
entertainment companies 266, 272,
    285–6
Esterhas, Joe 281
Et Dieu créa la femme 252
Etats Généraux du Cinéma 293–4
Europe:
    Americanization of 148–50; anti-
        Americanism 195, 204; cinemas 51,
        126, 158, 243, 247, 290, 315, 317;
        economy 103, 204; finances
        Hollywood 324–5; and GATT 5;
        government intervention 132, 142;
        post-war 204; protectionism 150–3,
        157–8; subsidy 256; talkies in 142
'Europe Pitted Against America' 48
European film industry 161, 248, 331–3,
    346, 353
    Balachoff Plan 326; budgets 313;
        collaborations 102–4, 258–60, 321–2,
        326–7; creativity in 332; crisis in
        5–6, 327–8, 333, 346; and culture
        79–80, 142, 150, 157, 181, 194, 204,
        344–5; distribution 32, 64, 103, 112,
        158, 199, 211, 311, 327–8, 345;
        émigrés 64, 112–14, 346; exhibitors
        72, 205, 209, 211, 242–4, 317–18;
        exports 49, 75, 87, 219; and film
        libraries 184–5; finance 324, 332–3,
        341; and GATT 5; independents 180,
        199, 312; influence on Hollywood
        274, 323–4; interests in US 49;
        internationalization of 324; launches
        in US 290; producer's role 180;
        production 64, 79, 94, 102–4, 180,
        244, 327–8, 345; and star system 58;
        and television 241–7; values of
        200–1; and World Wars 76–7, 82,
        86–8, 94–5, 194
European Cinema Owners Union 242

European Union 8, 320–1, 326, 343, 346,
    351–2, 356, 359
    Commission 5–6, 352; *Growth,
        Competitivity and Jobs* (White Paper)
        352; MEDIA programme 326–7;
        Parliament 344; *Television Without
        Frontiers* 338
Evans, Robert 275
exhibitors:
    and anti-trust legislation 187–90,
        216–18, 318; and Edison's Trust 47,
        52, 55–6; fairground showmen 25,
        30–2, 34; independent 189, 217; and
        levies 257; showmen 27, 35, 40, 52,
        123–4; and television 239; *see also*
        cinemas
L'Express 7, 252

Fairbanks, Douglas Snr 92, 94, 106
Famous Players 71, 100, 107, 121, 163
Famous Players-Lasky 84, 102, 126
fan magazines 57, 173
Fassbinder, Rainer Werner 299–300
Fayed, Mohammed 307
feature films 66–7, 71–2, 98–9, 101, 190
    and television 232–3, 237, 240
Federal Communications Commission
    (FCC) 230, 270, 272, 286
Fédération Internationale de la Press
    Cinématographique (FIPRESCI) 298
Fellini, Federico 161, 244, 257, 258
Feuillade, Louis 33–4
Fidelity Pictures 218
Fields, Freddie 279
Film Daily Yearbook 132
Film d'Art 66, 72, 80
Film Europe 102–4, 195, 326
Film Industry Defence Organization
    (FIDO) 242–3
film libraries 184–5, 238, 240–1, 244,
    345–6
Filmkreditbank 194–5
Films Acts 153, 161–2, 312
Fin-Syn rules 218, 271–2
finance:
    banks 31–2, 83, 94, 104, 117–22, 194,
        265, 283, 312; budgets 313; of
        cinemas 123–6, 317, 319;

finance – *cont.*
 banks – *cont.*
  collaborations 321, 332; foreign
  259–60, 270; international 324–6,
  347–8, 351; investment 26, 36, 160,
  308–9, 312–13; levies 211, 253, 255,
  257, 341; loans 160, 283; profit
  margins 283; sale and leaseback 308;
  subsidy 7, 207, 211, 213, 253–9, 269,
  301, 320–1, 333, 341; tax incentives
  and shelters 267–70, 272, 308, 312
First National 118
A Fistful of Dollars 258
Flint, Motley 122–3
Fonda, Henry 174, 224, 279
Foolish Wives 179
Ford, Henry 171
Ford, John 113, 179, 181, 183, 297, 300
Foreign Film Service 92
foreign-language films 322–3
Forman, Milos 268
Forsyth, Bill 335
Fortune 141
The Four Horsemen of the Apocalypse 112
Four-Minute Men 90
Four Weddings and a Funeral 290
Fox, Richard 285
Fox, William 61–3, 86, 167, 247
Fox Film 102, 113, 127, 167, 168, 176
 see also Twentieth Century-Fox
France:
 anti-Americanism 206, 268, 291, 304–5,
 320; cinemas 34, 65, 155, 207, 254,
 315, 319–20; as export market 193,
 204, 290; film criticism in 294–5,
 298–9; and GATT 3–4, 340, 343;
 Government 155–6, 205, 207, 253,
 291–2, 294, 319; Hollywood
 production in 255; investment in
 Hollywood 325–6; Ministry of
 Culture 253; Ministry of Industry and
 Commerce 207, 253; *see also* French
 film industry
Freddi, Luigi 196
French film industry:
 auteur theory 100, 181, 249–52, 297–9;
 company funding 259–60;
 collaborations 103–4, 321–2; cultural
 orientation of 7, 64–6, 80, 99, 154–6,

207, 249, 253, 326, 333; *dirigisme* 207;
 early technology 14–24; export markets
 38–40, 42–3, 70; finance 7, 31–3, 207,
 211; fragmentation of 156, 180;
 Gaumont's role in 33–4; independents
 180; and May '68 291–4, 298; New
 Wave 100, 252–5, 292, 295–6, 298–9;
 Pathé's role in 29–33, 40–4; political
 cinema 293–7; pornography 299; post-
 war 204–7; protectionism 150, 153, 158,
 204–6; relations with Hollywood 7,
 23–4, 39–40, 75, 154–5, 251; subsidy 7,
 207, 211, 253–4, 320–1; talkies 145; and
 television 243; during World War I
 76–7, 86
Friese-Greene, William 24–5
Frohman, Daniel 71
Fuller, Samuel 300
Fulton, Robert 10

Gable, Clark 174, 227, 239
Gammon, Frank 14
Gance, Abel 103
Gandhi 307–8
Garbo, Greta 113, 155, 174, 346
Gaulle, Charles de 291, 294
Gaumont 47, 145, 316, 319
Gaumont, Léon 33–4, 87, 137
Gaumont-British Picture Corporation 145
G-B Animation 199
Geffen, David 287
Geissler, Dieter 344n
Gelin, Daniel 298
General Agreement for Trade in Services
 (GATS) 343
General Agreement on Tariffs and Trade
 (GATT) 3–8, 15, 48, 339–44, 357, 360
General Cinema 287, 317
General Film Company 61
General Teleradio 238
German Expressionism 109, 113
German film industry:
 Autorenfilm 80, 100; co-productions
 321–2; and culture 108, 114; émigrés
 112–13; exports 105; finance 98,
 101–2, 194; in Nazi Germany 196;
 New German Cinema 299–301; New
 Wave 252–3, 255; post-war 213–15;

protectionism 111, 150, 158, 213, 215; renaissance of 158; rivalry with Hollywood 95, 107–8; stars 98; studios 101, 106–7; talkies 142–3, 145; and television 243–4; Ufa 98–104, 106, 109, 111–12, 180, 194, 196; and World War I 96–7

Germany 92
  Americanism in 110–11, 114; cinemas 98, 100, 243–4, 319–20; as export market 193, 208, 213–14, 290; Foreign Office 97; and GATT 340; government 97–8, 101, 142; hyper-inflation 107, 111; nationalism 101, 112; Nazi 104, 194–6; Weimar Republic 110; see also German film industry

Germi, Pietro 257
Germinal 7
The Ghost Goes West 161, 306
Ghostbusters 319
Giannini brothers 115–20, 127, 289
Giroud, Françoise 252
Giscard d'Estaing, Valéry 299
Gish, Lillian 109, 114
globalization 324, 346–8
Globus, Yoram 282
Godard, Jean-Luc 249, 252, 274, 293, 295–9, 302, 331
The Godfather 274–6, 277–8
Goebbels, Joseph 194–6
Goizueta, Roberto 336
Golan, Menahem 282
Goldcrest 307–12, 314, 335
Goldenson, Leonard 236
Goldfish, Samuel, *see* Goldwyn, S.
Goldman, Sachs 122–3
Goldwyn, Frances 139
Goldwyn, Samuel 78, 84–5, 112, 118–19, 233, 242
Gómez, Andrés Vicente 344n
Gone with the Wind 173, 183, 225
Good Earth 181
Goodheart, Billy 221–2
Goodtimes 335
Gorin, Jean-Pierre 296
Goskino 105
Grade, Lord Lew 242, 307
The Graduate 260

Granada 197, 242
Grauman, Sid 124
Great Britain:
  Americanization of 148–9, 318; anti-Americanism in 152; cinemas 145–6, 197, 199, 211, 242–4, 305, 312, 315–20; culture in 99, 151; Dalton Duty 208, 211; educational potential 356–7; as export market 86, 90, 193, 202, 208, 214, 290; Foreign Office 146–7, 152; and GATT 339–40; governments 146, 162, 208–9, 307, 312; Hollywood production in 162, 255, 260; post-war 208–12; see also British film industry
The Great Liberty Bond Hold-Up 92
Great Northern 49
The Great Train Robbery (1903) 38, 69
Greater New York Film Exchange 62
Grierson, John 152–3
Griffith, D.W. 68, 75, 88–9, 94, 105, 118, 138, 169
Grimaldi, Alberto 258
Grivolas, Claude 31–2
Gulf and Western 263
Guy, Alice 33

Haeften, Lt-Col. Hans von 97–8
Hamburg-Amerika 98
HandMade 314
Handy, Professor Charles 355
A Hard Day's Night 260
Hardy, Thomas 151
Harmsworth, Cecil 151
Harriman, Edward 121
Harriman, Pamela 4
Hart, William 92, 124
Havermans, Charles 65
Hawks, Howard 181, 183, 251, 297, 300
Hays, Will 128–31, 133–4, 143, 153, 162, 188, 330, 358
Hays Organization, *see* Motion Picture Producers and Distributors of America
Hayward Deverich 224
Hecht, Ben 127, 174, 182–3, 214
Hello Dolly 264
Henry V 209, 210
Hepworth, Cecil 25, 28, 47

Herriot decree 153
Herron, Frederick 131
Hertz, Carl 26
Hertz, John 125, 167
Heston, Charlton 267
Heyman, John 270
Hiawatha 56
Hindenburg, Paul von 98
Hirschfield, Alan 269
L'Histoire d'un crime 33
Hitchcock, Alfred 181, 183, 264, 298, 346
Hitler, Adolf 196
Hodkinson, W.W. 82-4
Hollywood 94, 129, 330
    ambassadorial role of 213, 215, 352; anti-
      trust law-suit 187-92, 203, 216-18,
      231; blockbusters 276-7; budgets 313;
      businessmen in 265, 277-8;
      collaborations 258-60, 344;
      commercialism of 331-3; crisis in
      263-7; cultural revolution in 273-4,
      278; distribution 34-5, 43-4, 54-5,
      61-2, 70-1, 75, 158-60, 190, 210,
      213, 218-19, 238, 240, 247, 259-60,
      265, 267, 313; during Depression
      166-7, 172; early film industry 34-6;
      as entertainment industry 334;
      European émigrés 64, 108, 112-14,
      307, 347; exports 6, 76, 86-7, 90-5,
      99, 102, 111, 131-4, 140-4, 157-8,
      161-3, 190, 193-4, 200, 202-15, 220,
      228, 241, 245-7, 265, 268, 271, 285,
      320, 334, 336, 352; finance 36, 83, 94,
      115-34, 141-4, 166-8, 184, 324-6;
      genres 174-5, 263-4; impact of
      330-1; independents 47, 60, 69, 73,
      75, 86, 170, 188-9, 218, 227, 233-4,
      243, 246, 270-1, 282-3, 324-5; and
      language 322-3; movie brats 274-5,
      278; movie industry moves to 77-80;
      and national culture 79-80, 92-3,
      95, 140-1, 148-9, 162; overseas
      expansion 286, 290; producer system
      175-82; Production Code 273-4;
      production figures 276; relations with
      Europe 208-12, 251, 258-60, 274,
      323-4, 344; relations with
      Washington 88-95, 187-91, 203-4,
      212-13, 215, 228, 266-70, 339, 342,
      351-2; revenues 6-7, 158, 203;
      runaway production 86, 208, 210-11,
      255-9, 267, 347; scandals 59, 128;
      screenwriters 180-3; self-regulation
      59, 128-30, 133; sequels 277; and
      sound 139-40; studios 42, 76, 80-2,
      85, 109, 166-85, 187-93, 216-20,
      256, 260-1, 263, 265; and subsidy
      257; and television 229-41, 246, 268,
      271, 276, 285-6; values of 149-50,
      200, 330, 334, 346-7; and World War
      II 191-4
Hollywood Chamber of Commerce 59
Hollywood Reporter 173
Hollywood Ten 214
Hong Kong 163, 214
Hoover, Herbert 91, 127-8
Hopkins, Anthony 346
Hopkins, Harry 190, 192
Hopper, Hedda 173
horizontal integration 266
Hotel Imperial 113
House Un-American Activities
    Committee (HUAC) 214
How We Advertised America (Creel) 91
Howe, Al 265
Hudson, Hugh 304
Hugenberg, Alfred 96-7, 112
Hughes, Howard 168, 238
Hungary 143, 158, 253
Huntington, Professor Sam 350

I Love Lucy 234
In Which We Serve 197
Ince, Thomas 109
Independent Manufacturing Company
    (IMP) 56-7, 60, 73, 75
India 163-4, 195, 286, 323, 350
information technology 355-9
Informational Media Guaranty Program
    (IMG) 213
Ingram, Rex 112
Inherit the Wind 330
Inslee, Charles 57
International Congress of the
    Cinématographe (Brussels, 1911) 65
International Creative Management
    (ICM) 279

International Famous Agency 279
International Film Chamber 195
Italian film industry:
  Church and 67–8; collaborations
    257–9, 321–2; downturn in 150; and
    Edison's Trust 47; exhibitors 244;
    exports 68; fascists and 196–7;
    feature films 67; Film Commission
    213; finance 67, 104; neo-realist
    movement 207–8; New Wave 255;
    post-war 207–8; protectionism 153,
    207; spaghetti westerns 258; stars 58,
    68; studios 196; subsidy 258–9;
    talkies 145, 150; and television 243–4;
  UCI 104–5; and World War I 77, 86, 104
Italy:
  Christian Democratic Party 208;
    cinemas 68, 150, 319; as export
    market 193, 213; fascism 104, 194,
    196; and GATT 340; government 196;
    Hollywood production in 208, 255,
    257–9; *see also* Italian film industry
It's Our Choice 6
ITV 242, 245, 318

Jannings, Emil 98, 112
Japan:
  electronics companies 144; film industry
    163–4, 193, 195, 252, 257; finances
    Hollywood 270; Hollywood films in
    290; television in 243
Jaws 277, 298
The Jazz Singer 139, 141
Jeanne, René 155
Johnson-Reed Act (1924) 107
Johnston, Eric 203, 209, 214–15, 256–7,
  358
Joinville 144
Jolson, Al 139
Josephson, Marvin 279
Le Journal des Savants 64
Jurassic Park 7, 283, 287, 314, 323
JVC 144, 324

Kael, Pauline 277–8
Kahn, Otto 120–2, 127
Kansas City 314–15

Kantor, Jay 260
Kantor, Mickey 8, 340, 342–3
Karmitz, Marin 297
Katz, Samuel 125–7
Katzenberg, Jeffrey 285, 286–7
Kazan, Elia 330
Kennedy, Edward 269
Kennedy, Jeremiah 47, 62, 71
Kennedy, Joseph 162, 168
Kent, Sidney 167
Keough, Don 336
KFWB Radio 137
The Kid 118
The Killing Fields 308–9
Kinetoscope 12–14, 16, 25, 28, 31, 136
Kinney National Services 265
Kirch, Leo 244
Kitner, Robert 233
Klein, Jules 131
Kleine, Georges 47
Klitzsch, Ludwig 97, 101, 104, 112, 194
Korda, Alexander 158–61, 199, 305, 306,
  309
Korda, Vincent and Zoltan 160
Kramer, Karl 235
Kramer, Stanley 242, 330
Kristl, Vlado 300
Kubrick, Stanley 306
Kuchel, Thomas H. 257, 266
Kuhn Loeb & Co 120–2
Kurtz, Gary 306

Lacan, Jacques 294
Laemmle, Carl 52–60, 70, 76, 80–2,
  86–9, 112, 118, 135, 179, 184, 199, 247,
  334
Laemmle Film Service 54
Lake, Anthony 4
Landis, Judge Kenshaw 130
Lang, Fritz 106, 108–10, 112, 114, 180, 300
Lang, Jack 338, 343
Langlois, Henri 292
language 140, 142, 144–5, 322, 357
Lasky, Jesse 78, 83–5, 87, 118, 121–2, 182
Lasky Company 78, 84
The Last Days of Pompeii 68
The Last Emperor 324
Lastfogel, Abe 220

Latin America 86, 192
Lawrence, Florence 57, 171
Lean, David 197
legislation:
    anti-trust 186–91, 203, 261; on cinema
    construction 319–20; fin-syn 218,
    270–2; moral right 302; protective
    157–8, 162, 207; tax 267–8, 272
Lelouch, Claude 259
Lenin, V.I. 105, 110
Leone, Sergio 258
The Leopard 258, 322
Le Prince, Augustin 11
Lesser, Sol 116–18
Lester, Richard 260
Levine, Joseph 257, 297
Levinson, Major Nathan 137
Lewis, Daniel Day 346
Liberation 302
Lieberson, Sandy 305
Life 217
Linsk, Eddie 'The Killer' 223
Lion Hunt 50
The Lion King 283, 285, 347
Local Hero 308, 335–6
Loew, Marcus 91, 112, 118, 124–6, 168–9
Loews 124–5, 168, 218
London 21–2, 25, 87
London Films 159–60, 306
Loos, Anita 182
Los Angeles 77–81, 124
Los Angeles Times 264
Ludendorff, Erich 97–8
Lubin 39–40, 118
Lubitsch, Ernst 98, 113, 124
Lucas, George 274–5, 305, 306
Luce, Henry 331
Lumière family 15–24, 27–8, 38, 56, 138,
    329, 334
Lyne, Adrian 304

McAdoo, William 94
McCarthy, Frank 203
McDonald, Mac and Dick 109
McKinley, William 15, 23
Madame Dubarry (Passion) 107, 113
Made in the U.S.A. 297
Malle, Louis 259

Malraux, André 253, 292
Mankiewicz, Herman 127, 177–8, 231
Mann, Anthony 259
Marconi, Guglielmo 229
Marey, Tienne Jules 12
marketing 172–4, 276–7, 284, 288–90,
    305, 313–14, 334, 345
Markgraf, William 41
Marvin, Harry 22
Marx, Groucho 184
Mason, James 198
Mastbaum, Jules and Stanley 125
Masterman 311
Matsushita 63, 144, 167, 281
Maxwell, John 145
Mayer, Carl 113
Mayer, Louis B. 125, 135, 142, 168–70,
    175, 179, 183, 194, 233, 334
MCA (Music Corporation of America)
    220–5, 235, 260, 266, 267, 279, 281
Mean Streets 274
Melbourne 67
Méliès, Georges 17–19, 39–40
Mengers, Sue 279
Le Mépris 297
merchandising 173, 236, 266, 277, 284,
    285, 290
Mesguich, Félix 20, 23, 329
Metro-Goldwyn-Mayer, see MGM
Metro Pictures 125
Mexico 163
MGM 112, 125, 127, 226
    crisis in 263; ends studio system
    218–19; Mayer and 168–70, 175;
    recovery 269; takeover 283; talkies
    141; and television 231, 237, 239, 240;
    Thalberg at 178–80
Middle East 350
Midland Bank 146
Midnight Express 305
Milan 68
Miles Brothers 34
Milestone, Lewis 221
Milton Keynes 318
Minnelli, Vincente 251
Miramax 289
The Mission 309–11
Mitterrand, François 7
MK Productions 297

Moisson, Charles 16
Le Monde 206
Monogram 170
Moreau, Jeanne 252
Morning Post 151, 157
Morse, Samuel 10
Motion Picture Association of America
    (MPAA, MPA) 6, 203, 209, 228, 272,
    273, 338–9, 344, 351, 358
Motion Picture Export Association
    (MPEA) 203, 215
Motion Picture Patents Company
    (MPPC) 47–9, 51, 52, 55–6, 60–3,
    70–3, 75, 187, 218
Motion Picture Producers and
    Distributors of America (MPPDA)
    128–9, 131–4, 195
Motion Picture Story 57
Motion Pictures in Argentina and Brazil
    163
Mottershaw, Frank 33
movie, use of term 46
movie theatres, see cinemas
Moving Picture World 57, 60, 76, 86, 117
Moyne, Lord 162
MPAA 133
Murnau, F.W. 112–13, 300
Mussolini, Benito 196–7, 258
Mussolini, Vittorio 196
Mussolini Speaks 197
Muybridge, Eadweard 12
My Four Years in Germany 137

The Name of the Rose 322
National Amusements 287, 319
National Association of the Motion
    Picture Industry 90, 128
National Bank of Commerce 123
National Broadcasting Company (NBC)
    229–30, 270–1
National Film Finance Corporation 211
National General 261–2
National Recovery Administration (NRA)
    186
nationalism 19, 97, 99, 101, 108, 112, 153
Negri, Pola 98, 113, 155
Neilan, Marshall (Mickey) 180
Nelson, Harman 223

Netherlands 92, 143, 245
Neubabelsberg 101, 107
New German Cinema 300
New Line 289
New Wave (Nouvelle Vague) 100, 252–5,
    292, 295–6, 298–9
New York 22, 40, 50, 62, 68–9, 85–7, 123
New York Motion Picture Company 109
New York Times 22, 183
The New Yorker 277
New Zealand 86, 162, 193, 202
Newman, Paul 279, 281
Newsweek 261
Neyret, Jean 31–2
nickelodeons, see cinemas
Nielsen, Asta 98
Nixon, Richard 267
Nordisk 47, 49–50, 87, 97–8
North, Clarence J. 132
North American Review 157
North German Lloyd 98
Notes for English Producers (Grierson)
    152–3
Nouveau Roman 252
Nouvelle Vague, see New Wave

Oakley, Laura 81
Odeon Theatres 199, 209–10, 316
Office of War Information, Bureau of
    Motion Pictures 191–2
Olsen, Ole 49–51, 87, 98
Omnia 65
On the Waterfront 330
One Plus One 296
Open University 356
Ophuls, Marcel 302
Oppenheimer, George 178
Orion 310
Orlando 313
Orr, William 237
Otterson, John 166–7
Oury, Gérard 254
Ovitz, Michael 280–1

Pacelli, Ernesto 67
packaging 279–80
Paint Your Wagon 264

Palace Pictures 309
Paley, William 226, 230, 233, 261
Paramount decree 217, 220, 227–8, 231, 318
Paramount Pictures 113, 127, 168, 182, 275
    court case 282; creation of 76, 82–5; in crisis 263; during Depression 167; Joinville studio 144; talkies 141; and television 230, 238; and Ufa 112
Paris 17, 19, 21, 27, 206
Parker, Alan 304, 346
Parretti, Giancarlo 283
Parsons, Louella 173
Parufamet 112
The Passion Play 70
Pathé 34, 47, 283, 319, 346
Pathé, Charles 29–32, 40–43, 65–6, 158
    as distributor 75–6; and Edison's Trust 48, 51, 70; move to US 77; quotas proposal 150; and vertical integration 41–2, 99, 334
Pathé, Emile 31
Pathé-Consortium 103
Pathé Frères 31, 54, 180
Pathé-Westi 103
Paul, R.W. 47
Paul, Robert 25–8
Pearson, George 106
Pearson Longman 308
peep-shows 12–14
Penn, Arthur 273
Petsch, Maurice 156
Phono-Ciné-Gazette 65
Photoplay 58, 117
Piccoli, Michel 292
Picker, Arnold 220, 260
Pickford, Mary 57, 59, 92, 94, 113, 128, 138, 149, 171, 278
Pinewood Studios 198, 306
Pittsburgh 36
Plagnol, Henri 3
The Player 171
Poland 214, 253
political cinema 293–7
political lobbying 133–4, 153, 162, 267, 269, 272, 339
Polygram 285, 345–6, 347–8
Pommer, Erich 102, 109, 113, 327
Ponti, Carlo 257

pornography 255, 269, 299
Porter, Edwin 38, 69
Positif 250
Powell, Michael 198, 274
previews 118, 180, 288–9
The Private Life of Henry VIII 159, 309
producer 302–3, 310–11, 332
    system 109, 175–83
production 54
    costs 276; mass production 41, 43, 109–10, 171, 184; Production Code 273–4; runaway 86, 208, 210–11, 255–8, 267; by television companies 261–2; of television programming 271
propaganda 89–91, 97–8, 101, 105, 155, 191–2, 194–5, 213
protectionism 23, 150–3, 207, 339, 345
    foreign exchange restrictions 213; and GATT talks 4–5, 339–44; import restrictions 150, 204–5, 264; quotas 111, 145, 150, 153, 158, 162, 215, 246, 331, 338; of studios 188; tariffs 15, 107, 131, 158, 338; tax incentives 267–8; in television 246, 338–9; trusts 48
Prudential Assurance Company 160, 309
Publix 126
Puttnam, David 304–5, 308–9, 318, 329–30, 334–8, 341, 344n

Quarrier, Iain 296
Quo Vadis? 68, 87

radio 173, 222
Radio-Keith-Orpheum 168
Rafelson, Bob 268
Raff, Norman 14
Raise the Titanic 307
Rank, J. Arthur 197–200, 209–10
Rank Organization 242, 272, 306, 309, 311, 315–16, 318
Rappe, Virginia 128
Rathenau, Walter 98, 101
Ray, Nicholas 251
RCA 141–4, 230
Reagan, Ronald 223, 226, 235, 266

Redstone, Sumner 287
Reichenbach, Harry 172
La Reine Elizabeth (Queen Elizabeth) 71, 87
Reliance Pictures 75
Religious Film Society 198
Renoir, Jean 250
Republic 170
Revenue Acts 226, 267–8
Revolution 309–10
Revue Productions 235
The Rivals 63
Rivette, Jacques 249, 296
RKO 168, 175, 182, 221, 238
Roach, Hal 197
Robert, Yves 254
Robinson, Edward G. 170
Rock, William 'Pop' 48
Rohmer, Eric
Rome 67, 105, 207, 258
Roosevelt, Franklin D. 186–8, 190, 229
Rosaspina, Carlo 80
Rosenwald, Julius 125
Ross, Steven 265–6
Rossellini, Roberto 207
Rothapfel, S.L. 'Roxy' 123
Russia 43, 87, 105–6

Saetta Contro Golia 105
Salvation Army 67
San Francisco 116
Sanders of the River 161
Sapène, Jean 103
Sarnoff, David 168, 229–30, 233
Sarris, Andrew 251, 274, 278
Saturday Evening Post 147
Saturday Review of Literature 215
Saura, Carlos 293
Saussure, Ferdinand de 295
Scandinavia 50, 58, 87, 99, 193, 253, 299
Schenck, Joseph 118, 168
Schenck, Nicholas 118, 168, 170, 224
Scherl group 112
Schoenberg, Arnold 181
Schulberg, B.P. 182
Scorsese, Martin 5, 268, 274, 278

Scott, Ridley 304, 346
Screen Actors Guild 235, 240, 267
screenwriters 65, 100, 180–3, 249–50, 298, 334
Seabury, William Marston 159
The Search 330
Seastrom, Victor 113–14, 155
Security First National Bank 122
Seitz, Raymond 350
Selfridge, Gordon 151
Selznick, David 123, 175, 176–7, 182, 184, 217, 225, 228, 242, 289
Selznick, Irene 184
Selznick, Myron 221
Semel, Terry 286
Servan Schreiber, Jean-Jacques 358
Seven Arts 265
Shauer, Emil 86
Shaw brothers 214
Shearer, Norma 139, 174, 175
Shochiku 164
shorts 49, 75–6, 97, 98, 162
Showgirls 324
showmen, *see* exhibitors
Siegfried 106, 108
Siemens 103, 143
Signoret, Simone 292
Sjöström, Victor, *see* Seastrom, V.
Skelton, Red 178
Skouras, Spyros 240, 257
Smith, Albert 27, 61
Smith, Richard 287
Snow White and the Seven Dwarfs 235
Société Cinématographique des Auteurs et Gens des Lettres (SCAGL) 66
Société Populaire des Beaux-Arts 64
Sommersby 324
Sony 63, 144, 167, 281
La Sortie des Usines Lumière 17
sound, *see* talking pictures
The Sound of Music 264
Soupault, Phillipe 77
South Africa 162
South America 144, 163
South-East Asia 286, 320
Soviet Union, *see* Russia
Sovkino 105
Spain 193, 243, 319, 340
special effects 18, 39, 284, 306–7

Spielberg, Steven 5, 7, 274, 278, 286
Spraos, John 316–17
Stanford, Leland 12
Stanley Company 124–5
Star! 264
Star Films 39
Star Wars 277, 298, 306
stars 56–9, 144, 163, 171–4, 228, 289
    contract system 156, 172, 220, 225–6,
       233; German 98; of Hong Kong 214;
       independent 218; Italian *divismo*
       system 68; percentage deals 226–7,
       282; salaries 278–9, 281–5; and
       television 234
Stars Over Hollywood 235
Stauss, Emil Georg von 98–9, 110
Stead, William 148
Stein, Jules 220–4, 241
Stewart, James 223, 226–8
Stiller, Mauritz 113, 180
Stinnes, Hugo 103–4
Stone, Admiral 213
The Story of the Kelly Gang 67
Stroheim, Erich von 179
Stuart, Halsey 167
studios:
    anti-trust suit 187–90, 216–18; Big Five
       168–70; ; classics divisions 289;
       distinctive character of 174–5, 182; as
       distributors 219, 247, 256, 268;
       divorcement 218–19, 239; executives
       264;
    Hollywood 42, 76, 80–2, 85, 109,
       166–85, 187–93, 216–20, 230–3,
       236–41, 246–7, 256, 260–1, 263–4,
       285, 317–18; Hong Kong 214; Little
       Three 170; publicity departments
       172–3; reorganization 265–6; studio
       system 41–2, 156, 164, 170–1, 181,
       214, 218–20, 227–8, 233, 278, 284;
       and television 230–3, 236–41,
       246–7, 268
subtitling 144–5, 322–3
Sunrise 113
Svenska 104
Svenska Bio 50
Swanson, Gloria 292
Sweden 50, 100, 193, 245, 260, 317, 320
Switzerland 92, 143, 193

Tait Brothers 67
talking pictures 12, 104, 117, 137–46,
    164–5
    cultural impact of 140–1; first 139;
       language problems 140, 142, 144–5;
       technology of 137–8, 140
Tati, Jacques 250
Taxi Driver 268, 278
Taylor, Elizabeth 273, 279
Taylor, Frederick W. 110
Taylor, William Desmond 128
technology 8, 50, 99, 101, 110, 184, 195
    cameras 16–17, 24–5, 31–2; early
       9–28; information technology 355–9;
       new 340–1; phonograph 12, 30;
       photography 11–12, 14–15; projectors
       16, 18, 22, 25, 31–2; of sound 137–8,
       140
telecommunications industry 143–4, 350
television 164–5, 229–47, 289
    alliance with movie industry 285;
       American 143, 229–41, 261–2, 270–1;
       American programming 245–6, 353;
       and cinema attendances 316;
       commercial 286, 338; and crisis in
       Hollywood 185, 228, 264, 268, 276;
       European 6, 241–7, 272, 286, 318,
       338, 353; export markets 245–7,
       271–2; fin-syn regulations 270–1; and
       GATT 5, 8; impact of 351;
       independents and 234, 271; new
       technology 285; pay-television 284;
       production companies 261–2; quota
       system 338–9; residuals 235, 238,
       240; revenues from 226, 354; rights
       238–9, 242, 244, 318; satellite 350;
       stars and 227; syndication 234, 271
Television Without Frontiers 338
Tempelhof 101
Temple, Julien 309
Terminator 2 324
Thalberg, Irving 113, 139, 168, 175,
    178–84, 289
Thanhauser, Edwin 75
Thanhauser Company 75
Things To Come 306
Thomas, J. Parnell 214
Thomas, Jeremy 324
Thomson, Lord 245

Thorez, Maurice 206
Thorn-EMI 314, 319
Three Men and a Baby 324
Thring, Frank 162
The Times Educational Supplement 65
Tinker, Edward 167
Titanus 259
Tobis-Klangfilm 142–3
Tocqueville, Alexis de 154
Toho 164
The Torrent 113
Totó 208
Tourneur, Maurice 180
trade papers 56–7, 107–8, 173
trade wars 204, 209
The Tramp 61
Trewey, Félicien 21, 25
A Trip to the Moon 39
Truffaut, François 249–50, 252, 259–60, 293, 296, 301
Truman, Harry 192
Trumbo, Dalton 147
Trust, *see* Motion Picture Patents Company
Tumulty, Joseph 90
Turin 67
Turner Entertainment 241
Twentieth Century-Fox 230, 237–8, 257, 263, 296, 307
20,000 Leagues Under the Sea 236
2001: A Space Odyssey 306

Ufa 98–104, 106, 109, 111–12, 114, 180, 194, 196
Ufi (Ufa-Film) 196
Unione Cinematografica Italiana (UCI) 104–5
United Artists 94, 159–60, 168, 170, 220, 258–60, 287
United Cinemas International 319
United International Pictures 290
United Kingdom, *see* British film industry; Great Britain
United States:
    anti-trust legislation 186–91, 216, 231; cinemas 62, 69, 124–7, 210, 320; Commerce Department 4, 90, 127–8, 131–2, 190, 215; Congress 266;
Depression in 166–7, 172, 186; economy 95, 264; as export market 44; and GATT 5, 339–43; Government 23, 73, 88–95, 129–34, 186–92, 203–4, 212–13, 215, 256, 266–70, 338–9; immigration 107–8, 347; Information Agency 213; Internal Revenue Service 267; Justice Department 187–8, 190, 202, 230, 270; New Deal 186, 187; protectionism 15, 23, 48, 107–8, 131; relations with Europe 23–4, 107–8, 205; Senate committees 192, 220, 269; social change in 232, 273; State Department 212, 215, 338; technological innovation in 9–14, 21–4, 110; telecommunications industry 143–4; urbanization in 44; War Department 204; and World Wars 74, 76, 87–9, 91–2, 191; *see also* Hollywood
Universal Pictures 170, 179, 218
    British stake in 199; creation of 76, 80–2; marketing strategy 314; MCA take-over 225, 279; overseas activities 86, 102; Stewart deal 226, 228; studio system 284; studios 81–2; UK subsidiary 152
Urban-Eclipse 47
US Army Psychological Warfare Division 204

Vadim, Roger 252
Valenti, Jack 6, 133, 273, 317–18, 338, 341–4, 358
Valentino, Rudolph 171
Variety 48, 108, 173, 188, 189, 190, 219, 237, 239, 267, 290
Veblen, Thorstein 149
Veidt, Conrad 112
Venice Film Festival (1935) 195
Verhoeven, Paul 346
Verne, Jules 39
vertical integration 41–2, 50, 76, 99, 124, 188, 217, 266, 346
video 143–4, 164–5, 239, 241, 283, 284, 285, 289, 299, 305–6, 313, 323, 341
Viertel, Salka 181

Village Roadshow 320
Vincennes 30
Virgin 309, 314
Visconti, Luchino 207, 258
Visual Programmes Systems (VPS) 305–6
Vitagraph 46–7, 48, 118, 123
Vitascope 22
Vogel, Harold 283
Volpini, Monsieur 19

Wald, Jerry 219
Waldman, Bernie 173
Wallis, Hal 175
Walt Disney Productions 235, 266–7, 270, 281, 284–6
Warner, Albert 137
Warner, Harry 137–8, 190
Warner, Jack 135–7, 174–5, 191–2, 194, 204, 218–19, 225–6, 231, 236–7, 240, 265, 273
Warner, Sam 136–9
Warner Brothers 168, 182
cinemas 127, 319; in crisis 265–6; as entertainment conglomerate 266; financiers 122–3; Puttnam and 335; stars 225–6, 286; and studio system 170, 174–5, 218–19; and talkies 135–9, 141, 143, 354; and television 230, 233, 236–8, 261; in wartime 192
Warner Brothers Presents 237
Wasserman, Lew 220–1, 223–8, 235, 267, 342
Webb-Pomerene Export Trade Act (1918) 203
Wegener, Paul 98, 100
Welland, Colin 147, 308
Wells, H.G. 173, 359

Wenders, Wim 5, 297, 300
Wengeroff, Vladimir 103
Western Electric 137, 138, 141, 143–4
Westi 103–4
Who's Afraid of Virginia Woolf? 273
Wiene, Robert 109
Wilcox, Horace 78
Wilder, Billy 114, 228, 300, 346
William Morris Agency 220, 279–80
Williams-Jones, Michael 290
Williamson, James 33, 49
Wilson, Harold 209, 211
Wilson, Woodrow 88–91, 96, 157, 331
Winchell, Walter 173
Winchester 73 226
The Wind 114
The Wizard of Oz 240, 263
World's Fairs 12, 15, 229–30
World Trade Organization 359
World War I 74, 76–7, 86–9, 91–2, 94–7, 149, 190
World War II 191–4, 201, 204
Worthington-Evans, Sir Laming 152
Wright, Robert L. 191
Wrigley, William Jr 125
Wyler, William 300

Yugoslavia 214
Yule, Lady 198

Zanuck, Darryl 170, 175–6, 182, 192, 204, 231, 232
Zecca, Ferdinand 32–3, 41
Zinnemann, Fred 330
Zoopraxiscope 12
Zukor, Adolph 68–72, 76, 83–6, 91, 93, 108, 121, 135, 138, 167, 179, 333, 334